A History of Early
Southeast Asia

A History of Early Southeast Asia

Maritime Trade and Societal Development, 100–1500

Kenneth R. Hall

ROWMAN & LITTLEFIELD PUBLISHERS, INC.
Lanham • Boulder • New York • Toronto • Plymouth, UK

To Randy, Jason, Jeremy, and Rachel

Published by Rowman & Littlefield Publishers, Inc.
A wholly owned subsidiary of The Rowman & Littlefield Publishing Group, Inc.
4501 Forbes Boulevard, Suite 200, Lanham, Maryland 20706
http://www.rowmanlittlefield.com

Estover Road, Plymouth PL6 7PY, United Kingdom

British Library Cataloguing in Publication Information Available

Library of Congress Cataloging-in-Publication Data

Hall, Kenneth R.
  A history of early Southeast Asia : maritime trade and societal development, 100–1500 / Kenneth R. Hall.
      p. cm.
  Includes bibliographical references and index.
  ISBN 978-0-7425-6760-3 (cloth : alk. paper)
  ISBN 978-0-7425-6761-0 (pbk. : alk. paper)
  ISBN 978-0-7425-6762-7 (ebook)
  1. Southeast Asia—Commerce—History—To 1500. 2. Southeast Asia—Commerce—Social aspects—History—To 1500. 3. Southeast Asia—Civilization—To 1500. 4. Southeast Asia—History—To 1500. I. Title.
HF3790.8.H348   2011
959'.01—dc22   2010043612

♾ ™ The paper used in this publication meets the minimum requirements of American National Standard for Information Sciences—Permanence of Paper for Printed Library Materials, ANSI/NISO Z39.48-1992.

Printed in the United States of America

Contents

Figures and Maps

FIGURES

MAPS

vii

Preface

The research for this book is rooted in my study of the early history of Southeast Asia begun forty years ago at the University of Michigan, under the guidance of John K. Whitmore, Thomas R. Trautmann, Alton L. Becker, Peter Gosling, and Karl Hutterer, with adaptive methodological input from Marshall Sahlins, Aram Yengoyan, and Sylvia Thrupp. The new scholarship of that era was represented in O. W. Wolters's *Early Indonesian Commerce*, which focused on the activities of those Southeast Asians who responded to the presence of traders and other foreigners—on their own initiative—by optimizing their opportunities, in contrast to the earlier ideas represented by George Coedes's *The Indianized States of Southeast Asia,* which was concerned with Indian culture as the basis for state development. Unlike Coedes, however, Wolters and other revisionist scholars from the 1970s normally examined specific areas within the region without coming to terms with the larger regional patterns.

Whitmore challenged me to approach early Southeast Asia civilizations not as extensions of India ("Indianized States") and China (Vietnam as a "Lesser China"), but as the products of indigenous agency, via their conscious adaptation and synthesis of the external in ways that reinforced indigenous cultures rather than displaced them. This new scholarship reconstructed social and economic history and attempted to balance the picture of outside forces by addressing indigenous responses. Archeological research had achieved the sophistication necessary to supply reliable new data. My work with Whitmore was focused on the inclusive maritime world rather than a specific civilization, though based in my previous Indonesian and Old Javanese language studies. My interactions with my fellow Southeast Asian

ix

studies graduate students Michael Aung-Thwin (Burma), Keith W. Taylor
(Vietnam), and Nidhi Aeusrivongse (Thailand/Cambodia) evolved as a part-
nership that is represented in our collected volume *Explorations in Early
Southeast Asian History: The Origins of Southeast Asian Statecraft* (1976).
Bennet Bronson of the Field Museum made possible my first field work in
Southeast Asia by inviting me to join his archeological team excavating Srivi-
jaya-era sites at Palembang, Sumatra (1974).

These initial studies, subsequent field experiences, and preliminary journal
articles formed the core of my *Maritime Trade and State Development in
Early Southeast Asia* (1985). The *Cambridge History of Southeast Asia*
"Economic History of Southeast Asia" extended chapter (1992) went beyond
the *Maritime Trade* book in my initial synthesis of Vietnam and Cham history, with substantial input from Whitmore and Keith Taylor. My several
years at Elmira College in New York in the late 1970s allowed me to work
with John Echols, David Wyatt, Stanley J. O'Connor, and especially O. W.
Wolters, who challenged me to constrain my propensity for wider synthesis
by better rooting myself in the indigenous primary sources.

The point of this introductory reflection is foundational to this new book,
which demonstrates how far the scholarship of early Southeast Asia has come
since the publication of *Maritime Trade* twenty-five years ago. This is certainly not a second edition of that book, though it incorporates some of its
essence. It is a reflection, however, of how the study of early Southeast Asian
history has progressed over that time. Above all, new studies by prehistori-
ans, archeologists, linguists, art historians, and technology specialists have
made us more keenly aware of how early civilizations emerged, developed
material bases, and evolved intellectual and cultural foundations pre–100 CE.
Recent shipwreck recoveries have been vital to our understanding of ceramics
and other material artifact distributions (e.g., textiles, beads, and metal
objects) and regional technology, which pairs with sophisticated multidisciplinary work undertaken at archeological sites throughout the region to provide us with essential primary source data. Following postcolonial regional
instabilities, the maturing of indigenous scholarship from the 1980s is a
major byproduct of favorable local government initiatives. New archeological
research, discoveries, and studies of other indigenous historical sources by
native language speakers have added insightful local voices to international
discussions of early Southeast Asia.

Purposely there is no reference to the ca. 100–1500 period as the "classical
era" of Southeast Asian history. In part this avoids referencing a "classical
era" that is based in a Western chronological categorization and that then
invites comparisons to Western civilizations rather than viewing Southeast
Asia as having inclusive regional characteristics, which justifies its study as

a distinctive region. Thus, this book is a study of Southeast Asia as an "indigenous" essence and region of "stand-alone" entities. It does not dismiss the local voices in the primary sources as fictional, biased, romanticized accounts of the past that have no historical validity, as was too often the case among colonial-era Western scholars. Secondly, avoidance of the "classical era" label discourages the conceptualization of a definitive regional timeline boundary. Though the book is focused on the ca. 100–1500 era—and thus acknowledges the importance of the initial regularization of the east-west Indian Ocean maritime passage in the earliest era considered in this book and anticipates the regional consequences of the Portuguese seizure of Melaka in 1511—each chapter is framed by periodization appropriate to local and regional events.

Though some chapters address specific civilizations, there is no intent to regard these societies as existing in isolation, or as having well-defined geographies in which singular ethno-religious groups reside. While studies of "states" may provide a potential basis for understanding an inclusive era of a civilization, the boundaries of the early states were ill-defined and, as this book will establish, extremely fluid. There were political heartlands but fluctuating state peripheries, both real and imagined, in the pre-1500 era, which require thinking outside the vocabulary and images associated with the "nation-state" of the modern era. As a case in point, the thirteenth-century Java-based Majapahit state claimed sovereignty over a vast maritime realm called Nusantara, which in local minds extended over most of the Java Sea and Straits of Melaka region, but critically portrayed T'ai-claimed territories in the northern Malay Peninsula as outside Majapahit's sovereignty over the southern peninsula. Against this, a following chapter introduces the alternative view in the contemporary Samudra-Pasai state chronicle, acknowledging Majapahit's interests on the Sumatra coastline, but not its authority. The Angkor realm's borders beyond its modern-day Cambodian heartland were continuously in question, as was similarly the well-documented case in contemporary Burma and Vietnam.

While focusing on the regional importance of maritime trade, this book's chapters offer a wider consideration than might at first seem implied. By necessity the book addresses a series of significant related issues such as the development of written languages of state; the creation of religious traditions unique to a civilization, via local adaptations of Hindu, Buddhist, and Islamic religions; the evolution of local notions of leadership, legitimacy, and rightful authority, based in a foundational sense of patron-clientage and familial loyalties; the development of economic systems based in agriculture, hunting and gathering, commerce, trade, craft production, and mixtures of these; participation in layered local and wider networks often linked by religious and political institutions; the initiation of the initial codes of civil and criminal law by integrations of local custom and religion; and, of course, the creation of patterns of social organization.

Appropriate chapters will demonstrate that the thirteenth-century "decline" projected in numerous previous studies of the pre-1500 era was in reality the beginning of an upward spiral based in a new regionwide internationalism that was set in motion by evolving economic and social opportunities. Thirteenth-century Mongol invasions had less regional significance in Southeast Asia than elsewhere, and instead provided opportunities for the multidimensional east-west linkage consequent to the Mongol-era Silk Road, as well as presenting the potentials of a more integrative Indian Ocean maritime network due to the Yuan dynasty's support of China's trade connections. In this corrective view, the thirteenth century was not an age that isolated the old elite, but offered new potentials for participation in generalized societal prosperity. The thirteenth century was about change, not due to that era's crisis, but because of new opportunities. Certainly the time witnessed the demise of old polities, such as Angkor, Pagan, Srivijaya, and the Kadiri-based monarchy in Java, but these were more the consequence of the previous orders' internal decay rather than being due to an external source. The documentation of this transition is best demonstrated in the new studies of Vietnam, Champa, and Angkor that are the basis of the present text, representing substantial revisions of my 1985–1992 characterizations of these civilizations. This book purposely, in contrast to the earlier *Maritime Trade and State Development in Early Southeast Asia* that concluded in 1400, embraces the fifteenth century as a continuum of previously established patterns of economic and social development. It also addresses the emerging fifteenth-century civilizations of the eastern Indonesian archipelago and the Philippines, which the previous book did not.

While the focal issue in this book is maritime trade and its consequences, maritime trade is only one motor for change—as this book's title equally embraces societal development in acknowledgment of the vitality of local initiative in the evolution of Southeast Asia's pre-1500 regional civilizations. As such, the book is intended as an entry point for nonspecialists, specifically university undergraduates and graduate students encountering Southeast Asian history for the first time. Since the inclusion of photographs in this text was cost prohibitive, there is an accompanying website that provides a photographic core, as well as thematic PowerPoints to illustrate the book's chapters.

I thank my faculty colleagues and students at Elmira College, Tufts University, SUNY–Binghamton, the Massachusetts College for the Liberal Arts, Williams College, Anderson University, Gadjah Mada University, and Ball

State University, who have in various ways and times contributed to my development as a multidisciplinary scholar and teacher. This book benefits from my partnership with Fred Donner of the University of Chicago in the presentation of a series of National Endowment for the Humanities Faculty Summer Institutes in the post-9/11 era; Fred shared his cutting-edge revisionist history of the early Islamic era in the Middle East and encouraged me to similarly reconsider the origins of the early Islamic states in Southeast Asia. Robert Wicks of Miami University in Ohio introduced me to Southeast Asia numismatics; at various times John Miksic (University of Singapore), Jan Wisseman Christie (Hull University), Barbara and Leonard Andaya (University of Hawai'i), Pierre-Yves Manguin (École française d'Extrême-Orient), Hermann Kulke (Kiel University), Eric Tagliocozzo (Cornell University), and E. Edwards McKinnon critiqued my understanding of island Southeast Asia.

John Chaffee of Binghamton University connected me to the revisionist studies of Tang-Ming maritime trade, with follow-up support from my Ball State University Ming-era specialist colleague Kenneth Swope. Sun Laichen (University of California–Fullerton), Charles Wheeler (Hong Kong University), and Tana Li (ANU) shared their new studies of Vietnam coastal communities. Elizabeth Lambourn (De Montfort University, Leicester, UK) introduced me to the revisionist scholarship on the pre-1500 western Indian Ocean trade. Edwin Zehner (St. Lawrence University) and Craig Lockard (University of Wisconsin–Green Bay) offered suggestions on the development of new T'ai sections of the book; Michael Aung-Thwin (University of Hawai'i–Manoa) provided updates on the Burma sections and shared discussions on the application of revisionist historiography to the study of early Southeast Asian history; and John Whitmore (Michigan) did extensive review of the Cambodia and Vietnam sections, made available his and others' backlog of "in press" studies of the early Champa and Vietnam realms.

Michael Hradesky, staff cartographer at Ball State University, prepared the maps for this book; Jason Higgs, graphics designer at the Ball State University Teleplex Complex, recreated the several graphic displays, and Cynthia Nemser-Hall compiled the index. Susan McEachern at Rowman & Littlefield patiently guided the manuscript through the various stages of its preparation, assisted by Carrie Broadwell-Tkach and Jehanne Schweitzer.

I encourage discussion of this new book and invite others to test my hypotheses in their own studies of Southeast Asia's early history.

Southeast Asia to 1500

Trade and Statecraft in Early Southeast Asia

Through the first centuries CE, Western and Chinese records portrayed Southeast Asia as a region of exotic lands that lay between India and China on an Indian Oceanic passageway of which little was known. This book addresses the developing interactions between Southeast Asian peoples and foreign cultures that were the consequence of the Southeast Asian archipelago's strategic position along the major premodern maritime route and the critical point of connection between East and West. Southeast Asia's earliest centers of power emerged between the first and early fifteenth centuries CE, as their leaders faced issues relative to ruling their domains, which were commonly transitioning from highly localized tribal and clan-based societies. Two forms of transitional traditional polities are contrasted in this book: those of the riverine coastal states of the Indonesian archipelago, the Malay Peninsula, and the Philippines; and those of the lowland wet-rice states of the Southeast Asian mainland (Burma/Myanmar, Thailand, Cambodia, Laos, and Vietnam) and of Java.

The chapters that follow will approach the sources of Southeast Asia's pre-1500 history with the multidisciplinary tools of the modern scholar of Southeast Asian history, highlighting the consequences of Southeast Asia's participation in the international trade relative to the evolution of regional cultures. The view taken here is that Southeast Asia's positive response to the economic and cultural opportunities afforded by the international trade was conditioned by and consistent with preexisting patterns of civilization. Both well-developed and developing internal socioeconomic and political networks existed in Southeast Asia before significant foreign penetration took place; this book highlights local initiative rather than foreign intervention as foundational to the emergence of more centered regional polities. With the growth of external interest in Southeast Asian commodities and the refocusing of the major East-West commercial routes on the region during the early centuries of the Christian era, internal conditions within Southeast Asian states changed to take advantage of the increased external contacts. The juncture of the trade routes and the existing or developing forms of exchange and state polity in Southeast Asia suggest the way this adjustment was made.

As in other scholarship by Western historians, inevitably this study tends to impose Western concepts and values on what constituted advanced civilizations in early Southeast Asia. In the modern West, temple complexes, urban centers, centralized and bureaucratic state systems, and sophisticated literary texts are generally accepted as signs of advancement. The impressive remains of the ritual and court centers of Angkor (Cambodia), Bagan/Pagan (Burma/Myanmar), and Majapahit (Java) seduce us with their massive stone and brick edifices reminiscent of the great pyramids of Egypt. The early civilizations of the Mediterranean basin thus become standards for comparison and the basis of attempts to make Southeast Asia's history conform to Western cultural prejudices in which physically impressive architectural remains and evidence of large concentrations of a diverse resident population in urban centers are the standards (Said: 1979; Miksic: 2000). But were the nonurban, multicentered, yet cohesive early societies less deserving of being labeled advanced or civilized, and was it necessary for an advanced civilization to leave impressive archeological or textual remains (Wheatley: 1979)?

In response to this Western bias, the standard here is evidence of cultural integration rather than political centralization. The evolution of Southeast Asian societies needs to be understood on their own terms. One way to understand local development is to look at instances of cultural transition and continuity that took place whether or not there was outside stimulation or the development of a highly centralized polity—that is, a state in which an administrative center dominated and effectively integrated its subordinate population centers under its elaborate system of administration, justice, and protection. The states of Southeast Asia's pre-1500 age will not be depicted as highly administered (rather than bureaucratic) polities, even in the case of the prosperous Cambodian, Javanese, Burmese, or Vietnamese wet-rice realms. Rather, this portrayal explains why a higher degree of political centralization was not possible, despite the opportunities for economic development and consequent cultural and political innovation afforded by participation in international trade. Instead, the continuing tendency of early Southeast Asian civilizations to empower the local over an all-powerful urban political center did not, however, diminish the political, cultural, and economic accomplishments of Southeast Asia's pre-1500 courts. These early courts provided meaningful linkages among networked population clusters through a variety of initiatives, and consequently submissive populations thought of themselves as sharing membership in a common civilization that was centered in a court (Hall: 2010c).

EARLY ECONOMIC DEVELOPMENT

In the premodern world, the Southeast Asian region was initially portrayed in international sources as a land of immense wealth; developments there were thought to be of crucial importance to the entirety of world history in the pre-1600 period. Writers, travelers, sailors, merchants, and officials from every continent of the Eastern Hemisphere knew of Southeast Asia's exotic products, and by the second millennium of the Christian era, most were aware of its ports of trade and major political centers (Park: 2010).

In the early centuries CE Indians and Westerners called Southeast Asia the Golden Khersonese, the "Land of Gold," and it was not long thereafter that the region became known for its pepper and the products of its rainforests: first aromatic woods and resins, and then the finest and rarest of spices (Wheatley: 1961). From the seventh to the tenth centuries Middle Easterners and Chinese thought of Southeast Asia as the vital passageway between India and China, as well as the source of spices and jungle products that had substantial market value. By the fifteenth century sailors from ports on the Atlantic, at the opposite side of the hemisphere, would sail into unknown oceans in order to find these Spice Islands. They all knew that Southeast Asia was the spice capital of the world. From roughly 1000 CE until the eighteenth century, all world trade was more or less governed by the ebb and flow of spices in and out of Southeast Asia (Reid: 1988, 1994). Throughout these centuries the region and its products never lost their siren call. Palm trees, gentle surfs, wide beaches, steep mountain slopes covered with lush vegetation, and birds and flowers of brilliant colors, as well as orange and golden tropical sunsets, have enchanted its visitors as well as its own people through the ages.

The story of economic development in early Southeast Asia begins long before the Christian era. Southeast Asia had already been for centuries a region with a distinct cultural identity. By the early Christian era, Southeast Asia had skilled farmers, musicians, metallurgists, and mariners. Even though they had no written language, no large urban concentrations, and no administrative states of recognizable proportions, they were nevertheless a highly accomplished people who had already assumed a significant role in the cultural development of the southern oceans of the Eastern Hemisphere.

Their expertise was in three general areas. First, they were innovative farmers. It is possible that Southeast Asians were the first to domesticate rice and to develop wet-rice cultivation. Early archeological evidence from the era of known rice cultures, as early as 2000 BCE, has been identified in Southeast Asian sites (notably northeastern Thailand), and archeologists have found evidence of a rice plant that could be classified as an intermediate stage between wild and domesticated rice that has been dated to ca. 3000 BCE. But these people never developed a rice monoculture. In addition to rice, local populations also harvested a number of other crops, including sugarcane, yams, sago, bananas, and coconuts. And they apparently were among the first (if not the first) to domesticate the chicken and pig (Bellwood: 1997; O'Connor: 1995).

It may be that Southeast Asians independently discovered bronze and developed their own sophisticated metallurgical techniques based on the special qualities of bamboo. Since the trunk of this plant grows in hollow segments, they were able to use it to fashion a fire piston that produced the heat required to liquefy metal. Archeologists have dated bronze objects uncovered in northeast Thailand to 1500 BCE, and iron bracelets and spearheads to about 500 BCE. By 200 BCE many peoples in the region possessed a sophisticated metal technology that allowed the production of bronze, brass, tin, and iron, although in most cases the tin, copper, and iron raw materials were not locally available and in some cases had to be imported. Beautiful large bronze ceremonial drums like those found in Dong Son (in modern Vietnam) could be found all over Southeast Asia. That these drums were so widely dispersed throughout the region is clear evidence that there existed an extensive and efficient exchange mechanism within the Southeast Asian world prior to any significant trade with imperial India or China (Bronson: 1992).

Their third area of expertise, that of sailing, may explain in part how these drums, among other material objects, became so widely dispersed. The people of the maritime realm were the pioneers of early watercraft developed on the southern oceans (Manguin: 1994). From before the historic period, they knew how to ride the monsoons, the seasonal winds that pulled across the continent during the hot months of the Central Asian summer and pushed away during the cold Central Asian winter. This basic rhythm of the Central Asian bellows offered an opportunity that the seaborne sojourners of Southeast Asia seized. They sailed thousands of miles from their homes, navigating by means of swell and wave patterns, cloud formations, winds, birds, and sea life. This sophisticated and complex knowledge was passed orally from generation to generation. They measured their peoples by "boatloads," and on the slightest pretext, boatloads would leave islands where they were already heavily concentrated and sail off to set up new communities on uninhabited islands, so that these Malayo-Austronesian peoples eventually stretched halfway around the globe, from Madagascar on the East African coast to Easter Island in the Pacific.

They were the nomads of the Southern Ocean, and they played a role in history that in some ways resembles that of the nomads of the northern steppe. They were prime movers in the links created between larger centers, as well as potential impediments to those links once they were created. Exactly when this far-reaching maritime activity began is unknown, but "Malay" (*Kunlun*) sailors were known in China by the third century BCE, and there is evidence that they were settling along the East African coast by the first century CE. By the time of the Roman Empire, there were permanent communities of Malayo-Polynesian–speaking peoples on the coast of Malagasy, where they remain to this day (Taylor: 1976).

The Malay sailors did not cover these routes empty-handed, and in the process of sailing across the thousands of miles of Southern Ocean from Africa to Easter Island, they moved the specialties of one place to others. Cinnamon, a product that originally came from the south China coast, may also have reached the markets of India on the vessels of these sailors, and the markets of Southwest Asia and the Mediterranean through Malay trading stations in East Africa. The Roman historian Pliny, writing in the first century CE, described cinnamon traders between Africa and Asia who rode the winds "from gulf to gulf" (see chapter 2). Pliny describes their craft as rafts. What he was no doubt referring to was the double outrigger canoe of the Malays. This same craft is still used today along the routes that these ancient mariners sailed. The cinnamon they brought was then traded north by the Africans until it reached Ethiopia, where the Europeans obtained it.

Since Malay sailors were known in China by the third century BCE, it was probably not long after that they began to sail through the Straits of Melaka (Malacca) and Sunda into the Indian Ocean and on to India, and thus it is quite possible that the Southeast Asians themselves were responsible for the earliest contacts between Southeast Asia and South Asia. Historians do not know exactly when the first ships based in Indian ports went to Southeast Asia, but many believe that it was sometime in the last two centuries BCE. It has been suggested that from the late fifth century BCE beginning of the Mauryan period India's supply of gold came from Siberia, from the northern reaches of Central Asia, but that after the Mauryans fell in the second century BCE, the movement of steppe nomads cut them off from these sources and forced them to look elsewhere. It was then, they think, that merchants based in India's ports began to sail into Southeast Asian waters, looking for the "Islands of Gold" (Wheatley: 1983; Ray: 1994; Sen: 2003).

The early Southeast Asian populations shared a relatively common physical geography, wherein ample and readily accessible productive land could support the basic economic needs of the indigenous society. The exceptions were the several dry and infertile islands of the eastern Indonesian archipelago, like Timor and northern Maluku (the Moluccas). Southeast Asia had no substantial grasslands, no pastoral tradition, and thus low dependency upon animal protein; meat and milk products had little importance in the traditional diet. Houses were constructed from the seemingly inexhaustible local supply of wood, palm, and bamboo; they were usually elevated on poles above the annual floods of the lowlands, and this also provided a sense of security from human and animal predators in the highlands. The ease of building and rebuilding these shelters and the abundance of unoccupied fertile land meant that the population was inherently mobile. Indeed, the shortage of labor relative to land produced a social pattern in which additional labor rather than land became the object of competition.

Traditional household-based production in early Southeast Asia consisted of clearing woods, planting, weeding, harvesting, cooking, feeding pigs and chickens, and fishing. Men and women performed daily chores according to local tradition, but everyone participated in food production. As more stratified societies emerged, productive activities became more differentiated. Work was often assigned by local leaders ("big men/women," chiefs, or religious elite who tended to distance themselves from the physical labor involved in food production) to their social subordinates, as well as to prisoners of war and debt slaves (Reid: 1983). When states began to emerge there was a corresponding dissociation of a small or large group of state elite, inclusive of religious functionaries and courtiers, musicians, dancers, and dramatists as well as craftsmen and traders.

Millet and dry rice were highly adaptable and predate Southeast Asian wet rice as the staple grains. The late Roman-era geographer Ptolemy's reference to *Yavadvipa* probably equates with *Yawadvipa*, "millet island." But millet or dry rice and *sawah* (wet) cultivation were incompatible; as sawah production spread it displaced this earlier grain production, which did not do well in waterlogged soils (Wheatley: 1965; Setten van der Meer: 1979; Dove: 1985).

Initially, millet probably was produced in the uplands, by means of what is commonly called "slash-and-burn," "shifting," or swidden cultivation (Geertz: 1963). Shifting cultivation of this grasslike grain was ideal for sloping highland areas with adequate drainage. It required little labor and was able to produce a substantial surplus relative to the size of the workforce. Local populations supplemented their diet by hunting, gathering, and fishing.

They cleared and burned a new patch of forest each year. Planting normally consisted of using pointed sticks to make holes, into which they placed two or three grains. Nutrients added to the soil in the initial burn-off were washed away by rain within two seasons, thus necessitating the shifting culti-vation cycle. Slash-and-burn regions could usually produce a stable food sup-ply, but their populations were not usually as spatially confined as were those of their lowland neighbors. Fields, rivers, and lake productive centers might be some distance apart rather than coincident, thereby making their aggregate revenue potential less. Local migration cycles, together with the relatively low yield per acre, limited highland population density to twenty to thirty persons per square mile and made it difficult to collect surplus for urban development or for export.

Transition from upland shifting to settled lowland rice cultivation may have been necessitated by population pressure, but was more likely due to a sup-portive physical environment. It is generally believed that wet-rice cultivation was becoming common in the early first millennium CE, although surviving records can definitively substantiate only that wet-rice agriculture in perma-nent fields was practiced in eastern Java and the Kyaukse area of Burma by the eighth century. On the mainland (Cambodia, Thailand, and Burma), seed was more commonly broadcast on a bunded and plowed floodplain, and grew quickly and needed little work. In Java, however, the transplanting method came to be preferred; this gave higher yields per unit of land used, though not the highest per labor input (Dove: 1985; O'Connor: 1995). By either the broadcast or seedling method, a Southeast Asian lowland wet-rice farmer could normally expect an annual output of twenty to twenty-five bushels of grain per acre. In early times one rice crop proved adequate to supply local needs, although a second could be harvested, if weather and irrigation facili-ties permitted and there were incentives to produce a surplus for external con-sumption.

On Java, seed was annually sown in small seedling beds at the approach of the rainy season. While seedlings took root, farmers and family prepared nearby fields; they weeded and broke up soil with wooden, stone, or metal-tipped hoes until the monsoon rains soaked the earth. Then seedlings were transplanted by hand, with enough space between for each plant to grow. As the crops matured, farmers repaired the local irrigation system and regulated the flow of water as rains reached their peak. As water receded, fields were drained, and the sun ripened the grain. At harvest, the entire community worked side by side. Javanese women sometimes harvested using a finger knife that cut only one stalk at a time, rather than use a sickle, which might offend the local rice spirit and thus jeopardize future production. During the subsequent dry season, fields were cleared and tools repaired, and feasts, fes-tivals, and marriages were celebrated.

Sawah cultivation was effectively maintained only where dissolved volca-nic matter was brought into the fields with irrigated water, in rich alluvial plains, or where fertilizer (such as water buffalo and duck excrement) was added. Initial Southeast Asian wet rice may have been cultivated without plows, in part because some areas, such as Java, did not have local access to iron (which the maritime trade networks eventually provided). But by the late first millennium CE water buffaloes plowed the irrigated fields to make the land suitable for the reception of seeds and seedlings. Cultivation with wooden or metal-tipped plows puddled the flooded soil and turned it into a creamy mud; it also produced a dense layer of soil to a depth of seven to twelve inches (thirty to fifty centimeters), which reduced the percolation of irrigated water. As the water buffaloes worked the fields, their droppings added to soil fertility, as did those of domesticated ducks, which were more important relative to their role in field fertilization and control of algae than as a consumable food.

In sawah regions there were three food staples: rice, fish, and coconut. Rice might be affected by periodic disease and plagues; mice plagues are shown in Borobudur (Java) and Angkor (Cambodia) temple relief. But fish (from rivers, tanks, or sawah fields) and coconut (when properly maintained) were virtually free of pests and diseases. Rice was eaten by preference to other grains or other kinds of starches. Reliance upon other staples was looked down upon except during rice famines when sawah cultivators could normally turn to tubers (taro, which grew in sawah areas) and yams (which were gathered from nearby forests or were grown in the rain-fed fields) as well as to sago palms, which were another stable source of starch. The three staples were supplemented by a wide variety of vegetables, pigs, and fowl that could not be preserved, except in coastal zones where salt was readily available. Properly prepared, rice and fish—which was usually dried or fermented and was the major garnish to rice—could be preserved more than a year; coconuts (the source of fruit, sugar, oil, and palm wine) could not be stored as long, but were available at three-month intervals.

Sawah agriculture could thus support a high population density and high yields from small areas—a field of two and a half acres (one hectare) could well support a household. But large population centers in the early sawah regions were the exception. Small housing clusters (one house and one field, or several houses and nearby fields) were more practical for flooding and draining the fields. Too much water flow would damage the dikes, while too little would result in algae growth. Rights to occupy and use land were characterized by long-term commitment to a soil plot.

Such a stable food source was ideal to feed non–food producers, that is, state officials, priests, and traders. There is thus a general coincidence of sawah cultivation and temple and state development in early Southeast Asia. Sawah cultivators could occupy the same lands for generations; because they had little need to move, they were ideal producers of surplus. Taxing the early small and scattered agricultural units of production must have been a time-consuming task for emergent states, yet sawah cultivators could not easily escape their revenue cesses. Leaving their fields uncontrolled was not an option among sawah cultivators, except just after harvest, and developing new lands for cultivation (bunding, etc.) might take several seasons. But early armies and state administrative corps were not large enough to constantly threaten sawah producers. Instead, would-be elite had to offer inducements, such as protection, although this was not always needed in areas where population centers were geographically isolated from their neighbors or foreigners, as in volcano-ringed central Java, the Tonle Sap "great lake" region of central Cambodia, and the upstream Irrawaddy River basin of Burma. More commonly subordinate sawah cultivators received material rewards (foreign luxury goods) or ideological/symbolic rewards (titles, temples, rituals) as reimbursement for their food and labor.

Control of water was important in dry areas, but in regions where rainfall was plentiful, or where there were multiple water sources useful for irrigation, an elite would have had to employ too many functionaries to dominate a water system. Even in eastern Java, water control as the basis of the indigenous agrarian system does not seem to have been a major factor, although rulers based in east Java did build hydraulic networks that gave them better control of agricultural production. One incentive to develop this control was the more significant position that long-distance trade assumed in the east Java economy, particularly the rice-based trade to the eastern Indonesian archipelago via the Solo and Brantas rivers that had developed by the second millennium CE. In contrast, in central Java, overland transport from the volcano-ringed Kedu plain heartland to north coast harbors was more complicated.

Early Southeast Asian trade involved highland hunters and gatherers who exchanged their forest products (e.g., woods, bamboo, and lacquer) and services with lowland rice cultivators. Salt from the coast was a key commodity in this upland-lowland exchange. Another type of exchange network involved hinterland populations and coastal peoples; the hinterland supplied local agricultural or forest products that were in turn dispensed externally to international traders. Coastal-based traders returned goods of foreign origin or specialized services (for example, transport) to the hinterland producers. In exceptional cases merchants worked from a coastal base to organize the necessary trade mechanisms that allowed them to extract local products from their hinterlands. In normal trade, agricultural and imported commodities entered the markets and trading system either laterally, through direct barter between producers and consumers, or vertically, through political or religious institutions or developing hierarchical commercial networks, and only rarely through monetized commercial transactions (Wicks: 1992).

As is the case today, women assumed a significant role in the local market systems. A ca. 1300 Chinese source reports that women were in charge of local market trade throughout the region (Pelliot: 1951, 20; Mills: 1970, 104). While males normally dominated port-based and large-scale wholesale trade, there are counterexamples. The most notable exception was Nyai Gede Pinateh, a female Muslim of Sumatra, China, or Khmer origin, who was the harbormaster (*syahbandar*) of the major port of Gresik on the north Java coast around 1500 (Meilink-Roelofsz: 1962, 108).

Because land was plentiful in the Southeast Asian region, and additional labor was always in demand, women enjoyed a high degree of economic and social status—certainly by contrast with the low economic and social esteem of Chinese and Indian women. Our ability to precisely define the role of women in early Southeast Asian society is clouded by the epigraphic records, our major written sources for the earliest era, which were preponderantly recorded on Indic temples, or on stone slabs or metal plates that were associated with these temples, and were initiated by an elite who were emulating Indic culture. True to the Indian epics and religions that promoted male superiority and female dependency, there are infrequent references to women, and the inscriptional vocabulary is male or universal generic. A discrepancy between Indic-inspired court ideal and reality is conspicuous in contemporary temple relief that portray everyday life, wherein females are participants in scenes that involve not only agriculture and home, but also market, diplomacy, warfare, entertainment, literature, and even court political affairs (Miksic: 1990; Jacques: 2007; Jacques and Lafond: 2007; Zoetmulder: 1974).

In everyday life, male work included plowing, felling trees, hunting, metalwork, house building, statecraft, and formal (Indic- or Sinic-based) religion; females transplanted, harvested, grew vegetables, prepared food, wove cloth, made pottery, and marketed local produce. Because of their control over birth and crop growth, women were believed to have magical powers relative to fertility. Women were deemed to have special capacity to mediate between humankind and the spirit world, and were called upon to heal the sick and to change unfavorable weather conditions.

Bilateral kinship was a common feature of the early Southeast Asian socioeconomy. In determining inheritance, for instance, equal value was accorded the mother's and father's relatives, and sons and daughters usually both received rights to their deceased parents' estates (including land). The value of daughters was never questioned in early Southeast Asia. Bride wealth passed from male to female at marriage (the reverse of the European dowry custom, but very much like bride gifting that was widely practiced among the

Western nobility), and it was normal practice for a married couple to reside with the family of the bride. Temple iconography as well as the earliest literary records portray the marriage ritual as involving the escort of the male, with his bride price, to the residence of the female for the marriage ceremony. Should the husband leave his wife, the bridal wealth, as well as at least one-half of their mutual resources (including their land), remained in her possession. From the perspective of the woman's family an absent husband created no substantial hardship, as the abandoned wife and children were quickly assimilated into the family work unit (Reid: 1988, 146ff).

While the conjugal relationship tended to be strong, and the woman's predominance in the family gave her a major sense of responsibility for its survival, divorce was relatively easy. The Chinese envoy Zhou Daguan, commenting on daily life in the Khmer realm around 1300, writes, "If the husband is called away for more than ten days, the wife is apt to say, 'I am not a spirit; how am I supposed to sleep alone?'" (Pelliot: 1951, 17). Another display of the power and autonomy of women was the widespread practice among men of painful surgical implants of penis balls to enhance the sexual pleasure of their women. For example, the Candi Sukuh and Candi Ceto fifteenth-century mountain temples northeast of modern Solo in north-central Java prominently display *lingas* (male phallic symbols that symbolize sexual fertility) with three or four small ball implants. The Chinese Muslim Ma Huan (1433) provides the earliest written record, reporting that among the Thai:

> when a man attained his twentieth year, they take the skin which surrounds the *membrum virile*, and with a fine knife . . . they open it up and insert a dozen tin beads inside the skin; they close it up and protect it with medicinal herbs. . . . The beads look like a cluster of grapes. . . . If it is the king . . . or a great chief or a wealthy man, they use gold to make hollow beads, inside which a grain of sand is placed. . . . They make a tinkling sound, and this is regarded as beautiful. (Mills: 1970, 104)

In the Cambodian Khmer state, inheritance of the throne of the Angkor-based realm was neither patrilocal nor matrilocal. Although males held monarchical authority, when they assumed power they would record their official descent from either their father's or their mother's family, dependent upon which genealogical faction was most critical to their successful acquisition of the throne. With considerable royal polygamy, wherein marital alliances to regionally powerful families were an important source of political stability, there were numerous offspring who might step forward to assert their claims of rightful descent, backed by their armed maternal relatives. That this was the case is documented in the frequent epigraphic references to the female links of Khmer monarchs, and corresponding failure in such cases to mention the male lineage (Kirsch: 1976). Bilateral succession was also common among the rulers of Java; by the fourteenth century the female lineage was the most prominent and was celebrated in realmwide rituals that proclaimed the Majapahit ruler's maternal roots (Hall: 1996b; Noorduyn: 1978).

STATECRAFT IN INDIANIZED SOUTHEAST ASIA

An examination of Southeast Asia's geography reveals two dominant patterns. The island world is characterized by numerous river systems that flow from interior highlands to the ocean, a feature that has had significant impact upon the island world's social and economic evolution. Over time people settled among these various river systems, populations becoming concentrated only in the broad delta regions at river mouths. This diffusion of the population had important implications for the island realm's political systems, as those who attempted to govern the island world found it necessary to bring multiple river systems under their authority in order to implement their political hegemony. Because it was impractical to control an entire river system, a pattern more common than complete political subjugation emerged—the establishment of partial hegemony through direct rule of only coastal plains and river mouths. By controlling the river mouth it was possible to influence movement up and down a river system. A river-mouth ruler was able to utilize his control over the riverine communications network to forge various alliances with upriver groups.

In contrast to the geographical inaccessibility of the island world caused by the multiple-river-system pattern, Southeast Asia's mainland, along with a small number of island locales, is dominated by major river systems with corresponding broad river plains, which are relatively flat, fertile, and extremely productive agriculturally. These river plains were conducive to the development of population centers by those seeking to cultivate rice in the rich soil of the plains. Rice plain population centers also proved easier to dominate politically than the more diffused population centers of the multiple-river-system geography. Southeast Asia's conspicuous political systems of the past all had a geographical base in the fertile rice plains: for example, the royal center of Pagan Burma was strategically located adjacent to the Irrawaddy River, surrounded by three core productive agricultural zones (*kharuin*); the Angkor-based realm was centered in the Tonle Sap (Great Lake) floodplain of Cambodia; and the Dai Viet state's Thang Long (Hanoi) capital lay between the Red River delta and its fertile upstream in Vietnam.

In the island world this great plain geographical pattern is found in central Java, again in the Brantas River basin of eastern Java, and in the rice plain on the island of Luzon in the Philippines (Hutterer: 1977; Boomgaard: 2007). As on the mainland, population centers and early states evolved in both regions. While the majority of the island world shared the multiple-river-system geography and thus what may be characterized as a riverine political system, the rich-soiled rice plains of central and eastern Java allowed the development of a higher degree of social and political integration than was possible elsewhere in the island world.

The problem of defining what commonly constituted a classical Southeast Asian state may be approached by a careful comparative description of the statecraft—the management of state affairs—of the riverine and wet-rice plain systems. Based on Western and Chinese prejudices that equate advancement with the evolution of elaborate state systems, successful Southeast Asian wet-rice cultures of the mainland and Java are assumed to have become centralized administered polities (Coedes: 1968; Mabbett: 1977a). Historians have also minimized the level of integration between the coast and hinterland of both the wet-rice plain and riverine states (Wolters: 1967). But the wet-rice states were not as centralized as most Western historians have believed, and the riverine states were not as isolated from their hinterlands as previously thought. And the two systems were not totally unrelated, as the mainland states had both a settled rice production aspect and a mobile coastal international trade sector that acted in agency with the economy of the hinterland, and the riverine/coastal states needed the agricultural produce of the upstream, notably rice, to sustain their dietary needs. Thus, the two alternative systems were not at opposite poles but formed part of a continuum. In both, local statecraft was organized to control people and their production, not boundaries. Indeed, the accumulation and control of manpower was the basis of economic and political power.

As noted, pre-1500 Southeast Asia was generally underpopulated. Would-be rulers competed among themselves to attract the labor supply necessary for them to assume power. The continued existence of a state and its management polity—that is, a state in which a court center dominated and integrated its subordinate population centers under its system of administration, justice, and protection—depended on the ruling elite's ability to maintain the allegiance of its population centers. The authority a state claimed and its actual control over people, however, were quite different (Wolters: 1999). The core of the domain was that area of land, usually near the capital, that was administered directly by the state's central administration or its authorized representatives. The king was usually a major landholder in this core, but the landholding rights of others—normally familial or individual rights to a share of the produce from the land under their authority rather than ownership in the modern sense—were also protected (Barrett Jones: 1984). Peripheral populated clusters in those regions bordering the core were in a tributary relationship to the state. Although the state might claim to have administratively annexed these areas, its real control was minimal, as local elites remained in power while paying homage to the center—as long as the center had something to offer them. Although the records of monarchs might be widely distributed, the wording employed in engraved inscriptions found in areas outside the state's core domain, where the ruler's power was not direct, honored the authority of the strong local elite. It was through the support of such secondary leaders of local populations that the ruler could command the loyalty of population centers outside the state's core.

Early states showed little capacity to absorb the populations of regions beyond their core. People of various regions could be brought under the state's sovereignty, yet although a regional population might be swallowed up by a state even for several centuries, with the decline of that state, this same group of people was capable of reemerging with its local traditions intact—a pattern not unique to Southeast Asia. The key to a center's authority over manpower was its ability to form personal alliances with the locally based elite. The ruler, acting from his royal center, fragmented his potential enemies by reaching agreements with the leaders of local population centers, and these potential opponents became subordinate allies of the state. In return for their patronage of the state's monarch, the local elites enjoyed enhanced status in the eyes of their followers, and the allied population received the protection afforded by the state's armies and the symbolic benefits of the state's ritual cults, and shared in a successful state's prosperity.

This characterization of early states as dependent on the interactions of a court center and its surrounding periphery differs from the historiography of the pre-1500 period that depicts the capitals of Southeast Asian states at the summit of a hierarchical societal pyramid, with the monarch and his elite on top having little personal contact with the people below. In this view local populations were subjugated, continually exploited, and generally remained in awe of the elite who resided in the state's court (Heine-Geldern: 1942; Mus: 1975). In contrast, this book asserts that a more intense interaction, interdependency, and ongoing networked negotiations existed between state centers and their subordinate populations (Vickery: 1998). O. W. Wolters applied the term *heterarchy* in characterizing a horizontal networked relationship as the alternative to the conceptual vertical hierarchy, against historians "who detect . . . change in the form of centralizing tendencies" (Wolters: 1999, 152). In some cases the rulers of the earliest states were able to appoint their own clan members to administer key provinces, and thereby maintain a personal local presence on the court's behalf. In contrast, established regional elite and ancestral clans normally became submissive networked allies of a state center, to their mutual advantage (Tambiah: 1976; Geertz: 1980; Wheatley: 1983; L. Andaya: 1993a, 2008). In Java, for instance, state polities (*rajya*) ruled by great kings (*ratu/maharaja*) were divided into numerous regional provinces (*watek*), each governed by provincial chiefs (*rakrayan*), who initially emerged out of the local community (*wanua*) council of elders (*rama*), but who in later times were often the sons of the states' monarchs (Buchari: 1963; Barrett Jones: 1984). In the Sumatra-based state of Srivijaya, key regional population clusters of this realm that was centered in the Straits of Melaka were ruled by chiefs (*datu*), some of whom were relatives of the king, while others were local *datu* with no royal background. The distinction between the powers of the two is never clear in the remaining Srivijaya inscriptions, although it appears that the Srivijaya monarch was quite willing to accept strong local leaders as his subordinate datu, as long as they were legitimately submissive to this authority (see chapter 4).

Srivijaya, Angkor, and other early Southeast Asian states merged traditional indigenous symbols of divinity and power with Indian cosmological symbolism and religious theory to form an ideological basis for their kingship. The blending of indigenous and Indic traditions is seen, for instance, in the universal significance of the mountain in the mainland and Java wet-rice states. In the Angkor Cambodia realm, a symbolic "Mount Mahendra/Meru" temple mountain became the ritual home of the *devaraja* in the cult of Jayavarman II in the early ninth century—a cult that inclusively incorporated and subordinated worship of local deities to the king's worship of Siva (see chapter 6). As the traditional abode of ancestor spirits, mountains were already considered sacred by indigenous tradition. By patronizing the external god Siva, who was known in Indian philosophy as the Lord of the Mountains and for his association with fertility, the kings reinforced their local stature. It remained for Cambodian kings to link themselves ritually with this mountain, the domicile of the ancestors and Siva, and thereby make a profound statement about their ability to guarantee the flow of life-power from the realm of the ancestors—and Siva—to their subjects. In Burma, the various *nat* spirits were integrated into a similar cult that also came to be focused on a Lord of the Mountain, the Mahagiri spirit of the ritual Mount Popa. In both the Cham and Vietnamese realms, kings were regarded as descendants from the union of the *naga*/dragon (water) spirit and a maiden who resided on a mountain inhabited by powerful mountain spirits. The importance of this ritual incorporation of indigenous folk belief is well shown in the case of Vietnam, where one reason for the failure of the early Sino-oriented elite of the upper Red River Delta to form a lasting state was their unwillingness to integrate local folk traditions into their sinic ideology (Taylor: 1986). All the early Java capital complexes were strategically located in close proximity to a sacred mountain, and state ritual complexes were at the foot of a mountain, in a highland plateau, or on a mountainside.

The early Southeast Asian monarch's powers were bestowed and periodically renewed in the course of ceremony. The royal court, its activities, and its style recreated the world of the gods—in theory, a heaven on earth. Here all greatness and glory were possible. By successfully fulfilling his role as the hypothetical focus of all earthly sanctity and power, the king maintained the orderliness of the world. The king's court attempted to develop ritual links to its subordinate centers of power by integrating local religious cults into the state religious network, whereby local deities were acknowledged in the court's ceremonies and were frequently allowed to become subordinate residential deities in the court's core temples, symbolized by placement of an icon that represented the local spirit's submissive presence. The subordinate centers in turn imitated the ritual style of the royal center (Geertz: 1968, 36–39, 1980; Wisseman Christie: 1986). In a combination of top-down and bottom-up networked syncretism, local deities and, of most consequence, local ancestor worship were blended into the state's religious ceremony. The state made great use of Indian (or, in the case of Dai Viet, Chinese) ceremony, performed by religious specialists or elites who assumed the role of priests. These state ceremonies, however, were built on traditional beliefs of how spirits and ancestors were to be addressed to guarantee the prosperity of the living. Indic or sinic patterns were thus utilized to enhance local religious views to the advantage of the elite at all levels of society; the elite's ritual magic was presented to their subjects as being greater than that of earlier practice.

Throughout the pre-1500 era, including the Dai Viet realm, the Southeast Asian elite's patronage of the Hindu and/or Buddhist traditions that had their origin in India brought them into a wider universe of symbols and attachments and provided an Indian framework for their statecraft. Southeast Asian kings utilized Sanskrit and Pali vocabulary, described the world in the idiom of Hindu and Buddhist thought, and sponsored art and architecture that expressed the Hindu and Buddhist worldviews (Tambiah: 1976; Wheatley: 1983; Taylor: 1986). Royal monuments were cosmological symbols redefining the boundaries of time and space to the advantage of the state's elite. A vast and orderly cosmos was substantiated by the most advanced mathematical astronomy of the time and was the foundation for Hindu and Buddhist thought (Lansing: 1991). States were patterned on the order of the cosmos and linked the sacred and secular orders. A ruler and his capital were at the center of the universe; cosmological and magical symbols expressed royal power. In the Hindu and Buddhist concepts of state the ruler facilitated the establishment of a secular society that was more nearly in harmony with the natural cosmic order (*dharma*). In a successful state, society was harmonious as well as prosperous. The most effective ruler did not force conformity by use of physical might (*danda*), but achieved success due to his righteous victory (*dhammavijaya/dharmavijaya*) and continued peaceful leadership. The just ruler was the *cakravartin* (universal monarch), whose illustrious moral force uplifted his subjects and established the secular conditions necessary for the attainment of their salvation (Tambiah: 1976; Reynolds: 1978).

Summarizing their perceptions of the Hindu and Buddhist traditions, early Southeast Asian rulers fused these cosmological principles with Indic topographical formulas (*mandala*—a geometric, typically rectangular or circular "contained core") that provided a design for the integration of village or lineage-based groups into more complex centralized polities. In the Indian philosophical tradition a mandala was a sacred diagram of the cosmos that was normally depicted in art as a geometric construct of encompassed circles and rectangles. The worldly mandala (state) in early Southeast Asia was defined by its center, not its perimeter, as there was no notion of a firm frontier (Tambiah: 1976, 102–131; Wisseman Christie: 1986). Subordinate population centers surrounding the center were variably drawn to participate in the ceremony of the state system. One theoretically moved from the mundane world toward the spiritual one by approaching the sacred axis from one of the four quarters (defined by the points of the compass). The devotee/subject was to become caught up in a psychological state that grew in intensity when drawn to this sacred core of the universe and its "world mountain" (normally a central temple or court complex) that joined the celestial powers with the fertile soils of the earth. Frequently a state water or blood oath formalized this sacred bond.

While in a theoretical sense the king's only duty was to maintain the world order—to protect his realm, promote its prosperity, and facilitate passage to the realm of the ancestors—in practice the monarch's duties sometimes involved the application of customary law regarding land and labor. In an inscription from central Java dated 860, for example, state administrators were asked to intervene in a local dispute when the village elders and representative of a temple could not resolve the method of repaying a considerable debt owed to the local community. In this case the state administrators ruled in favor of the community elders and their foundational rights to secular production over the sacred authority of the temple (Casparis: 1956, 330–38). Early Southeast Asian epigraphy in Cambodia and Java contains many such references to the adjudication of local disputes over land and income rights, which document the important role the early courts assumed as an administrative force providing order to challenges of a local elite's position or a corporate community's land rights by the newly wealthy and upwardly mobile.

Normally, however, courts discouraged all but major disputes from clogging the state's administrative system, and settlements encouraged the continuity of local custom (*adat*), which the state generally left untouched as long as it was not disruptive to state harmony (Higham: 2001; see chapters 6 and 8). Above all, however, the fact that local communities and elites turned to the royal court to settle such disputes reflected their acceptance of their secondary place within the inclusive court-centered network (mandala).

The effective ruler also took an interest in his state's economic affairs. Besides being the ideological center of the state, and in addition to the importance of the court relative to its subordinate centers' acceptance of the court's authority in the resolution of legal matters, the royal capital and its surrounding core was frequently the economic center of the monarch's domain. The economic resources of the state were very important to its ability to maintain power. Rulers of wet-rice states therefore attempted to increase the agricultural output of their core domain. The construction of water tanks and irrigation systems might be undertaken under state mandate or supervision, and courts looked favorably on economic development in general. In Java, for example, to develop economically peripheral lands, reward loyal followers, endow and maintain temples, and extend the control of the throne, kings and other royalty gave royal land grants known as *sima* (freehold). Although such land was considered to be outside the administrative authority of the king—freeing it from royal demands for taxes and service—a ceremony dedicating the sima tax deferment emphasized that the grantee was expected to remain loyal to the Javanese state. This ceremony involved an oath in which the grantee pledged his loyalty, and it culminated with the pronouncement of a curse by a religious official threatening those present who were not committed to their monarch (Boechari: 1965; Veerdonk: 2001). There are similar records from Angkor Cambodia, wherein the remaining inscriptional records detail the Khmer kings' acknowledgment of land rights that are tied to expectations of higher cultivation yields (frequently associated with mandated construction of new water reservoirs locally) and linked transfers of local production to sustain rituals in the state's temple network (Higham: 2001, 152ff).

Although more open to direct international networking, the economic center of the Srivijaya riverine state was functionally similar to those of the wet-rice producing states. It served as a locus for economic redistributions, fulfilling roles both as a trade entrepôt and as the central treasury for a series of ports. A downriver port on the edge of the Sumatra hinterland, the Srivijaya capital was more vulnerable to attacks from outsiders as well as to the rebellions of its upstream hinterland inhabitants than the land-based states that were established inland well away from the coast. Yet the capital's economic control over its disparate subject population—upriver tribesmen and coastal sea sojourners—was similar to that of the land-based states. Because it was difficult to control directly tribal producers who were distant from the court, the Srivijaya state relied on either physical force or alliance relationships, symbolized by a water oath administered to state subordinates, to establish and maintain its economic hegemony in peripheral areas. While a royal navy of maritime sojourners based at the Srivijaya port who had sworn their allegiance maintained the capital's position as the dominant port on the Sumatra coast, a network of ritualized alliances with its hinterland tribesmen allowed a flow of goods from the interior to the ports to sustain the port's resident community as well as provide them with desirable commodities for export—giving Srivijaya its economic and thus its political strength (Bonatz: 2006; L. Andaya: 2008, 49–81 and passim).

The pre-1500 political systems, whether wet-rice or riverine, commonly attempted to draw the resources of their realms—in the form of tribute, talent, men, and goods—to their centers. Central Java states, for instance, expected both taxes in kind and labor service from their subjects (see chapter 5). Inscriptions report that rulers of east Java's states received specified shares of local products such as rice and cloth, as well as goods supplied regularly by domestic traders, such as spices, ceramics, and cloth of foreign origin. Resources acquired from a state's own core, when added to tribute extracted from politically subordinate peripheral areas, supplied the centers with large quantities of wealth. This wealth was in turn redistributed to maintain loyalty to the state. One type of reciprocal investment was the regional construction of large temple complexes that emphasized the state's theoretical powers. Often such construction was financed by the transfer of the royal right to a share of local products and labor to a community, and the community acknowledged this gift, as well as also agreeing to apply this designated income from tax-free "estates" to finance local temple construction and the temple's maintenance. In such instances the royal investment also provided for economic development in the vicinity of the temple, and the construction of elaborate temple complexes contributed to the growth of an indigenous artisan community (Aung Thwin: 1985).

Payments to various state armies and administrators were important revenue outlays of the state. Military power was essential in the process of concentrating as many resources as possible at the center. Military strength allowed the state to protect its subordinate territories—whether in theory or in fact—which in turn facilitated the establishment of the state's economic base, the administration of oaths, and the formulation of the various royal cults. To ensure the flow of revenues that supported the pre-1500 state, a system of recordkeeping was initiated and in the more developed wet-rice states a council was formed to handle it. This royal administrative council, concentrated at the center, was composed of a small group of administrators who were generally literate and capable of dealing with a variety of matters (Robson: 1995, 76–87; Coedes: *IC*, 4:149–50; Ricklefs: 1967). Periodically they were sent out individually or as members of a mobile royal retinue traveling from place to place within the realm to act on disputes that could not be solved locally or on affairs that were considered to be in the state's interest (see various chapters below; Aung Thwin: 1985; Taylor: 1983; Wyatt: 2003, 50–85; L. Andaya: 2008, 82–145). State administrators also participated in the various state ceremonies. In a system of statecraft in which ritual links were a vital tool of integration, it was essential that the state's revenues were sufficient to finance a variety of impressive secular and religious ceremonies. Elite who knew how to conduct the required ceremonies properly performed the ritual at the center, both in appropriately setting the stage as well as in their flawless performances (Tambiah: 1976; Geertz: 1980).

To achieve political integration, the leaders of a pre-1500 Southeast Asian state had to diversify the state's economy as well as manipulate a set of symbols that would distinguish themselves from other elites in the state. Therefore, the ruling elite of a coastal-based riverine state with ambitions of political grandeur, for example, had to promote their state's external role in the international trade community. To accomplish this, they first had to establish their economic and political authority over upriver populations as well as over the maritime-oriented inhabitants along the coasts. To depend only on the redistributions—the allocation of rewards and resources that served to help integrate the society—derived from facilitating trade in a downstream port with limited upstream ties made a coastal-based riverine political system vulnerable to the periodic fluctuations of international trade. If revenues derived from international trade diminished, local political and economic alliances that depended on the ritualized redistributions of trade goods could no longer be sustained. As the international trade diminished, the state's maritime allies frequently turned to open piracy to maintain their personal livelihood, thereby further destroying the coastal center's viability by discouraging sojourning traders from navigating the state's waters (Wheeler: 2006).

Likewise a state too dependent on income derived exclusively from its wet-rice plain base was also limited in its development potential. The rice plain–based state elites of Java, Angkor, Dai Viet, and Ayudhya shared land control with rival landed elites and institutions. Some of the competing institutions had been created by the state's elite to reinforce the state's legitimacy. For example, temples and temple networks were heavily endowed with economic resources by pre-1500 rulers. Initially this patronage returned merit and bestowed superior status on the state elite, but over time the continued endowment of temples had the capacity to concentrate in temples income rights exceeding those of the state. A network of temples could—and in the case of the Burmese state of Pagan did—use their wealth and their control over large segments of the state's land and labor to influence if not dictate state policy (Aung Thwin: 1991).

Since income derived from the land was the major source of a rice plain–based elite's ability to exercise political sovereignty, providing the would-be rulers with material as well as symbolic capital with which to construct alliance networks, a successful sovereign had to have either immense personal prowess or greater economic resources at his personal disposal than did potential sovereigns from other elites within the realm. Trade provided an alternative means to concentrate wealth at the center. By becoming more actively involved in external commercial affairs, those claiming sovereignty in a rice plain state could secure their and their court's authority relative to competing regionally based elites and institutions. Economic leadership in the commercial sector provided a new source of income for wet-rice plain monarchs and in turn enhanced their political accomplishments. Development of an international trade sector also promoted the further prosperity of the wet-rice sector, providing new markets for local rice production and facilitating the expansion of wet-rice agriculture, which then stimulated the development of a more integrated political and economic order (Dove: 1985; O'Connor: 1995; Whitmore: 2011b).

STRUCTURES OF TRADE IN THE PRE-1500 SOUTHEAST ASIAN WORLD

Two models may be used to explain the ways that external trade came into contact with existing and developing internal forms of exchange. One reflects the riverine political system, in which upriver exchange networks connected with foreign trade at coastal centers through the agency of river-mouth rulers, who shared trade-derived prosperity with their downstream and coastal allies as well as with the upstream populations of their interiors. The second model attempts to show how trade was conducted in the river plain realms of the early states of the Southeast Asian mainland and Java. Here, contact with foreign merchants was similar to that in the riverine states, in that it was concentrated on the coast rather than the agrarian hinterland. Local trade gravitated toward these coastal centers, and the state's share of the trade's profits was redistributed to emphasize the ruler's hegemony. But the geography of a rice plain economy held greater potential for the evolution of an integrated and hierarchical system of market exchange, which was capable of facilitating coincidental political and social integration. In both economic systems the inherent potential for conflict with foreigners was minimized because international trading activities were confined to the coastal ports, where business was transacted by locally resident and itinerant merchants who supplied the rice, pepper, and other products the seasonal sojourning seafarers desired (Reid: 1988, 1994; Wisseman Christie: 1998a; Heng: 2009).

RIVERINE AND RICE PLAIN EXCHANGE NETWORKS

Figure 1.1 diagrams exchange in decentralized Southeast Asian riverine political systems (Bronson: 1977). In this model, an economic system's trade center (A) is a coastal base located at a river mouth. Points B and C are secondary and third-order centers located at upstream primary and secondary river junctions. Point D identifies distant upstream centers, the initial concentration point for products originating in more remote parts of the river watershed. Points E and F are the ultimate producers—the nonmarket-oriented population centers of the hinterland and upland or upstream settlements whose loyalty to the marketing system dominated by A is minimal. A_1 represents a rival river-mouth center and its marketing system. A_1 can compete for the loyalty of E and F as well as for trade with X, an overseas center that consumes the exports and supplies imports for A and A_1.

This riverine marketing system is integrated by coercion, where practical, or can be directly administered or colonized by A. A holds the loyalty of its

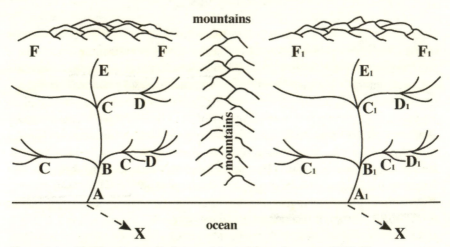

Figure 1.1.   Riverine System Exchange. Adapted from Bronson: 1977, 42

marketing system by exacting oaths and/or tribute or through exercising its ability to select or confirm local leadership. A must also compete with B to establish and maintain dominance over the hinterland network. A relates to B and the other upriver centers via emphasis on traditional mechanisms of alliance, but also depends on X as a consumer of local products or as a supplier of foreign luxury goods, and as the source of the entire network's prosperity. X, though, can likely acquire goods from each of several As, concentrating upon a coastal center where foreign merchants can acquire the best quality or the best deal, or ideally both. X can shift its trade to a rival, without regard for the acute economic or political hardships suffered by a center temporarily deprived of trade, or X can even attempt to deal directly with the interior centers of supply. Points A and A_1 are thus natural enemies, and it is in the interest of one or the other to establish political hegemony over the other. In this instance A's control of A_1's entire marketing network is not even necessary. Bennet Bronson makes the important observation that to conquer a rival coastal center and profit from its commerce, a riverine state needed only to seize its rival's river-mouth center, not its hinterland, in order to dominate the communication network of its rival's entire drainage system. As long as A controls A_1, A will dominate the flow of trade goods to and from A_1's river mouth. A's dominance over B could also conceivably accomplish this same objective. Wars of conquest and even "extermination" were not only predictable but actually made better economic sense than they would for an inland kingdom because the cost-benefit ratio was more favorable. There was no need to subsequently fund the residual overhead of administrating newly won territories, nor to defend against what no longer existed.

This riverine system model can be applied to the Srivijaya maritime state as documented in the early seventh-century inscriptions discussed in chapter 4. Initially Srivijaya's center was in the Palembang area of Sumatra, a point at the intersection of several river systems upriver from the coast, a strategic position that allowed Srivijaya rulers to dominate commerce flowing upstream and downstream from its harbor. Palembang's control over its hinterland was based on its own physical might, but was especially dependent on an oath of allegiance that was administered to the state's subordinate elites, inculcations, the systematic redistribution of wealth from the royal treasury, alliances with local chieftains (*datu*), and the assignment of royal princes to leadership positions in the hinterland. Srivijaya's marketing network was based more upon alliances and the common sharing of the wealth derived from foreign trade than on direct coercion. The Srivijaya monarch was recognized as the source of the system's prosperity.

Palembang's natural enemy was Jambi, a rival coastal center dominating the adjacent Batang Hari River system. Consequently, one of the Srivijaya rulers' first expeditions of conquest was against Jambi in 682 CE. Srivijaya's victory over the rival river-system center and subsequent victories over other river-mouth centers on the Sumatra, Malaya, and western Java coasts guaranteed Srivijaya's control over the flow of goods within the Straits of Melaka, as well as from the region into the international trade route.

The riverine system model implies that the riverine system was by nature impermanent, and indeed some historians believe that the Srivijayan political entity was characterized by a shifting center. The Srivijayan core port may have initially been on the Musi River system but in the eleventh century was at Jambi and was likely based in other riverine centers in the Straits of Melaka region at times in between as well as after (Wolters: 1966a, 1983; Bronson and Wisseman: 1976; Manguin: 1993a; Kulke: 1993; L. Andaya: 2008, 58, 84).

Chinese dynastic records document this internal competition among the various Malay river systems. Numerous river-mouth centers sent tribute missions to the Chinese court in hopes of receiving recognition as a preferential trade partner of the Chinese (Wolters: 1970, 39–48). Such recognition would seemingly have reinforced a riverine center's ability to trade not only with the Chinese but also to assume a special intermediary position in trade with Western merchants who would stop in the Southeast Asian archipelago on their way to China, and who could subsequently claim that they were the trade agents of the local monarch (Kee-long: 1998, 303; Heng: 2008).

While the riverine system diagram provides a model for understanding trade relationships within the island world, the geography and historical records of the river-plain realms of the mainland and Java do not lend themselves to this analysis. The second model (see figure 1.2) better characterizes commercial networking in the rice plain economies of Java and the Southeast Asian mainland. Although discussion of the model in this chapter is specific to Java, the model is intended to illustrate a rice plain state's trade structure in general, and it will be applied to the evidence of exchange in the rice plain states of the mainland in subsequent chapters.

Contemporary Javanese inscriptions portray networks of clustered villages called *wanua* as the most important units of local integration in the pre-Islamic Javanese hinterland. These village networks are generally viewed as units of social and political integration; what is not understood is how the indigenous village networks provided for the flow of goods from coastal ports to village cluster markets. Merchants who had external ties and who were encouraged by Javanese monarchs had a role in providing this commercial linkage (Wisseman Christie: 1998a, 1999). Such encouragement may be seen, for example, in the royal grants to merchants that freed them from royal tax assessments on their transactions within specified village cluster markets

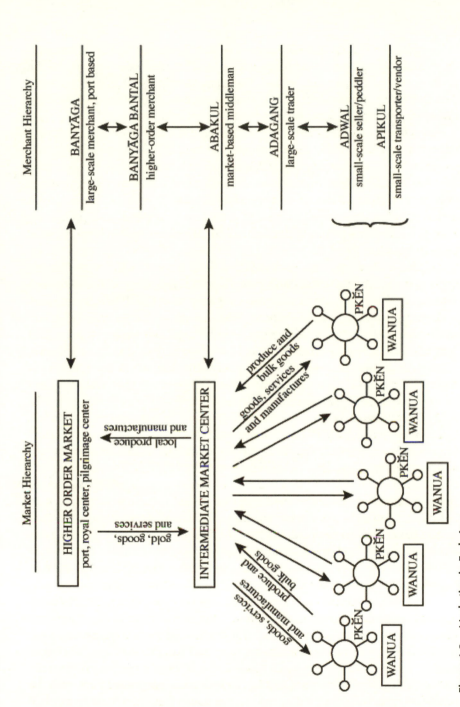

Figure 1.2.   Marketing in Early Java

(Wisseman: 1977, 202). However, the village clusters may be equally understood as local marketing networks whose nucleus was in every instance a
periodic market, identified as *pken* in Javanese inscriptions.

   In pre-Islamic Java, pken village markets operated on a five-day weekly
cycle; itinerant merchants circulated among groups of tightly knit village
clusters within this cycle. Figure 1.2 shows the resulting hypothetical marketing hierarchy. At the base of the marketing system were the wanua, local village clusters ("communities of exchange") that converged at a market center
(pken) where the village cluster's inhabitants gathered once every five days.
The pken markets were centers of local exchange. Market participants
included farmers and artisans who sold their products and who purchased
local goods or those commodities transported to the market by itinerant peddlers (Wisseman: 1977, 211; 1992, 182–85). To facilitate easy access for the
population, a pken marketplace would have to have been located within walk-
ing distance of the homes of the village cluster's inhabitants, thus dictating
the pken market's position near the geographical center of the village cluster.
A local official controlled access to the marketplace, collected taxes on goods
offered for sale, and in general represented the village cluster's interest in
dealings with the itinerant peddlers. It is not clear if this official (*apken*) was
a member of the local community or an outsider appointed by a monarch.
Apken were normally mentioned in lists of *mangilala derwaya haji* (collectors of the king's due), documenting royal interest in local exchange, but
apken clearly belonged to a list of local wanua officials who were paid for
their services in usufruct of wanua land. For example, income from *lmah kap-
kanan* land was a subsidy payment to the office of a market official in one
inscription (Wisseman: 1977, 201, 211).

   These itinerant peddlers, identified in the inscriptions by the titles *adwal*
and *apikul*, linked village clusters horizontally into marketing networks composed of multiple wanua communities of exchange. Peddlers circulated
among pken markets and made their travels conform to the indigenous five-
day marketing cycle—or the local marketing cycle conformed to the travels
of the peddlers. In either case the various village cluster communities of
exchange were integrated into market cycles, which allowed one wanua community's pken market to hold its transactions on a certain day of the week
and others one each on the other four. A band of roving peddlers could thus
have potentially served five wanua communities, participating in a different
pken market every day and trading in each village cluster once every five
days.

   The peddlers and their pken market networks, in turn, were integrated by
intermediate full-time market centers. Unlike the pken markets, the intermediate centers of exchange had permanent shops or at the minimum a market

that met every day. Such centers were inhabited by *adagang*, large-scale traders, who conducted both a retail and wholesale trade, as well as groups of artisans ("Waharu Inscription of 931," in Wisseman: 1977, 203; 1998a, 350). Also based in the intermediate center were *abakul*, market-based middlemen, who were the key to the natural flow of commodities between village clusters and the intermediate market center. Both adagang and abakul serviced the needs of the pken-focused itinerant peddlers, supplying goods of various sorts in exchange for local products acquired by the peddlers on their circuit. Abakul were wholesale specialists who traded in bulk for local production, especially for the rice, salt, beans, and dyes that figure so prominently in lists of Java's major exports (Wheatley: 1959a, 67–86; Wisseman Christie: 1998a, 364–65).

Goods acquired by abakul intermediate traders were transmitted to adagang, the large-scale traders, who in turn transferred goods to "higher-order" merchants, identified by the title *banyaga bantal*, who connected the intermediate marketing centers to higher-order markets that were inhabited by *banyaga*, "large-scale and seafaring traders—"those who encircle the sea, those who travel throughout the sea" (Wisseman Christie: 1977, 205; 1992; 1998a, 365). These higher markets were major commercial centers integrating the various networks of exchange below them during this age and were normally located at coastal ports rather than at a royal court or a major ritual center—the negotiation of major commercial transactions would have been inappropriate to such sanctified centers of elite residence (Wisseman Christie: 1998a, 373–78). It is noteworthy that banyaga do not appear in lists of those participating in pken market exchange, implying that there was a hierarchy of merchant and marketing activity within the early Javanese economy. Banyaga were clearly functioning only at the topmost levels of the marketing system, integrating the intermediate and local levels of commercial exchange to the "foreign" realm of trade. In the Javanese plains, free of physical constraints on the movement of goods from the hinterland, a hierarchy of specialized and large-scale traders connected a number of small, periodic market centers to intermediate and higher order centers of exchange by a hierarchy of specialized and large-scale traders, thus expediting the logical flow of goods destined to be sold to sojourning seafarers (Hall: 2010b).

Javanese kings, especially in the post-tenth-century era of the east Java courts, played a key role in facilitating this trade. They encouraged and legitimized the incursions of port-based traders (banyaga) into the Javanese hinterland to collect specified amounts of produce. The royal stance in relation to the trade is reflected in an inscription that elaborates five royal instructions on the conduct of trade, quality control, and the use of standards and approved weights and measures at warehouses and rice granaries ("Mananjung Inscription," Sarkar: 1971, 2:227–47; Wisseman Christie: 1991, 38–40; 1998a, 373–74; Hall: 2010b). In the tenth century, according to one inscription, a Javanese ruler removed royal taxes from twenty vessels and the shippers of goods of twelve different classes—a total of 135 vessels were operating from one north coast port, reflecting a sizeable trade ("Dhinanasrama Inscription," Wisseman Christie: 1998a, 372–73). Another tenth-century inscription records a royal grant to encourage settlement along the river and roads leading to an east Java port to lessen the danger to merchants and coastal people from banditry ("Kaladi Inscription of 909," Barrett Jones: 1984, 178–94). Development of a port in east Java under royal patronage is also shown in an eleventh-century royal project that dammed the Brantas River to "reduce the threat of flooding to benefit shiphandlers, pilots, and gatherers of goods at Hujung Galah, including ships' captains, and merchants (*banyaga*) originating from other islands and countries" ("Kamalagyan Inscription of 1037," Wisseman Christie: 1998a, 206). Port-based merchants were granted royal charters, and in the era of east Javanese hegemony port-based merchants were even employed as royal tax collectors in areas near their port of residence (Wisseman Christie: 1992, 190–95; 1998a, 363ff). This was a further means of facilitating the movement of goods from the hinterland, and also an attempt by the Javanese monarch to penetrate local political autonomy. The use of foreign tax collectors may also indicate internal political instability, revealing the political system's need to depend on foreigners at that time to support the king's authority, as royal agents might better ensure the profitable flow of commercial commodities between the coast and their Java hinterlands.

It is important to remember that the centralization of trade constituted not only a convenience for all participants but also served as a mechanism for minimizing the penetration of the hinterland by outsiders. Control of the activities of higher-order merchants strengthened the social cohesion of the local village cluster communities of exchange by protecting the interests of indigenous merchants and producers. For a river plain state desiring to participate in the international commercial networks, the aid of foreign merchants and seafarers was a necessary source of extended economic contacts with China and India. Indeed, eleventh- and twelfth-century inscriptions from the Straits of Melaka reflect considerable interaction with a south India–based international trade consortium (Wisseman: 1977, 208; Wisseman Christie: 1998b; Hall: 1978). In subsequent centuries Straits of Melaka communities had similarly beneficial networked relationships with Middle East– and China-based maritime sojourners. The use of seafarers as maritime allies was a double-edged sword, however. These allies could be a source of support or a serious threat to the political system's stability, if they chose to act independently of the ruler's authority. There was always the potential for a port community to initiate a successful challenge to the state's leadership. The port could do this by establishing its autonomy from royal control or by undermining royal authority by supporting one royal faction against another. Further, successful trade made the coastline vulnerable to naval attack. Southeast Asia's early history is full of references to maritime raids, among these the south India Chola raids on Srivijaya's ports in 1024–1025, the retaliatory 1292 maritime expedition of the Mongols against Java after the local ruler beheaded China's court envoys, and the early fifteenth-century maritime interventions of the Chinese fleet led by the eunuch general Zheng He in the Straits of Melaka region (Mills: 1970; Levathes: 1994; Robson: 1995, 57; Wade: 2005).

Thus foreign merchants and seamen who were integral to a ruler's ambitions could also destroy his state. Merchants and seafarers of foreign origin are described in Cham epigraphy from the southern Vietnam coast as "demonic" and "vicious," and are justifiably seen as "a threat to established order" (see chapter 3). To protect itself, and to remain consistent with the essentially inner focus of the Javanese state, the Javanese royal capital was situated upstream and well within the Javanese hinterland. Merchants and seafarers of foreign origin were largely confined to Java coastal ports where the potential danger of their commercial activities could be isolated. Local marketing networks and merchants provided the intermediary links to supply the sojourners' needs and demands for goods. Ultimately, with the coming of more powerful armed foreign traders fortified with gunpowder firearms in the sixteenth century, penetration beyond these ports became possible, with disastrous consequence to the traditional Javanese way of life.

MARITIME TRADE IN EARLY SOUTHEAST ASIA: ZONES AND ERAS

Premodern maritime exchange in Southeast Asia was transacted in five commercial zones (see map 1.1). Zone I, South China Sea Network, encompassed the northern Malay Peninsula and the southern coast of Vietnam and was the first to openly solicit and facilitate East-West trade during the last millennium BCE. In this age Southeast Asia was regarded by foreign seamen as an intermediate and virtually unknown region lying between the riches of India and those of China. The initial agents of foreign contact were Malayo-Polynesian sailors who made voyages to as far west as the African coast and as far as China in the east (Taylor: 1976). Passage through Southeast Asia by international traders became important in the second century CE, as the central

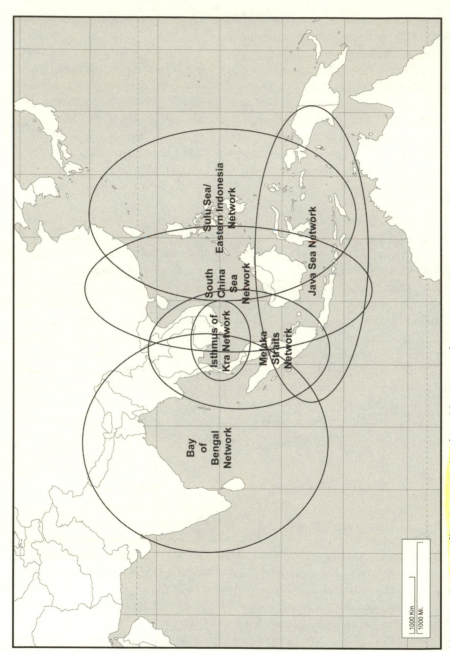

Map 1.1. Eastern Indian Ocean Regional Maritime Networks, ca. 100–1500

Sulu Sea/
Eastern Indonesia
Network

South
China
Sea
Network

Java Sea Network

Isthmus of
Kra Network

Melaka
Straits
Network

Bay
of
Bengal
Network

1000 Km
1000 Mi.

Asian caravan routes, the previously preferred connecting link between East and West commercial networks, fragmented due to internal strife. During the second and third centuries the transport of goods shifted to the sea, and shipping flowed along a maritime route between the southeastern coast of China to the Bay of Bengal via a land portage across the upper Isthmus of Kra. Merchants' transit through Southeast Asia crossed the Gulf of Thailand between the Isthmus of Kra, eastern Malay Peninsula ports, and an emporium on the western edge of the Mekong Delta, known in contemporary Chinese records as Funan, which the Chinese courts considered to inclusively control the critical Gulf of Thailand regional passageway (see chapter 2).

It is unlikely that the same group of second- and third-century sailors made the complete journey from the Middle East to China or vice versa, in part due to the seasonal nature of the monsoon winds, which were critical to navigation. Westerly winds from the southern Indian Ocean begin in April and peak in July. In January the wind flow reverses direction as the northeastern monsoons bring easterly winds. This means that voyagers had to wait at certain points until the next season's winds could take them to their destinations. Because the complete transit from one end of the route to the other was not possible within a single year, sailors found it expedient to travel only one sector of the route. One group would make the trip between Middle Eastern ports and India, and another made the Bay of Bengal voyage to the Isthmus of Kra, where their goods were transported across the isthmus and shipped from the western to the eastern coastline of the Gulf of Thailand, to Funan on the lower Vietnam coast. There commodities from the West were exchanged for those of the East. Another group of sailors then made the voyage from Funan to south China (Wolters: 1967). By the time fleets arrived in Funan ports, those ships traveling the China leg of the route had already departed. Initially no local Southeast Asian products were exported from Funan's ports (Miksic: 2003a).

During this second- and third-century era a second commercial zone emerged in the Java Sea region. This Zone II, Java Sea Network, was chiefly involved with the flow of gharuwood, sandalwood, and spices such as cloves among the Lesser Sunda Islands, the Maluku, the eastern coast of Borneo, Java, and the southern coast of Sumatra. The development of a commercial center, known in Chinese records as Koying, on the northern edge of the Sunda Strait region, was critical in connecting the riches of the Java Sea region with the international route (Wolters: 1967, 55–58). The Sunda Strait location was ideal as a point at the end of the Java Sea where the flow of commerce within the Java Sea and beyond Java could be concentrated. Likewise a Sunda Strait entrepôt offered easy access to Funan and its international clientele. Malay sailors initiated the transport of spices from Koying to

Funan's ports. There they also began to supplement Eastern and Western products with products from the forests of the Indonesian archipelago. Koying well represents the indigenous response to the potential for trade provided by the new maritime activities (see map 2.2).

By the early fifth century the southern Sumatra coast assumed an additional importance, due in part to Java Sea spices. The principal East-West maritime route shifted from its upper Malay Peninsula portage to a nautical passage through the Straits of Melaka, making direct contact with the northwestern edge of the Java Sea (Wolters: 1967, 34–36; Wisseman Christie: 1998a). Zone III, Straits of Melaka Network, thus became the third zone of Southeast Asian commerce, and its center on the southeastern Sumatra coast soon became the focal point for Malay trade in western Borneo, Java, and the eastern islands, as well as the upper Malay Peninsula and its hinterland, the Chaophraya and Irrawaddy river systems (Wheatley: 1959, 67–86). Historians describe southeastern Sumatra in this era as a "favored coast" that aided the flow of commerce, marketing its own Sumatra forest products and Java Sea goods and utilizing Malay ships and crews to connect indigenous riverine and coastal exchange networks with the international route. It was also strategically located relative to contemporary developments in west Java (Wolters: 1979a, 35–36).

Under the Srivijaya maritime state, which dominated straits commerce until the early eleventh century, a pattern of riverine statecraft emerged built on alliances with Malay coastal populations and balanced by an expanding inland power base (L. Andaya: 2008, 49–81). In the eyes of the Chinese, Srivijaya was the perfect trade partner. It was able to keep goods moving into south China ports by servicing vessels voyaging through the Southeast Asian archipelago. Srivijaya's ports were utilized as centers of exchange for those ships traveling over but one segment of the maritime route or as ports of call for ships awaiting the appropriate monsoon winds to take them to their destination. Srivijaya also successfully protected the Southeast Asian zone of the international commercial route from piracy. In recognition of Srivijaya's power the Chinese granted the maritime state preferred trade status, suggesting that those who utilized Srivijaya's ports were given preferential treatment when entering Chinese ports. Historians believe that this Chinese connection was critical to Srivijaya's prosperity and that Srivijaya's power was dependent upon the fluctuations of the Chinese economy (Wolters: 1979a, 39–48). When trade with China's ports was prosperous, Srivijaya thrived. But when China's ports periodically closed, the economic repercussions were disastrous to Srivijaya's political authority. With declining trade revenues Srivijaya was unable to maintain the loyalty of its seafarers, who shifted their energies to open piracy.

The Srivijayan era of economic hegemony came to an abrupt close in 1024–1025, when the south Indian Chola dynasty successfully attacked the Melaka region's ports and shattered Srivijaya's authority over the straits (Spencer: 1983; Kulke: 1999; Sen: 2003, 220–27). This raid began a two-century restructuring of the patterns of Southeast Asian maritime trade. In this era not only Indian but also Chinese and Middle Eastern traders began more openly to penetrate Southeast Asia's markets, moving more directly to the sources of commercial goods. Foreign merchants began to travel regularly into the Java Sea region to acquire spices, a movement that encouraged the development of Java's ports on the northern and eastern Java coasts as trade intermediaries and as ports of call for foreign merchants from the West. The destruction of Srivijaya's hegemony also increased the significance of the southern Vietnam coastline as a commercial power, as coastal centers in the Champa domain that extended from the central Vietnam coastline southward to the Mekong River delta became more prominent intermediary ports of call on the way to China (Lockhart and Phuong: 2010).

The relationship of the river plain–based and previously more internally focused Javanese state to the outside world changed radically during the eleventh and twelfth centuries. During the eighth and ninth centuries the Javanese capital and the territory under its control had been situated in and around the Kedu Plain of central Java, to the south of the Merapi-Perahu mountain range. After the shift of the Javanese state's political center to the lower Brantas basin of eastern Java in the tenth century, and the subsequent consolidation of the eastern and central Javanese plains under one authority, Java rulers began to take a more active interest in overseas trade. This change was in part due to the shift of the royal center to the Brantas River basin and in part due to the increasing economic potential that direct interaction with the maritime traders provided (Boechari: 1979).

Not only was this the era of the Srivijaya network's demise, it also coincided with a significant increase in the volume and economic importance of trade with China during the reign of China's Song dynasty. At the same time that the Java Sea zone flowered as a commercial power during the eleventh and twelfth centuries, the penetration of Chinese seamen from the north through the Sulu Sea to acquire the products of the Spice Islands brought the development of the Philippines and northern Borneo as Southeast Asia's commercial Zone IV, Sulu Sea/Eastern Indonesia. While previously China's rulers had utilized the tributary trade network of non-Chinese to secure international products—because China's rulers had been reluctant to release Chinese seafarers from China's ports, preferring to keep them where bureaucrats could police their overly commercial activities—in the late Song era Chinese commercial specialists were for the first time encouraged to sojourn into the

Southeast Asian region to market Chinese products (e.g., porcelain and silk) and to acquire foreign goods for China's marketplace (Schottenhammer: 1999, 2001; Chaffee: 2008; Heng: 2008). Chinese traders became permanent as well as part-time residents of Southeast Asia's ports and established trade bases in the Philippines and beyond to more directly secure the profitable spices of the eastern Indonesian archipelago, rather than depend on the Java Sea spice trade network (Ptak: 1992, 1993, 1998a). To distribute imports and to gather the forest products the Chinese traders desired, an intensive and extensive network of native trade evolved in this age, and it stimulated major changes in Philippine society (Hutterer: 1974; Morrison and Junker: 2002). The archeological remains of early Laguna, Mindoro, and Cebu society document the rapid growth of Philippine trade centers, as people from the interior and other islands congregated around ports fortified with brass artillery—to protect against the piracy rampant in this region's sea channels—in response to the opportunities and demands afforded by foreign trade (Hutterer: 1973; Diem: 2001, 2010).

The growing interest among the mainland powers at Angkor and Pagan in directly participating in international maritime trade activities resulted in the development of the Southeast Asian trade Zone V, Bay of Bengal Network, during the post-Srivijayan age. Bay of Bengal regional trade encompassed the Burmese, Cambodian, and Thai mainland polities and the variety of domains on the upper Malay Peninsula and the northern and western coasts of Sumatra; India's eastern and southern coasts and Sri Lanka were the regional points of contact with the western Indian Ocean. There was also an overland trade network between Burma and southern China. Southern Sumatra and the lower Malay Peninsula remained principal Southeast Asian landfalls where Western and Eastern Indian Ocean international traders intersected. A mixed ethnic community of Indian Ocean–based Muslim and Tamil traders focused their contact on the Burma and Kedah coasts of the Malay Peninsula, and shifted their activity from Palembang to Jambi on the southern Sumatra coast and Barus on the northern Sumatra coast in the late eleventh century (Wisseman Christie: 1998a; Kulke: 1999).

By the thirteenth century Southeast Asia's regional trade was in the hands of Southeast Asians and Southeast Asia–based traders, inclusive of resident communities of non–Southeast Asian Muslims and Chinese ethnicities, as international sojourning merchants found it once again more expedient to deal with Southeast Asia–based intermediaries at major international emporia rather than attempting to deal directly with those who controlled the sources of supplies (Hall: 2004b: Heng: 2008). This was due in part to the growing efficiency exhibited by Southeast Asia's marketing networks in capably providing goods for the foreigners at selected ports. As opposed to the Srivijaya era, when trade was dominated by a single Malay state and its ports, by the thirteenth century all five Southeast Asian maritime zones had become prosperous and independent economic networks, not as competitors for maritime dominance but representing an integrated commercial prosperity within Southeast Asia. The strongest of the Southeast Asia island realm's political systems, Majapahit, was centered in east Java. Javanese rulers facilitated the Java Sea spice trade but found no need, nor were they able, to physically dominate the more numerous functional ports of the Straits of Melaka region as Srivijaya had in the earlier age (Hall: 2000). Majapahit's rulers established a loose regional hegemony that saw the emergence of new potential challengers, notably among the northern Sumatra ports that depended heavily upon their role as intermediary centers of commercial exchange with Middle East and India-based seamen, and at the end of the fourteenth century, Melaka on the Malay Peninsula side of the Straits (Hall: 2001a).

Java's limited control over the Straits region was also linked to the rise of Straits piracy, which resulted in China's direct military intervention in the early fifteenth century (Wade: 2004; Hall: 2006). The eventual establishment of Melaka as the focal regional emporium was in part the result of initiatives taken by the Chinese Ming dynasty to fill what they perceived to be the absence of a major political power in the area that could be depended upon to contain piracy, which was jeopardizing the steady flow of profitable commerce into China's ports (Wolters: 1970, 47; Heng: 2009). By the 1430s, however, Melaka's prosperity depended less on Chinese support and more on interaction with intermediary maritime sojourners; Champa, Ayudhya, and Java-based merchants; and Java-centered commercial networks that extended eastward to Indonesia's Spice Islands. Java-based seafarers controlled the island traffic to and from the Straits and used Melaka as a trade intermediary through which to market Java's rice as well as eastern archipelago spices (Hall: 2008).

A new era of Southeast Asian commerce unfolded after the Portuguese entry into the Straits region in 1511. Not only did the Europeans take over Melaka, they also penetrated the Java Sea sphere in the eastern archipelago, attempting to assert their control over the spice trade. Over the next four hundred years the Portuguese and other Europeans who followed attempted to impose their hegemony over the sources of the products and to eliminate the indigenous and resident diaspora intermediaries who had controlled trade in Southeast Asia since its inception. Although the Europeans' attempts to monopolize Southeast Asia's trade failed, they did successfully open the archipelago trade to a variety of competing groups, both Eastern and Western. By the seventeenth century ports on Java's north coast, which had emerged as independent economic centers during the decline of the Majapahit state in the late fifteenth and early sixteenth centuries, were destroyed by the emerging inland power at Mataram in central Java. This victory effectively internalized Java's commerce and minimized the role of Java-based merchants in the Java Sea trade. Henceforth control over the international trade was assumed by others. In the Straits of Melaka, in Aceh on the northern tip of Sumatra, and in Johor on the southern Malay Peninsula there emerged successors to Melaka and the Java port-polities, and in the eastern archipelago Malay seamen based in Brunei, Sulu, and beyond assumed control over the regional and Chinese trade with the Spice Islands.

On the mainland new successor states emerged at Pegu in lower Burma, at Ayudhya on the lower Chaophraya River in Thailand, and at Phnom Penh on the Mekong River in Cambodia, all strategically located to profit from the heightened international trade of that era. In Vietnam, the Thang Long–centered Dai Viet state defeated their Vijaya central Vietnam coastline Cham rivals in the late fifteenth century, and thereafter asserted a greater role in the Vietnam coastline's maritime trade from their northern Red River delta port of Van Don (see chapter 7). In the sixteenth century the new rival Nguyen Vietnamese court at Hue reestablished the prominence of the central Vietnam regions, and mixed ethnicities of maritime sojourners based in their Hoi An port were active competitors on the South China Sea maritime passageway, with solid networked connections to southern Japan, south China, and the archipelago regions to their south and east (Wheeler: 2008).

The waxing and waning of states in various parts of Southeast Asia were directly tied to transitions in the international trade, just as the trade routes themselves shifted in response to local power configurations and local initiatives. The following chapters study the multiple patterns of growth and decay as these routes developed out of regional contact with the international trade, and how these contacts affected transitions in Southeast Asian civilization during the pre-1500 era.

2

Early International Maritime Trade and Cultural Networking in the Southeast Asia Region, ca. 100–500

As discussed in chapter 1, international maritime trade and coincident cultural networking in Asia developed in stages. Initial prosperity was centered in the maritime Middle East–India route with overland connections to the Silk Road that connected the West with China. The Indian Ocean maritime route (the "Maritime Silk Road") developed after Rome established its Pax Romana in the first century of the Christian era, corresponding to a diffusion of knowledge among sailors of Greece, Persia, and the Roman Orient on the use of the monsoon winds for navigation, which navigators based in South and Southeast Asia had used in earlier centuries to reach the western Indian Ocean coasts. The point here is that heightened Indian Ocean trade was not exclusively due to the agency of Westerners or Chinese (Begley: 1996–2004; Miksic: 2003a).

When Westerners reached India in the first century they found that there was already regular maritime networking between India and Southeast Asia's Straits of Melaka region. Southeast Asia–based seamen and Indian and Middle Eastern traders routinely made the voyage from India's eastern coast or Sri Lanka to Southeast Asian ports, which provided access to China's rich markets. In the earliest era of maritime trade, ships from Indian ports touched land on the upper western coast of the Malay Peninsula rather than the Straits. They portaged their trade goods across the Isthmus of Kra to the Gulf of Thailand, reloaded them on ships, and navigated the coastline to ports on the western edge of the Mekong Delta, which by the second century CE the Chinese thought to be dominated by the Funan polity. According to the Chinese

37

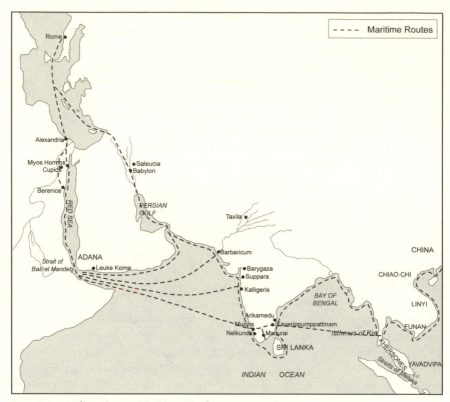

Map 2.1.   Indian Ocean Maritime Trade, ca. 100–600

records, the lower Vietnam coast–based Funan port polity dominated trade in this sector of the commercial route until the fifth century. From Funan, ships departing for south China might make stopovers at Linyi ports on the central Vietnam coastline or in northern Vietnam's Red River delta region, which China's dynasties controlled from 111 BCE to 938 CE.

Traders in the Roman Empire eventually joined the ships on this route, and Western maritime contacts thereafter extended beyond India and Sri Lanka to Sumatra and other commercial centers at the western end of the Java Sea, which in the post-Funan age displaced the upper Malay Peninsula and Gulf of Thailand–adjacent mainland as the principle Southeast Asia centers of international trade. The full development of the maritime route by international traders making regular use of the Straits of Melaka and the South China Sea came in the late fourth and early fifth centuries. By the fifth century commercial networking between East and West was concentrated in the maritime route.

As a consequence, during the first five centuries of the Christian era international trade in Southeast Asia became well defined, regular, and prosperous as trade relationships extended to include new members and products. This expansion of trade in turn stimulated significant transitions in Southeast Asian economic and political organization as well as cultural practices. Once established through the region, route interaction between Southeast Asian peoples and foreign merchants was inevitable; the populations of the region were thus exposed to foreign cultures and ideas. Initially, the role of Southeast Asia's ports in the international trade was simply to provide facilities for foreign merchants who were passing through on their way to China or India or lying over until the next season's winds allowed a return voyage. Coastal port-polities on the edges of settled hinterlands served as commercial entrepôts providing suitable accommodations for sailors and traders; food, water, and shelter; and storage facilities and marketplaces, thus facilitating the exchange of Eastern and Western goods, as well as ideas (Manguin: 2009).

In the initial era of the trade an international sojourner might make the entire journey, but from the end of the first millennium CE, once the volume of trade increased, it was economically inefficient for a trader to travel from one end of the route to the other, and instead a trader might specialize in one segment of the route. There were partnerships among merchants; instead of functioning independently when he arrived in a foreign port, a sojourner could depend on a trade partner, who would act as his local commercial agent. This agent could also store commodities in anticipation of his partner's arrival. The sources tell us that merchants were likely to bond based on family, merchant association, common ethnicity, and/or commodity specialization: for example, Romans, Parthians ("Persians"), Sogdians (eastern Iran-based traders who were prominent traders along the overland Silk Road), Jews based in Egypt and the Persian realms, and Malayo-Austronesians in the earliest era; members of the multiethnic trading brotherhoods based in south India; and specialists in the trade of frankincense, who were collectively highlighted in the early Chinese trade records (Sims-Williams: 1994).

While Southeast Asia's earliest ports seem to have initially developed as commercial stopovers, local merchants took advantage of the opportunity to market their own spices and aromatics as substitutes for foreign commodities and then built upon this substitution to introduce other indigenous products to the international sojourners. Demand for Southeast Asian products quickly followed when spices from Indonesia's eastern archipelago began to flow out of the Java Sea region to international markets in the fourth and fifth centuries. The new marketing opportunities required more formal political and economic relationships between hinterland populations and coastal commercial communities than had hitherto been necessary. At that time the international trade began to act as an impetus to state-building efforts in the broader region, whether as a consequence of or as a reaction to the international trade.

From at least the seventh century BCE, goods from India arrived in Babylon along two well-traveled commercial routes. The preferred overland route, often called in modern writings the Silk Road, crossed the mountains and steppes of Central Asia. By the fourth century BCE, however, Aramaic language inscriptions from the Middle East recorded an active maritime trade along the coast, with goods transported by sea from India's northwestern coast to Seleucia in Mesopotamia via the Persian Gulf and the Tigris River. Alexander the Great's admiral, Nearchus, employed local pilots and commissioned a fleet of thirty-oared galleys that used the same coastal route to transport Alexander's troops from India back to Mesopotamia in 321 BCE (Ray: 2003, 2004).

Such coastal shipping rather than transocean voyages was typical of the early maritime contact between Middle East and Asian ports. Until the first century CE, there was limited knowledge or use of the seasonal monsoon winds, except by Southeast Asia–based seamen who were sailing between the Indonesian archipelago and Madagascar. The small-oared galleys making these ocean voyages tried to stay within sight of land as they hopped from port to port between Mesopotamia and India. Early Middle Eastern literary references speak colorfully of six-month voyages during which trained birds were used to guide ships to land; sailors navigated by the stars and by watching the flight of birds. Merchants and other sojourners commonly booked space for themselves and their goods on the ship deck.

Regional political fragmentation at first limited Mediterranean markets for goods transported along this coastal route; the real blossoming of maritime trade between East and West awaited a stable Mediterranean Sea–centered marketplace. The consolidation of Roman rule provided this peaceful setting. Rome's political growth heralded a demand for luxury goods, among them spices, scented woods, resins, and cloth from the East, which substantially encouraged the expansion of Indian Ocean shipping. Technical advances soon followed as innovations in Western ship construction provided sailing rigs capable of undertaking voyages with larger loads and ultimately promised a means of using the ocean monsoon wind currents, thus enabling navigators to make transoceanic voyages.

Too frequently recent Western secondary sources tend to collectively categorize Middle Eastern traders as "Arabs" (Sen: 2003, 174, 234). This generalization ignores the multiethnic communities from the Middle East who participated in the Indian Ocean trade since its inception. In the earliest era, Parthian merchants predominated, from the period of the Persian king Mithradates I (r. ca. 171–139 BCE) onward. Parthians supplied Indian iron,

Chinese silk, and Asian hides to Rome, and competed with Roman merchants to maintain their monopoly over the maritime trade between India and the Red Sea and Persian Gulf—and even went so far as to try to block Roman envoys from traveling to China and discouraging Chinese embassies from traveling to Rome (Sen: 2003, 161). In the first century CE the Parthian dominance over the Silk Road caravan trade faced a challenge when the Kushanas consolidated their control over the northern India and Central Asia region, and the Parthians further isolated themselves by maintaining their own silver standard rather than accepting the Kushanas' preference for the gold standard as the basis for commercial exchanges. Gold was becoming the more valued precious metal in the remainder of the ancient world, while China retained its preference for silver well into the twentieth century. Then, in the late second century, wars between the Romans and Parthians diminished Parthian fortunes further, and when the Parthian Empire eventually fell to the Sassanids in 225 CE, Persia-based Sassanian and eastern Iran–based Sogdian merchants emerged as the new leaders among Western traders active in the Indian Ocean and the Central Asian caravan trade. The Sogdians were the most prominent Western traders in Asia from the fourth through the eighth centuries (Sims-Williams: 1994). Following the seventh-century fall of the Persian Empire to Islamic armies, many other Persian Gulf–based traders converted to Islam and thereafter became one among numerous Middle Eastern Muslim merchant communities who competed on the Indian Ocean maritime network. New Arabic-language literature described those travels to a receptive public (Sen: 2003, 160–68; Park: 2010).

INITIAL INTERNATIONAL MARITIME CONTACTS WITH SOUTHEAST ASIA

Early references to trade with Southeast Asia are rather ambiguous. Indian literature from the first centuries CE refers to Southeast Asia in general as Yavadvipa or Suvarnadvipa, the "Golden Island" or "Golden Peninsula." The *Ramayana*, India's classical-era mythic epic poem about Rama's attempts to rescue his wife, who had been abducted by the evil king of (Sri) Lanka, records seven kingdoms on the "Gold and Silver Islands" beyond Sri Lanka. The Buddhist Jataka fables from contemporary popular Sanskrit literature mention Indian merchants who went to Southeast Asia in search of wealth. The Egypt-based Roman geographer Ptolemy, writing in the mid-second century, uses *Yavadvipa*, "the Golden Peninsula," in describing the lands beyond India. He makes it quite clear that few Roman sailors were making the passage to Yavadvipa, and indeed Indian evidence indicates that not many Indian sailors were making the passage either.

Chinese records provide a more satisfactory yet still incomplete view of the burgeoning commercial networks that connected China with the West in the era of the Roman Empire (Liu: 1988; Ray: 1994). By 111 BCE, the Han dynasty controlled southern China, and Han emperors, following the lead of the illustrious emperor Han Wudi (140–87 BCE), who was responsible for the development of the Central Asian caravan (Silk Road) route, came to control Guangzhou (Canton), a coastal city with strong commercial interests. Together with Quanzhou to its north, Guangzhou would serve as the early terminus for China's maritime trade with the West. During a break in Han rule from 9 to 25 CE, south China became a haven for refugees escaping from the turmoil in the north, among them northern aristocrats who further encouraged the development of Guangzhou as a commercial center. These aristocrats constituted a growing market for Western goods.

The Chinese used the term *Da Qin* in reference to the Roman provinces in the Middle East stretching from Syria to Egypt. From these western regions "precious and rare objects of all foreign countries" were said to come (Hirth: 1885, 42). The Han history (*Hou Han-shu*) dating from 125 CE vaguely describes Da Qin's trade with the northwestern coast of India. Profit to Da Qin's traders from this trade was said to be tenfold, but "honest" (Wolters: 1967, 40). Da Qin products reaching China included glass, carpets, rugs, embroideries, piece goods, and precious stones. Among these, manufactured goods—notably glassware in the form of costume jewelry, ornaments of colored glass, and glass beads—were especially valued (Wolters: 1967, 39–40; Miksic: 2003, 18–22).

The decline and fall of the Han dynasty between 190 CE and 225, and the corresponding collapse of the Silk Road network, increased the Chinese gentry's need for a maritime link between East and West to supply them with exotic goods. The south China–based Wu dynasty (220–264 CE) encouraged the import of Western textiles (mainly Indian cotton), tree resins, coral, pearls, amber, glassware, jewelry, and other manufactures. When in 226 Da Qin merchants from the West visited the Wu court, they were questioned extensively by the emperor himself, who sent an official to accompany them on their return voyage (Wolters: 1967, 42). The Wu governor of the Chinese province in northern Vietnam was subsequently delegated the special role of advertising south China's interest in this trade. When envoys from the lower Vietnam coastal states of Funan and Linyi paid official visits in 226 and 231, respectively, the emperor congratulated the Wu governor for his "meritorious performance." In 240, the Wu court dispatched envoys led by the court's appointed agent Kang Tai to Funan's ports to view firsthand the nature of

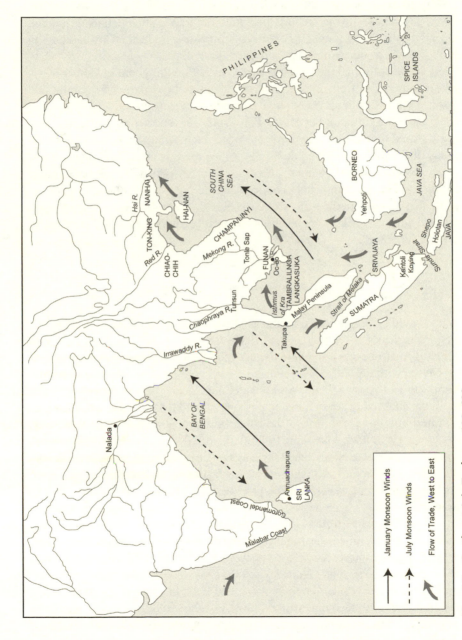

Map 2.2. Southeast Asia Trade, ca. 100–600

trade with the West—and seemingly as well to evaluate whether conquest down the coast beyond the Red River delta would be worthwhile (Wang: 1958, 33). These envoys' reports provided the first written details on Funan, Da Qin, and the networked centers of maritime trade that lay beyond in Southeast Asia, northern India, and the Middle East.

Kang Tai informed the Chinese emperor that the kingdom of Funan was a prosperous realm from which great merchant ships departed for China and India. Funan's authority stretched along the trade route beyond the lower Mekong Delta to the upper Malay Peninsula. He reported that after a major naval expedition in the early third century, Funan had assumed authority over many of the trade centers on the Malay coast, thereby consolidating its dominance over the flow of commerce through Southeast Asia. By the early fourth century, however, significant changes were taking place on the international route that resulted in the fifth- and sixth-century demise of Funan and its networked northeast Malay Peninsula commercial centers (Manguin: 2009; Miksic: 2003a, 28–33).

THE EARLY CHINA TRADE

Who provided passage from Southeast Asia's ports to China and India in the first centuries of the Christian era? Early Chinese records make it clear that Malayo-Austronesian seamen (*Kunlun*) and ships (*kunlunpo*) based in Southeast Asia, with the ships described as extending to two hundred feet in length, rising up to twenty feet above the water level, and said to be able to hold from six hundred to seven hundred passengers and ten thousand bushels (nine hundred tons) of cargo, sailed the route between Southeast Asia and China (Wolters: 1967, 154; Manguin: 1994; Miksic: 2003a, 22). Until the eleventh century no Chinese ships made the voyage on a regular basis, and until the sixth century Persia-based ships went no farther east than Sri Lanka. There is disagreement, however, on who provided the passage from South Asia to Southeast Asia.

Many Western historians initially thought that Indian seamen in Indian-made ships developed the route. In reiterations of this view, it used to be argued that Southeast Asian seamen were not capable of building the great ships making the voyage (Wheatley: 1975, 154). In this West-prejudiced view Indian craftsmen copied the more advanced Persian ships in shipyards along the Indian coast and Indian sailors, most of them Buddhists, then sailed the vessels with their international passengers and cargoes to the "Land of Gold." Other historians now believe that it was not Indians but multiethnic Southeast Asians, piloting ships (kunlunpo) built in Southeast Asia from the

Southeast Asian archipelago to India and back, who provided this early linkage for international merchants (Wolters: 1967, 154). In their view Southeast Asian seagoing populations were responsible for opening the entire sea route from India to China. They point to Western accounts from this age that record voyages by "Malay" seafarers as far west as the African coast and draw the conclusion that if Malay ships could reach Africa, they could certainly reach India (Manguin: 1980).

When the need for a maritime route increased, international sojourners were able to turn their maritime skills to financial gain. Because Western traders at this time were primarily interested in exchanging Western goods for Chinese products without voyaging beyond South or Southeast Asia themselves, access to the ports of south China was a critical factor that allowed Southeast Asia–based sojourners to expand their Western trade. By securing Chinese commodities and transporting them to Southeast Asian and South Asian trade depots, Southeast Asian seamen effectively eliminated the need for Western ships to venture beyond South Asia.

Southeast Asia–based seamen, however, were not only facilitators of international trade; they could be a serious detriment to it as well. They had the potential to be shippers and/or pirates. Chinese records recognized this duality in their report that "merchant ships of the barbarians" piloted by Kunlun seamen were used to transfer the early third-century Chinese envoys to their destinations in the archipelago, and that these seamen profited equally from the trade and from plundering, enslaving, or killing people (Wang: 1958, 20). The Chinese considered Southeast Asia to be generally unstable politically and a potential threat to the efficient flow of commercial goods into China. The Chinese government was most interested in having its political legitimacy and dominance recognized—above all to ensure the stability of their southern borderlands—as it was in establishing commercial goals as the basis of relationships. The Chinese thus looked for a strong, dominant port-polity in the area that would be able to maintain trade and prevent plundering by the sea pirates based in Southeast Asian waters.

The Chinese apparently favored consistency, preferring not to shift alliances from one port-polity to another. They would recognize one port and attempt to maintain a tributary relationship with it. If the state stopped sending envoys to the Chinese court, the Chinese would try to reestablish contact with that tributary state before granting official recognition to another. Southeast Asian states in a tributary relationship with China received token reciprocal material gifts from the Chinese court and the even more valued Chinese recognition of their legitimacy and trading status. Appeals for direct military aid or patronage were almost always ignored. Southeast Asian states did capitalize on Chinese recognition, however, to attract trade to their ports. Chinese support bestowed on them a legitimacy that contributed to their rise. Traders who frequented a "legitimate" coastal trading center were given preferential treatment in their trade with China. The Southeast Asia–based seamen who provided shipping for goods and merchants saw the potential for acquiring great wealth in the China trade and joined forces with the legitimized states. They turned to policing rather than pirating the sea channels and in return for their loyalty shared in the trade-derived prosperity.

So critical was Chinese recognition that any coastal trade depot wishing to share in this prosperity regularly sent a tribute mission to the Chinese court. According to one historian's analysis of these political missions, which were dutifully recorded by Chinese scribes, when they were few it meant stability in the area; that is, when one trade depot's authority over the sea lanes was unchallenged (Wolters: 1970, 38–48). Periods of internal dissension and political turmoil are reflected, on the other hand, by numerous tribute missions, as various coastal commercial centers competed for the preferred status the Chinese could bestow. For example, in the era of Funan's supremacy, Funan ports were officially recognized by the Chinese court and sent few tribute missions. But by the fifth century, when the pattern of trade was shifting from Funan to the Melaka and Sunda Strait region, numerous tribute missions from the former economic subordinates of Funan appeared at the Chinese court soliciting favorable trade relationships. Funan attempted to regain Chinese favor, sending both tributary missions and trade envoys to the Chinese court, but the Chinese, fully aware of the transition taking place in trading patterns, chose to ignore the Funan initiative and to give official recognition instead to the ports of a southeastern Sumatra state as well as to those of Funan's northern neighbor, and potential rival, the Cham state of Linyi.

THE INDIANIZATION OF EARLY SOUTHEAST ASIA

We have seen that the growing importance of the maritime route through Southeast Asia had a significant impact on the political and economic systems of the region. Just what that impact entailed can be illustrated by a case study of the earliest known Southeast Asian political entity, Funan.

As reported above, when in the 240s the first China envoys on record traveled to Southeast Asia to explore the nature of the sea passage, doing so at the behest of the Wu dynasty, they went to Funan on the southern Vietnam coast. The reports filed by the court's agent Kang Tai and his compatriot Zhu Ying offer a window on the origins of Funan (Wheatley: 1961, 114–15; Vickery: 1998, 33–37). Kang Tai's report provides a contemporary glimpse of the prosperous state, informing his emperor that the people of Funan

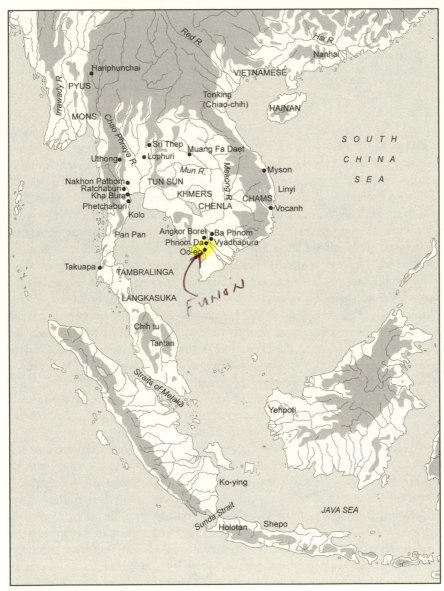

Map 2.3. Southeast Asia in the Funan Age

live in walled cities, palaces, and houses [that are built on wooden piles]. . . . They devote themselves to agriculture. In one year they sow and harvest for three [i.e., they leave it in and it will grow back three years before they have to replant]. . . . [Customs] taxes are paid in gold, silver, pearls, and perfumes. . . . There are books and depositories of archives and other things. Their characters for writing resemble those of the Hu [a Sogdian people of Central Asia whose alphabet and script was of Indian origin]. (Pelliot: 1903, 252)

At the beginning of the first millennium, ports on the lower Vietnam coast, said by the Chinese to have been under Funan's authority, were among the coastal centers in the vicinity of the upper Malay Peninsula that quickly developed to service the growing numbers of merchants traveling the sea and overland Isthmus of Kra route. Revisionist historians, citing new archeological data obtained since the 1990s from extensive excavations and surveys in the lower Mekong River basin, believe that the Funan realm was populated by a mixture of ethnicities. Largely Khmer agricultural societies developed in the Mekong River upstream in modern Cambodia, while mixtures of Mon, Cham, and Malayo-Austronesian fishing and hunting groups populated the lower Mekong and the coast (Vickery: 2003–2004; Bourdonneau: 2003). Already building their own ships, Funan-based seamen recognized that the location of their coast in relation to the new international route across the Isthmus of Kra enabled them to provide passage for Indian and Chinese goods. Soon a Funan port was booming. The latest archeological evidence documents the construction of the port facilities, including buildings for storing goods and hostelries for merchants lying over until the next season's monsoon winds allowed their return voyage (Manguin and Khai: 2000; Miksic: 2003a; Vo: 2003, 47–69; Manguin: 2004).

Archeological data from the Óc Eo site on the northwestern edge of the Mekong Delta supports the Chinese ambassadors' early third-century reports on the evolution of Funan as a commercial center for the maritime trade destined for China; it also connects the Funan polity's rise to the parallel or previous development of Funan's agricultural base. Favorable water resources, soil, and seasonal weather allowed Funan's agriculturalists in the upper delta and lower Mekong River basin to produce multiple rice harvests annually, supplying sufficient surplus to easily feed foreign merchants resident in Funan ports and to provision their ships (Vickery: 1998, 300–1). Clearly Funan's rise had two sources: the productivity of its agrarian system and the area's strategic location opposite the Isthmus of Kra. A network of canals connect the coast to Funan's agricultural upstream, centered on its urban "capital" at the archeological site of Angkor Borei in modern southern Cambodia. It is unclear whether this canal network required a new level of technological competence or a central leadership for its construction (Malleret:

1959–1963; Liere: 1980; Stark: 1998, 2003, 2006a, 2006b; Stark and Sovath: 2001). The question arises whether Funan's emergence was the consequence of indigenous evolution or the result of a significant input of foreign expertise, especially Indian. To answer this question, it is necessary to examine Funan's earliest history.

INDIANIZED FUNAN

According to the Chinese sources, the Funan state was founded in the first century CE. Its origin is suggested by a local legend that was already old when Chinese visitors recorded it in the 240s. According to this legend, Funan began when a local princess (whom the Chinese called Linyeh) led a raid on a passing merchant ship of unspecified nationality. The ship's passengers and crew managed to fend off the raiding party and make a landing. One of the passengers was Kaundinya, a man from a country "beyond the seas" (India). Linyeh subsequently married him, and the legend says he drank of the local waters, suggesting an oath of loyalty. As Funan was a matrilineal society, Kaundinya thereby became part of the local lineage, and as its heir he became the first Funan monarch. The realm that Kaundinya and Linyeh inherited consisted of several settlements, principally along the Mekong, each with its own local chief. Kaundinya and Linyeh later transferred seven of these to their son, while retaining the rest as their own (Pelliot: 1925, 246–49).

During their reign, according to the legend, Funan began attracting merchant ships by providing secure facilities and harbor improvements. The Kaundinya myth suggests that Indians were using Southeast Asian ships on their passage through Southeast Asia, for the myth does not specify that Kaundinya was traveling on an Indian ship, but says simply that a man from beyond the seas was on a ship of unremarkable and thus presumably local origin. This is certainly plausible, for Chinese records report that ships were being built in Funan's ports, including the ships that the Funan monarch Fan Shihman had ordered constructed for his third-century expedition of conquest against Malay Peninsula port-polities (Miksic: 2003a, 22).

Legends like the Kaundinya story cannot be taken too literally, but as symbolic if not metaphoric references. Early societies did not compose oral or the earliest written history as "fact" in our modern sense, but as mythical references that were attuned to their audience, or what their audiences were preconditioned to hear relative to their own lifetime experiences. In this light the Kaundinya myth, and others to be encountered in subsequent chapters of this book, above all provide meaning relative to a specific local space, in references to mountains, water, and sky. The upstream homeland leading to the mountainous interior offered security, while the coastal realm adjacent to the sea, which was the most physically threatening as the source of seasonal typhoons and subsequent flooding, was also the borderland to the unknown, from which came strangers.

This particular story combines a myth of the Indian origin of Funan's rulers with an older myth, common among the Malayo-Austronesian peoples, which described a marriage between a sky god and a foam-born *naga*/snake princess (or sometimes a princess born from a bamboo shoot). The Kaundinya legend parallels this latter myth, as Kaundinya, and the Indic celestial religious tradition he represents, is the "sky god" (foreigner) who unites with the naga (local) earthbound princess, representing local worship of animistic spirits, which together (the celestial Indic religious tradition that is localized with the preexisting indigenous animism) become the basis of Funan's future. The basic elements of the Kaundinya legend are reiterated elsewhere in Indic and Southeast Asian folklore, but historians have not been in agreement on its interpretation (Przluski: 1925; Vickery: 1998, 36). What seems most likely is that it suggests that the rulers of Funan began a cultural dialogue with India at the same time as they were integrating their settlements into larger domains.

The details of this cultural dialogue are a matter of dispute. It used to be argued that Indian Brahmans, or perhaps Indian traders claiming to belong to this Indian upper caste, traveled to Southeast Asia and presided over an Indianization of the region. According to this view, South Asians united in marriage with the daughters of the local chiefs and then converted the rulers and their subjects to Indian ways. Because the local population had no equivalent vocabulary or understanding for the social, moral, and religious innovations brought by the foreigners, the Indians used their own terminology as they worked to uplift the native population culturally. Indic culture soon engulfed the more primitive local civilization, and the local population became subjects of Indianized states.

While not denying the role of South Asians in stimulating the formation of early Southeast Asian states, revisionist historians opposing these South Asian agency theories have more recently stressed the active role of Southeast Asia's indigenous rulers in forging the initial linkages with the bearers of Indian culture (Miksic: 2003a; Tingley: 2009). Some scholars have reasoned that the maritime traders most likely to have initiated contact with the Southeast Asians would have been incapable of transmitting the more subtle concepts of Indian thought, due to their lack of formal training. Revisionists, therefore, stress the idea of a mutual sharing process. According to this view, local rulers, having learned of Indian culture through their trading relationships with South Asia, invited trained personnel from India who then guided the Indianization process. One of these revisionist proposals has it that the original contacts had been with Indians traveling to Southeast Asia, while according to another proposal the initial contact came through the agency of the Southeast Asian sailors who seem to have dominated the earliest East-West maritime routes.

Whatever the manner of the initial contacts, Southeast Asian rulers recognized in Indian culture certain opportunities for ritual, administrative, and technological advantages useful against local rivals. They also recognized that by Indianizing their courts they could facilitate trade with South Asia–based merchants and thereby increase their income. To obtain those advantages, the Southeast Asian rulers therefore encouraged the immigration of literate Brahmans to help them administer their realms. Thus, the early era of trade contact was one of adaptation and learning—an apprenticeship period during which rulers of emerging states were curious about Indian and other foreign cultural traditions and were in the habit of looking overseas for cultural and economic benefits. In this view the initiative was Southeast Asian, not Indian, and Indianization itself was a slow process of cultural synthesis dictated by local need, not a rapid imposition of Indic traditions caused by a massive influx of Brahmans (Wisseman Christie: 1995; Wolters: 1999, 107–25).

As discussed in chapter 1, the motives for these developments are clarified when we realize that the early Southeast Asian polities were not states in the modern sense. Rather, they were tribal societies that from time to time produced chiefs who were able to impose their hegemony over neighboring chiefs by mobilizing military power through family networks, clans of relatives and their allies, and marriage alliances to other chiefs' groups. Certain teachings from the Indic religious tradition would have supported these chiefs' efforts to distinguish themselves from their peers. In particular, the chief could build on the notable heroic accomplishments that had demonstrated his military prowess by referring symbolically to the Indic philosophical notion of ascetic achievement through meditation and ritual performance. Thus, after consolidating his position, whether by force or by offering access to new economic and culturally meaningful resources, the successful Southeast Asian chief would begin to practice Hindu asceticism to further enhance the local perception of his spiritual superiority. The local ruler's ascetic achievements and ritual performances demonstrated his close relationship not only with the indigenous ancestors and spirits, but also with the celestial and universal Indic deities.

In the early Southeast Asian polities the most significant of these deities was the god Siva, whom early mainland inscriptions depict as not only the source of fertility but also the patron of ascetic meditation and the supreme lord of the universe. Rulers of ascetic achievement were characterized in their inscriptions as Siva's spiritual authorities on earth, and since Siva's authority over all that exists was absolute, in theory the rulers' own powers on earth had no limit (Tingley: 2009, 132, 144).

The ruler's claims to partake of divinity took his followers beyond their existing relationships with ancestors and local chthonic spirits, holding out the potential rewards of a relationship with an omnipotent Indian divine. Due to the political attractiveness of these notions, Southeast Asia's early rulers focused not on the development of state institutions of secular scholarship, but rather on the institution of religious cults that allowed followers to draw inspiration on the leader's spiritual relationships. Local populations responded by rallying behind these spiritually endowed leaders, who were supported by a blend of local and Indian cultural symbols and values. Successful leaders were therefore able to use these symbols and values to mobilize local populations for various intraregional adventures.

Economic relations were also important. Whatever our precise understanding of the process of Indianization—whether imposed by Indian immigrants or invited by Southeast Asia rulers—there is general consensus today that Funan's political development was stimulated in some way by contact with the entrepreneurial activities of traders of various cultures. Funan's chieftains were hardly passive actors in this process, for they oversaw the initial commercial transactions with foreign traders. The local chieftains were the instigators and organizers of Funan's ports. Furthermore, as mediators between the traders and the local population, they selectively adapted Indian-derived vocabulary and concepts for their own purposes.

This in turn had implications for the development of Funan's political culture, for as the international trade through its ports increased in volume, Funan's rulers were subjected to a range of experiences that expanded their statecraft capabilities beyond those of other land-based mainland populations, such as the Mons who were evolving in modern-day Thailand to the northwest. There smaller settlements called *ra* in seventh-century inscriptions were clustered around larger "urban centers" called *dun*, among these the U-Thong, Nakhon Pathom, and Khu Bua settlement sites; these sites and other archeological remains scattered across the Malay Peninsula and central and eastern Thailand are collectively referenced as marking the first-millennium CE Dvaravati civilization. Dvaravati artifacts include refined Buddhist statuary in the Indian style; Wheels of the Law, symbolizing the Buddha's first sermon and teaching, that were erected on the pillars of Buddhist temples; and distinctive pottery, all similar to the evolution of religious practices indicated in the remaining Funan artifacts (Vickery: 1998, 83–138; Dhida: 1999; Robert Brown: 1996; O'Reilly: 2007, 65–90).

Through their international contacts, Funan's leaders were exposed to new life goals and new perceptions of the cosmos, becoming especially aware of new organizational possibilities. The local ruler thus became a cultural broker, while also being the principal beneficiary of profits directly derived from the commercial route. The Funan monarch's material rewards included ceremonial regalia, beads, textiles, and wealth that could be shared with clients (particularly precious metals, the cash of the period, and other items that could be useful to a submissive local chief attempting to stress his own superiority over potential competitors for power). Funan's paramount chief thus had a vested interest in continuing and expanding the evolving commercial system. The trade gave him the material means to consolidate his rule, while the Indian notion of divine kingship enabled him to assume a more illustrious personal status by using Indian-derived symbols and rituals to reinforce and enhance prior notions of legitimate and empowered leadership.

As previously discussed in chapter 1, Southeast Asia's local rulers traditionally had mobilized followers through ties of marriage and kinship. It is significant, therefore, that the Funan origin myth of Kaundinya and Linyeh, which localizes Indic religion, also weds the local social system with the culture of India. In this myth, the local princess married a foreigner and thus established for him a place within local matrilineal society. He subsequently "drank the waters," which suggests that he took an oath of loyalty to the local ruler (i.e., he entered his/her service), or that he in some way assisted in the development of the local agrarian system. The prominence of the local princess/chief in the legend denotes the importance of women in Funan society prior to its adoption of the Indianized style of patriarchal statecraft, in which males normally assumed leadership roles.

The story also carries the important moral that good things come not from attacking and plundering passing ships, but from befriending and servicing them. Funan's prosperity was ultimately tied to maintaining good relations between its own populations and the assorted traders and religious pilgrims who passed through the area. Note that the initial contact was a raid in which the princess Linyeh led a band of local seamen from the Funan coastline against the passing merchant ship. This is symbolic of initial efforts to bring shipping to Funan's ports by force, and it may demonstrate an early pirate stage in Funan's development (Wheeler: 2006). However, the myth ultimately rejects piracy, as only by the marriage of the local ruler with the ship's traveler was Funan's future prosperity guaranteed. The marriage of the princess and the foreigner therefore sealed a commercial and a cultural compact with foreign merchants and their Indic culture.

Though the Funan origin myth may not document an actual marriage between a native princess and a foreign traveler, it symbolizes a marriage of interests. In order to develop into a successful entrepôt, Funan had to present a cosmopolitan character. The Kaundinya myth suggests that Funan's ports became such a neutral meeting ground. This transformation of the Funan realm's coastal centers into networked international ports depended on the local ruler's initiative in organizing and inspiring his supporters to facilitate this trade. First, port facilities had to be built. Second, these would-be commercial centers had to establish themselves as purveyors of the goods desired by international traders. In the case of Funan this was initially done by providing superior facilities or, if necessary, by using force to build up a supply of desirable goods in its ports.

Chinese and Western goods were the initial staples of the trade passing through Funan's ports, as traders from Funan went to China to exchange Mediterranean, Indian, Middle Eastern, and African goods (such as frankincense and myrrh, other plant resins, and assorted substances used to manufacture perfumes and incense) for China's silk and ceramics—critically, China was an indirect participant in the local marketplace, as China's products were exported rather than locally consumed (Miksic: 2003a, 18–22; Manguin: 2009). However, Funan also increasingly imported Southeast Asian goods that supplemented these staples. For example, copper and tin were transported downriver from the uplands of modern Thailand to supply the workshops of Óc Eo in Funan, where, according to the results of recent excavations, there was no lack of raw materials (Wolters: 1967, 52; Bronson: 1992; Miksic: 2003a, 18–22; Tingley: 2009, 138–39). In addition, a growing flow of goods was brought by Southeast Asian sailors from the islands of the Indonesian archipelago.

Initially, neither the Indians nor the other international traders using the ports of Funan were interested in the Southeast Asian specialties. But as the international transit trade at Funan grew, sailors from the Sunda Strait area to the south (in western Indonesia) began to introduce their own products for the Chinese market, beginning with some that might be construed as substitutes for goods from farther away. Sumatran pine resins were substituted for frankincense, and benzoin (a resin from a plant related to the laurel family, also known as gum benjamin) was substituted for bdellium myrrh. Soon the sailors from the western Indonesian archipelago began introducing their own unique new products.

One of the most important was camphor, a resin that crystallized in wood and that was valued as a medicine, as incense, and as an ingredient in varnish. The most highly prized camphor came from Sumatra's northwest coast (Ptak: 1998b). Products also began to arrive from Indonesia's eastern archipelago. Aromatic woods such as gharuwood and sandalwood (a specialty of Timor) became important commodities, as did Borneo's camphor, and the fine spices of the Maluku Islands also began to appear in international markets. Charaka, a court physician of the northwest Indian monarch Kanishka at the end of the first century CE, references eastern Indonesian cloves in his medical text, as do fourth-century Gupta court poets (Wolters: 1967, 66).

Trade was not the only basis of the early Funan polity, for it was also generating an agricultural surplus. In addition to its references to the cultural and commercial compact on which Funan was based, the origin myth's depiction of the foreign traveler drinking the water of the land can be interpreted as an allusion to the construction of a Funan hydraulic system, which was the critical link to support the flow of hinterland produce to the coast. Air surveys of the Funan region substantiate the archeological evidence to show a network of skillfully laid out channels between the Bassac estuary and the Gulf of Thailand—hundreds of canals, estimated to cover 120 miles (200 kilometers), connecting at least a dozen population centers whose people lived within earthen ramparts in houses built on stilts (Paris: 1931, 1941; Bourdonneau: 2004; Sanderson: 2003).

The Funan origin myth in its different versions describes the early Funan domain as being comprised of several settlements, each ruled by its own chief. This would be consistent with the view of many scholars that early Southeast Asian states, including Funan, derived their power from networked control over manpower rather than from landholding rights (Wolters: 1979a, 1999). In the Chinese citation of the origin myth the first Funan king was said to have retained authority over the core sector of his realm, while eventually assigning to his son seven "centers" that together became a subordinate secondary "realm." These seven networked population centers were thereafter ruled indirectly through the son. Whether they had been networked and ruled as a unit before this assignment is unclear. Were these new settlements that had come into existence when rice cultivation spread into unoccupied land, later grouped into a new administrative unit/region under the delegated authority of the Funan monarch's son? As networked territories under the authority of a subordinate Funan chief, how far would their loyalty have extended beyond the familial ties between Funan's ruler and the son who was their initial regional ruler/chief? More generally, what, beyond such personal ties and accompanying oaths of allegiance, would have created the continuing desire of regions beyond Funan's heartland to affiliate with the Funan monarch's leadership?

Some answers to these questions are suggested in the revisionist work of Southeast Asia specialist historians (Vickery: 1998; Higham: 2001, 13–35; Vickery: 2003–2004; Bourdonneau: 2003). Drawing attention to the archeological evidence of dispersed communal population centers ("villages") in the area, there is common agreement that early Funan was a polity composed of networked villages, a vision consistent with the picture presented in the third-century Chinese records. Drawing from later seventh- to eighth-century Khmer and Cham inscriptions and working backward to the Funan-era Chinese sources, scholars posit that Funan's influence extended over the scattered areas of fertility in the delta region, reaching roughly from Óc Eo near the coast to Angkor Borei on the northern edge of the Mekong Delta. Mountains separated this region as a whole from the developing Cambodian agricultural plain to its north.

In one scholar's view, in this early Mekong Delta domain, as was also the case in the neighboring Khmer regions to its north, local chieftains, known in the Khmer language as *pon*, held authority over networks of village population clusters that grew enough rice for self-sufficiency. The earliest inscriptions show that the traditional pon's (chief's) power over the local population derived from his ritual strength rather than control over land. The pon was backed by his lineage group, whose familial guardian deity was locally preeminent. Pon and their kinsmen controlled the clan spirit house, where they worshipped a locally prominent female deity (*epon*) on the behalf of other community residents. (Vickery: 1998, 22, 258). Villagers committed to a pon's authority because they believed the pon and his lineage group were more spiritually empowered than others. Initially, then, local authority was not economically derived except as it related to local agricultural communalism, for in purely economic terms the pon and his kinsmen were merely the highest among economic equals.

This local system of ritually empowered chieftainship changed with the rise of maritime trade, because the trade provided opportunities to accumulate wealth beyond the scope of the pon's traditional share of communal production. This further enhanced the importance of family ties, while structuring them in new ways. The traditional system was a matrilineal one in which inheritance passed from the father's brother (the uncle) to the sister's son (the nephew); a man never inherited from his father (Vickery: 1998, 19, 23). By contrast, new externally derived wealth could be passed directly to the chief's own children or parceled among a network of client chiefs. While traditional wealth and production were subject to group/familial rights, the newer goods were subject to personal rights of possession. Thus, the new wealth from outside the community could be used to support personal authority over traditional community entitlements, and it enabled creation of broad alliance networks and concentrations of power that might sustain seizures of land and manpower. These contrasts between communal and individual conceptions of the basis of rights and power could lead to conflicts, as happened with the accession of the king Fan (pon) Shiman as described below. Though this externally derived wealth had made it possible for chiefs to build more powerful self-centered networks, Funan was hardly a tightly organized, centrally controlled realm.

The Óc Eo archeological site remains document Funan's wide-ranging web of trading networks. The archeological remains include an abundance of Indian and western Indian Ocean artifacts, jewels, gold rings, merchant seals, and Indian ceramics and tin amulets with symbols of Visnu and Siva. There are also Roman materials dating to the second through fourth centuries, including glassware fragments, a gold coin minted in the reign of Marcus Aurelius (r. 161 to 180 CE), and a gold medal of Antoninus Pius dating from 152 CE. Imports from China include a bronze mirror dating from the Later Han dynasty (first to third centuries) and several Buddhist statuettes from the Wei period (386–534 CE) (Malleret: 1959–1963; Tingley: 2009, 120–22, 136–45, 162–71).

In addition to objects of Western and Eastern origin, there is ample evidence of local craft production. Glass beads, possibly produced by a local application of Western glass technology, are abundant in the Óc Eo excavations, as are significant quantities of local ceramics. More impressive, however, are the numerous molded and engraved tin decorative plaques, as this type of tin-working is not known to have been practiced elsewhere at the time.

In addition to these Western objects and local crafts, there are local adaptations of Indian religious art, especially in the sculptured stone architecture found in Funan's core area. These adaptations show features that are unique to Funan. While Indian stone carvers in this early era normally sculpted statues that were part of wall relief or were backed or enclosed by a stele or a wall, Funan sculptors developed their own freestanding style, which is demonstrated in several wooden standing Buddhas, believed to date to the sixth century, that were miraculously preserved in the mud near Binh Hoa (Tingley: 2009, 126–27, 134–35, 154–55). The standing wooden Buddha statues impressed one art historian with their "delicate and graceful [bodies], soft and smoothly rounded, with muscles indicated only slightly, yet with astonishing sensitivity, so that one feels the swing of a body motion, or the balance of a gently bending body at rest" (Groslier: 1962, 63). This sculptural expression reached its height in the early sixth century, as documented in a variety of stone carvings of Visnu and Buddhist statues discovered at multiple Funan sites. The sexless style of this statuary is characteristic of later Southeast Asian Buddhist sculpture, which was seemingly modeled on that of the Funan-era craftsmen (Vickery: 1998, 45–46; Christie: 1979; Cooler: 2010).

Also demonstrative of local initiative is a building ("K") at Óc Eo where local architects constructed a temple modeled on the rock sanctuaries that were popular in southern and central India during the late Gupta period (fifth and sixth centuries). The crafting of this brick and granite temple in an area with no cliffs or large rocks demonstrates the sophistication of local technology. The skill by which the granite slabs were joined together shows the local control of technique. Such artistic initiative impressed the Chinese court, which received several stone Buddhist statues that the Indian monk Nagasena brought from Funan in the late fifth century. In 503, a Funan monarch also sent the Chinese emperor a coral statue of the Buddha and an ivory stupa as "tributary" gifts (Pelliot: 1903, 257–70, 294).

The coinage found at the Óc Eo excavations further substantiates Óc Eo's contacts with the regions to its west (Malleret: 1959–1963, 3:948–49; Gutman: 1978; Wicks: 1985, 196–99; Miksic: 2003a, 23–24). Notable among the coins recovered, most of which date to the second-to-fourth-century period, are silver conch/Srivatsa (an auspicious Indian symbol of fertility and abundance usually associated with Sri Laksmi or a tuft of hair on Visnu's chest) weighing 8.3 to 8.6 grams, as well as later Rising Sun/Srivatsa coins weighing 9.2 to 9.4 grams, all of which originated in the coastal region of southern Burma. At Óc Eo, sixty-eight to seventy wedge-shaped pieces cut from Rising Sun/Srivatsa coins were recovered, and it is thought that the cut portions were used as fractional coinage in local marketplace transactions. Since no similar cut portions of the Burma silver coins (or of any other coinage from that era) have been recovered in Burma or Thailand, this evidence substantiates the Funan coast's greater importance at this time, due to its need for smaller-denomination currency to sustain local exchange (Wicks: 1985, 196–99; Miksic: 2003a, 24).

The Óc Eo archeological evidence, together with information from recent study of Bengali scripts and seals, also provides important information on trade with South Asia. Kushana merchants from northwest India assumed an important role in that trade. The Óc Eo remains include unique seals of South Asian origin, similar to those found in sites associated with contemporary lower Burma, which are attributed to Kushana merchants. The scripts and seals of Gupta-era Bengal (fourth to sixth centuries) substantiate especially the existence of a luxury trade in horses, which were transported overland from India's northwest frontier down the Gangetic plain to Bengal, where they were shipped by boat to south China via the Funan emporium. The archeological remains from Bengal, notably terra-cotta seals found there, depict the sea trade in horses and highlight the Kushana horse traders who were their source (Chakravarti: 1989, 348; 1999, 194–211). This and other evidence—consisting of plaques, seals, pots, and coins—supports the conclusion that Kushana merchants, whose trading network extended across the Gangetic basin from northwestern India, were present at the mouth of the

Ganges during the time of Óc Eo's commercial prominence (Ray: 1994, 87–120).

The horses that were shipped through Funan from northwest India were a very important item of trade for the Chinese, and their availability may have been an important factor in Funan's development as an entrepôt. During the second century, especially, the Chinese Han dynasty had required horses for their wars against the Xiongnu, seminomads who inhabited the steppe region of Central Asia (Creel: 1965). These wars in Central Asia, together with the political confusion in China that reigned in the chaotic years (190–225 CE) leading to the demise of the Han dynasty, created a need for a new trade link between China and the West. The need for the horses became even more acute when the Wei dynasty took control of the Silk Road approaches to China, forcing the southern China–based Wu dynasty (220–64 CE) to develop a maritime trade route that would also allow its elite to continue their consumption of the desired Western products.

The discovery that the maritime route could supply horses apparently came by accident. As was discussed above, Funan's contacts with China were said to have begun when Lu Tai, the Wu governor on China's southern frontier, was ordered to advertise China's interest in trade by sending envoys "to the south." As noted above, Funan and neighboring Linyi responded by sending diplomatic missions to the Wu court in 226 and 231 CE. In turn, the Wu envoy Kang Tai, who visited Funan ports to evaluate their potential for trade, reported that among the commodities available in Funan were Yuezhi (Arabian, Indo-Scythian) horses from Central Asia. In Funan, according to Kang Tai, "There is a saying [that] in foreign countries there are three abundances, the abundance of men in China, the abundance of precious things in Da Qin [the Roman West], and the abundance of horses among the Yuezhi" (Wolters: 1967, 41). Kang Tai reported that the Yuezhi horses were continually being exported to Funan by South Asia–based merchants and said that when he visited Funan he encountered a Persian Sogdian merchant with whom he explored the possibility of entering a horse importing partnership (Sen: 2003, 162; Wolters: 1967, 59–60).

Thus it was that the horses of Central Asia, which had made their way to the Bengal region of India and thence to Funan, were now reexported to China. This documentation, in addition to the archeological remains—particularly Funan's crafts and the evidence of its trade with China, central Thailand, southern Burma, Bengal, and points farther west—not only demonstrate Funan's economic prominence but supply part of the rationale for considering it a state.

FIFTH-CENTURY TRANSITIONS

In the fifth century, Funan's maritime dominance was crumbling and it consequently needed to refocus on developing its agrarian base as the principal source of royal revenue collections. Funan's irrigation innovations thus date to this fifth- and sixth-century era of Funan's transition to a more agrarian lifestyle, and Indianized statecraft, which favored a settled agrarian society, was potentially supportive of this transition from the earlier maritime focus to the agrarian sector. However, these adjustments were not enough to prevent the Funan state's collapse.

The changes came as improvements in navigation made it possible for ships sailing from distant ports to bypass Funan and deal directly with the Chinese. Chinese records make it clear that by the fifth century Holotan in western Java and Koying in the Sunda Strait were trading directly with China, rather than through Funan's intermediary ports (Wolters: 1979b). Funan and the east coast Malay Peninsula were thus being cut out of the India-to-China trade. The Isthmus of Kra portage had fallen into disuse, as ships from Sri Lanka and India were now sailing via the Straits of Melaka directly to these ports on the western edge of the Java Sea, putting them closer to the source of the Indonesian archipelago spices that were beginning to find an international market (Wolters: 1967; Miksic: 2003a, 28–33). The more direct sea passage from the Sunda Strait region north to China incorporated a stopover on the central (Linyi) and northern Vietnam coastlines rather than on the Funan coast of southern Vietnam.

Whether this refocusing of the international trade was directly responsible for Funan's dynastic crisis is not certain, but it had profound consequences for Funan's future. The shifting of the commercial shipping route to the Straits of Melaka passage and the subsequent omission of stops at Funan's ports in the Gulf of Thailand and the Mekong Delta region of the lower Vietnam coastline denied the Funan rulers important revenues. Deprived of this major source of royal income, the ruler as well as his followers, including subordinate chiefs and their supporters, found their prosperity diminished. Such a decline in royal income available for redistribution to their followers could well have touched off a dynastic crisis as rival claimants, promoting their ability to restore Funan's prosperity, attempted to gather enough supporters to seize the throne. As they did so, they competed for a shrinking realm.

By the end of the fifth century, Funan was losing ground to its northern neighbor Linyi (the future Champa), the sailors who had provided Funan's navy had turned to piracy, and the Malay entrepôts had begun sending their own embassies to China. In this same period, as noted earlier, Funan's canal and irrigation networks were expanding rapidly in the Mekong Delta, as part of its transition to a more intensive agricultural economy. However, Funan's decline continued, as midway through the sixth century its Khmer vassals to the north broke away, and by the seventh century Funan was no more. Its irrigation networks in the Mekong Delta were reclaimed by jungle as the farmers moved northwest to the new Khmer-ruled centers in the central Cambodia Tonle Sap area.

The fall of Funan and the importance of this watershed is substantiated in a series of fifth- and sixth-century sources, which are cited here in detail as an example of the level of Chinese and China-related documentation of China's increased contacts with Southeast Asia and the importance of these early Chinese sources in the absence of this level of itemization in the early Southeast Asian written sources. China's court records record the arrival of Funan's embassies to China in 434 and 484. As noted above, some historians have argued that Southeast Asian embassies to the Chinese court increased in times of local upheaval or political transition, or in response to the ascension of a new Chinese emperor or a new Chinese dynasty. While O. W. Wolters placed emphasis on Funan embassies being sent in times of Funan crisis, this study has also taken into account political unrest in China to explain interruptions in tributary missions (Wolters: 1970, 39–48). This pattern can be seen in the dispatch of the earlier Funan embassies, notably the embassies sent in 268, 286, and 287, in a period marking the fall of the Wu dynasty and its replacement by the Jin (Pelliot: 1903, 251–52). These three embassies were apparently meant to ensure continued Funan commercial interaction with southern China under the new Jin rulers. Apparently the effort was successful, and Funan did not send another embassy until 357, which was reactive to the succession of a new Jin emperor.

In contrast, both of Funan's fifth-century embassies were associated with an era of crises, this time with crises in Funan itself. Since the 434 embassy took place around the time that the ruler of the previously subordinate Pan Pan port-polity on the Malay Peninsula coastline began to declare independence by sending his own diplomatic missions to the Chinese court, it is likely Funan's 434 mission was dispatched in an attempt to renew Funan's favored Chinese commercial relationship (Coedes: 1931). The one in 484 (described below) was understood by the Chinese sources as a vain attempt to recover the commercial business that Funan had already lost to other centers, and it was shortly followed by an equally vain attempt to gain Chinese assistance against Funan's neighboring Vietnam coast competitor Linyi.

Significant changes in the international trade networks from the mid-fourth century had a profound impact on Funan. When the Jin dynasty (265–420) came to power in the late third century, it briefly reunified China and thereby gave southern China access to the central Asian overland trade routes. However, by the second half of the fourth century this unity was lost, and with it south China's access to the Central Asian trade. In response, the Jin redoubled their efforts to promote the maritime trade routes. They sent embassies to a wider array of Southeast Asian trade centers, including Holotan in western Java and Koying in the Sunda Strait, both of whom responded positively. The Chinese Buddhist pilgrim Faxian (337?–422?) and the fifth-century Indian Buddhist prince Gunavarman provide first-hand evidence that Funan was being bypassed. In 413–414, Faxian sailed directly to Guangzhou from Yehpoti, an Indianized port on the Borneo coast, without a stopover at a Funan port (Giles: 1959; Naerssen and de Iongh: 1977, 18–23). In the midfifth century, Gunavarman sailed nonstop to China from Shepo, a trading center on the north Java coast (Coedes: 1968, 54; Wolters: 1967, 35). Coincidently, neither Faxian nor Gunavarman used the Isthmus of Kra portage in their travels, further evidence that ships were then sailing directly through the Straits of Melaka to and from Sri Lanka and India and bypassing Gulf of Thailand ports.

In 449, the Chinese emperor sent embassies to confer titles on the rulers of three new Indonesian "states." This is significant because, as noted above, normally the Chinese tried to maintain established commercial relations with a particular Southeast Asian port-polity instead of actively seeking out new ones (Wolters: 1970, 39–48). Also significant was that at this time the Chinese refused to recognize the embassy of the ruler of Funan, their old trade partner, implying that the Chinese court fully recognized by 449 that Funan's ports had been replaced by Java Sea emporia as the dominant ports in Southeast Asian commerce.

That Funan was being replaced by Linyi as the most important trading center along the Vietnam coastline was already apparent in the mid-fifth century, when Gunavarman traveled from the Javanese entrepôt of Shepo to China, for his ship was originally to have made an intermediate stop on the southern Vietnam coast above the Mekong Delta, not at Funan (see above). However, the most significant evidence of the change in Funan's fortunes is the record of a 484 embassy on Funan's behalf by the Indian Buddhist monk Nagasena. Apart from the 434 embassy, this was Funan's only recorded contact with China in the fifth century. Actually, Nagasena's 484 embassy followed a commercial embassy sent around the same year, when King Jayavarman of Funan had dispatched a group of merchants to Guangzhou to solicit Chinese trade. Nagasena had accompanied them on their return and then was sent back to the Chinese court to plead for the Chinese court's aid against Linyi. His entreaties brought no result. Nagasena's comments to the Chinese emperor acknowledged the lack of regular interaction between Funan and China, and they hint that Funan no longer traded with any part of the coast of present-day Vietnam. Speaking on behalf of Funan, Nagasena reported that the realm he represented was "ceaselessly invaded by Linyi and has [therefore] not entered into relations with [the Red River delta region]. That is why their embassies so seldom come" (Pelliot: 1903, 267).

By then China was increasingly favoring Linyi. In 491, the Chinese court bestowed an important title upon Fan Tang, the ruler of Linyi, proclaiming him "General Pacifier of the South, Commander-in-Chief of the Military Affairs of the Seashore, and King of Linyi" (Maspero: 1928, 77–78). Clearly, by this time Linyi had surpassed Funan as the most important trade ally on the southern Vietnam coast, as Fan Tang's new title put more emphasis on his role as protector of the Vietnam seacoast than on his role as Linyi's monarch. Even the report of Funan's envoy Nagasena accepted that by this time it was Linyi, and not Funan, that was considered responsible for curtailing acts of piracy on the lower Vietnam coast. In his report to the Chinese emperor, Nagasena related that he had been shipwrecked on the Linyi coast, where his possessions had been stolen. That he should have reported this to the Chinese court and that the Chinese should subsequently have invested Fan Tang as Commander of the Seashore indicates that it was Linyi, and specifically its ruler Fan Tang, who were now considered accountable for this area.

Even earlier evidence of Funan's diminished power along this eastern coast comes from the 430 petition to the Chinese court of the Holotan port-polity, which was seeking protection for its ships sailing from the Sunda Strait coast to China. Sailors from Holotan and what is thought to have been the contemporary west-coast Borneo port-polity of Shepo had both been sailing within range of the lower Vietnam coastline on their South China Sea passage in order to avoid the navigational hazards associated with the Paracel Reefs south of Hainan Island (Manguin: 1976; Wheeler: 2006). Holotan's petition suggests that by this time shipping along the route was threatened by piracy. Either this piracy resulted from Funan's attempts to retain control over the maritime channels by forcing ships to utilize its ports (unlikely as evidenced in the case of Nagasena), or else it signaled Funan's decline as a major commercial emporium, a decline that had forced its resident maritime supporters to resort to piracy. If the latter were the case, as seems likely, Funan's loss of trade-derived revenue would have left its rulers unable to pay subsidies to the locally resident sailors, for whom piracy then was the more lucrative alternative, albeit a risky one.

In this period, Linyi may have been no more coherently organized than was Funan (Mabbett: 1977a, 154; Coedes: 1968, 59). Nevertheless, Fan Tang's investiture by the Chinese court was not an arbitrary move. Rather, in response to the instabilities precipitated by Funan's commercial demise, China was recognizing the local leader who seemed best positioned to restore order along the Vietnam coast. China's interest in Southeast Asia was at that time to keep the flow of shipping moving into south China's ports rather than any sort of political hegemony. It was interested not only in commercial trade, but also in facilitating the flow of Buddhist pilgrims, sacred texts, and relics to and from India, as in the fifth century the Chinese aristocracy was increasingly Buddhist, and the movement of religious items and travelers via the maritime passageway was therefore vital to its self-definition (Liu: 1988).

Thus it was that, despite the fact that throughout the third and fourth centuries Linyi had, with Funan's aid, continually contended for the control of the northern Vietnam coastline by harassing the Chinese Tongking (Giao Chi/Chiao Chau/Jiaozhi) Province in the Red River delta to the north, the Chinese emperor in 491 found himself able to overlook this unfortunate past misbehavior (Stein: 1947). However, in his doing so, it is also significant that the Chinese, always on the lookout for continuity, explained this transfer as an acknowledgment of the relocation of Funan's rightful patriarchal line of kings to Linyi, for which reason they cited Fan Tang's supposed descent from Funan's rulers. Significantly, Fan Tang's move to the Linyi domain and the growth of Linyi's maritime prominence coincided in the Chinese eyes, making even more plausible China's decision to recognize Linyi as the dominant port on the Vietnam coast.

Thus, by the mid-fifth century Funan was no longer a major international trade center. As it declined, its resident seagoing populations shifted to more prosperous Linyi ports, among others. By 431, Linyi's ruler had already been able to launch a force of over one hundred ships to pillage the northern Vietnam coast (Coedes: 1968, 56–57). Meanwhile, the remnants of the Funan realm began to internalize. The Chinese acknowledged this reality in their 491 eulogy of the Linyi ruler Fan Tang.

The emergence of Khmer civilizations coincided with the final demise of Funan, either destroying or incorporating its village communities. Funan's lands in the Mekong Delta were depopulated as cultivators shifted their labor to more productive and secure lands upstream, initially at and around Sambor Prei Kuk. By the eighth century what remained of the mixed agrarian populations to the south moved either by choice or by force to the Khmer rulers' developing economic base in the Tonle Sap area to the north and west. With Funan largely depopulated, Funan's hydraulic system fell into disuse, and Funan's downstream ricelands over the next five hundred years reverted to swamp and jungle (Liere: 1980, 271).

Nevertheless, Funan lived on in the traditions of the successor civilizations of the Chams and the Khmers. Both traced their lineage to Funan and rooted their evolving polity on the Indianized patterns of statecraft initially developed by Funan rulers. In this they went well beyond the beginnings that Funan had made. While it was true that Funan's rulers had begun to bridge the gap between tribal politics and Indianized statecraft, it remained for the Chams and especially the Khmers to initially develop the mainland Southeast Asian state to its fullest.

EARLY BUDDHIST NETWORKING
AND THE MARITIME ROUTE

By the sixth century Buddhism had become especially important to the Chinese, and Southeast Asia assumed a key intermediary role between South Asia, the source of Buddhism, and China. Buddhist monks passed along either the international sea network or a land route through the mountainous regions of Burma and Yunnan (Changli: 1993; Stargardt: 1971; Howard: 1989); Chinese monks traveled to India by sea with stopovers in Buddhist pilgrimage centers in Vietnam, Java, and Sumatra to acquire deeper understanding of their faith and of the Sanskrit and Pali languages, and Indian monks journeyed to China to share their knowledge with Chinese patrons (Sen: 2003, 15–101).

The first account of this passage comes from the Buddhist pilgrim Faxian (337?– 422?), noted above, who traveled from China to India overland but returned by sea from Sri Lanka in 413–414 CE via the Straits of Melaka passageway. His description of the return voyage provides a vivid picture of the fateful fifth-century sea passage.

> [I] took passage on board a large merchant vessel, on which there were over two hundred souls, and astern of which there was a smaller vessel in tow in case of accidents at sea and destruction of the big vessel. Catching a fair wind [i.e., the monsoon], [we] sailed eastwards for two days; then [we] encountered a heavy gale, and the vessel sprang a leak. The merchants wished to get aboard the smaller vessel; but the men on the latter, fearing that they would be swamped by numbers, quickly cut the tow-rope in two. The merchants were terrified, for death was close at hand; and fearing that the vessel would fill, they promptly took what bulky goods there were and threw them into the sea. . . . The gale blew on for thirteen days and nights, when [we] arrived alongside an island, and then, at ebb-tide, they saw the place where the vessel leaked and forthwith stopped it up, after which we again proceeded on [our] way. This sea is infested with pirates, to meet whom is death. The expanse is boundless. (Giles: 1959, 79)

After sailing through the Straits of Melaka, Faxian landed at the trade depot known to the Chinese as Yehpoti, on the west coast of Borneo (Naerssen and de Iongh: 1977, 18–23), and voyaged directly from Yehpoti to Guangzhou, which he claimed to be a voyage of fifty days under normal conditions.

There was an economic as well as an intellectual dimension to this earliest Buddhist networking, as the Chinese sought religious artifacts and ritual objects as well as religious texts, all of which would, in their mind, allow them to legitimately perform Buddhist rituals in China. By the seventh century, for example, the Chinese Tang court's envoys exchanged coral, pearls, glass, and silk to acquire Buddhist relics; one envoy paid four thousand bolts of silk to purchase a small parietal bone of the Buddha from a Buddhist monastery in northwest India (Liu: 1996, 47; 1995). Patronage of Buddhism bestowed membership in the international Buddhist movement on Southeast Asian realms. Consequently early Southeast Asian civilizations raised their status above the "barbarian" image normally held by the Chinese of their southern neighbors and provided the basis for international and regional intellectual linkage as well as commercial exchanges among the numerous Buddhist communities that participated in the international maritime route.

As early as the third century an urban community near modern Hanoi on the edge of the Red River delta in Vietnam had become a center of Buddhism, with at least twenty temples and over five hundred monks in residence. By the seventh-century voyage of the Chinese pilgrim Yijing (635–713), this community was viewed as an important stopping point prior to one's entry into China, not only because it was a commercial layover of note, but also because it had become one among a network of Southeast Asia religious centers for Buddhist pilgrims traveling between China and India.

According to legend, Buddhism came to Vietnam in the first century CE, and by the end of the second century resident Indian monks led the important Luy Lau international intellectual center (in the modern Bac Ninh Province north of present Hanoi), at the capital of the Jiaozhi (Giao Chi/"Vietnam") Han administrative district. Luy Lau was the last stopover for Indian monks traveling to China along the international maritime passageway, as it was also for Chinese monks who had traveled to study in Buddhism's homeland. Here a number of important texts were translated into Chinese scripts (e.g., the Anapanasati, the Vessantara-jataka, and the Milinda-panha) prior to their delivery in China. Since Buddhism was initially imported directly from India, the original Vietnamese word for Buddha was *Bụt*, which is still used in Vietnamese folktales. Bụt was popularly localized as a folk deity who helped the good and punished the bad. By the fifth century, when Chinese Mahayana Buddhism became prominent, and Chinese rather than Indian monks dominated the maritime route, Bụt had lost its Buddhist association and *Phật*, the Chinese pronunciation of Buddha, prevailed (Cadiere: 1989; Cuong Tu: 1998).

3

Competition on the East Coast of the Mainland

Early Champa and Vietnam Political Economies

The previous chapter's discussion of Funan's history has shown that early Southeast Asian monarchies gained control over population clusters by conquering or networking with a number of allied and competing regionally based elites. Funan's resulting political system was based on the interdependence of political, economic, and religious institutions, a form of hierarchical networking that culminated in a royal court. Funan's sovereignty was, though, inherently unstable because it overly depended on the fortunes of the international maritime trade routes rather than on the income from its productive hinterlands.

This chapter will initially examine the Champa successor network of port-polities on the central and southern Vietnam coast, which were subject to the ebb and flow of the international trade, reflected in the fluctuations in Cham sovereignty. The Cham "state" was dispersed among several competing river valley courts centered in productive downstream river valley ricelands that not only provisioned international traders making stopovers on their Straits of Melaka-to-China voyages, but also linked their coastal ports of trade to productive upstream highland sources of commodities in high international demand. In contrast, Champa's Dai Viet neighbor to the north, which was initially based in the fertile Red River plain and delta in and around modern Hanoi, exhibited developmental patterns toward centralization. When the Vietnamese Dai Viet state declared its autonomy from Chinese overlordship in the tenth century, its court's proactive support of economic expansion in both its agricultural and commercial sectors would ultimately reinforce royal hegemony relative to competing elites and institutions.

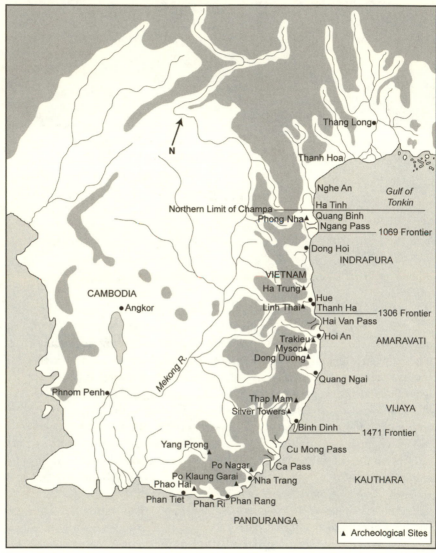

Map 3.1.   Champa and Vietnam in the Pre-1500 Era

THE CHAMPA REALM IN OVERVIEW

It is now widely accepted that the Champa realm was never a unified kingdom, but was instead the name of a collection of ports of trade and their adjacent Truong Son mountain-range plateau hinterlands, from roughly above

modern-day Hue in the north to the northern edge of the Mekong River delta in the south (from the eighteenth parallel in the north to Phan Thiet and Bien Hoa at the eleventh parallel in the south). The earliest Sanskrit inscription in the Cham realm dates to the fourth century, at Vo Canh near the Nha Trang port. In roughly this same era most of the archeological evidence is in the vicinity of Tra Kieu to the north, which consisted of an offshore port complex on Cu Lao Cham Island linked to the sheltered coastal cove in modern-day Hoi An, known later as Cua Dai Chiem, "Port of Great Champa," and the adjacent Thu Bon Valley rice basin of the modern-day Quang Nam Province. While there are some fifth- and sixth-century remains, in the seventh century the Cham realm was a flourishing multicentered Indic civilization. Most of the inscriptions and archeological evidence from the fifth to the eighth centuries are from the areas surrounding Tra Kieu, which was the political and economic center of the region; My Son was the region's most sacred religious center and Dong Duong was alternately a fortified walled political and religious center.

In the earliest era the Nha Trang basin to the south and its temple center at Po Nagar was a secondary center, as was Phan Rang; its eighth-century Hoa Lai temple complex had a Cambodian architectural style that differed from that of the earliest temples at the My Son temple complex to the north. This was also the case with the Phu Hai temple near Phan Thiet even further to the south (Vickery: 2009, 47). Collectively these differences in architectural styles reinforce the conclusion that the river-mouth centers and their adjacent river systems were autonomous identities making independent adaptations of Indic culture. Phan Rang is also the site of the later architecturally distinct thirteenth- to fourteenth-century Po Klaung Garai and the very different sixteenth-century Po Rome temple complex, a reflection of its prominence as a Cham port of trade in this later era. Similarly Quy Nhom near the Binh Dinh port, between Tra Kieu in the north and Phan Rang to the south, has temple towers that date from the eleventh to fifteenth century. Known at that time as Vijaya in both Cham and Cambodian inscriptions, its temples used the same mixed stone- and-brick construction techniques as their contemporary Khmer neighbors, but their architectural system is distinct; nearby Thap Man has sculptures of monstrous animals that show Vietnamese/Chinese similarities (Vickery: 2009, 48; Guy: 2009).

From south to north the Champa realm consisted of what is called Panduranga in the south, consisting of Phan Thiet, Phan Rang, and sometimes Nha Trang, which was otherwise known as Kauthara and was the site of the sacred Po Nagar temple complex. To the north was Vijaya, centered in the Quy Nhon region, variously called Campanagara, campapura, and campadesa (Champa country, city, or region) in its inscriptions. In the Champa middle was Amaravati, which consisted of Indrapura, the Thu Bon Valley sites of Tra Kieu (then known as Simhapura), My Son, and Dong Duong, which was the center of new Mahayana Buddhist patronage by Cham kings who lived in a walled city from the ninth century, following a period in which the region seems to have been marginalized in favor of Panduranga in the late eighth to early ninth centuries. This transition of the favored port of trade/polity on the Cham coastline is reflected in Chinese sources, which had earlier distinguished Panduranga in the south from the middle Huan Wang (the circle of the king; i.e., Indrapura) in the earlier century and, significantly, dropped earlier references to the collective Linyi for the regions south of the northern Red River provinces that were subject to Chinese sovereignty. But from the ninth century the Chinese called this middle region *Zhan Cheng*, Cham city, and developed separate tributary relationships with Zhan Cheng and Huan Wang. Cham records confirm this division, as separate kings were ruling from the Indrapura central regions of Amaravati in the north and the collective Panduranga Nha Trang/Phan Rang southern regions. In the eleventh century, the Nha Trang–based king Pramabodhisatya claimed a victory that consolidated Panduranga's authority over the south. In the eleventh and twelfth centuries the southern Nha Trang– and northern Tra Kieu–centered polities began to interact on several levels with their Khmer neighbors to their west, notably as trade partners as overland commercial networking between Angkor and the Champa realm heightened. In the north were the port-polities of Amarendrapura, centered at Lai Trung near modern-day Hue, and Visnupura, centered at Nhan Bieu.

Nineteenth-century French archeologists were highly impressed with the remains of Cham urbanism and regional networking as they explored their new Indochina colony. They found primary and secondary centers linked in the Tra Kieu region, connected by road networks on raised embankments paved with stone; stone bridges built over canals; and urban ruins 16 feet (5 meters) high on stone foundations on a rectangle 984 feet by 1640 feet (300 by 500 meters). These were not exclusively military fortresses, but protected palaces, temples, and the general populace (Aymonier: 1891b, 21–22; Hardy: 2009, 109–10, 121).

Chinese records substantiate recent archeological excavations in their descriptions of early Cham urbanism. In the sixth-century *Shui Jing Zhu* geographical account of China's waterways and those of its borderlands, the author Li Daoyuan (d. 527) includes this account of the fortified Cham urban center at Hoa Chau (Thira Thien Hue) near modern-day Hue, where the ramparts, over 1.24 miles in length (2,000 meters) are still visible (Hardy: 2009, 121).

The ramparts were made up of a first brick foundation, six *li* and 170 paces in circumference, and measuring 650 paces from east to west; this foundation was [twenty feet] high; above, there was a ten-foot high brick wall, pierced by square slits. This brick wall was itself topped with a stockade, and the entire structure dominated by pavilions and belvederes attaining a height of up to 70–80 feet. The city had thirteen gates; all the public buildings open towards the south; we counted more than 2,100 residential houses. (Pelliot: 1904, 191; Hardy: 2009, 108)

A ninth-century Cham inscription describes a secondary town to the larger Dong Duong temple/administrative complex.

The town bedecked in the splendour of Indra's town, sparkling with white lotuses . . . founded by Bhrgu in ancient times . . . [this town] called Campa keeps here its invincible fortune. This illustrious [town] protected by His Majesty Jaya Sinharvarman, whose power unceasing renews its prosperity, [this town] inseparably untied with good fortune shines here. The king is the shelter of the virtues. (Finot: 1904a, 109; Hardy: 2009, 108–9)

This Cham self-image is authenticated in the collection of ninth-century stories circulating in Baghdad, collated in the *Kitab al-Aghani* by the Persian scholar Abu al-Faraj (897–967), which describes Buddhist worship at Dong Duong ca. 875: "The Indians have, in the town of Champa, a different temple from the above, . . . this temple is ancient and . . . all the Buddhas found there enter into conversation with the faithful and reply to all the requests made to them" (Ferrand: 1913, 123; Hardy: 2009, 109).

Similar to the contemporary regions of Southeast Asia, the Cham temples were equally sustained by meritorious tax-free transfers of income from designated lands that were dedicated to support the temples. The referenced Buddhist temple is an example, wherein a ninth-century Dong Duong temple stele inscription reports:

King Indravarman gave these fields with their harvests, slaves of both sexes, silver, gold, brass, copper, and other riches, to [the Divine Lord] Sri Laksmindralokesvara, for the use of the [resident monastic] community of monks, for the completion of the propagation of the Dharma. Those who . . . kings, ksatriyas . . . brahmans, ministers . . . merchants, who remove, destroy, or . . . [these goods], may they all go to Maharaurava ["Hell"]; on the other hand, keep them, reveal [those who have removed them], may they all go, according to their desire, to the City of Heaven and the City of Deliverance. (Finot: 1904a, 95; Hardy: 2009, 109)

CHAMPA AND INTERNATIONAL COMMERCE IN THE EIGHTH CENTURY

The Cham polities had compelling reasons to assert themselves as Funan's successor in the international commercial channels. This Malayo-Austronesian people, ethnically, linguistically, and culturally related to the maritime regions to their south and east, developed into a series of Indianized civilizations from the second into the sixteenth centuries CE. As cited in chapter 2, the earliest Chinese references to a Cham state date to 190–193 CE. Then and later, it appeared in the Chinese records as the state of Linyi, but the state's own later epigraphy refers to the realm as Champa, after the Champa region of northeast India with which the Chams were in trade and cultural contact, for which reason the people are known as Chams (Vickery: 1998, 48–51, 64–69; Guy: 2009, 128–29).

Caught between the domain of Funan to the south and the Chinese province of Jiaozhi to the north, the Cham realm's early history was characterized by shifting alliances among regional centers that were concentrated at the river mouths of the Cham coast, a situation not unlike that of the Straits of Melaka Srivijaya realm that will be examined in chapter 4 (Coedes: 1968, 17; Stein: 1947). In contrast to Srivijaya, however, the Cham realm had major neighbors to its north (Jiaozhi) and west (the Khmer realm that would become Angkor). According to Chinese sources, during the early third century the great Funan ruler Fan Shihman brought the Chams under his authority. This report is corroborated by the earliest Sanskrit inscription in Cham territories, a third-century inscription that was placed in Cham territories and that has been interpreted by historians, based on the corresponding Chinese sources, to record that Linyi was then a networked territory under Funan hegemony. The third-century Sanskrit stele inscription of Vo Canh in the Linyi region of Nha Trang references the reigning king Sri Mara, who some scholars argue to be the prominent Funan king Fan Shihman, whose consolidations of the Funan realm are highlighted in Chinese sources (Coedes: 1968, 40; Gaspardone: 1965). Revisionist historians are now asserting that the Linyi in Chinese references was not referential to the entire Champa coastline, but was referential exclusively to the borderlands south of the Chinese Jiaozhi Province, whose population was always a threat to their northern neighbors, as these borderlands were continuously contested by the Chams and Vietnamese over the centuries (see chapter 7). Reports of the Chinese envoys Kang Tai and Zhu Ying, who visited Funan about the same time (arriving there in the 240s), say that Funan's ruler, whom they call Fan Hsun, had already established an alliance with the Chams around 220 and that together the Chams and Funanese were making naval raids and land attacks against the coast of the northern Red River delta region (Maspero: 1928: 54–55).

About a century later, in the mid-300s, the semiautonomous Cham ruler known to the Chinese as Fan Fo took the Sanskrit title Bhadravarman, developed a Sanskritic administrative core, and erected the first temples in the Cham holy city of My Son. This temple city focused on their fictitious Mount

Vugvan, the Cham equivalent of Mount Meru, the abode of the ancestors. Almost all the My Son temples, like elsewhere in the Cham realm, center on a core temple, known to Cham as a *kalan*, surrounded by smaller temples. Almost always Cham temples face east, from where the sun rises and believed to be the realm of the gods, and where cosmological movement begins. Here at My Son, Bhadravarman consecrated the Siva-linga Bhadresvara, thereby beginning the Cham tradition of assigning to the polity's central deity the reigning king's Sanskrit name, thus proclaiming the monarch's potential for achieving divinity upon his death, and he reinforced this by the strategic pairing of the most important Cham royal temples with a specific sacred mountain (Maspero: 1928, 53; Vickery: 1998; Phuong: 2009, 176).

Shortly afterward, in the fifth century, the Cham realm was an independent entity, responding in part to the new circumstances afforded when China's Jin dynasty rulers encouraged traders from the Southern Seas to trade in China's ports. Cham ports became intermediate stops for merchant ships navigating the South China Sea, and ships regularly put into Cham ports prior to their entry into China's harbors. This is demonstrated in the fifth-century travel itinerary of the Indian prince Gunavarman, who made a Cham port stopover sailing from the Java coast to China (Wolters: 1967, 35). According to Chinese accounts, perhaps trying to see a continuity of power, during the mid-fifth century a dynastic crisis in Funan resulted in the flight of a Funan prince to Linyi, where he became king of the Chams (Coedes: 1931). As noted above, the Chinese throne officially recognized this king, Fan Tang, in 491, when he was granted the title of General Pacifier of the South, Commander-in-Chief of the Military Affairs of the Seashore, and King of Linyi (Maspero: 1928, 77–78). Chapter 2 makes the case that this late fifth-century recognition was due to China's perception that Funan was no longer the dominant commercial center in the Southeast Asian realm, and that Linyi regional ports had become the major commercial powers on the lower Vietnam coast. Fan Tang's title of Pacifier reflected the Chinese court's view that he was responsible for maintaining control over Cham coast piracy that otherwise threatened international shipping. This was done by successfully engaging the loyalty of the coastal seamen.

This Cham state's effectiveness in controlling piracy was intermittent, however, and in 605 a Chinese general tried to forcibly open the Southern Seas region for commerce, most likely seeking to make the Cham coast fit for trade by deterring piracy (Coedes: 1966b, 77). According to the Chinese sources the Cham state reacted favorably and soon became a secondary entrepôt on the main international route, servicing shipping and sailors traveling between the Malay world and Guangzhou. At the time, a Cham capital was located at Tra Kieu near present-day Hoi An, and by 758 the Chinese reported that the Cham state, which they mistakenly viewed as a unified polity, had also developed secondary commercial centers at Kauthara (present-day Nha Trang) and Panduranga (present-day Phan Rang). As previously noted, around this time the Chinese began to call the Cham state Huan Wang (Wang: 1958, 90–91). According to Chinese sources, around 875 a new Cham dynasty came to power at Indrapura (Quang Nam), and reference in Chinese accounts is henceforth made to Zhan Cheng, "the Cham city," or Champapura (Maspero: 1928, 6).

The Chinese apparently thought of the Cham domain as principally a maritime state, possibly due to its place in their own commercial preoccupations. This preoccupation is reflected in the fourteenth-century *Annam Chi Luo*, written by a Vietnamese, Le Tac, who gives the following brief note on Champa (*Zhang Cheng Kuo*): "[They] established [their] state on the shore of the sea. Chinese merchant ships cross the sea. The outer barbarians who come and go all congregate here to take on fuel and water" (Le Tac: 1961, 31; Taylor: 1983, 350). However, early Cham epigraphy well documents that the Cham downstream river plains were productive centers of rice agriculture. Scholars are currently agreed, based on the considerable archeological work done in the former Cham realm over the past twenty years, that Champa was never a centralized single state except in the minds of the Chinese, but instead was a series of variable networked river valleys that sometimes worked as allies, and at other times were in competition (Hardy: 2009). We know from archeological and epigraphic evidence that Champa had a river valley focus to its agriculture. Politically, the leader of a Cham riverine network practiced Indic-inspired statecraft, initially drawing legitimacy from Hindu-Buddhist cults that emphasized the Cham king's association with Siva and his consort Bhadrapatisvara. As with its Angkor neighbor to the west (chapter 6), temples were often responsible for bringing the lands of the Cham political elites under cultivation (Sox: 1972, 60; Wachtel: 1998).

As was the case with their Srivijaya and Khmer contemporaries, the naga/snake motif remained a prominent Cham visual connection between the Indic and indigenous religious traditions. The Siva-linga was a male divine figure, symbolic of creative energy of the celestial realm, seated with legs partly crossed, hands on hips, on the coils of a naga or seated on a five-headed naga throne, symbolic of natural deities (*yaksa*) in Brahmanical imagery of the subterranean world of the naga presided over by the yaksa Kavera, protector of riches and treasures (Guy: 2009, 122ff; Guillon: 2001, inscription 62). Linga, the focal phallic ritual centerpieces in Cham temples, are also a syncretism of the Indic and the local. The male linga rises from the receptive female *yoni* circular bowl-like base. Cham linga are often three-tiered, as the foundational Hindu divine Brahma and Visnu are symbolized in staggered rectangular or square bases for the culminating rounded penis head of Siva. Cham scholars assert the acceptance of the Indic linga as a powerful symbol in local culture, as the linga is the traditional male spiritual force (Ahier) and the yoni is the female (Awar), which together are the two most powerful dualistic creative forces in the Cham animistic realm. This male/female duality is also the basis of the ritual relationship between the most sacred My Son (Indrapura) and Po Nagar (Vijaya) temple complexes: My Son was the sanctuary of the god Siva (male/father), while Po Nagar was the sanctuary of the goddess of Po Inu Nugar (female/mother) (Nakamura: 2009, 103).

By the seventh and eighth centuries the Cham realm had evolved a loose balance between its wet-rice economy and its participation in the international trade. An important factor necessitating this balance was the fact that the Cham coast was by then strategically located on the principal maritime route between the Srivijaya Melaka Straits–based realm and China, a position that allowed the Chams the opportunity to take advantage of the economic benefits offered by participation in the trade as the trade heightened in the Tang and Song eras (618–1279). In doing so, to some degree Champa inherited the entrepôt position filled in earlier centuries by Funan to the south, though it was Srivijaya that assumed the primary emporium role, maintaining this position generally from the seventh century until the eleventh century. In the eyes of the Chinese, Champa, though important, was ultimately a region of intermediary ports, the last stopover between Srivijaya and China before ships reached China's ports of trade. In time, however, the Cham realm would become increasingly important as a source of commodities desired by the Chinese elite (Hardy: 2009).

A rare oblique reference to external commerce comes from eighth-century Cham inscriptions reporting two sea raids that threatened the state's very existence. A Sanskrit inscription from Nha Trang informs us that in 774 "ferocious, pitiless, dark-skinned men born in other countries, whose food was more horrible than corpses, and who were vicious and furious, came in ships . . . took away the [temple *linga*], and set fire to the temple," thus desecrating the Po Nagar temple near Nha Trang in the Kauthara region (Barth and Bergaigne: 1885–1893, 253). This was followed by a second raid by a similar group in 787, when a Panduranga temple to the south was burned (Aymonier: 1900–1904, 191; Barth and Bergaigne: 1885–1893, 217). The desecration of these temples represented the destruction of the Cham kings' legitimacy, and in the first of these raids the temple's sacred linga was taken away. The Po Nagar temple inscription recording this event reports that the Cham king followed with his navy and defeated the raiders in a sea battle. He was unable to recover the original linga, which was said to have been lost in the battle, but he used the booty acquired from the defeated marauders to reconstruct the damaged temple, where he installed a replacement linga, the symbol of his legitimacy (Barth and Bergaigne: 1885–1893, 253).

Historians have traditionally identified these dark-skinned and demonic raiders with Javanese or Malay sailors, though they are most likely a multi-ethnic group similar to the Malayo-Austronesian sea nomads who were the strength behind Srivijaya's hegemony (see chapter 4), but who were also a maritime diaspora active along the entire Cham and Vietnam coastline. These sea nomads were seasonally resident oceangoing sojourners who could be used by local rulers to control shipping, but who in times of political turmoil might turn to piracy as the source of their livelihood (Wolters: 1967; 1970). It is notable that the two referenced raids were directed at the southernmost of the Cham regions, the two port areas recognized by the Chinese as being of greatest commercial importance in that time. The maritime raids therefore reflect three possible conditions. First, the Srivijaya state may have seen the rise of the Cham ports as a threat to its economic hegemony (Barth and Bergaigne: 1885–1893, 252). Alternatively, if Srivijaya was not such a powerful force at this particular time, as some historians have proposed, then the raids on the Cham ports may have been undertaken by the very sea pirates who in more settled times might have supported Srivijaya's control over the Southern Seas, but who now would have seen Cham ports as attractive sources of plunder (Bronson and Wisseman: 1976). A third possibility is that the attack could have been mounted by rebel seamen based in the variety of settlements along the lower Cham coast and numerous offshore islands.

CHAMPA AND INTERNATIONAL COMMERCE IN THE TENTH AND ELEVENTH CENTURIES

After these eighth-century records, there is little documentary evidence of the Cham realm's commercial activities until the eleventh century, when several inscriptions, supported by Chinese records, allow further consideration of the Cham relationship with international commerce. Moreover, we know a good deal about Champa's internal structure during this period. Champa's multi-centered civilization was distributed among several river valleys and their upstream highlands, each of which was separated from the others by rugged mountains. In this regard, the state's geographical features were similar to those of the earliest multiple-riverine-system polities in the Straits of Melaka region. Yet despite this similarity to Srivijaya, the Cham polity also resembled contemporary Java (chapter 5), in that its river systems had settled downstreams that were adjacent to fertile upstream centers that lay between the coast and the upstream highlands, as the downstream produced sufficient rice surpluses to support the expenses of networked temples. By contrast, as described in chapter 4, the internal economic and political development of the Srivijaya realm was hampered by its region's extensive downstream swamps. Champa's economic and religious networks reinforced their multiple river systems' upstream and downstream cultural and economic linkage, while also proclaiming the legitimacy of their Cham elite patrons (Quach-Langlet: 1988, 28–37).

By the tenth century Champa was divided into five core regions. The northern region that bordered Vietnamese territory, which had port sites known as Amarendrapura (Lai Trung/Hue) and Visnupura (Nhan Bieu), was a narrow, sandy coastal plain of scattered agricultural settlements that was punctuated by numerous short streams connecting the coast with its mountainous interior. Amaravati incorporated the earlier Indrapura middle region. This was the site of the important port now known as Hoi An (Redfern: 2002; Wachtel: 1998; Wheeler: 2001). Its multiple short, fertile river valleys were sealed by steep mountain ridges, a geography affording the security necessary for the development of the local wet-rice works that supported these early religious and political complexes.

Amaravati's prior leadership was superseded in the twelfth and thirteenth centuries by its southern neighbor, Vijaya, which developed overland links with the evolving Khmer realm of Angkor, which used Vijaya's port, now known as Sri Banoi/Sri Banoy, as a point of contact with the South China Sea international trade, as an overland road network connected the Khmer heartland with the western Cham highland region, and from there via upstream river valleys to the coast. Continuing southward, the fourth region was Kauthara, which was situated in a narrow coastal strip with little agricultural hinterland between the rugged mountains and the rocky seacoast, but which also developed overland commercial and cultural connections to the Khmer heartland via Sambor (Sambhupura) on the Mekong River. Though the topography was less hospitable for large-scale agriculture, it had several bays (notably, Nha Trang and Cam Ranh) that afforded accommodation for assorted maritime communities. Here, too, was the important early cult site of Po Nagar. To Kauthara's south lay the fifth region, Panduranga (Phan Rang), which had a mixed economy based on hydraulic agriculture, salt production, and fishing. This mixed economy and distance allowed Panduranga to enjoy a degree of autonomy from its northern neighbors.

The five core regions were surrounded by border zones in each of three directions. On the northern periphery of the core was the Nghe Thanh region, which was long contested between the Vietnamese and the northern Cham polities. Although the Chams occasionally raided into this borderland, they verily controlled it. To the west of the core was an autonomous region of

mountains and highland plateaus (now known as the Central Highlands) populated by an assortment of highland tribal populations, some of whom were
closely related to the Chams (Quach-Langlet: 1988, 37–42; Hickey: 1982,
78–120). To the south of the core was the sparsely populated Mekong Delta
region, occupied largely by a mixture of Chams and Khmer, which served as
a buffer zone between the Chams and the upstream region controlled by
strong Khmer polities (Brocheux: 1995, 1–11).

The northern border zone was especially significant during the tenth and
eleventh centuries, when there was ongoing hostility between the Chams and
the emerging Vietnamese state after it had won its independence from Chinese authority (see below). While this chapter attributes Vietnamese-Cham
warfare to commercial competition and to compensatory aggression, Keith
Taylor's studies of eleventh-century Vietnam provide an alternative interpretation, attributing the Vietnamese raids on Champa to competition over settlement of the agriculturally rich frontier regions that lay between settled Cham
and Dai Viet territories (Taylor: 1983, 297; Taylor: 1986). There were likely
elements of both. In the Vietnamese chronicles' retrospective view, the warfare in the south was of secondary consequence to the Vietnamese, who were
more concerned with their need to defend the Dai Viet state's newly won
autonomy and northern borders from the Chinese. In Taylor's view, as discussed below, recurrent Vietnam-Champa conflict resulted from competition
to settle and control this productive agricultural frontier; agricultural expansion took priority over international commerce as the Dai Viet monarchy
attempted to conform to the sinic agricultural state prejudice.

An increasingly important element of these hostilities was the use of naval
warfare. Vietnamese responded to two major Cham naval campaigns as well
as using naval warfare to enhance their own trade interests on the coastline.
In 979, a naval expedition attributed to the Chams, said to have been led by
a rebellious Vietnamese, attacked the Vietnamese capital of Hoa Lu in the
Red River delta. According to the Vietnam chronicle account, only the Cham
king's vessel survived a gale on the fleet's return voyage (Maspero: 1910,
678). In response, the Vietnamese destroyed the Cham capital of Indrapura
in 982. Cham raids against the northern Vietnam coast in 1042 again brought
retaliatory action against the Cham capital at Vijaya; the Vietnamese emperor
Ly Thai Tong led a 1042 seaborne expedition that was said to have routed the
Chams, killed their king, Jaya Simhavarman II, and returned with five thousand prisoners who were resettled in new agricultural villages in the southern
borderlands of the Ly domain (Coedes: 1966b: 83).

Raids against Dai Viet were not the only source of conflict. In 1050, for
example, a Cham inscription recorded a Cham royal expedition against the
southern Cham port of Panduranga. The people of this port were described

as "vicious, threatening, and always in revolt against their sovereign," and they refused to recognize the Cham ruler's authority (Aymonier: 1891b, 29; Finot: 1903b, 634, 643; 1909, 205, 208). At the time, Panduranga had a significant commercial presence, as two Arabic script (Kufic) inscriptions, dating between 1029 and 1035, document that Panduranga was a major port with a sizable commercial community (possibly some three hundred strong) (Ravaisse: 1922; Manguin: 1979). The inscriptions also suggest Panduranga's degree of political independence. One of them records that this community selected one of its members, a Muslim, as "agent of the bazaar," having the duty of representing and protecting local merchants' interests when dealing with Cham authorities.

The latter inscription is not the first reference to Muslim traders in the Cham realm. An earlier mention appears in a tenth-century Chinese court reference to a 958 diplomatic mission to China by a Muslim named Abu Hasan (Bu Hosan), who was traveling as the ambassador representing the Cham king Indravarman III. On this trip he presented the Chinese emperor rosewater, flasks of "Greek fire," and precious stones (Tasaka: 1952, 52). In 961, Abu Hasan again traveled to the Song court, this time bearing a letter from the new Cham king Jaya Indravarman I. On this second occasion the Cham ambassador presented the Song monarch with fragrant wood, ivory, camphor, peacocks, and twenty Arab vases, all items from Arabia, Persia, and other western regions that were supposedly available in Cham ports as commercial products (Schafer: 1967, 75). Abu Hasan's visits were a response to the opportunities afforded when Guangzhou was fully reopened to foreign commerce under the Later Zhou (951–959) and then the Song (960–1279) dynasties.

This commercial activity by Muslims and others was profitable to the Cham realm. Chinese sources from the Song era reveal that ship cargoes were inspected by a king's agent upon arrival in Champa's ports. After registering all commodities carried by the ship and noting how many goods were unloaded, the king's agents collected one-fifth of each kind of commodity in the name of their monarch before authorizing the sale of the rest. Concealed and undisclosed freight was seized (Maspero: 1928, 29). The income from these inspections financed various royal activities, not the least of which was Cham ambition for military conquest, especially against their Dai Viet neighbors to the north, who were seen as both a political and economic threat.

However, the Vietnamese were also experiencing increased trade and were doing so in direct competition with Champa. There were two primary avenues for this trade. The first, an interior trade route connecting Vietnam with the Khmer realm to its west, was an especially serious threat to Cham trading, notably with their Khmer neighbors. In the tenth and eleventh centuries the

overland trade route from the Vietnamese Nghe An region ran west through
the Ha Trai pass and turned south along the Mekong River into the Khmer
heartland (Maspero: 1918). Khmer inscriptions describe traders of Vietnamese origin using this route. The development of this overland route is likely
to have been especially threatening to Cham ports, which were linked to the
Khmer heartland either by riverine links, or more likely by overland trade
across the Central Highlands. For example, Vijaya was linked to the Khmer
heartland via an overland network via the highland center of Kon Klor, where
there are a Cham temple and epigraphic and archeological remains from this
era that substantiate this overland cultural and trade connection. A Khmer
inscription dated 987 (Coedes: *IC*, 6:183–86) mentioning Vietnamese use of
the interior route found at Phum Mien on the lower Mekong documents this
threat, demonstrating that Cham ports were then bypassed entirely, with negative consequence to Champa ports. A 1050 Panduranga naval raid up the
Mekong River into the Khmer heartland, sacking Sambupura on the Mekong,
may have been more than a plunder raid, but was potentially intended to reas-
sert its trade relationship with the Khmer realm (Osborne: 1966, 449). Any
war with the north was likely popular with the Cham commercial community,
to reclaim lost territories in the north, to plunder the region and take back
captives for Cham slave markets and to work Cham lands, and also to destroy
commercial port competition on the Dai Viet coastline.

Champa's sea-mounted attacks on Vietnam could have drawn on ethnically
diverse peoples, most prominently on a relationship with maritime sojourners
based in Cham coastline ports. As was noted earlier, the Chinese had continuously depicted the Cham coast as a center of disorder and piracy, as well as
a source of slaves since earliest times (Whitmore: 1986, 121–22). However,
as will be described in the chapter 4 discussion of Srivijaya, these very same
"pirates" could sometimes be turned to the service of the state. The Champa
realm was clearly a naval power in this period. A ninth-century Khmer
inscription, for example, refers to a victory over "thousands of barks with
white sails," a navy that historians attribute to the Chams (Coedes: 1968,
114; Barth and Bergaigne: 1885–1893, 492n3). The source of tenth- and
eleventh-century Cham maritime strength must have come from populations
similar to those who in the eighth century had pillaged the Cham coast; that
is, the sojourning seafarers. Indeed, a relationship with multiethnic sojourners, or at least with peoples from the southern islands, is suggested by the
Javanese influence upon Cham culture from at least the ninth century onward.
This influence is most visible in Cham temple architecture of the ninth century, at My Son and elsewhere (Stern: 1942; Guy: 2009, 147–49). There is also
a two-part Cham inscription from Nhan Bieu (Visnupura) north of modern-day
Hue, dated 908–911, which reports two official diplomatic missions to Java

(Yavadvipa) by a favorite of the Cham monarch Jaya Simhavarman (Huber: 1911, 299). On the other side of the sea, Java inscriptions from this late ninth- and tenth-century period make specific reference to the regular activities of both Khmer and Cham merchants in Java's ports, as there are also Khmer inscriptions that reference their Java contacts (Wisseman Christie: 1998a, 244; Coedes: 1968, 93, 97–98, 100; Finot: 1915; Higham: 2001, 59). This Javanese contact no doubt equally attracted sojourning traders and seafarers to Cham ports, making them available for various maritime expeditions against the prosperous contemporary Vietnamese domain to the north.

Though this first raid benefited the Cham state, relative to plunder and manpower returns, continuing hostilities resulted in Vietnamese reprisals (Coedes: 1968, 139–40). In the retaliatory Vietnamese attack of 982, the Cham capital at Indrapura was destroyed. As a result, between 982 and 1050 the southern Cham domain, including the port of Panduranga and its seafar- ing groups, were the beneficiaries, as is evidenced by the two Arabic script inscriptions cited above (dated 1029 and 1035).

Seafarers from Panduranga, as well as those associated with each of the other enumerated ports associated with the other Cham coastal regions, were likely participants in a major Cham naval expedition against the Vietnamese in 1042. Indeed, it is quite possible that a number of the naval raids attributed to the Chams during this period were initiated not by a royal center but by semi-independent piratical sojourners who used Cham ports as their base of operation (Maspero: 1928, 29). Whatever the case, the Vietnamese held the Cham centers responsible for the attacks and aimed their retaliation accord- ingly, both in the earlier instance and in this one. In the earlier case, the Cham capital at Indrapura (Tra Kieu) was destroyed. In the present case, as noted, in 1044 the Ly mounted a return expedition at an unspecified northern Cham center to vent their wrath upon the Chams and killed the Cham king.

The Po Nagar temple in Kauthara (just north of Panduranga) gives us a Cham perspective on these events. We already saw the eighth-century inscrip- tion that referred to the 774 desecration of this temple by dark-skinned people from the sea. A subsequent Po Nagar inscription describes this 1050 expedi- tion by the Cham king against Panduranga. This latter inscription noted that the king celebrated the restoration of his authority over Panduranga by rebuilding the sacred Po Nagar temple complex and assigning "slaves"— Khmers, Chinese, men of Pukam (Pagan [Burma]), and Thais (Syam)—to the temple (Aymonier: 1891b, 29). These "slaves" were most probably war captives who had formerly been residents of Panduranga; in the case of the Thai and Burmese, having come to be in this Cham marketplace via trade from someplace else. Since Champa's ports were widely recognized interna- tionally for their slave markets, it is likely that such war captives from a vari-

ety of sources would normally have been marketed in Cham coast ports and
that some of these slaves were present among Panduranga's maritime community at the time of its subjugation to Kauthara. Equally likely, the Kauthara
monarch's victory over Panduranga allowed him to enslave the conquered
population, which would have included the enumerated members of the multiethnic maritime sojourning community that had fought on Panduranga's
behalf.

The Cham realm sent three embassies to China between 1050 and 1056
and five to the Ly Dai Viet capital between 1047 and 1060 (Maspero: 1928,
138–39). This sudden flurry of diplomacy after 1050 is best characterized as
an assurance to the Chinese and the Vietnamese that the Cham monarch now
had his domain firmly under control, including Panduranga and its marauding
seafarers, as well as also an assurance to his powerful neighbors that his
aggression against the Khmer realm would have no negative consequence to
them. Nevertheless, when a Cham army launched a land attack against the Ly
in 1068, and Dai Viet responded with a naval attack against the Cham capital
at Vijaya, the Vietnamese found it remarkable that they met resistance only
from a Cham army and not from a Cham fleet, indication that at that time the
Cham ruler did not have sufficient naval forces to take on his 1068 campaign
(Maspero: 1928, 141–42). Whatever had enabled the king to attract seafarers
in 1050, those tools had become ineffective.

CHAMPA'S POLITICAL ECONOMY
OF COMPETITION

Champa was a culturally integrated yet multicentered polity. Like its contemporary Southeast Asian civilizations, Champa left impressive temple complexes and numerous inscriptions (composed in both Sanskrit and the Cham
language), which are the main source for early Cham history. Yet based on
the surviving evidence, Champa state systems were weakly institutionalized
and dependent on ritual and personal alliance networks to integrate their geographically fragmented populations.

We have already noted the multiple Cham royal centers (capitals) at several
river-mouth urban centers bearing Indic titles. First Nha Trang in the southward section of Kauthara was prominent, then in 875 it was in Indrapura (Tra
Kieu) in the north central region, which by 982 was the inclusive Amaravati.
Based on Cham inscriptions and archeological sources rather than Chinese
dynastic records, historians now conclude that there was never a single, continuous Cham state. Rather than representing shifts from one dynasty's rule
to that of another, one river system's elite periodically became more promi-

nent than those of other river-mouth port-polities of the Cham coast. As such, the Cham polities were more like the Malay riverine and archipelago states characterized in chapters 1 and 4 than like its mainland wet-rice plain neighbors to the west and north. As with the rulers of the archipelago riverine-based political economies, the authority of a Cham monarch was concentrated within his own river-mouth plain, while beyond that river-mouth port-polity base the monarch's sovereignty depended on his ability to construct alliance networks with the leaders of the populations in his upstream hinterland as well as with those of the Cham coast's rival riverine systems.

There was an important difference, however, for, unlike most of the Straits of Melaka polities, the Cham coastal centers had immediately adjacent networked productive agricultural communities that could be self-sufficient while also supplying the basic needs of the Cham ruling elite and their sustenance of the Cham temple networks and royal centers. Thus, the Cham realm that had emerged by 1000 CE had much in common both with the Malay polities of Srivijaya (chapter 4) and with its contemporaries in east Java (chapter 5) and their Khmer neighbors to their west (chapter 6), possessing the river-mouth orientation of the Malay polities and the agricultural hinterlands of Java and Angkor. The Cham polity's hinterlands were not nearly as extensive as those of east Java and Angkor, and overall had less production capacity. Furthermore, Java's political centers were located upstream and were therefore better insulated from the threat of coastal raids, while the Cham political centers were constantly subject to the raids of both their riverine neighbors and their Dai Viet neighbors to the north and the Khmers to the south and west.

Throughout the periodic fluctuations of Cham river-mouth centers, there was one constant—the Cham sacred centers at My Son and Po Nagar, located on the edge of the highlands and upriver from the Cham port-polity centers in Hoi An and Nha Trang respectively, which served as the locus of Cham royal ceremony that promoted a sense of cultural homogeneity among the disparate populations of the Cham realm. Thus, although Cham society was weakly linked institutionally, it was united by common cultural values and a mutual ritual core. In addition, the communal values expressed in Champa's widely distributed inscriptions demonstrate a level of societal integration, reinforced by Cham ritual networks, that provided the foundation for a functional Cham polity (Wachtel: 1998).

John Whitmore has recently argued the importance of the need for protection as the motivation for early Cham political development, in reaction to political developments to the north among the Vietnamese and to the west among the Khmer (Whitmore: 2010b). He notes in support of this view that the earliest Cham inscriptions, after first reporting successions to the throne, focus on the capacity of a monarch to defend his realm and then detail the supernatural qualities that allow him to establish or reaffirm local cults to achieve a cosmic partnership with a supreme deity, especially with Siva. Accordingly, the earliest inscriptions are usually linked with specific temples and their cults, as, for example, the great cult of Sambhubhadresvara (based at My Son) which, according to an inscription found there, "protected Nagara Champa." According to this inscription, the king and the goddess of the cult lived in a symbiotic relationship calling for their mutual protection: "May the king . . . protect you in order to rule the Cham people. May the Goddess of Sovereignty in her turn always protect him, [as also to] protect these riches [of the temple]" (Majumdar: 1927, inscription 31).

Just as the monarch was enjoined here to protect the cult, so, too, the Cham kings declared themselves protectors of the entire realm, erecting stone steles inscribed with proclamations of their capacity to protect all the Cham people. For example, that King Indravarman II (875–ca. 898) was "equal in prowess to Visnu, who protected without fear the kingdom of Champa" (Majumdar: 1927, inscription 43; Coedes: 1968, 122–23) and "skillful in protecting Champa" (Majumdar: 1927, inscription 45). His successor Jaya Simhavarman (ca. 898–ca. 903) "protect[ed] the entire world" and especially "protect[ed] his subjects . . . by his strength" (Majumdar: 1927, inscription 46). An inscription of Paramasvaravarman I (d. 982) asserted at its beginning that he was "the protector of Champa," and went on to detail his role in providing protection from the Khmer (*Kambu*) and in "protect[ing] the ten regions from fear," a phrasing that also reflected the composite nature of the Cham realm (Majumdar: 1927, inscriptions 52–53). An inscription of the following monarch, Harivarman (ca. 1081) declared that he was "the protector of Champa" (Majumdar: 1927, inscription 62) while in another case an underaged successor was removed from the throne and replaced by a veteran warrior on the grounds that the former was incapable of providing the necessary defense (Majumdar: 1927, inscription 65).

Whitmore's study of early Cham kingship speculates that by the twelfth century Cham kings had a more stable style of networking than in earlier times (Whitmore: 2010b). Ultimately, however, the successful ruler had to generate income for his direct subordinates and secure material well-being for his subjects. Whenever economic prosperity was lost, serious questions arose regarding the successful magical qualities of the ruler's cults, and in such situations the autonomy of regional units soon would be reasserted. In fact, throughout Champa's history periodic regional autonomy and resistance to the centralizing ambitions of would-be Cham monarchs were coincident with an inability to provide expected economic returns.

As we have just seen, according to Cham inscriptions the king's place was not in the palace managing the day-to-day affairs of his state, but in the battle-field protecting his subject communities and thereby securing their prosper-ity. This is signaled not only by the references to the Cham king as protector, but also by the administrative functions that are left out of the records. Cham monarchs are never referenced in records of local water management, nor did they assume a role as supervisors of communal granaries, which together with the local water-management networks were the source of unity among local peasant communities. They were not entirely aloof from these arrange-ments, however, as they did periodically assign the responsibility for the supervision of new or existing public granaries to newly established temples (Wachtel: 1998).

Inscriptions report that, in return for securing his subjects' prosperity, the Cham monarch was entitled to receive one-sixth of local agricultural produc-tion. But they also repeatedly proclaimed that, due to the ruler's "benevo-lence," the state expected to collect only one-tenth. Since such references appear in inscriptions reporting transfers of the ruler's remaining income rights on property to temples (which, like in Angkor and Java, were signifi-cant centers for the concentration of economic resources), it can be inferred that the state was either unwilling or unable to collect a share of local produc-tion even in its own river system base and thus assigned its token one-tenth share in the hope that a temple, an institution with local roots, might have better luck making such collections. What were normally assigned were income rights to uncultivated and unpopulated lands, further indication that the state had only limited rights over cultivated lands. Manpower (war cap-tives or other bondsmen and bondswomen) was frequently assigned to sup-port the extension of agriculture under the direction of a temple and its staff. Such consolidation of control over land and existing granaries and their assignment to temples provided indirect access to local production that was otherwise inaccessible to the state, and in turn temples promoted the king's sovereignty in their religious cults, thereby providing Cham kings with sym-bolic rather than direct material dividends (see chapter 5).

There is an inconsistency between the inscriptions' stress on the ruler's moral and physical prowess and their conclusion that this prowess was insuf-ficient to guarantee the future security of endowed temples. Cham inscrip-tions continually use curses to protect temples rather than threatening a monarch's physical retribution against offenders. While they glorify the physical capacity and personal heroism of Cham rulers, they normally end with the proclamation that those who plunder temples (which, given the con-sistent references to the practice, would seem to have been a common occur-rence) would be subject to divine retribution—normally a shortened and unprosperous life and the certainty of hell in the afterlife. One such endowment inscription ends with the following fairly typical warning: "Those who protect all these goods of Indrabhadresvara in the world, will enjoy the delights of heaven along with the gods. Those who carry them away will fall into hell together with their family, and will suffer the sorrows of hell as long as the sun and moon endure" (Barth and Bergaigne: 1885–1893, 226ff).

Such statements give the impression that even during a king's reign, and especially after his death, his territory and notably his richly endowed temples were subject to pillage by his various political rivals. It is not surprising, then, that the inscriptions of Cham monarchs should so frequently report the restoration of the temples of previous Cham rulers; temples were especially vulnerable to the demonic "foreigners" who attempted to plunder local material resources and labor. Acts of restoration were statements of royal legitimacy, proclamations that the new monarch had sufficient resources to guarantee his subjects' (and a temple's) future livelihood.

Since Champa possessed an extensive coastline, an alternative source of income for Cham monarchs was the sea. There was certainly potential for trade income. During the summers, monsoon winds propelled sea traffic north to China, while from the autumn to the spring winds from the north made the Cham coast a natural landfall for the merchants traveling south to the archipelago and beyond. Though Chinese sources always considered Cham ports to be secondary centers of international commercial exchange, they did have important products that Chinese and other international traders desired, notably luxury items such as ivory, rhinoceros horn, tortoiseshell, pearls, peacock and kingfisher feathers, spices, and aromatic woods, including eaglewood (Maspero: 1928, 29; Wade: 2010; Li: 2006; Hardy: 2009).

Chinese and Vietnamese sources say a good deal about these commodities, many of which came to the Cham coast from the mountainous hinterland. Elephants and their tusks, for example, were highly desirable, and fourteen times were included among the tribute gifts Cham monarchs sent to the Chinese court between 414 and 1050 (Hardy: 2009, 115). These elephants came from the highland regions upriver from Amaravati (Hoi An), Kauthara (Nha Trang), and Panduranga (Phan Rang). Rhinoceros horns (ground rhinoceros horn is a prized aphrodisiac among the Chinese), cardamom, beeswax, lacquer, resins, and scented woods (sandalwood, camphor wood, and eagle or aloeswood) came from the same upstream region (Maspero: 1928, 57, 67, 87–88, 99, 120, 133, 138). As for areca nuts and betel leaves, the chewing of which gave teeth a distinctive red color, they came from the highlands upriver from Indrapura (Tra Kieu), while cinnamon was a product of the region upriver from Vijaya (Binh Dinh), and gold was said to be mined at a mountain of gold some thirty *li* from modern Hue in the Amaravati region.

Highland oral histories provide valuable insight into the nature of Cham commercial exchange, which is ignored in all the local written sources, focused as they are on political and religious activities as they relate to temples rather than on Champa's commercial activities. Indeed, such early lowland-highland exchanges are rarely referenced anywhere in Southeast Asia. Legends told among highlanders near Cheo Reo in the Dar Lak (Darlac) Plateau region substantiate that the highlands were the source of the trade items enumerated in external sources. They also report that the Chams attempted to integrate highlanders into their political economy by negotiation rather than by force, offering the protection of the Cham armies and the privilege of becoming the Chams' trade partners (Hickey: 1982, 116).

In turn, the Cham monarchs were entitled to receive locally woven cloth as tribute (Hickey: 1982, 446). Apparently, the most valuable of the trade commodities offered by the downstream-based Chams was salt, which was critical to the highland diet and in local animal husbandry (Hardy: 2009, 115). Among the highland populations in the Panduranga region north of the Mekong Delta the local headmen were said to have organized a band of men to assist the Chams in the search for eaglewood, valued for its fragrance when burned in Cham, Vietnamese, and Chinese rituals. Tribal legends report that local leaders became Cham vassals and received a Cham saber and seal, and a title that roughly translated to lord/master and thereby confirmed their leadership status (Hickey: 1982, 117).

Also important were the coastal populations, the maritime sojourners who sometimes provided navies and yet who sometimes engaged in piracy. The Chinese court was always trying in vain to compel Cham monarchs to assume responsibility for the behavior of their coastal populations; judging from the frequency of Chinese demands, it would seem that this coastal population was only marginally under the Cham monarch's control. Cham coast piracy was widely known among the international trade community. International voyagers were often warned to avoid the Cham coast when traveling from the Melaka Straits region to China. This weakened the appeal of Cham ports to international traders.

While some of this piracy was motivated by sea populations acting on their own, some of it may also have been organized directly by the Cham state as part of a self-sustaining social economy of plunder (Wheeler: 2006). Being unable to secure sufficient revenue income from their subordinate river valley agricultural communities or consistent return from internal or external trade, Cham monarchs had to seek alternative sources to finance the alliance networks that were critical to their sovereignty. Plundering raids were therefore waged on a regular basis both against rival river-mouth population centers on the Cham coast and also against Champa's neighbors, particularly the Khmer to the west and the Vietnamese to the north. These raids are reported not only in Cham epigraphy but also in Vietnamese chronicles and, from the tenth century onward, in inscriptions from the Khmer realm. In local Cham inscriptions these raids are honored as demonstrations of the Cham ruler's capacity to protect his realm (a good offense was considered a good defense), and also for the resulting material and human resources that were then redistributed among Cham temples and among the monarch's supporters (the latter included both the coastal populations and the various warriors who figure so prominently in Cham epigraphy as the monarch's principal political allies). This dynamic of plunder explains why Cham history is dominated by seemingly constant military expeditions.

Not only did this plunder—in the form of goods and captured labor—help bind together the internal realm, it also provided a source of external income, for Cham ports were widely known as a major source of slaves; that is, war captives, who were traded there to various international buyers (Hardy: 2009, 114; Li: 2006; Maspero: 1928, 16–17, 30, 34). Furthermore, in addition to helping the Cham monarchs validate their local cultural image as the source of their subjects' well-being, successful plundering expeditions provided the practical resources—particularly labor—for rewarding warriors and other key participants, who in turn strengthened the temple networks. Cham inscriptions suggest that supporters of successful expeditions were often assigned jurisdiction over land that was either undeveloped or needed redevelopment. In turn, suggest the inscriptions, these supporters acted immediately to strengthen the local temple networks, for one of their first acts was the lavish endowment of temples, whose staffs subsequently assumed supervision of the land development projects. Thus local development was itself rooted in the political economy of plunder, as the warrior elite donated, or redistributed, a portion of the objects, money, and "slave" labor won in successful royal expeditions (Barth and Bergaigne: 1885–1893, 218, 275).

The endowment of temples in newly (re)developed territory had economic, social, and symbolic value, for royal subordinates sanctified their development projects by instituting lingas and establishing new temples that not only honored the temple's benefactor, but also proclaimed the glory of past and present Cham monarchs, for whom the temple lingas were named. This promoted local appreciation of the monarch's accomplishments and encouraged local subordination to the Cham state's sovereignty even in the absence of the kind of administrative structure that was being developed in the contemporary Khmer realm to its west (chapter 6) and the Vietnam polity to its north (see below) (Wachtel: 1998).

The early Cham realm may thus be understood as a loose and marginally interdependent networked polity that encompassed a series of politically linked river-mouth urban centers and their upriver hinterlands. Lacking a resource base sufficient to support their political aspirations, if not responding to threats from their Khmer and Vietnamese neighbors, by the eleventh century some Cham kings by necessity launched periodic military expeditions to acquire plunder that could be redistributed, both directly (by sharing booty with their warrior allies) and indirectly (via temple endowments made by those allies), for these arrangements were necessary if the monarchs were to maintain the loyalty of the leaders of the local inhabitants. Cham monarchs maintained the loyalty of their direct military allies by keeping them "in the field" on various plunder expeditions. Lacking a royal administration that could directly control the various regions of the Cham realm, Cham monarchs instead depended on the willingness of local elites to recognize their sovereignty via participation in expeditions of conquest and by support of local religious cults that proclaimed the ruler's superior prowess. While these arrangements might sustain the Cham state for a while, they also fostered an inherent vulnerability in the realm's political economy, notably to retaliatory attacks. We have seen some of this instability in the fluctuating histories of the realm's capitals. As we will see in chapters 7 and 9, the inherent vulnerability of the economy of plunder would eventually lead first to the demise of the Cham polities consequent to Vietnamese expansion, supported by a successful mix of agricultural productivity and overseas trade.

THE DEVELOPMENT OF THE
DAI VIET POLITICAL ECONOMY

The widely held notion that Vietnam has never been anything other than a reflection of China is no longer taken seriously. Today early Vietnam is described as a unique society straddling the southern border of China. The rise of the Vietnamese civilization as a linguistic, cultural, and political entity is, however, deeply indebted to the prolonged association between the inhabitants of the Red River delta and their neighbors immediately to the north, collectively known to the Chinese as the Yue, who were a variety of ethnic populations inhabiting the mountains of south China and its borderlands. But Vietnam's southern and western connections with populations on the Southeast Asian mainland cannot be ignored. This includes the Chams and Malays, who shared the South China Sea coastline. Vietnamese traits—such as tattooing, betel chewing, a pluralistic concept of ancestry, and the use of a material culture distinctive to the Southeast Asian locale—bear witness to connections with Vietnam's nonsinic southern neighbors (Taylor: 1983).

Located on the border of both the Chinese and the Southeast Asian realms, Vietnam drew from both cultures, yet belonged to neither. No other Southeast

Asian population experienced centuries of Chinese rule as the prelude to the foundation of their own independent political existence. In the post–tenth century era independent Vietnam polities repeatedly rebuffed the advancing armies of their neighbors. Chinese armies of the Song, Yuan, and Ming dynasties each unsuccessfully attempted to reannex Dai Viet. Neighboring Cham, Khmer, and tribal populations periodically tried to plunder Dai Viet's wealth and carry off its manpower.

In premodern times early Vietnamese civilization moved spatially from higher, upland areas of the Red River valley into the delta region, and then south into previous Cham territory in the second millennium CE. Early Vietnamese society consisted of small communal groups who farmed the area above the delta, using the natural ebb and flow of the tides of the Red River system to support local irrigation networks (Taylor: 1983, 1–44). By the tenth century Vietnamese society was based in villages and had developed elaborate dike and drainage systems to control the raging monsoon-fed waters of the Red River delta. Staples of Vietnamese life were fish and rice; twelfth-century Chinese writers report that the Vietnamese grew the special early-ripening strain of rice that had come into Vietnam from Champa, although an indigenous type was preferred (Whitmore: 1986, 130).

Early Chinese political interest in Vietnam included Han rulers' desire to secure their southern borderlands and southern trade routes to gain access to international luxury goods (Taylor: 1983, 78). Han-era outposts in Vietnam at the beginning of the first millennium were primarily commercial centers rather than fortified military or governmental capitals. Han rulers never demonstrated an elaborate administrative commitment to their Jiaozhi/Jiaozhou Province; Vietnam was viewed as being too remote. In the symbolic early first-century CE Han-era political order, the pre-Chinese Vietnamese Lac lord elite remained in charge. They remitted tribute, especially rare objects and valuable consumables, and in return received seals and ribbons from their Han overlords that legitimized their collections from their dependents and in theory added prestige in the eyes of their peers. The Lac elite was more or less allowed to rule in traditional ways, although there were attempted modifications to aspects of their social system that the Chinese found inconsistent with the Chinese sense of morality, notably their disregard for Chinese-style patriarchal marriage and their preference for the bilateral kinship patterns practiced throughout the Southeast Asian region. The Lac lords enjoyed the labor services and a share of the local agricultural and craft production, which were supplied by their subject client communities (Taylor: 1983, 45–84).

During Wang Mang's first-century China interlude (9–23 CE), Han ruling-class refugees reinforced the authority of the local Han officials, and new patterns of Chinese rule evolved. In the aftermath, in 40 CE, Trung Trac and

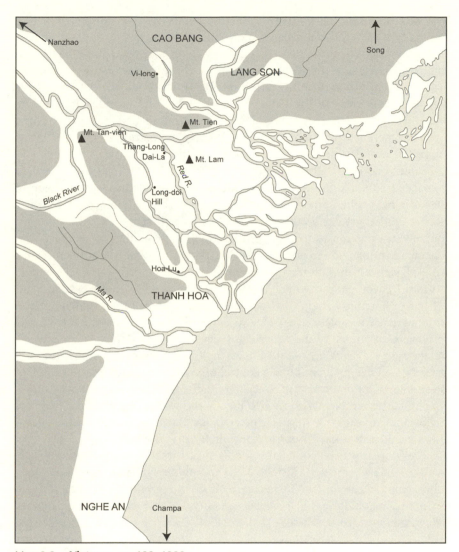

Map 3.2.   Vietnam, ca. 100–1200

Trung Nhi, daughters of a Lac lord, led an uprising against the restoration of Han authority and temporarily drove Han administrators out of northern Vietnam and parts of southern China. The Han general Ma Yuan captured and beheaded the sisters in 42–43—local legend differs from the official Chinese sources, reporting that to avoid capture and certain execution the sisters heroically committed suicide. This rebellion was the final attempt of the pre-Han

Vietnamese ruling class to resist Chinese authority, and subsequently Han authority over Vietnam became more direct. From that time forward Lac lords were no longer mentioned, and their Dong Son civilization had ended by the conclusion of the second century. The Trung Sisters Rebellion reflects the importance of women in early Vietnamese, if not wider Southeast Asian society, since many of the Lac clan leaders who followed the Trung sisters were also women. Subsequently, the spirits of the sisters and many of their female generals were honored as early Vietnamese patriots and are still worshiped in various Vietnam villages today.

Chinese administrators especially addressed their need to pay for their expanded administration. To cover the additional expenses they began to develop the local agrarian economy as a stable tax base. Chinese administrators promoted greater productive efficiency as well as the extension of agriculture into previously uncultivated lands. To support their objectives, they encouraged transition to a formal patriarchal society as a way to increase the role of men in agricultural production, which had traditionally been performed by women as "women's work." Hunting and fishing were the focus of male economic activity, but produced no taxable surplus; settled agriculture was a predictable source of tax revenues. This society in which men were predominantly hunters and fishermen seemed, from the Chinese perspective, to have no stable family system. The male role in agriculture, or the lack thereof, and the apparent female control of cultivation were difficult for Chinese administrators to accept. One Han official tried to combat this by ordering all men aged twenty to fifty to marry; the would-be elite were expected to pay for Chinese-style marriage ceremonies. Subsequent registration of new family units made kin groups responsible for tax payments.

The Vietnamese responded to new Han post-rebellion initiatives, but not as the Chinese expected. Instead of becoming an agrarian society comfortably settled in one place, Vietnamese retained the frontier spirit of their previous hunting culture. Vietnamese readily moved into and developed previously uncultivated lands. This mobility supported periodic Chinese (and subsequent Vietnamese) government efforts to extend wet-rice cultivation into new territories. Similar to Chinese society, Vietnamese possession of land rights was considered essential for the well-being of a family, and for the continuation of the family line. Sons needed to have land to keep the family unit together and readily extended cultivation into previously uncultivated land to enhance their family's collective income. Family property and family ancestor cults were mutually interdependent. Substantial houses that would endure for generations rather than makeshift dwellings become the norm.

Ancestor spirit houses were also constructed, with a central sanctuary honoring ancestors of the paternal line. This was the center of family rituals and feasting. Stone tombs, too, were reminders of generations past. Neglected ("unnourished") ancestral spirits became hostile, untrustworthy spirits that wandered endlessly in search of offerings. Designated cult lands collectively farmed by members of the family lineage supplied income to finance rituals and feasts meant to acknowledge ancestors, who in turn were expected to reciprocate by bestowing good fortune on the living. The head of the kin group, usually the oldest male, was the guardian over the ancestor rituals (Taylor: 1986). Vietnam's elite had previously built spirit shrines (*dinh*) for the guardian deities of local agricultural fertility, and also ancestral shrines to honor past generations of locally based clans.

Han bureaucrats viewed traditional Vietnamese landholding patterns, which were based on communal usage rather than family ownership, as incompatible with their desire to establish new statewide revenue systems based on private ownership. Han-era land taxation in Vietnam was unorthodox and underwent constant evolution. Since it ultimately depended on the personal skill of the Chinese bureaucrat, the system was inherently vulnerable to personal greed and corruption. The Chinese government would on occasion police itself, as for example when two officials were executed for extorting bribes and filling a storehouse with improperly seized possessions, which were subsequently redistributed among local court officials (Taylor: 1983, 59).

Han soldiers settled in newly built walled outposts to govern new administrative prefectures and districts and to negate the attempts of the old Lac aristocracy to stand in their way by their assertions that they held hereditary rights over all previously uncultivated property. Soldier-farmers supervised the digging of local ditches to irrigate the fields surrounding the frontier population clusters that were on the northern edge of or in the Red River delta rather than the previously developed regions in the upper river plain. It was Han policy to keep soldiers in place, as they settled in and became part of the local social fabric. The resident military was self-sustaining and was empowered to regularize the revenue flow from conquered territory, and also to subdue disaffection over newly imposed Han revenue demands among prior residents. Moreover, Han rule established a coordinated authority over the Jiaozhi (Vietnam) Province irrigation systems, which they helped to extend, and a merging of Chinese and Vietnamese societies began to take place. A powerful Han-Viet landlord class came into existence as government tax demands forced peasants to sell land to rich officials and become tenant farmers on their private estates; or, as Han soldiers received communal lands in return for their service, previous populations who were driven off this newly assigned land began to settle uncultivated lands, based on the new family landholding policies.

In the new Han-Viet culture, status derived from wealth and the private

ownership of land. Great families lived in fortresslike compounds and supported a private community of "guests" that included scholars, technical
experts, spies, assassins, and private armies. The elite ruled by virtue of the
validation of their character marked by seals given them that they attached to
the rooflines of their houses, replacing the Lac-era seals and ribbons as symbols of their authority. The remaining tombs of the elite reflect a cultural
intermix between Chinese and Vietnamese. It was then normal for Chinese
men to take Vietnamese wives. This was a means of interconnecting the two
groups and cultures.

As the Han dynasty fell in the third century, the Han-Viet elite took greater
interest in seaborne trade as a secondary source of income. Commerce in luxury goods was especially a major preoccupation of local administrators
(Giap: 1932; Taylor: 1983, 196–99; Taylor: 1986). During the post-Han era,
Chinese officials posted in Vietnam were said to have normally extorted
20–30 percent of the merchandise's value as it moved through Vietnam's
ports (Taylor: 1983, 107). There were fine lines between piracy, corruption,
and appropriate state service. Chinese records characterize war booty Chinese troops collected when they raided Linyi's ports in the mid-fifth century
as an "economic inspiration" (Taylor: 1983, 121). Among that same era's
Chinese records is a summary statement that "men who go to Jiao [Vietnam]
abandon the thankless task of government for more lucrative occupations of
commerce." This account also reports that "barbarians of the Jiao regularly
assemble for plunder" (Taylor: 1983, 148). That era's south China–based rulers, eager to secure the luxuries of the Vietnamese coast, gave special titles
to local leaders who helped them collect slaves, pearls, kingfishers, elephant
tusks, and rhinoceros horns, and also policed the coastline to inhibit piracy,
so that the lucrative international shipping and cargoes could make their way
to south China's ports (Taylor: 1983, 167).

China's occupation of Vietnam between the third century BCE and the
tenth century CE also left a considerable cultural and intellectual legacy in
the form of Confucian thought. Vietnam's Confucianism had to compete with
other belief systems, especially the continuing importance of Buddhism and
local animism among Vietnam's elite (Taylor: 1986; Nguyen: 1997). And
Confucian influence in Vietnam was far from uniform, varying considerably
according to the historical period, geographical region, and social class. No
Vietnam-based ruler or aristocrat, however deeply committed to Chinese tradition and Confucian thought, would have attempted to deny Vietnam's own
cultural heritage and separation from the Chinese Middle Kingdom. Vietnam's rulers' honoring of important local deities constituted an important
part of their legitimacy. Such spirituality posed a subtle threat to the intellectual and moral orthodoxy of Confucian humanistic philosophy, which for the

ruler and the scholarly elite represented the basis of the secular political and social status quo. Among China's legacies to Vietnam were the Chinese written language and artistic, philosophical, and political forms, which would eventually lead Vietnam to be more Sinified than Indianized. But below the elite level, Chinese influences did not deeply penetrate. Local populations retained their disdain for Chinese sovereignty and Chinese culture and were determined to maintain their separate identities.

THE EMERGENCE OF THE INDEPENDENT DAI VIET POLITY

The Dai Viet polity of the Red River delta region became definitively independent of China in the tenth century. The resulting intensive development of Vietnam's Red River delta environment in the tenth and eleventh centuries was important not only for its additional agricultural productivity, but also because of its proximity to the sea. Like its Southeast Asian contemporaries, the Dai Viet state of this period depended on the production of its wet-rice economy. However, aided by its location, it also devoted itself to the development of international commercial networks. Song rule in China was a great boon to this latter effort, for the Song welcomed international commerce, and the resulting efflorescence of international trade benefited Dai Viet along with the other overseas centers. Meanwhile, like the mainland wet-rice states to its west, Dai Viet's rulers enhanced their resource base by encouraging the development of the Red River delta, their south, and the highlands, economically and administratively, but also pursued the cultivation of external trade contacts.

The development of Dai Viet's independence was a side effect of the collapse of the Tang dynasty in 906/7. After his 938 victory against regional Chinese forces in the battle of the Bach Dang River (the major riverine route into the Red River plain from the north), Ngo Quyen established the initial capital of the Dai Viet kingdom at Co Loa, north across the river from modern Hanoi, at a site that was symbolically linked to the pre-Chinese era of the Lac lords. After his death five years later twelve regional warlords competed for control. In the 960s, the victorious Dinh Bo Linh (r. 968–980), working in alliance with the Buddhist monkhood and the general Le Hoan, proclaimed himself the first emperor of the independent realm he renamed Dai Co Viet (Great Viet State), now based at Hoa Lu in the hills at the southern edge of the Red River delta. Dinh Bo Linh was succeeded by his infant son, who, with his mother's approval, was quickly replaced by his new stepfather Le Hoan. Le Hoan (r. 980–1005) defeated a Song dynasty (960–1279) expeditionary force in 981, and then tried to unify his realm, notably by defeating a number of revolts and providing the infrastructure for future political stability by building a series of roads to connect Vietnam's diverse regions to his capital.

Following Le Hoan's death, in 1010 the capital relocated at Thang Long, the site of modern Hanoi, a former Tang provincial center surrounded by Buddhist temples and fertile ricefields. There allied aristocratic leaders proclaimed the establishment of the Ly dynasty (1009–1225) under Ly Cong Uan (known posthumously as Ly Thai To, r. 1009–29). Ly Cong Uan's son and successor Ly Phat Ma (posthumously known as Ly Thai Tong, r. 1028–1054) is remembered as one of Vietnam's greatest kings. He consolidated and institutionalized the king's powers, implemented the *Minh-dao* (clear way) code of common laws in 1042, and, in 1044, personally led a naval expedition against the Chams. The latter initiative was explained in the Vietnamese chronicles as necessitated by the Chams' failure to maintain proper order on the southern coast, a situation that was, as we have seen, endemic to the Cham style of rule. According to the chronicles, Ly Phat Ma's successful raid on the Chams ensured Vietnam's security, and thereafter Vietnam enjoyed a period of prosperity in which taxes were reduced, foreign merchants accommodated, and markets opened in the mountains. Ly Phat Ma's son succeeded as Ly Nhat Ton (posthumously known as Ly Thanh Tong, r. 1054–1072) and began to confer official titles and ranks on his officials and on members of the royal family, while also conferring posthumous titles on the royal ancestors. Vietnam chronicles reporting his reign also highlight his trade initiatives, which included contact with sojourning merchants and especially Java—he was said to have paid a substantial sum to a Java-based merchant for a pearl that "glowed in the dark" (Taylor: 1992, 140–45).

The Vietnamese and their rulers concerned themselves with lowland-highland relations even before the Dai Viet period. In the ninth century, for example, Li Cho, protector-general of the Vietnamese territory on behalf of the Tang dynasty, was said to have changed the terms of trade between the Vietnamese lowlands and the mountain chiefs. Previously, the mountain chiefs had been bartering horses and cattle for salt from the lowlands. Li Cho took control of salt production in the tidewater villages, hoping thereby to obtain a larger number of horses that he could sell to accumulate a fortune. Other local officials were aware of the advantages of such arrangements, and one of them is quoted as saying: "If we cut off the salt and iron trade on the southern coast [we would] cause the ruination of their [the highlanders'] market . . . after two years they can be crushed in a single battle" (Taylor: 1983, 96, 239–40). These sources reflect the importance of Vietnamese expansion into the delta, which gave them access to salt, the key commodity in lowland-highland exchanges.

Initially, both the Chinese and the Vietnamese administrators were uninterested in expansion into the highlands, and were it not for the demands of commerce and governance, the Vietnamese might have remained content to stay in the Red River delta. But commercial and revenue needs forced the Vietnamese to reevaluate their traditional disregard for this region as well as the south, where the river systems between Vietnam and Cham territories could provide access to the highland sources of numerous trade goods. This desire for better access to the highlands in part explains Vietnam's eventual commitment to southward expansion, which paired with their need to develop agricultural lands and their desire to be more aggressively involved in international trade. The first Vietnamese annexation of Cham territory took place in the eleventh century, shortly after Dai Viet's independence and 981 victory against Song dynasty efforts to reclaim Vietnam.

As we have seen, the early years of the Vietnamese state in the tenth and eleventh centuries were especially critical in the transition to a more externally focused Vietnamese political economy. The political unity achieved by Dinh Bo Linh, the founder of the independent Vietnamese state, made large regional markets possible, encouraging commercial expansion and attracting foreign merchants. His capital at Hoa Lu, strategically located on the Red River downstream rather than the traditional political core in the Hanoi region at the northern edge of the Red River delta, was itself an important market for trade where, as was reported for the year 976, merchant boats from various nations beyond the sea arrived and presented the goods of their countries (Taylor: 1983, 287–88). Over time, the port at Bo-hai, near the mouth of the Red River, also grew in importance, especially after the Dai Viet capital shifted to Thang Long (Hanoi) in 1010. This was where inland trade met the southbound seaborne trade (Wang: 1958, 82; Whitmore: 1986, 130).

The Hoa Lu court (969–1009) provided the initial market for the luxury goods in which foreign merchants specialized, as an edict of 975 prescribed types of clothing to be worn by civil and military officials at the court. To meet these clothing needs, as well as the other material requirements of the emergent Vietnamese court, foreign trade was a necessity. To this end, envoys were sent to China with many gifts, presumably to proclaim Vietnam as an international marketplace and secure political recognition, but also to gain access to the Chinese marketplace, which became the source of the ceremonial paraphernalia, cloth and clothing, and other material objects necessary to sustain the new Vietnamese court's aristocratic culture and cults of legitimacy (Taylor: 1983, 146). The Vietnamese economy was thus transformed to serve the needs of a strong king lifting himself up in a place hitherto considered insignificant.

Additional development supported the economy in the eleventh century. In 1048, Ly Thai Tong (r. 1028–1054) began the aggressive extension of his Dai Viet state's agricultural base. In doing so he instituted a China-inspired agricultural cult in which the monarch was the highest officiate. As the symbolic source of fertility, the Vietnamese emperor led springtime rites in which he would plough the first furrows, and he also symbolically assisted in the gathering of rice at harvest. At the south gate of his new capital of Thanglong he made offerings to bring rain and to guarantee crops at the Esplanade of the Gods of the Soil and Harvest. To sustain the substantial expenses of his new ritualized monarchy, in the 1040s, as previously noted, five thousand Cham war captives were assigned to land and resettled in undeveloped, unpopulated areas of the Dai Viet borderlands, where they were allowed to name their new communities after their native Cham settlements (Khôi: 1955, 164). Road and temple construction programs linked the capital and the regions in a realmwide communication network that had both favorable political and commercial transport implications.

The periodic Cham raids on their former territory challenged the local bases of Vietnamese imperial authority by carting off numbers of Vietnamese villagers, while plundering what remained of local villages and their temples. In addition to depleting the state of needed resources, these raids challenged Vietnam's royal stature. As portrayed in the Vietnamese chronicles, the main issue in the Vietnamese rulers' punitive actions against the Chams was that Cham rulers failed to properly acknowledge Vietnamese imperial "virtue." Thus, though the Vietnamese state benefited economically from its own military expeditions against the Chams, it justified these counterraids as acts of reciprocity that were necessary for the future security of the Vietnamese people. Victory in these exchanges was tremendously important to the Vietnamese monarchs; they engaged in elaborate preparations for these reciprocal "defensive" acts, for to lose against the "rival" Chams was unthinkable.

In contrast with the Chams, the Vietnamese state leadership was ideologically opposed to the use of plundering raids as a regular source of state financing. This would have been inconsistent with the state leadership's intended development of a moral Vietnamese administration, which would seek to foster a harmonious state system under the leadership of an educated land-based and moral Buddhist aristocratic gentry (Hall: 2010c). Though the Vietnamese state actively linked with the East-West sea trade as an acceptable source of state finances, in so doing they were like their fellow rulers of Southeast Asian wet-rice states in perceiving these trade-derived revenues primarily as an attractive alternative to squeezing additional tax revenues from their lands.

CHAM AND VIETNAMESE COMMERCIAL
DEVELOPMENTS IN PERSPECTIVE

During the tenth and eleventh centuries the political authorities in the Champa and Vietnamese states supported external commercial involvements. Rulers hoped to acquire a share of the profits from commerce, or the luxury goods derived from the trade for ritualized distributions, and therefore attempted through diplomatic means to expand their external commercial contacts. To this end, they sent official embassies and gifts to the emperors of China at the eastern polar end of the Indian Ocean trade network. But while, at least in the tenth and eleventh centuries, the Vietnamese kings generally benefited from their embrace of external trade, the interaction of the Cham domain with the commercial channels had mixed results.

Though the Cham political economy has been described above as fragmented, at its core a Cham society emerged in the first millennium CE that was also hierarchically structured according to the norms of a localized Indic tradition. The Chams were overtly conscious of status distinctions, and the Cham social hierarchy was clearly defined as "aristocrats" or "commoners." Merchant compounds were the residencies of those who did not do any of the things that might lead to the community's composition—those who did not engage in populating villages or making temple endowments, or participating in military expeditions unless assured of an opportunity for personal gain rather than achieving or defending the collective good of the community. Merchant and sojourner occupancy of the lowest rung on the social ladder was justified, as was also their negative mention in the temples of the Cham aristocrats—but, it should be noted, this was not unusual regionally, even if the products of their activities were valued. Similarly in the Vietnamese chronicles, the rare references to merchants occur only when one might supply a ruler with exotic products.

Though retrospectively the Vietnamese chronicles do not provide clear documentation of the hierarchical nature of their early trade networks and commercial specialists, in contrast to the inscriptions of contemporary Java that do (chapter 5), there is at least ample circumstantial evidence of thriving internal trade, especially in the documentation of the eleventh- and twelfth-century roadways that linked the major Vietnamese population, ritual, and political centers, an evolving network that provided the opportunity for a variety of internal exchanges, both cultural and economic. We can be fairly certain that vital, internally integrating Vietnamese marketing networks were in place and spreading from at least the eleventh century, if not earlier (Wicks: 1992, 194–99; Taylor: 1992, 140ff).

On the other hand, the remaining evidence of the Cham realm as discussed above does not show a similar internal integration of commercial activity, despite the many cultural and social parallels to the Vietnamese realm to its north. At least at the river mouths and their connected upstream river valleys, the Cham state has been considered a wet-rice, temple-building civilization that favorably compares to that of the developing Angkor-based Khmer state to its west (chapter 6) (Maspero: 1928; Coedes: 1968; Sox: 1972). Furthermore, like Angkor, Champa used Indic vocabulary and religious styles in the service of the state. Champa had impressive central temple complexes at My Son and Po Nagar and other networked Indic temples in each of its five riverine zones, and Cham inscriptions portray Cham administrative capacity in a vocabulary similar to that of the Khmer.

Yet though Cham inscriptions speak of centralized administrations and present the image of an integrated wet-rice socioeconomy, Cham epigraphy as well as external sources reflect an incomplete synthesis of the early wet-rice state tradition on the part of Champa, and as a result its political and economic networks were complex, often disconnected, and highly contested. Therefore, despite the obvious parallels to the other wet-rice states of mainland Southeast Asia, Champa's political dynamics were actually more similar to those of the riverine and archipelago networks of island Southeast Asia, and better understood as a polity based in the riverine exchange network system as introduced in chapter 1 (see figure 1.1) and detailed in the initial sections of chapter 4 (Taylor: 1992, 153). In its combination of the two systems—wet-rice agricultural on the one hand and multicentered riverine on the other—Champa is in some ways analogous to post-1000 Java, where, as will be seen in chapter 5, the east Java–based monarchy was beginning to blend its riverine and rice plain sectors. In Java this blending would produce a highly productive political economy that would culminate in the fourteenth-century Majapahit polity. In Champa, however, the rice economy did not have nearly the productive capacity as that of Java, its strategic position relative to the trade route was less vital, and its expansion into bordering fertile rice plains was blocked by its powerful Khmer and Vietnamese neighbors. For this and other reasons, among them being Champa's multicentered geography, the political and economic integration achieved in Java was never achievable in Champa, and in the following centuries this lack of integration would eventually lead to Champa's demise.

But it was not only Champa that would feel the strains of change in the next centuries. The eleventh and twelfth centuries would bring significant

political and economic change to a number of Southeast Asia's polities, particularly on the mainland. Along with these changes would come the growth
of Buddhist cultures. Though the Cham elite generally remained committed
to Hinduism, there was earlier patronage of Buddhism at Dong Duong that
was foundational to a robust Mahayana Buddhist monastic community in
eleventh- and twelfth-century Champa (Maxwell: 2007; Schweyer: 2007;), as
Buddhist monarchies would develop in the Vietnamese and Khmer realms in
this same age (Hall: 2010c). Post-1000 Champa Buddhism was a mix representative of its diverse maritime and overland connections to Yunnan, Tibet,
China, and Java, in which religious networking and commercial networking
overlapped (Guy: 2009, 144–52). This same period would see the rise of yet
another strong Buddhist realm, the Pagan polity in Burma, west of Angkor.
Chapters 6 and 7 detail these developments and their implications for the
future of the Southeast Asian mainland.

4

The Foundations of Indonesian Polity

Srivijaya and Java to the Early Tenth Century

The previous two chapters demonstrate the problem of reconstructing early Southeast Asia's history due to limited internal written documentation prior to the tenth century. This absence of a local voice has forced scholars to depend on and interpret external primary sources, notably to balance the Chinese dynastic and Middle Eastern geographic accounts. What was once thought to be "truth" revealed in these external sources has regularly been discounted by new archeological discoveries and better linguistic analysis. Written sources inevitably reflect the cultural prejudices and interests of their authors. Therefore the surviving early Chinese dynastic records and the Middle Eastern geographies and travel accounts were shaped by their "outsider" interests, specific to assessments of the Southeast Asia region's trade potential and securing the necessary diplomatic footing to access Southeast Asia's valuable products. In contrast, the early Southeast Asian epigraphic sources utilized the vocabulary of local and state elite, which was sensitive to local interests in ways that legitimated the process of state building.

In earliest times the coasts of southeastern Sumatra and northern Java frequently interacted commercially and culturally. Historians have had considerable interest in the first of these, the southeastern Sumatra-based Srivijaya maritime state that dominated the Straits of Melaka passage between the seventh and eleventh centuries. Because the Srivijaya realm has few remaining inscriptions, historians have depended on external sources to reconstruct Srivijaya's history (Manguin: 1993a; Kulke: 1993; Coedes and Damais: 1992). In contrast, the history of the Java coastline of this same era is perhaps

103

the least understood and most controversial, because there are so few known epigraphic and archeological records. The history of the central Java hinterland is better, due to its impressive monumental remains, notably the Borobudur and Prambanan temple complexes, and the increasing frequency of epigraphic sources from roughly CE 800. Historians today generally agree that these historical treasures were produced by a civilization governed by indigenous Javanese monarchs, but debate whether there were contemporary networked cultural and political links to the Straits of Melaka–centered Srivijaya polity that were contributing factors. Above all, there is discussion of whether the Javanese civilization that produced these complexes was governed by strong, unifying centralized states or is better understood as based in multiple competing semiautonomous agricultural zones governed by regional chiefs (Wisseman Christie: 2001).

This chapter overviews the evolution of Straits of Melaka civilization from the fifth to the tenth centuries, an era that corresponds to the greatness of the Srivijayan maritime polity. It also considers the earliest evidence of Indic civilization on Java's northwest coastline and the subsequent Javanese civilizations in the Dieng Plateau and Kedu Plain regions of central Java, and examines the economic, political, and cultural relations between central Java and the contemporary Srivijaya polity. It will also devote special attention to the economic organization of the Srivijaya realm. Chapter 5 will continue the story with the shift of Javanese civilization to east Java and its eventual displacement of Srivijaya as the dominant regional force in the Straits of Melaka region in the fourteenth century. This outline of contemporary developments in Javanese statecraft will include a section on the Javanese economy and the post-900 rise of Java's external trade.

EARLY REFERENCES TO JAVA

The earliest written reference to Java is found in the Roman geographer Ptolemy (100–170 CE), who provides separate references to *Yavadvipa* (*Iabadiou*) and *Jawadvipa* (*Sadadibai*). Ptolemy's Yavadvipa is associated with the Jelai River system of southwestern Borneo, an area known by the Chinese as *Yehpoti* and that was said to be located next to *Shepo* (Java) (Meulen: 1975). Archeological evidence from the presumed site of Yehpoti, notably carved sacrificial posts known as *yapas*, substantiate a Borneo cultural link to Funan, indicating as with other archipelago coastal centers that early interactions between these depots and the Chinese and Indian commercial markets had been funneled through Funan's ports, as described in chapter 2 (see map 2.2). By the fifth century, however, Chinese sources reported that emerging coastal

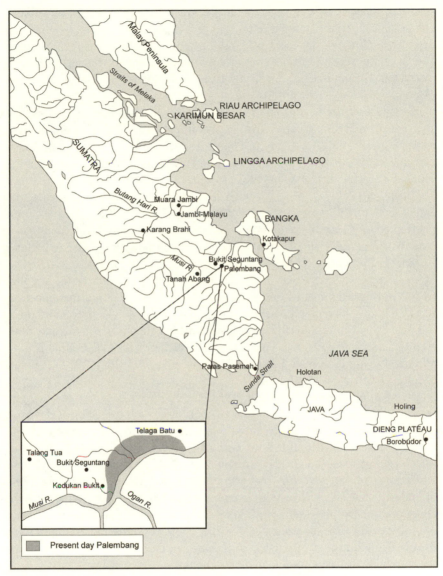

Map 4.1. The Srivijaya Age, ca. 600–1200

centers on Java's northern coast had absorbed Yehpoti commerce; Chinese sources subsequently omitted references to Yehpoti and referred thereafter to the Shepo (Java) realm alone as China's preferred trade partner (Wolters: 1967). There were two fifth-century Javanese centers with which the Chinese interacted: Holing in central Java and Holotan on the northwestern Java coast (Meulen: 1977; Wolters: 1967).

The story of the north Indian Buddhist pilgrim Gunavarman records the emergence of Holing (central Java) as a political entity. In 422, Gunavarman stopped at Holing on his way to China. He stayed there for several years, patronized by the queen mother and preaching Buddhist doctrine with great success; the king of Holing asked Gunavarman's advice on whether to attack his enemies (Pelliot: 1904, 274–75). Herein in the Chinese accounts, the emergence of Holing from what was previously a tribal society involved competition among several communities and the productive outreach by one to a potential Indian advisor. This, like the Funan origin myth detailed in chapter 2, reflects the actual or symbolic use of Indic culture as the basis for the establishment of one enterprising chiefdom's supremacy over its regional rivals. Holing sent envoys to China in 430 and 440 but is not mentioned in sixth-century Chinese records, suggesting that international contact with central Java was limited until two centuries later, when in the 640s and 660s Holing again sent embassies and around 640 welcomed a Chinese monk who remained to study under a Javanese Buddhist master (Pelliot: 1904, 286–88; Meulen: 1977, 90).

Meanwhile, Holotan (in western Java) sent seven missions to China's court between 430 and 452, a pattern that is consistent with the Chinese dynastic assessments that Holotan was in an unstable transitional condition. In the report of a 436 tribute mission the king of Holotan, who held the Indic royal title Visamvarman, was said to live in fear of his enemies both inside and outside his realm, and thus requested diplomatic assistance and weapons (metallic, since Java had no iron) from the Chinese. According to the Chinese court record, Holotan was once a peaceful and prosperous land but at that time was being attacked from all sides; its people (the king's supporters) were fleeing the country. A subsequent 470s entry in the *Liu Tung shu* (*History of the Early Sung*) reported that when the king's son usurped the throne Visamvarman went into exile (Pelliot: 1904, 271–74; Wolters: 1967, 151, 313n92, n95).

These Chinese references to Holotan (western Java) are thought to be related to four undated mid-to-late fifth-century inscriptions of the King Purnavarman who ruled the Tarum River basin just east of present-day Jakarta, a land known in the inscriptions as Tarumanagara (Vogel: 1925; Casparis: 1975, 18–20; Sarkar: 1971, 1–12). Employing Sanskrit verses written in an early south Indian script, these inscriptions are similar in style to the earliest regional yapa inscriptions of Kutei on the southern Borneo coast, epigraphy associated with the previously noted Yehpoti coastal center. One of Purnavarman's inscriptions, discovered near the shore of Jakarta Bay, notes that in the twenty-second year of his reign Purnavarman gave his attention to the drainage problems of the coastal area, altering the course of the river to provide a new outlet (Noorduyn and Verstappen: 1972). These downstream coastal initiatives foreshadow the successful late tenth- and early eleventh-century downstream initiatives of east Java kings in the Brantas River basin, as discussed below. The other three inscriptions were found on a hillside near Bogor, south of modern-day Jakarta, and are associated with footprints carved in stone symbolizing "the three conquering and victorious footprints of Visnu." These footprints proclaim a great victory by Purnavarman, who is described as being "ever efficient in destroying hostile *kraton* [courts/states] and salutatory to princes who are devoted subjects." These Purnavarman inscriptions collectively document several characteristics of earliest Javanese statecraft.

Western Java did not develop a wet-rice (sawah) agricultural system until the seventeenth century, but at the time we are discussing dry-rice (*ladang*) cultivation was already being practiced (Naerssen and Iongh: 1977, 28). While a wet-rice society was by necessity more deeply committed and bound to a specific agricultural area, as would be true of the populations inhabiting the river plains of central and east Java in a later age, west Java's dry-rice agricultural population was more mobile and was therefore capable of escaping the grasp of an oppressive court elite or an unsettled political environment. These are the very kinds of situations that are reported in Chinese references to Holotan in Visamvarman's time, when Visamvarman's subjects were said to have fled the country because of constant disorder. The likelihood of having sufficient local agricultural resources to sustain an agrarian-based royal court (*kraton*) in west Java was thus limited; the alternative was to build a maritime-focused court/state, like the Srivijaya polity that would arise on nearby Sumatra, and this required the establishment of a coastal port and the recruitment of maritime populations.

Accordingly, Purnavarman's inscriptions in the mid-fifth century assert that he supervised the construction of a new river outlet, possibly because of the silting up of the mouth of the Tarum River, to make his port more accessible for trading vessels (Noorduyn and Verstappen: 1972). Another benefit deriving from this project was that it alleviated the potential of riverine flooding, and this increased the dry-rice production capacity in Purnavarman's upstream hinterland. Significantly, Purnavarman's fifth-century development project on the west Java coastline corresponds to the southern refocusing of the international maritime route from the Isthmus of Kra and the Funan realm in and around the Gulf of Thailand and southern Vietnam to the Straits of Melaka region as described in chapter 2, and its consequences to the mainland coastland as described in chapter 3.

The emergence of the Tarum River estuary as an economic center, with a coastal port supported by upstream dry-rice cultivators, facilitated the Tarumanagara ruler's rise and allowed him to proclaim his kingly status. This networked river system also provided sufficient surplus rice to feed foreign merchants who utilized the local port facilities. Consistent with the noted Chinese dynastic reports, Purnavarman's Bogor inscriptions report that his initial political consolidations were achieved via wars "destroying hostile *kraton* [courts/states]," more likely the bases of rival chiefdoms within the Tarum riverine system, and constructing alliance networks by being "salutary to princes [i.e., subordinate chiefs] who are devoted subjects." Such victories and alliances guaranteed the security of the international traders who visited the new port, but also encouraged the flow of local production (rice) from upriver population clusters to Purnavarman's would-be coastal emporium.

A further dimension of Purnavarman's inscriptions was his association with Indic religion, as documented in recent archeological research (Manguin and Indrajaya: 2006; Dalsheimer and Manguin: 1998). Consistent with the rulers of other emerging early Southeast Asian centers, Purnavarman utilized Indian religious tradition to reinforce his legitimacy and to elevate his ritual status above that of his fellow chiefs. Purnavarman's inscriptions glorified his victories by the symbolic localization of both Indic and Javanese traditions; for example, Visnu's three footprints, which are associated with the Bogor inscriptions, were taken from early South Asian tradition, because they meaningfully corresponded to indigenous Javanese conceptions of feet as the locus of magical power (Meulen: 1977, 104). The economic development of the Tarum River estuary and Purnavarman's political and economic achievements were thus sanctified in the three Bogor inscriptions, which proclaim that Purnavarman was "tantamount to . . . Visnu," and was thus a semidivine worthy of being followed.

We know very little about the west Java–based successor to Purnavarman. Subsequently this region appears to have been submissive to its contemporary competitor, the southeast Sumatra-based port-polity of Srivijaya. It remained for the central Javanese ruler Sanjaya to provide further definition of Javanese sovereignty in the early eighth century, drawing from prior developments in western Java and neighboring Sumatra.

THE RISE OF SRIVIJAYA (CA. 670–1025)

The east Sumatra–based realm of Srivijaya would dominate the area around the Straits of Melaka, including western Java and the Malay Peninsula, from roughly 670 to 1025, in large part because during this time it was widely acknowledged to be the most prominent regional participant in the flows of East-West trade. As discussed in chapters 2 and 3, with the decline of the importance of the southern Vietnam coast in the fifth and sixth centuries, successive Chinese courts sought to establish commercial relationships with other Southeast Asian port-polities capable of maintaining the flow of East-West trade. As previously cited, early Southeast Asian entrepôts were responsive to the fluctuations of the international markets, especially those of China. The opening and closing of Chinese ports constituted a "rhythm of trade" that is reflected as well in the pattern of tribute missions sent to the Chinese court from Southeast Asia. Frequent missions from many states have been seen as representing times of political and economic competition—both in Southeast Asia and in China—during which states solicited Chinese profitable patronage. A period of few missions indicated relative stability, as the Chinese recognized one state that in their minds dominated others. When China was particularly interested in external trade, for example when its ports came under the control of a new, stable imperial government, there could be especially heated competition among Southeast Asian centers to receive recognition as the dominant emporium of the region. Thus, in the early seventh century the new Tang dynasty (618–906) selected the Srivijaya polity from among its rivals (Wolters: 1967).

The founders and rulers of the Srivijayan realm were local chiefs of Malay ethnicity, who ruled the port area that the Chinese Buddhist pilgrim Yijing visited in 671 on his voyage from Guangzhou to India and again on his return voyage from India in 695 (Takakusu: 1896). This earliest Srivijaya core is now generally accepted to have been at or near the modern city of Palembang, still a significant port city in southeastern Sumatra. It was this area that became the initial core of the Srivijayan expansion. In the traditional Malay view of the world, there was a powerful duality, influenced by a landscape dominated by high and steep mountains and seas whose horizons seemed unreachable. Both the mountain heights and the depths of the sea were the loci of powerful forces that shaped the lives of the people, forces that could be both generous and devastating. The same volcanoes that provided the most fertile land could and did on occasion destroy the villages that grew up on them. The sea, too, was a bountiful provider and a major means of communication, but its storms could also destroy the lives and livelihood of those dependent upon it, as demonstrated by the powerful 2004 tsunami that was set in motion by a devastating earthquake. This region is today called the Ring of Fire, which acknowledges this vulnerability to a variety of destructive forces set in motion by shifts in the major earth fault lines that lay beneath the earth and ocean surfaces.

In traditional Malay belief, both the source of the river waters and the home of the ancestral spirits were high on the upstream mountain slopes; the highest reaches of the mountains were thus thought of as the holiest places and the source of beneficent forces that bestowed well-being upon the people (L. Andaya: 2008). The Srivijayan king drew upon these beliefs as he took the title "Lord of the Mountain" (Tibbetts: 1979, 100–118). But he was also "Lord of the Isles" and able to commune with the "Spirit of the Waters of the Sea," a dangerous force that had to be propitiated and whose powers had to be absorbed by the king (Hall: 1976, 85–91). Thus he personally linked the spirits of the upstream and downstream in the person of the king. Contemporary Middle Eastern sources report that the Srivijayan monarch daily deposited a gold bar in the Palembang estuary as a symbol of his indebtedness to the maritime trade (Ferrand: 1913, 57; Wicks: 1992, 228–30). They did not understand the local ritual significance of this act, relative to the ruler's negation of the Spirit of the Waters' harm to them, but assumed that the monarch believed that if foreign merchants left the Srivijaya port, the ruler's treasure would surely fade away.

The critical link between these two forces of mountain and sea were the rivers, the channels through which the rainwater that fell on the mountains flowed down, ultimately to merge with the sea. These river basins contained the earliest polities of island Southeast Asia and shaped the political dynamic between them. The king's magical powers, closely associated with fertility, were also linked with the river. The magic of the association between the king and the water was so strong that it was dangerous for the king to bathe in ordinary water for fear of causing a flood. His bathwater had to be treated with flower petals before it was safe. And there were other fertility taboos. On a specific day each year the king could not eat grain. If he did, there might be a crop failure. Nor was he able to leave his realm, for if he did, the sun's rays might go with him, the skies would darken, and the crops would fail (Hirth and Rockhill: 1911, 61; Ferrand: 1922, 57; Hall: 1976, 85).

Palembang's significance as a port probably dates back to the prehistoric period when the metal culture of the mainland was spread about by the Malayo-Austronesian sailors from the more easterly islands (Bronson: 1992). Sailors moving down the 960-mile (1600-kilometer) length of the Malay Peninsula to the islands would have found local settlements at Palembang on the Musi River and Jambi-Malayu on the Batang Hari River. Both were across the Strait but near the tip of the peninsula. As river-mouth ports, they offered the sailors access not only to those people who lived near the coast but indirectly to Sumatra's sizeable hinterland and to all those who lived along the banks of these two rivers' many tributaries. Strategically, both the Musi and Batang Hari river upstreams had gold deposits, and Bangka Island, a source of iron, lay off the Palembang coastline (Manguin: 1982, 2004; Koestoro, Manguin, and Soeroso: 1994; Bonatz: 2006). Thus, both these ports probably began as small trading centers near the mouths of rivers that linked the peoples of the mountains with the sailors of the seas. There the sailors could exchange their goods for the produce and metals of the island region.

When the international trade began to grow between the Mekong Delta region and India sometime around the first century CE, these Sumatran ports emerged as small political centers that concentrated the resources of their rivers' drainage basins near the coast in order to attract traders. They could then use imported goods to enhance their own resources and as gifts or trade goods to be exchanged for the products of their upstream hinterlands. Since the maritime realm of Southeast Asia possessed many river systems that were separated by mountains, this dynamic led to the creation of many small riverine polities based at their mouths. As depicted in figure 1.1, these coastal centers tended to look back toward the mountains and forward to the sea, but they did not look kindly to their sides; they saw their neighboring river systems as rivals and enemies. And by about 350 CE some of them had already begun their dialogue with Indian culture.

The development from the 400s CE onward of open-ocean sailing from India to China made the Straits of Melaka passage tremendously important in East-West commerce. This led to centuries of competition among the many independent ports and polities of the southern maritime realm. In the early part of the seventh century, one of these centers, Srivijaya, based at Palembang, emerged victorious in a contest to dominate the others and thus become the core of an emergent state system. Why it was the local ruler of Palembang who became the paramount power in the region is not immediately apparent. Although its location about halfway between the Straits of Melaka and the Sunda Strait was significant, there were a number of other ports that enjoyed locations with similar advantages. Nor was either of the two major southeastern Sumatran ports, Palembang and its chief rival Jambi-Malayu, located near those places that produced the items most desired by international traders. Camphor, the Sumatran forest product most sought after in this early period, came from more northern and western parts of the island. Although some pepper was locally grown, it was at that time mainly a product of west Java across the Sunda Strait. Sandalwood, another product popular from the earliest period, came from Timor, about 1,500 miles (2,500 kilometers) to Sumatra's east. The cloves, nutmeg, and mace that would eventually become the maritime realm's most famous products came from still other islands that were equally far away to the east. And frankincense, which eleventh-century Chinese sources assert was Srivijaya's foremost product, was in reality a product of the Middle East that was reexported to China by Srivijaya-based merchants, or was a local substitute that Srivijaya merchants passed off as frankincense in China's markets (Wolters: 1967; Sen: 2003, 194–95).

Further, the archeological data currently available indicates a general absence of intensive rice cultivation near the early Sumatran ports, which were on the upstream edge of the downstream wetlands. Unlike Java, whose centers of power were in the vicinity of agricultural production centers, Sumatra's early downriver ports depended upon less direct means of collecting food and upland products. Unless food was imported from Java, which seems unlikely as the volume of trade was not yet substantial (B. Andaya: 1993b; Reid: 1988), early Sumatra emporia would have drawn upon lower river basin deep-water rice (*lebak*) and tidal irrigated rice (*pasang surut*) to feed transients. Palembang's hinterland consisted of the Pasemah Highlands and the upper Musi, areas well known today for their rice and whose natural conditions were very similar to Java's wet-rice areas; volcanic activity in these regions supplied fertile material for rice cultivation (Drakard: 1999). Megalithic archeological remains in south Sumatra come from Pasemah in what are now ricelands. One carved stone there depicts a man riding on an elephant and carrying a drum of the Dong Son type that had its origin in contemporary Vietnam. Such a stone monument, or at least its inspiration, may have been received as a byproduct of an early upstream-downstream exchange. Bronze bowls and bells found in the same area suggest early foreign relations and downriver contacts. Similarly, in the Jambi-Malayu upriver heartland, stone sculptures of the early Common Era depict male figures standing on another human, a traditional Indonesian symbol of power, which would also indicate downriver contact (Schnitger: 1937, 1939; O'Connor: 1972).

There were, no doubt, numerous factors that accounted for Palembang's victory over its rivals, but one of them probably was the agricultural productivity of the fields in the valleys of the Musi River and its tributaries. Although none of the river-mouth ports of the island realm had agricultural resources comparable to those contemporary in the upper Mekong Delta, Palembang did have the unusually wide, slow, and silt-rich Musi River behind it, a better agricultural base than any of its competitors had. A local legend claimed that civilization was founded at Palembang only after the waters of the various rivers were weighed, and it was determined those of the

Musi were heaviest. Obviously its founders were searching for a silt-laden river that could be depended upon continually to deposit the fertile silt on fields adjacent to the river. Today, the best rice land in the area is on the edge of modern Palembang, at Bukit Seguntang (see map 4.1). It is on and around this hill that some of the richest finds of archeological remains from the Srivijayan period have been made, and this hill appears to have been the location of the ceremonial center described in the late seventh-century account of Yijing where one thousand priests resided and where gold and silver Buddhas were offered golden vessels shaped like lotus flowers. These bowls were known to be a specialty of Srivijaya, and as late as 1082 there is a Chinese record of Srivijayan envoys bringing lotus bowls filled with pearls and other precious objects as presents for the Song emperor (McKinnon: 1979; Hall: 1985, 281–82n7).

Palembang also offered a fine natural harbor and a river that was navigable for long distances. Even in the nineteenth century, the largest oceangoing steamers had no difficulty in reaching the city, which is forty-eight miles (eighty kilometers) inland from the mouth of the Musi. Even above Palembang, the river and its tributaries remain navigable by small boats for many miles. This gave the Palembang area unusually good access to the Sumatran hinterland and the island's valuable forest products (Gonarz: 2006; Manguin and Indrajaya: 2006, 255).

In terms of indigenous understanding, the initial motivation for conquest most likely emerged from internal politics, an attempt to unite the surrounding Malay peoples, and not necessarily from a desire to control the Melaka and Sunda straits. The earliest image of the Srivijayan founder comes from a Talang Tua stone inscription dated 683 CE. What is revealed is a traditional Sumatran war chief, a local ruler who after assembling the surrounding chiefs and their forces selected from twenty thousand a force of two thousand men, which he led against Jambi-Malayu, the rival to the north and the only other important river system on this strategic coast. Srivijaya defeated its rivals; the ruler proved himself in battle, and thus he could claim in this inscription to possess supernatural power that allowed him to bestow prosperity upon his new subjects.

> The king expressed his concern that all the clearances and gardens made by them [his subjects] should be full [of crops]. That the cattle of all species raised by them and the bondsmen they possess should prosper . . . that all their servants shall be faithful and devoted to them . . . that, wherever they may find themselves, there be in that place no thieves, no ruffians and no adulterers that there arise among them the thought of Bodhi [wisdom] and the love of the "Three Jewels" [the Buddha, the Doctrines, and the monkhood]. (Nilakanta Sastri: 1949, 114)

Yijing's account of Srivijaya suggests that Palembang's subjugation of Jambi-Malayu and thus the Batang Hari River system occurred between his 671 visit and roughly 685.

The realm that Srivijaya ultimately commanded can be divided into three parts: the core area around Palembang; its Musi River hinterland, upriver and downriver; and those river-mouth ports and their hinterlands that had previously been its rivals. In each of these three parts, the manner of rule was somewhat different. The urban core centered at Palembang was directly administered by the monarch and his family. The monarch was assisted by royal judges, revenue collectors, land administrators, and various other officials. The king referred to the cultivators of the royal domain as "my bondsmen," and they were also the nucleus of his imperial army (Hall: 1976, 74–75; Kulke: 1993).

The second part of the empire, the Musi River hinterland, was ruled by more indirect means, through alliances with local chiefs (datu) who swore allegiance to the kings at the Palembang core. This relationship between the royal center and its upriver and downriver hinterlands was based on what was in reality a mutual self-interest. These relationships had to be consolidated and could not be neglected or abused, for it did sometimes happen that populations in the hinterland took over river-mouth ports and made them their own. The relationship between the downstream and its upstream hinterland was crucial since it was necessary to maintain the downriver flow of manpower (with its military implications), agricultural resources (which could provision the port), and forest products such as the resins that were exported overseas in order to uphold the royal center's special position.

Srivijaya's rule in the hinterland deserves more extended comment. Although Srivijaya was not reluctant to use military means when it had to, it more often secured hinterland alliances through the offering of benefits, material and spiritual, to all who attached themselves to its center. In return for their loyalty and their products, the leaders of these upriver and downriver populations received redistributions of wealth and provision of goods derived from the trade route, as well as the prestige and the reflected power of the Srivijayan center. Based on the use of Buddhist doctrine in Srivijaya's widely scattered epigraphic assertions of legitimacy, Buddhism must also have played a strategic role in the upstream-downstream networking of the Srivijaya polity. Religious ceremonies and societal pageantry implied in the Srivijaya inscriptions suggests that the monarch's Buddhist patronage persuaded networked elite to participate in the royal cults at the center, where public and religious edifices proliferated and where the oath-taking ceremonies were held.

At the same time that the Srivijayan center offered benefits to those in the

Musi River hinterland, it also resorted to traditional oaths and threats of dire consequences to those who broke them. One of the stone inscriptions found at Telaga Batu in the Srivijayan hinterland combined the traditional Malay water oath with Buddhist images of power. On the upper edge of the stone was a seven-headed snake, an Indian motif that evokes the serpentine naga as protector of the Lord Buddha. This image may have been particularly effective in the maritime world, since Southeast Asia's rulers, too, prior to any Buddhist presence, invoked the power of snakes to protect themselves and their realms, as documented in the previous discussion of the earliest mainland polities. Below the naga was an oath of loyalty to the king, and below the oath was a funnel. During the oath-taking ceremony, water was poured over the naga and the oath and then drained out through the funnel. The water must thus have been drunk by the oath-takers, for the text said, in part, that the water would kill anyone who was insincere in the oath he drank (literally, his insides would rot). On the other hand, if the oath-taker remained faithful, he would receive not only a secret formula for the final (Buddhist) liberation of his soul, but also the pledge, "You will not be swallowed with your children and wives," a reference either to snakes, which it was believed could swallow men, or to the possibility of being swallowed up by flood waters (Hall: 1976, 90–91; Casparis: 1956, 45).

In dealing with the third part of the Srivijayan realm, the formerly (and potentially still) rival river-mouth ports and their own hinterlands, the element of force played a much larger role. Although Indian-inspired formalities and techniques were employed and material advantages were shared, the crucial element in Srivijaya's control in these areas was force. Middle Eastern accounts claim that the Srivijayan monarch had bewitched the crocodiles in order to ensure safe navigation into the realm's ports, but the truth of the matter was that he had charmed the sea nomads of the straits region.

Historians assume that during the previous era shifting wind patterns, unpredictable water levels, and hidden rocks and shoals made the Straits area dangerous, and so did coastal resident sea nomads (Wolters: 1967, 188–228). Early Chinese accounts reported that local populations often engaged in piracy and preyed on any merchant ship that happened to come their way. In part Srivijaya became prominent because its coastline offered the most dependable passageway through the Strait, and it would seem that, based on the collective Srivijaya documentation, the Srivijayan monarchs, unable to suppress the regional maritime nomads, essentially bought them out. The kings made an agreement with some of them that in return for a portion of the port's revenues, these coastal populations would not raid the ships at sea. The kings could as well use their seaborne allies to patrol the local waters and ensure the safe movement of trading vessels. They could also enlist their services as peaceful carriers in the trade. But in order to succeed in their maneuver, the kings had to have sufficient trade goods and revenues to make it worth the sailor's while, which meant that they had to attract a steady stream of foreign traders into their ports. If their ability to provide on a regular basis were ever to decline, the sailors could strike new alliances with rival ports, or revert to piracy (Hall: 2006). Srivijaya's rulers depended on this navy in order to ensure Palembang's predominance and its development as the major international port and the central treasury for the entire realm.

Srivijaya's power in the outlying parts of its realm was also marked by monasteries patronized by its kings and by inscriptions. One 775 CE inscription on the east coast of the Malay Peninsula, which was then under Srivijaya's suzerainty, commemorated the dedication by a Srivijayan king of a Buddhist monastery at the site, while also referring to the king as "the patron of the snakes," a more traditional image of power. Srivijayan inscriptions with Buddhist elements can similarly be found at various strategic points along the Sumatran coast, including Kotakapur and Palas Pasemah, that overlook the Sunda Strait between Sumatra and Java (see below).

This patronage of Buddhist sites deserves special attention, for it is one of the most significant aspects of the Srivijaya realm. Certainly, Srivijaya's success was related to its good location on a major international trade route, its fine harbor, its "heavy" and navigable river, and the political and economic talents of its rulers. But it may well be that the most important secret in Srivijaya's success was its relationship with Buddhism. Buddhism was locally meaningful as a means to elevate the monarch's ritual status above that of his subject populations and thereby reinforce his local economic and political supremacy. Also, as patrons of the Mahayana Buddhist religious tradition, Srivijaya's rulers gained international prestige that no doubt increased the stature of Srivijaya's ports (Kulke: 1986). In Indic terms, Palembang was the center of the Srivijaya *mandala*. It was the new locus of contact between the realm of the spirits and humankind, as well as the center of the economic and symbolic capital redistributions that reinforced royal authority. Below the Palembang-based king was a network of semiautonomous datu ("chiefs"), who as holders of impressive Indian Sanskritic titles were allowed to take part in the magical Buddhist rituals of the Srivijaya monarch's court (Kulke: 1993; Hall: 1976, 67–79).

Yet, in their patronage of Buddhism, the Srivijaya monarchs also drew upon existing beliefs that local chiefs possessed magical qualities. Traditionally, a powerful chief's effective use of magic influenced his followers' prosperity in this lifetime as well as in the next (Hall: 1976, 79–92). The Srivijaya monarchs grounded these notions in conceptions drawn from Buddhism. For example, the late seventh-century Telaga Batu stone inscription, which was collected on the northern edge of present-day Palembang, stressed the locally defined power and also reinforced the hegemony of the Srivijaya monarch by associating him with a higher level of spiritual power, which derived from Buddhism. This inscription records the water oath of service that was sworn by the ruler's subordinates over the ceremonial stone that was protected by the seven carved serpent heads, representing the seven-headed naga that in Buddhist tradition had protected the Lord Buddha during his ascetic meditations.

> If you embellish this curse on this stone and . . . then you are not faithful to me . . . ; behave like a traitor . . . ; form part of the retinue of my enemies . . . [or] spy on their behalf . . . ; induce my harem women to get knowledge about the interior of my palace . . . ; spend gold and jewels in order to destroy my court . . . ; consort with those who know how to make people sick, . . . [if] you are not submissive to me and to my court, you will be killed by the curse. (Casparis: 1956, 15–46)

There are edited contemporary versions of this inscription at Kotakapur on the island of Bangka off the east coast of Sumatra (Hall: 1976, 81; Koestoro, et al.: 1994), at Karangbrahi on the Batang Hari River system (upriver from present-day Jambi), and at Palas Pasemah on the southeastern Sumatra coast adjacent to the Sunda Strait. These are all areas that were linked to the Srivijaya center by the inscription's oath and its promise of divine punishment (Kulke: 1993, 160n7; Coedes and Damais: 1992). Buddhism not only provided strong new magic that reinforced the monarch's legitimacy in the eyes and minds of his own followers, it also was foundational to the king's international prestige. The area adjacent to the royal court of Srivijaya became a major Indian Ocean pilgrimage center. The Srivijaya ruler and his representatives became participants in Buddhism's network of intellectual dialogue, which was coincidental to the seventh-through tenth-century Bay of Bengal and South China Sea international trade routes. From the seventh through the tenth centuries, Chinese pilgrims regularly studied and worked on their Sanskrit and Pali language skills at Palembang prior to traveling on to Nalanda in northeastern India, which was the foremost center of Buddhist scholarship in that age. In recognition of this connection, the Srivijaya ruler endowed the Buddhist retreat at Nalanda in northeast India around 860 (Nilakanta Sastri: 1949, 125–28; Caldwell and Hazlewood: 1994). Here and in the various other Srivijaya inscriptions the monarch's patronage of Buddhism and his personal merit were well publicized (Hall: 1985, 108–11). Locally the emphasis on his magically derived legitimacy was critical to ensuring that the king could maintain his authority during periods when port activity dropped due to regular fluctuations in the volume of international trade (Wolters: 1967, 1979a, 1986; Manguin: 1993a).

Srivijaya's rulers, as with other Southeast Asian rulers in this age, were less receptive to the teachings of the older Theravada "Way of the Fathers" tradition (which in the second millennium CE become the favored tradition of most of the Southeast Asian mainland) than to Mahayana Buddhism, which was patronized in contemporary China and was the faith of the Mahayana monks who made Srivijaya stopovers on their maritime passages between China and Nalanda (Takakusu: 1896; Wolters: 1983). Followers of the Mahayana school depended on the assistance of heavenly buddhas and bodhisattvas—those who had achieved enlightenment but postponed their ultimate salvation to assist their fellow mortals. Srivijaya's bodhisattva statuary personalized the Mahayana teachings by the conspicuous association of this statuary with deceased kings. Avalokitesvara, the male bodhisattva of compassion, whose powers to answer prayers reached even to the deepest hells, was especially popular—in contrast to in contemporary China and Vietnam, where, as noted in chapter 3, the female intercessor Guanyin was favored. Local Buddhist icons were a public statement about the ritual powers of the Srivijaya monarchs. The seventh-century Talang Tua inscription of 684 makes it quite clear that the Srivijaya monarch was a bodhisattva (Coedes and Damais: 1992, 43–52). This inscription recorded the dedication of a Buddhist deer park, which the inscription asserts was set aside by the Srivijaya monarch so that the merit gained by his deed, and all his other good works, could be shared with all creatures and would bring them closer to enlightenment.

Srivijaya rulers also patronized a third Buddhist way, the Vajrayana or "Vehicle of the Thunderbolt"—also called Tantric Buddhism. Vajrayana emerged in the late Gupta era of northeast India, contemporary with the development of Srivijaya's hegemony. The Tantric way depended on the supernatural; release was achieved through the worshipper's acquisition of magical powers. Sacred texts, tantras, were textbooks of mystical experience, secret documents written in a mysterious language that revealed magical formulas (mantras), symbols, rituals, and spirits. Especially important were goddesses (*Taras*) and the spirits of deceased ancestors. Activating an energy force allowed the devotee to achieve rebirth into a Buddhist heaven after death. Thus the Srivijaya Nakhon Si Thammarat 775 inscriptions, as discussed below, reference the Srivijaya monarch as "the patron of the nagas, their heads halved by the streaks [thunderbolts] of the lustre of gems" (Nilikanta Sastri: 1949, 44, 125).

The oath contained in the late seventh-century Telaga Batu inscription, cited earlier, embodied the localization in Srivijaya of the Mahayana and Tantric traditions. When they took this oath, the monarch's subjects drank water that had been poured across the stone, which was guarded by the naga spirits.

These nagas were the traditional local source of fertility, prosperity, and earthly wealth, and they were now also the guardians of the Buddha. The implication of this ritual was that if the one who took this oath were unfaithful, a naga guardian would bring magical retribution. On the other hand, promised the inscription, if one were loyal one might share in a sacred *tantra-mala* and thus gain access to prosperity in this life and in the life beyond death: "if you are [however] submissive, faithful (and) straight to me and do not commit these crimes, an immaculate *tantra* will be my recompense. You will not be swallowed with your children and wives . . . eternal peace will be the fruit produced by this oath which is drunk by you" (Casparis: 1956, 43–46).

The Srivijaya realm lasted for nearly four centuries. As will be described in later sections of this chapter, in the eighth and ninth centuries Srivijaya became involved in close relations with the Sailendra family that arose first in central Java and then became the dynastic rulers in Srivijaya. In this period Srivijaya continued to be the dominant economic power throughout the Indonesian archipelago. In the eighth and ninth centuries there was little resistance from Java, and indeed there seems to have been an "era of good feeling" between the two realms that was reflected in a common artistic output (as will also be described later). From the early tenth century onward, though, there was increasing strife between Srivijaya and the states of Java. In the early 900s Javanese rulers who had taken over from the Sailendras moved their primary court to the Brantas River basin in the east, from which they developed competing trade relationships of their own, leading to a series of raids and counterraids between Srivijaya and the Javanese.

At first, Srivijaya enjoyed the upper hand, for the most part. In the early years of the 1000s Srivijaya was paramount not only in its traditional realm of Sumatra and the Malay Peninsula, but also in western and central Java. However, Srivijaya's era of economic stature came to an abrupt close in 1025, when the south Indian Chola dynasty successfully attacked the Melaka region's ports and shattered Srivijaya's authority over the straits (Spencer: 1983). This raid initiated a two-century restructuring of the patterns of Southeast Asian communication. Srivijaya continued to be one of the leading trading centers of the region, but after the Chola raid it never regained its old hegemony (Wolters: 1970). Java then became the dominant port area in the straits region, while new ports in northern Sumatra and the Malay Peninsula also began to function independently as alternative secondary centers. In these new Straits of Melaka port-polities, the system of Buddhist patronage that had been associated with Srivijaya monarchs gave way, and by the twelfth century the rulers of the assertive newer port-polities had adopted a new religion, Islam, as the ideational basis for their sovereignty (as discussed in chapter 7).

Yet the legacy of Srivijaya remained strong in the Straits region. The seventeenth-century *Sejarah Melayu*, the court chronicle of the Melaka sultantate's history, purposely connected the genealogies of Melaka's rulers to Srivijaya in its description of the rise of Melaka to prominence in the fourteenth and fifteenth centuries. This substantiates the legacy of Srivijaya in Malay history, as well as the success of the early Palembang-based monarchs in establishing a localized Indic polity that was compatible with preexisting Malay-Sumatran culture. Thus, despite its political demise, Srivijaya remained a viable symbol of Southeast Asian unity and common prosperity and was the standard for all Malay riverine states that followed, both in local minds and also among the Chinese (So: 1998).

Furthermore, as we have just seen, Srivijaya was by no means an isolated entity. As discussed in the remainder of this chapter, from the eighth century onward there were significant cultural and political interactions between this realm and those of central and eastern Java. In the eighth and ninth centuries this included common attachment to Buddhism and Srivijaya's connections with the Sailendra family of central Java.

As a basis for understanding these interactions, let us begin by considering the early rise of the central Javanese states and the manner of their political composition. This material will not only help us see parallels and contrasts with the contemporary Srivijaya realm, but will also provide a baseline for understanding the further development of the Javanese realm in chapter 5 and later chapters. We already saw a brief prefiguring of the Javanese story at the beginning of this chapter, which described two fifth-century realms of central and western Java. Java is again a factor in the seventh-century Chinese sources, and new inscriptional evidence appears about the same time. We resume our narrative in the eighth century with the rise of two significant centers in central Java, Sanjaya's Saivite realm that had its ritual base on the Dieng Plateau and the Sailendra family's Buddhist realm centered on the south-central Kedu Plain. Both left significant monumental and inscriptional remains that provide important insights on early Javanese society.

CENTRAL JAVA IN THE SEVENTH TO NINTH CENTURIES

Sanjaya and the Dieng Plateau (ca. 732)

The center of Java's earliest Hindu rulers was initially concentrated in the temple complex on the north-central Java Dieng Plateau, north of the Kedu

Plain surrounding modern Yogyakarta that would become the base of subsequent seventh-century rulers. The Dieng Plateau was proclaimed to be a sacred Mountain of the Gods, a mountainous and mystical center for the worship of indigenous deities that by the sixth century had become the locus of a Javanese Saivite cult (Damais: 1952–1954, 36–37, 42–43, nos. 30, 35, 48, 64). The reign of the *rakrayan* (regional chief) Sanjaya in the early eighth century was a critical moment in the development of a central Javanese polity.

Sanjaya's Canggal inscription of 732 provides details about the roots of the developing central Java monarchy (Nilakanta Sastri: 1949, 117–19; Sarkar: 1971–1972, 15–24; Wisseman Christie: 2001). According to this inscription, Sanjaya erected a sacred linga that he associated with a mountain, praising the Hindu trinity Siva, Brahma, and Visnu and invoking the immortals residing in the cosmic universe "who used to inhabit an island (*dvipa*) of great prosperity known as Yava [i.e., Ptolemy's Yavadvipa]." But according to the inscription the celestial Yavadvipa land had disappeared; yet Sanjaya was invoking the spirits of this former Yavadvipa realm, suggesting an actual continuity from the earlier polity. Sanjaya claimed to be the current and intimate representative of the ancestors of Yavadvipa, and also the patron of the sacred "field of Siva," the Dieng Plateau temple complex (Naerssen and Iongh: 1977, 96; Pigeaud: 1924). Sanjaya thus established his legitimacy on the sacred ground of the Dieng Plateau, which still is a magical place that visitors reach by ascending into the mountains and passing through a series of prosperous valleys, until they finally make their way through a narrow mountain passageway, which opens into a fertile plateau that is often surrounded by clouds. Sanjaya's plateau still retains its magical qualities, reinforced by local steaming hot-water sulfurous springs that are sacred bathing sites lying adjacent to the plateau's temples.

Sanjaya consolidated several earlier cults into a new, inclusive Saivite cult, thereby drawing legitimacy from indigenous cults previously associated with the Dieng Plateau and integrating them with a localized Siva cult in which Sanjaya was Siva's semidivine worldly patron (Filliozat: 1967–1968). The 732 inscription notes that after Sanjaya had subdued neighboring raja, elevating his feet above their heads and thus symbolizing his sovereignty in a traditional Javanese way, all goodness prevailed, there was peace and prosperity, and there was no fear among men.

Then there came forth (one) who was rich in good qualities . . . who had his feet high above other kings of good family who were standing on the ground. This king was named Sri Sanjaya, son of the [rulers of Yavadvipa]; he was glorious, honored by learned men as a scholar in the subtleties of the *sastra*s [Indian legal texts that

focus on the maintenance of harmony among the social order], a ruler who had courage . . . and had . . . subdued many neighboring monarchs (*rajas*), and his fame like
the splendor of the sun spread in all quarters. He ruled the Earth [Java] who has the
waves of the ocean for her girdle and mountains for her breasts, . . . [all goodness
prevailed, there was peace and prosperity, and there was no fear among humankind].
(Nilakanta Sastri: 1949, 116–19)

By this time, Sanjaya was claiming status not only as the rakrayan of
Mataram, the initial reference to the realm of Mataram, which would thereafter become synonymous with a central Java–based polity, but also as ratu, a
Javanese equivalent of the maharaja title. Chinese references to Java during
this era describe a very different polity from that which had existed even during the previous century. The *Revised Annals of the Tang*, which report on
China's eighth-century regional contacts, continued to describe a Javanese
polity based on Java's north coast, known to the Chinese as Holing, which
historians assume to have corresponded to Sanjaya's realm in time and place,
rather than a contemporary southern Kedu Plain polity. At this time the Holing polity was "exceedingly rich."

The ruler lives in the [capital] city of *She-p'o* [Java]. . . . His ancestor Chi-yen [Ji
Yen] moved eastward to the city of P'o-lu-chia-ssu. . . . On the borders [of Holing]
are twenty-eight small countries, all of which owe allegiance to *Ho-ling* . . . . On top
of the mountain there is the province of Lang-pi-ya. The ruler frequently ascends
this mountain to gaze at the sea. (Wolters: 1967, 216)

This was a Holing polity superior to the modest political entity based in
central Java depicted in earlier Chinese accounts (Wolters: 1967, 215; 1983,
61–62). The new polity had an inland base, a mountain, and "twenty-eight
small countries" allied to it. Though it would subsequently be overshadowed
by the nearby Kedu Plain–based Sailendra Buddhist polity to its south, Sanjaya's realm never entirely lost its sense of regional identity, and in the early
tenth century its genealogy would reappear in the list of Javanese rulers when
the center of the Javanese realm moved eastward to the Brantas River basin.
Meanwhile, our narrative shifts to the Buddhist Sailendras, who provided the
cultural basis for the flowering of the Kedu Plain realm in the fertile plains
that lay among several active volcanoes south of the Dieng Plateau, initially
centered at Prambanan just northeast of modern Yogyakarta.

The Sailendras and the Kedu Plain

While Sanjaya was developing his Hindu Saivite complex on the Dieng Plateau, a competing Buddhist realm was developing to the south on the Kedu

Plain. This realm was led by the Sailendra family, which would later play an important role in the Srivijaya realm. The Sailendras may have been politically active since at least the early seventh century, when an inscription in north-central Java refers to the "Selendras" (Boechari: 1966; Miksic: 2003b). Whatever their origin, by the mid-eighth century the Sailendras were Java's paramount monarchs. As they extended power and influence from their base in central Java, they introduced the Indic title maharaja to distinguish themselves from other regional chiefs (rajas). Patrons of Mahayana Buddhism, though they were also tolerant of Hinduism in an era characterized by the coexistence of both Indic religions, during the height of their power the Sailendras constructed impressive monuments and temple complexes in central Java, the best known of which is the Borobudur northwest of Yogyakarta. The Sailendra court attracted Buddhist scholars from afar and was acclaimed internationally as a major center of Buddhist pilgrimage and learning (Miksic: 1993–1994). In sum, the Sailendras were the precursors of a new concept of statecraft in Java, the concentration of political power in a single authority. In practice, they were still merely the greatest among equals. Yet they also took the first steps toward a more centralized polity that would be more fully realized in the tenth century.

At the start, the Sailendras were merely a regional power. When they first emerged during the early seventh century, the Sailendra realm was but one among several important socioeconomic regional units (*watak*) in central Java. Like Sanjaya, initially the Sailendra leaders were rakrayan, or regional leaders, rulers of a watak that integrated village clusters (*wanua*) participating in a regional irrigation and/or otherwise networked society. As rakrayan, these earliest Sailendra rulers provided the political stability necessary to maintain the local irrigation and marketing networks, and through their patronage of Indic religion they constructed sacred cults to legitimize the regional integration of wanua into watak.

By the early seventh century central Javanese rakrayan regional authorities had begun to construct suprawatak networks, drawing together several horizontally linked rakrayan into vertically networked hierarchical alliances. In this period the alliance leader was the economic equal of his subordinate rakrayan. He came to his leadership role principally through his own initiative and familial support, and these leadership resources were reinforced by his patronage of a superior ritual cult. As the leader among the regional rakrayan authorities (some of whom continued to patronize the Hindu religion rather than the Sailendra monarchy's favored Buddhism), he enjoyed a superior magical prowess and thus could symbolically guarantee the prosperity of those who were willing to subordinate themselves to his leadership. Accordingly, subordinate rakrayan built local temples that mirrored the cult ritual of the leading rakrayan's central temple complex.

Thus, eighth-century Javanese monarchs such as the Sailendras were important as initiators of a networked cultural integration in central Java. Their power was limited, however. Because they were economic equals to their subordinate rakrayan, and because the developing central Java wet-rice economy was a local and regional one that required minimal centralized economic or administrative leadership by a higher authority, leading rakrayan had few opportunities to dominate except through their ritualized sovereignty and personal power.

Nevertheless, these ritual resources, though limited, were still significant, and the Sailendras made effective use of them. By the mid-eighth century the Sailendras had replaced Sanjaya's line as the dominant rakrayan among central Java's local rulers. Once they were prominent over their hierarchical network, they took the title of maharaja and introduced a Buddhist cult that was concentrated in new sacred centers located at their regional watak bases in the Kedu Plain. Their culminating central temple in the eighth century, the Borobudur, was a massive "cosmic mountain" that symbolized the Sailendra world order. Other newly constructed Buddhist temples in the Sailendra realm were in various ways preparatory to the higher-order Buddhist theology depicted on the terraces of the Borobudur complex. This temple was an important element of the Sailendra system of legitimacy, for the Borobudur sanctified Sailendra rule, while association with this "cosmic mountain" brought promised prosperity to the subjects of the Sailendra realm (Casparis: 1961; 1981, 74).

As previously discussed, during the Sailendra period central Java also became an internationally recognized pilgrimage center, and like its contemporary Srivijaya, an acclaimed center for Buddhist scholarship. The visits of Chinese and Indian pilgrims were no doubt used by Sailendra monarchs and their clerical staffs to validate the Sailendra maharajas' special patronage of Buddhism and their claims to subsequent magical powers. Sailendra patronage of Buddhism was also the hypothesized source of their multi-layered link with the Srivijaya maritime state, which by the eighth century held sovereignty over the previously autonomous river outlets on the west Java coast. The importance of the Srivijaya and Sailendra common patronage of Buddhism and sustenance of international Buddhist scholars was for both a symbolic source of each realm's sovereign legitimacy. While there is no substantive documentation, this common Buddhist link would have been foundational to peaceful intellectual and cultural exchanges between the two realms. International pilgrims, as well as the members of Srivijaya and Java societies, could have freely moved back and forth between that era's Srivijayan and Java Buddhist centers.

The Sailendras in Srivijaya and the Era of Good Feeling (Eighth to Ninth Centuries)

Buddhist and commercial networking between the two realms apparently led to diplomatic exchanges between the two courts. Indeed, it may be that an important foundation to Srivijaya's success was a networked relationship with the prosperous realm of the Buddhist Sailendras. The royal family of Srivijaya likely intermarried with the Sailendras, and eighth-century Srivijaya monarchs seem to have emphasized their descent from the Javanese lineage, rather than from their own accomplished Sumatran ancestors. A marriage alliance between the two royal families would certainly have been convenient. At the time, central Java was the most productive rice bowl in the island realm, and Srivijaya's ability to control the international trade depended upon its ability to provision the ships and feed the travelers who remained in its ports while waiting on changes in the winds. While it is most likely that Palembang's agricultural resources were superior to those of any other river-mouth port within its realm, it is unlikely that they were equal to this task on their own. Thus a relationship with the agriculturally productive central Java domain would have sustained Srivijaya's food needs, and a marriage with the Sailendra family would have formalized this.

This special relationship between Srivijaya and the Sailendras is thought to be documented in contemporary inscriptions. One from Nakon Si Thammarat on the Malay Peninsula, dated 775 CE, refers to the Srivijayan empire on one side ("side A"), while on the reverse of the same stone is an undated inscription that speaks of the Sailendra family that is known to have ruled in Java in that same eighth-century era (Nilakanta Sastri: 1949, 44, 125). Taking the two Nakhon Si Thammarat inscriptions as evidence that Srivijaya was the dominant political entity in the Southeast Asian archipelago in that age, some historians have proposed a Sumatran period in Javanese history: in this view the ruler of Srivijaya is seen dominating central Java's statecraft and culture in the eighth and ninth centuries CE, an age characterized by Srivijaya's Mahayana Buddhist influence as the foundation for Java's most impressive temple architecture.

However, an 860 inscription honoring the Srivijaya monarch who sponsored the religious retreat at Nalanda, the well-known north Indian Mahayana Buddhist monastery and center of international Buddhist scholarship of that age, suggests that this maharaja did not actually rule Java. Instead, the inscription merely says that he had descended from the Sailendra family of

Yavabhumi (Java) (Nilakanta Sastri: 1949, 125–28). On the basis of this inscription, the Dutch scholar W. F. Stutterheim suggested that it was Java, not southeastern Sumatra, that dominated the Southeast Asian archipelago during the eighth and ninth centuries (Stutterheim: 1929). This is unlikely, as all the other remaining evidence indicates that at the time Sumatra and Java were complementary realms. A cultural dialogue between these two contemporary polities is certainly reflected in the inspired Buddhist art of the period in the Srivijaya realms of Sumatra, the Malay Peninsula, and central Java. Art historians portray the art of this time as of neither Srivijayan nor Javanese origin alone but as a product of the interaction of both. This eighth- and ninth-century "good feeling" between the Sailendra and Srivijaya realms would explain the reference to the Sailendras in the Nakhon Si Thammarat inscription and adds credence to the belief that there was a marriage alliance between the Sailendra and Srivijaya maharajas, formalizing a political relationship that went beyond the economic and cultural relationships (Teeuw: 2001; Miksic: 2003b).

Early Java Administration

One reason that this peaceful interaction would have been possible was the essentially complementary nature of the pre-tenth-century economies of Srivijaya and central Java. While the Sailendra realm in central Java was a productive, regionally integrated wet-rice economy with limited supralocal economic linkages or ambitions, Srivijaya's economy and sovereignty depended primarily on international trade. While Java's rulers focused on local and regional economic affairs, the Srivijaya polity's elite had a strong interest in stimulating the flow of local production from upriver hinterlands to coastal entrepôts. Central Java inscriptions do not show great concern on the part of Javanese maharajas for wider economic integration or expand beyond the development of their watak ("regional") cores until the tenth century. Furthermore, except for Purnavarman in the fifth century, who did not create a lasting court, only in the eleventh century would Java-based rulers assume a conspicuous role as facilitators of international commerce, as in the prior era there is no epigraphic documentation of their coastal-hinterland networks.

One may speculate that Java monarchs of the pre-tenth-century period were willing to recognize Srivijaya's supremacy in the international commercial arena because they derived sufficient income and assistance as traditional rakrayan regional chiefs ruling watak regions to accomplish their desired ends, which were chiefly concerned with the construction of temples that enhanced their ritual sovereignty. Royal ambition in Java thus dictated a preference for symbolic rather than material ends. This was a stark contrast not only with Srivijaya but also with the polities that would rule Java in the coming centuries.

The early Javanese polity consisted of economic or ecological regions (*watak*/watek) that came to assume a subordinate role under the authority of a single leader (*rake/rakai*/rakrayan) who had gained the most prestige among his equals and could thus claim the indigenous title of monarchical authority (ratu) and the accompanying prestigious Indic title of sovereign (maharaja). The eco-regions (watak) were natural units of water management, trade, and spheres of personal authority rather than self-contained territorial or administrative units (Barrett Jones: 1984, 59–90; Naerssen and Iongh: 1977; Casparis: 1981; Wisseman Christie: 1991). They were comprised of village clusters (wanua) that were governed by councils of community elders headed by local individuals of distinction (*rama*) (Damais: 1970, 378–80; Barrett Jones: 1984, 108–9). In this early age there were two growth processes at work. Agrarian community expansion occurred at the village cluster level, while trade and initial social differentiation characterized relationships with the inhabitants of other village clusters and eco-regions.

The councils of community elders and the village cluster authorities began to appear in inscriptions in the eighth century. By the late ninth century the initial political expansion of supralocal authorities had resulted in the incorporation of neighboring village clusters into watak under the jurisdiction of regional lords or "elder brothers" (rake/rakai/rakrayan) through an interactive village-and-center networked relationship (Stutterheim: 1940, 4–5; Sarkar: 1971–1972, 51–52; Boechari: 1967–1968; Barrett Jones: 1984, 98–100). Foundational to a rakrayan or ratu lord's claim to sovereignty was his continuing ability to establish reciprocity relationships and redistribution net-

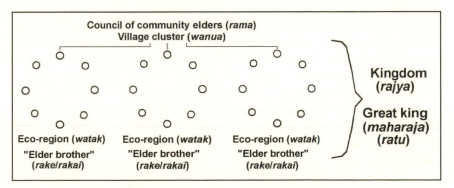

Figure 4.1.   Javanese Administration in the Eighth and Ninth Centuries

works in which material and psychological well-being were perceived to be a consequence of local submission to an overlord's authority. Power then seemed to be asserted downward to the eco-region and the networked village clusters, rather than handed upward by the village cluster to empower the monarch. Only in the ratu lord's own rakrayan territorial base was the passage of power from the bottom up; elsewhere it was at least symbolically horizontal or top-down. At the center of the vertically networked system was the great king's foundational realm, which consisted of a supportive familial network, possibly larger or more fertile lands, or linkage to translocal trade, or was strategically located relative to regional water distribution. A ratu/ monarch thus initially rose from this village cluster/eco-region base through combinations of personal, material, and ceremonial initiatives, which involved supportive individuals and groups willing to pool their efforts and resources on the behalf of their acknowledged leader (Casparis: 1956, 233, 251).

Nevertheless, the position of the monarch was still weak, or at least weaker than it would be in later times. This can be seen in some of the practices surrounding the granting of tax-free holdings known as *sima*. The institution of sima will be described in detail in the next chapter. The important point for the present discussion is that these sima grants were often accompanied by copper-plate charters that served as tangible evidence of the royal spoken word, considered the very breath of magical and spiritual power. The inscribed charters were treated with awe and reverence, not only as sacred relics, but also as royal and thus divine validation of an established system of rights and obligations. Holding a charter, this tangible proof of the divine, authorized the community to exercise the entitlements thereby enumerated. A commonly held belief was that the duties and prohibitions operational in a community had been imposed by divine sanction in the distant past, and that logically punishment for transgression came from the same source (Casparis: 1950, 24–50).

While these new copper-plate inscriptions validated kingship by their very existence, in the ninth and tenth centuries they included a high number of curses, supporting the conclusion that the Javanese monarchy was still weak. By the eleventh century, however, the dreadful curses would be omitted. This omission, together with a new tendency to elaborate the fiscal terms entailed by the sima obligations, suggested that at that time the monarchy had less need to intimidate and was much more self-assured. Nevertheless, this increased assurance was built on the base that the eighth- and ninth-century rakrayan had established. This base would soon become important, for in the tenth century there came an important shift in the relationship between Srivijaya and Java that made strong leadership essential in the latter realm.

THE RISE OF COMPETITION AND THE
FALL OF SRIVIJAYA (CA. 900–1025)

The tenth century saw a parting of the ways between Srivijaya and Java, which is reported in Middle Eastern and Chinese sources. In Middle Eastern references to the Javanese and Srivijaya realms during the eighth and ninth centuries, there was an important terminological development that signaled to Middle East observers both the separation of the realms and the end of Sailendra authority in Java, reported in Middle East sources as resulting from the transfers of Sailendra authority to Palembang in southeast Sumatra in the tenth century. Early Arab geographers' treatments suggested that the southeastern Sumatra and northeastern Javanese coasts formed a single commercial and cultural unit centered in southeastern Sumatra and encompassing Sumatra, Java, and the lower Malay Peninsula, while also including intense interactions with the Bangka Island and Sunda Strait areas (Wolters: 1967, 204, 219, 226). In these records the term *Zabaj* had been the first Arabic toponym for the island of Java as a whole and could be roughly equated to early Chinese dynastic references to *Shepo* (Java), as well as Indian references to *Javaka* or Yavadvipa (Tibbetts: 1979, 25–65, 104–17).

By the late ninth century Middle Eastern perceptions of the Indonesian archipelago were becoming more precise, being for the first time based upon personal experience rather than secondhand collations (Park: 2010). At this time Zabaj was specifically attached to reports of the maharajas who ruled central Java, as in the toponym "Maharaja [of] Zabaj." The end of the Sailendra line in Java and the subsequent transfer of Sailendra rule to southeastern Sumatra is thought by some historians to be reflected in the new tenth-century Arabic geographies, which began to reference the maharaja's base as being in Sribuza (Palembang) rather than in Zabaj, as had earlier works. Sribuza's ("Srivijaya's") capital in these post-tenth-century references was clearly a maritime center. Here the maharaja levied taxes on ships sailing to China, according to the *'Aja'ib al-Hind* (ca. 1000) (Tibbetts: 1979, 44, 113). Even in the thirteenth century, when Srivijaya had passed its prime, the Srivijaya maharaja's realm was still said by Ibn Sa'id (1274) to be "a city built on wooden piles at the edge of a large tidal river/bay," the largest commercial center of the Zabaj domain (Tibbetts: 1979, 57, 113).

Chinese sources similarly note a regional transition, if not their own clearer perception of the straits realm, at the beginning of the tenth century. While the records of the previous Tang dynasty had referred to Srivijaya as *Shih Lifoshih*, around 960, at the initiation of the Song dynasty, China's Srivijaya references changed to *Sanfozhi* (Tibbetts: 1979, 116–18; Wolters: 1979, 27). This new term, which is especially prominent throughout the records of the

Song dynasty (960–1279), literally refers to the "three *Vijayas*" (victories/cities of victory) of Palembang, Jambi, and Malayu, the latter a separate entity in the Melaka Straits, none of the three in Java.

Collectively, the Arab and Chinese records suggested that from the mid-tenth century onward Srivijaya (*Sribuza, Sanfozhi*) was the realm of the king of Zabaj, perhaps a Sailendra maharaja. But they clearly report that this ruler's authority encompassed the Straits of Melaka region, but not Java. By the mid-tenth century, however, political transitions had divided the old Zabaj realm into separate Srivijaya and Javanese commercial sectors.

This new post-Sailendra Java realm, which was based in eastern Java, had a more outward-looking economic focus that brought it into direct competition with Srivijaya (Wisseman Christie: 2001). In the ninth century merchants based in east Java had begun to actively secure spices in the eastern Indonesian archipelago, exchanging Javanese rice for spices and sandalwood that were then transported to Srivijaya's ports for sale to foreign merchants (Wisseman Christie: 1998b). By the tenth century east Java's ports were capable of acting independently of Srivijaya as commercial centers and competently attracting international traders. The hundred years following the reunification of China under the Song dynasty in 960 were an important watershed in the competition between Java and Srivijaya, for they saw a major upsurge in trade as China sought to enhance its communications with the Southern Seas (Nanyang), an effort that reached its peak in the twelfth century. The increase in trade combined with the enhanced importance of eastern Java to bring a serious weakening of Srivijaya's position as the dominant entrepôt in the Straits of Melaka region.

Anticipating these problems, Srivijaya's rulers reacted vigorously. Envious and fearing that rulers in east Java would establish a monopoly over the spice trade and that consequently merchants would begin to bypass Srivijaya's ports, they first sought to consolidate their position with diplomatic maneuvers in the direction of India and Sri Lanka (*ARE*: 1956–1957, inscriptions 161, 164, 166; *EI*: 22, 213–28). They followed these diplomatic initiatives with a series of wars against Java. As will be detailed in the next chapter, around 925 Srivijaya launched an attack on the new commercial centers of east Java. The repulse of this attack would play an important role in the development of east Java as a political center, as described in chapter 5. The warfare intensified in the initial years of the new Song dynasty. The Javanese counterattacked with an invasion of Srivijaya in 992, but in 1016 they suffered a devastating raid from their enemies, allowing the Srivijayan ruler to refer to himself as "king of the ocean lands" when he sent a richly laden mission to China in 1017; at this time he apparently controlled not only his traditional Straits of Melaka–centered realm but could also call on the allegiance of much of central Java (Wolters: 1970, 1, 14; Coedes: 1968, 130, 142, 144). Srivijaya's position seemed secure.

Yet less than a decade later Srivijaya would be knocked from its position of dominance. The decisive move came from neither of the two antagonists. It came, instead, from the west. In 1025 the Chola navy of India's Coromandel Coast sacked the legendary riches of the Srivijayan capital, and for the next fifty years the Cholas were to play a role in the politics of the straits area (Spencer: 1983). The attack of 1025 disrupted the concentration of the international route through the Srivijayan ports along the Straits, and as a result the trading pattern had become more diffuse by the last quarter of the eleventh century. No longer was the primary focus of the route on the southeastern Sumatra coast and its control of the Straits of Melaka. Though the coast was still important, it was considerably reduced in rank. In 1178, Chinese sources would state: "Of all the wealthy foreign lands which have great store of precious and varied goods, none surpasses the realm of Ta-shih (the Arabs). Next to them comes the She-p'o (Java), while San-fo-chi (Srivijaya) is third; many others come in the next rank" (Wheatley: 1961, 63; Wolters: 1967, 251).

Thus one of the major consequences of the 1025 Chola expedition was a shift in the main thrust of international commerce away from the produce of Sumatra and toward the developing ports of east Java and the imported spices they offered. The 1025 Chola expedition was critical to the Southeast Asian mainland as well. By removing Srivijaya's presence from the ports of the upper Malay Peninsula, the Cholas cleared the way for the expanding mainland states to fill the resulting power vacuum, as will be discussed in the chapters that follow (Nilakanta Sastri: 1949, 80; Kulke: 1999).

THE LEGACY OF THE SAILENDRA ERA IN JAVANESE HISTORY

Pre-tenth-century Java monarchs appear to have been quite willing to recognize Srivijaya's supremacy in the international commercial arena. Their limited interest in international trade at this time is partially explained by the fact that they derived sufficient income and assistance as traditional rakrayan regional chiefs ruling watak regions to accomplish their desired ends, which were chiefly concerned with the construction of temples that enhanced their ritual sovereignty. Royal ambition in Java thus dictated the priority of symbolic rather than material ends.

Nevertheless, it was the Sailendra era of eighth- and ninth-century Java that provided the foundations for the later flowering of Javanese civilization. The

Sailendra legacy to Java included the concept of the maharaja and a further definition of Indic-style rule. The Sailendras demonstrated the effectiveness of patronage to temples as the source of legitimacy and symbolic capital. Through the establishment of temple networks, they also began the process of political integration by drawing subordinate rakrayan and their temples into networked confederations. This stimulated the development of an integrated and ritually reinforced economic infrastructure whereby local products began to make their way, through supralocal markets as well as ritual networks, to Java's coastal ports.

Although at this time Srivijaya was more outward-looking than Java in its economic activities, archeological evidence does not support the assumption that the central Java heartland was economically isolated (Wisseman Christie: 1998b). Remaining Central Java epigraphy records the developing hierarchical marketing network described in chapter 1, which began with local periodic markets known as *pken/pkan* (Wisseman Christie: 1998b, 348). The pken marketing networks supported the integration of local peasant populations. Since pken marketing units were embedded within a watak region, watak have thus been understood to be self-contained irrigation and marketing units supporting the social, economic, and political cohesion of the unit as well as its autonomy relative to the centralizing ambitions of maharajas.

Yet at the same time the pken markets provided the forum for the watak's external commercial contacts, the place where "foreign" merchants were allowed to trade, and thus facilitated the flow of local production upward to supralocal market centers as well as receiving in return the downward flow of foreign goods for local consumption from the supralocal markets. These goods were then redistributed in linked transfers within the pken to participating wanua producers (see chapter 1). Such supralocal marketing links provided the basis for other types of integration beyond the watak level, interaction that was not inherent within the autonomous watak irrigation systems of central Java. To some extent they must also have facilitated the attempts of assertive rakrayan to develop the suprawatak-focused religious networks that were so critical to their claims of sovereignty as Javanese maharajas. These societal networks and their development have already been touched on in the present chapter, and they will be explored further in the next.

Inscriptions of the eleventh century and after reflect far greater and more regular interaction between rulers and ruled at various levels of the state system than was true in central Java in the eighth and ninth centuries. This was a consequence of the consolidations of the tenth and eleventh centuries that pressed the monarchs of east Java to take a larger role as agents of economic and political consolidation (Wisseman Christie: 1998b; Hall: 2010b). The emergence of the lower Brantas River basin wet-rice agricultural system in east Java would require their direct involvement, while also giving them more direct access to the northern coast. These initiatives enabled extended economic and political sovereignty, which is addressed in the next chapter.

5

Structural Change in the Javanese Community, ca. 900–1300

As discussed in chapter 4, Sanjaya (ca. CE 732–760), a patron of the Hindu god Siva, was the first significant Java monarch. He built his court and the first of Java's sprawling temple complexes on the sacred Dieng Plateau in north-central Java. Sanjaya was succeeded by a series of Sailendra monarchs (ca. 750–860), who followed his lead and built several major Mahayana Buddhist temples in central Java near modern-day Yogyakarta. These efforts culminated in the early ninth century with the Borobudur Mahayana Buddhist temple complex on the western edge of the Kedu Plain.

In the late ninth century, central Java–based Hindu kings defeated the Buddhist Sailendras and proclaimed their sovereignty over what they called the Mataram state (ca. 760–1000). These kings constructed their own equally impressive central temple complex dedicated to Lord Siva at Prambanan, north of Yogyakarta, near volcanic Mount Merapi.

As we will see in this chapter, historians believe that a devastating eruption of Mount Merapi in the tenth century temporarily made Mataram's central Java plains uninhabitable. The validity of such an eruption was well documented in 2010, with the announcement of the discovery on the edge of modern-day Yogyakarta of an intact ninth- or tenth-century Hindu Siva temple complex and its icons, covered by lava in the tenth century from nearby Mount Merapi (*New York Times*, Feb. 17, 2010). This natural disaster thus confirms one explanation for the shift of the center of Javanese civilization east to the Brantas and Solo river basins, but there are others, including the premise that the eruption of Mt. Merapi was in the aftermath rather than the primary cause of the transition. But there is no evidence to explain why such

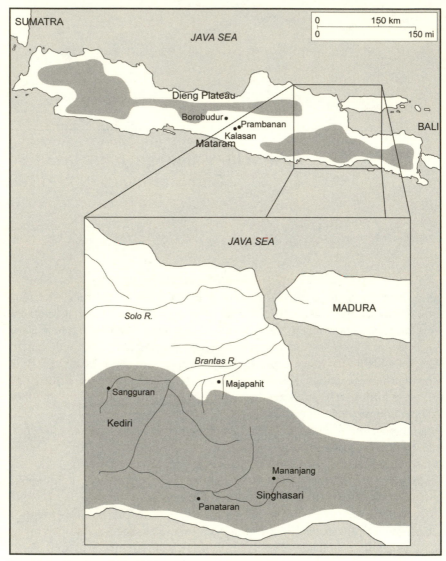

Map 5.1.   Java, ca. 600–1500

a transition to east Java would have taken place prior to the volcanic eruption. In east Java, for a time, temples assumed less importance as statements of royal authority. Instead, transitional kings through the reign of Airlangga (r. 1016–1045) encouraged the spread of wet-rice agriculture in east Java. They encouraged and initiated the construction of new water management projects and mountainside wet-rice terraces to support the development of new village societies. This move to the east also allowed Java monarchs to exploit east Java's strategic position adjacent the international maritime trade route to eastern Indonesia's Spice Islands.

Following Airlangga's death, the Java monarchy split into competing factions, with kings identified by their association with two rival courts. One regional dynasty ruled from Kadiri on the southwest edge of the east Java river plain, and the other at Singhasari to the southeast on the Malang Plateau. During this era kings came to possess a degree of direct administrative control over their subordinate regions in east Java that went beyond that of previous courts, in an age that was also noted for the emergence of a distinctive Javanese culture.

THE FOUNDATIONS OF EAST JAVANESE POLITY

The shift of cultural and political power from central to east Java was in part that of a particular ruling group that moved its residential base and was ultimately marked by the decline of the rulers of one region and the rise of those of another. Historians believe that the initially central Java–based monarch Balitung (ca. 907–ca. 913), who traced his ancestry to Sanjaya rather than to the Sailendras, extended his polity by conquering the independent east Java rakrayan territory of the Kanjuruhan, a fertile mountain plateau centered at Singhasari (Casparis: 1941; Sarkar, 1971–1972, 295–303). However, the central Java rakrayan territory of Watakura appears to have remained his base, as this is where most of his inscriptions were issued (Boechari: 1979, 475; Wisseman Christie: 2001). It was Balitung's successor Pu Sindok who established a permanent royal *kraton* in eastern Java and began in earnest the integration of central and eastern Java into a single polity. Around 928–929, according to a surviving 937 inscription, Pu Sindok fought off an attack by the Malayu-based army of Srivijaya. The inscription states that the Srivijayan forces landed in east Java and advanced to the area near Nganjuk, some distance into Java's hinterland, where they were defeated. The inscription eulogized Sindok for saving the east Java realm from the attack (Brandes and Krom: 1913, xlvi; Boechari: 1979, 474).

Evidence of Indic civilization in eastern Java predates this shift by more than a hundred years. A Sanskrit inscription dated 760 records the dedication of a temple to the sanctified Indian sage Agastya by Gajayana, son of "king" (*narapati*) Devasingha, who was said to rule from the *pura* (kraton or royal palace complex) of Kanjuruhan (Sarkar: 1971–1972, 25–33). East Java's economic and political development was made possible by the construction of wet-rice irrigation systems such as the Harinjing canal system, located northwest of Kadiri in the upper Brantas River basin region, which was established in ca. 804 (Naerssen and Iongh: 1977, 56–57).

The movement of the Javanese kraton from the center to the east was associated with a period of intensive development of the Brantas and Solo river basins under royal patronage. In an inscription dated 905, for example, King Balitung granted special trading concessions and sima (freehold) status to benefit two lords (rakrayan) in connection with the construction of an aqueduct and as a reward or boon (*anugraha*) because of their success in an earlier royal military expedition against neighboring Bali.

> Because the water of the [river] overflowed the irrigation pipes in [two named communities] . . . and [two village officials, one a *rama*, decided] to construct an aqueduct [with the assistance of the two named *rakrayan*] . . . The Rakrayan Hujung and Rake Majawunta were grateful that when intending to go to Bantan [Bali] they were accompanied by Sang Mapatih [Balitung] and thus Bantan was conquered by them, and that is the reason they received [this reward] from the king. (Barrett Jones, 1984, 168–71)

We know that between 900 and 1060 more than forty new communities were established by direct royal intervention in the developing Brantas River delta (Wisseman Christie: 1982, 496–531; 1994; Barrett Jones: 1984). As east Javanese polities grew, additional dams and canal systems were built closer to the Brantas River delta. Significantly, although wet-rice cultivation was extensively practiced in central Java well before the shift of Java's royal authority to east Java in the tenth century, most epigraphic records of the building of early Java's hydraulic systems were issued in east Java. Central Java inscriptions first reference officials responsible for the administration of irrigation systems (Casparis: 1956, 211–43) or the conversion of lands to wet-rice cultivation (Sarkar: 1971–1972, 278–87).

The tenth-century east Java inscriptions are related to the construction of major water management systems that would bring the Brantas River and its tributaries under control. The Brantas was a turbulent river with a propensity to cause major destruction of wet-rice fields when it seasonally overflowed its banks, and local efforts to protect the fields from regular inundation appear to have been insufficient. Indeed, in each of the early centers of wet-rice cultivation in the Brantas River system there is a corresponding post-ninth-century inscription that records the building of a major component (e.g., a dam, dyke, or canal) of a regional hydraulic system. Each of these inscriptions also records an east Java–based monarch's involvement in the system's construction or in organizing the continuing direction of local elders or regional political authorities to guarantee that the hydraulic system would be properly maintained or managed "for the benefit of the *rakrayan's* people." Local village elders were instructed by the rakrayan to see that farmers were fully aware of the significance of regulations affecting the use of this new irrigation system and that they were to abide by established rules applying to water distribution (Setten van der Meer: 1979, 51–52).

By the time Airlangga (1016–1045) came to power early in the eleventh century, not only had the status of the maharaja been elevated, but the possibilities for economic achievement implicit in the new east Java order had been consolidated as well. This is clear from a 1037 inscription of Airlangga reporting that the Brantas River had burst its dikes in 1033, flooding many local villages and making it difficult for trading vessels to reach the Java monarch's port (Naerssen: 1938). As a consequence, the maharaja's income, and also that of his subjects, was said to have greatly diminished. Although previous efforts by individual communities to control the Brantas had proven fruitless, the maharaja intervened and had two dams constructed at Kamalagyan and Waringin Sapta to reestablish the old river course. Through this effort and his continuing leadership, prosperity returned (Setten van der Meer, 1979, 80).

Airlangga's reign was critical to the evolution of a Javanese polity. The 1041 Calcutta Stone inscription reported that a "great catastrophe" took place in 1016, when Airlangga's predecessor on the throne, Dharmawangsa Teguh, was killed along with his kraton elite by an enemy (Srivijaya), who destroyed the kraton. By this time, Srivijaya had extended its authority to central Java itself, being supported by alliances with regionally based rakrayan who relied on Srivijaya's assistance to maintain their autonomy from the east Java–based maharajas (Chatterjee: 1933, 2:63–74). As we saw in chapter 4, the Chola raid of 1024–1025 then dealt a hard blow to Srivijaya, weakening its hold not only on central and western Java but even over its core areas on Sumatra and the Malay peninsula. Thereafter Airlangga began to "reestablish order" in his realms, consolidating his authority over all Java and Bali (Wicks: 1992, 281–83). Airlangga ascended the throne as the victorious Sri Maharaja Rakrayan Halu, establishing a kraton at the unidentified capital Kahuripan in the northeastern corner of east Java.

East Java–based kingship provided the opportunity for Javanese rulers to secure a more ample royal economic base than had been possible in central Java. There were several reasons for this. First, east Java's agricultural development potential was greater and more supportive of royal ambition, partially due to the fact that the area was less populated and free of previously existing claims to regional authority by rakrayan and other elites. In the post-tenth-century epigraphy of east Java the authority of a maharaja over land is more direct, and maharajas held rakrayan rights over a more extensive personal economic base. Second, there was greater access to the sea from the eastern Java hinterland. East Java had a wide coastal plain that could be developed as a center of wet-rice production.

The Brantas and Solo rivers that drained this plain were both navigable, allowing good internal communication among regions. They were especially important in facilitating the flow of local production from the highlands of the Brantas Plateau to the coast as well as goods from the coast back to the hinterland. Javanese monarchs based in the coastal plain or even in the upper Brantas region would be able to participate in and supervise international trade more directly than central Java–based monarchs, who had been more isolated in the interior. East Java monarchs thus had new opportunities for the acquisition of wealth, which in turn meant more ritualized economic redistributions as well as temple constructions that allowed them to accrue ritual merit and thus reinforce the ruler's power and prestige. Unlike earlier central Java monarchs who had to share the financing of such activities, usually depending on the support or initiative of the maharaja's allied rakrayan, east Java monarchs had greater economic resources at their personal disposal for such enterprises (Wisseman Christie: 2001).

It was good that they did, for more complex techniques of water management were necessary to develop sawah cultivation in the lower Solo and Brantas river plains than were required in central Java or even in the upper Brantas Plateau. In the coastal river plain the flow of water had to be regulated; otherwise the land was subject to devastating rainy-season flooding. This had to be accomplished by a complex regionwide water management network if these lands were to be regularly productive, a degree of management significantly greater than that required for the functioning of the less technically sophisticated irrigation networks of earlier Javanese civilization. According to eastern Java's epigraphic records, the eastern Java monarchs provided the expertise and management necessary to facilitate this development and were rewarded with the opportunity to assume reciprocal rights over this land. Thus, the personal powers of the eastern Javanese monarchs were significantly greater than those of the rakrayan who had served as overlords of watek regional networks in earlier times.

Surviving inscriptions document the certification of the Javanese monarchs' landholding and taxable rights during the extension of wet-rice cultivation into newly opened irrigated fields in eastern Java (Barrett Jones: 1984; Kulke: 1991, 12–14). Earlier, in central Java, symbolic statements of royal authority and societal integration had revolved around a regionally dominating Buddhist or Hindu ritual complex (e.g., the Dieng Plateau, Borobudur, and Prambanan complexes). In east Java, by contrast, the monarchs signaled a new sense of royal empowerment by encouraging the development of ritual networks focused less on a central royal temple than on the royal palace complex, which itself became the hub of ritualized exchanges between kings and their subordinate elites.

The precise reasons triggering the transfer of the kraton from central to eastern Java, other than a massive volcanic eruption, is a matter of dispute among historians. One popular explanation is that the burst of temple construction that took place from the early eighth through the early tenth centuries drained the central Javanese economy. According to this hypothesis, central Javanese monarchs weakened their base and their legitimacy by using all the resources at their disposal to build the temples (Schrieke: 1955–1957, 2:292–300). However, there are several problems with this notion of a reaction to central Javanese despotism. First of all, most of the temple construction had been done with the approval of regional chiefs (rakrayan), rather than having been initiated by those claiming maharaja status. Aside from the Dieng Plateau complex there were only five major state-level temple complexes known to be constructed in the name of a central Javanese maharaja: Candi Sewu, Candi Plaosan, Candi Ratubaku, and Candi Loro Jonggran (all at Prambanan), with the fifth being Borobudur. All of these show local cooperation. While the Borobudur was constructed under Sailendra patronage for the worship of the deified ancestors of the Sailendra dynasty, Candi Loro Jonggrang and Candi Sewu were built in partnership with various notables of the realm, especially networked rakrayan, while Candi Plaosan was built by the maharaja and his state administrators with the cooperation of local rakrayan, each of whom contributed one or more buildings (Casparis: 1950, 170–75; 1981; Miksic: 2003b).

Furthermore, discounting the notion that temple construction led to central Java's downfall is that the labor (*bwat hyang*) necessary for this temple construction does not appear to have been a burden, and indeed agriculturalists were not actively needed for the temple construction. Royal bondsmen and professional artisan groups provided the continuous labor for this construction; brahmans or other religious specialists laid out temples, sculptors carved the statues and reliefs, bondsmen carried stones and performed the preparatory shaping and chipping of stone, and local rakrayan provided the labor force for the construction of specific buildings by temporarily assigning their normal rights to labor (*bwat haji*). This labor need not have reduced local rice production, for work in central Java's paddy fields could, as now, have been done largely by women, freeing men to work on the temples—ideally men hoe and work the irrigation system; women plant, weed, and assist in the harvest; and children chase away birds to protect the maturing rice. Furthermore, temple construction could have been of a seasonal nature, corresponding to the slack periods of the growing cycle, with work schedules arranged such as to not diminish local agricultural productivity (Kaplan: 1963). Taking all this into account, and referencing the Borobudur and Prambanan temple relief depicting farmers happily at work as well as enjoying their leisure, Indonesia's senior historian Boechari found the "picture of a despotic ruler, forcing his subjects to build splendid edifices to his own glory, resulting in economic collapse" to be "rather improbable" (Boechari: 1979, 485).

A second hypothesis suggests that the eastward movement of the court was occasioned by a significant local crisis of some sort. The Java historical tradition treats the transfer of power to east Java as but one of numerous cyclical shifts of Javanese kraton that were triggered by various crises, such as invasion by an enemy who desecrated the kraton or the death of a monarch and a subsequent succession crisis. In cases such as these, the old kraton was considered to be spiritually polluted and was no longer acceptable as the center for the performance of sacred state rituals. It therefore had to be abandoned in favor of another, with the new kraton becoming the ruler's source of a new and more powerful prowess.

Javanese historiography suggests there may also have been a predisposition to move. According to Java's early literary traditions, a catastrophe would take place unless every fourth monarch established a new kraton, and this resulted in the periodic movement of the maharaja's palace compound, even though the movement was sometimes within the immediate area. This pattern of shifting the kraton approximately once every fourth generation continued to the fourteenth century (Boechari: 1979, 487–91). Such moves were elaborate, requiring the ritual creation of a new world order (mandala) in which the center of the cosmos was transferred to the new royal center, and there was a corresponding establishment of a new cosmic mountain via the construction of a new state temple as the replica of Mount Meru, the center of the universe.

Nevertheless, regardless of this possible predisposition, both internal and external evidence suggests that a major crisis in fact occurred in the first quarter of the tenth century, and this crisis, viewed by early Javanese historians as an omen that the current order had come to an end, was likely the substantive reason for the transfer of the Javanese royal kraton to eastern Java. The crisis earthquake and/or volcanic eruption is believed to have taken place some time around 925. Boechari postulated, based on his study of Javanese and foreign literature, that a cataclysmic explosion of Mount Merapi, located between the Prambanan and Borobudur complexes in central Java, produced ash rains and landslides, making the fertile Kedu and Mataram rice plains, on either side of the volcano, temporarily uninhabitable and triggering the abandonment of central Java in favor of eastern Java. In support of his case, and previous to the new 2010 discovery of the intact temple at Yogyakarta,

Boechari had referenced the 1966 discovery of the Candi Sambisari temple north of Yogyakarta, buried in an almost perfectly preserved state twenty feet (six meters) below the surface of surrounding fields, covered by layers of protective volcanic ash; the recovery of the Borubudur and other central Java temples from similar layers of ash by nineteenth- and twentieth-century Dutch archeologists; and the Middle Eastern geographer Abu Zaid's tenth-century Arabic account of Java that reports Java was "one of continuous habitation and uninterrupted cultivated fields, except near the volcano, where the land was deserted for the distance of a *parasang* [3.6 miles/6 kilometers]" (Tibbetts: 1979, 105). The incessant wars among various rakrayan local rulers, known from the epigraphy of the early tenth century, could well have been viewed as provoking the wrath of the gods, who had responded with this natural cataclysm. Whether or not this was the precise reason for the move, by the time of the Srivijaya raids of the early eleventh century, the Javanese population center and locus of royal power had shifted to eastern Java's Brantas River basin, a place from which Java presented a far greater commercial threat than it had in the past.

TAX TRANSFERS AND RITUALIZED FEASTS IN TENTH- AND ELEVENTH-CENTURY JAVA

Throughout the tenth and eleventh centuries, from Balitung to Airlangga and beyond, inscriptions recording transfers of "tax-free territory" (sima) demonstrate royal efforts to promote court authority in their hinterlands. The tradition of sima transfers had developed in the earlier era of the central Java courts; we have records of them since at least the early eighth century as they especially record the transfers of local income rights to sustain the expenses of temples (Sarkar: 1971–1972). In the highly personalized, early central Java–based polities, the monarch had limited revenue demands, which were consistent with his own inability to make large-scale revenue collections.

Because of insufficient court-centered administrative capacity, central Java–based rulers were more likely to redistribute their local production income rights to community temples that were associated with submissive lords, thereby allowing retention of "the king's due" in return for local recognition of royal beneficence. The early Javanese state was based on networks of ritualized reciprocity in which monarchs solicited local submission to their courts' authority by symbolic exchanges, wherein the local community, and especially its elite, accepted a place in the "orbit" of a court-centered hierarchy. As a consequence, the monarch was assured that he could regularly draw upon a local community's labor and produce to sustain his central temple or to accomplish projects of common value, such as extending irrigated agriculture or constructing roads that were of mutual benefit to the court and the local populace (Dove: 1985). Now, in eastern Java, the nature of royal development projects had wider significance. New sima grants were also used as a means by which the rulers could establish an enduring local presence that had political and economic implications. At face value such grants appear to reduce the influence of both the local lord and the overlord, but they were foundational to the formalization of Java's political and cultural integrity.

Sima were not gifts of land, for Java's monarchs did not normally possess local land rights, and even their tax rights were subject to negotiation with village elders and regional authorities (Barrett Jones: 1984, 59–60). When a court transferred entitlements to land, it had to first purchase the land from the villages affected. Sima, on the other hand, involved the alienation of all or a portion of the income rights to which a superior political authority was entitled from certain types of local land. Sima grants were the linked transfers that provided a continuing source of funding for a religious institution, a favored individual, or a group. The most common sima involved transfers to ancestor temples that honored deceased monarchs, regional lords, or village ancestors.

While land that had been made sima involved a relinquishing of all or some of the king's entitlement to income from the property, the sima registered the land and its legal status and thus was a means by which farmers and nonfarmers were brought into (and under) a dominant court. Sima grants of income rights to previously uncultivated lands were especially common, to encourage pioneer territorial expansion but also to clarify the ownership and income rights concerning the newly developed property. These sima charter registrations were the referenced legal record in later judicial challenges concerning land rights, as for example in thirteenth- and fourteenth-century epigraphic records of court cases upholding grants made by defunct ruling families (Casparis: 1981, 128–30; Wisseman Christie: 1986).

Sima grants in effect freed designated lands from numerous demands for taxes and services, prohibiting civil authorities, or the tax collectors and officials working for local rulers or village authorities, from entering domains to collect payments on their own behalf or on others' behalf (Sedyawati: 1994). Thus, while on the surface these tax transfers would imply the local surrender of royal power, they eliminated in addition a portion of the wealth directly available to local elite. Regional notables were, however, compensated for their lost income with assigned status rights and presents of gold, silver, or cloth. Although the sima transfers helped the monarch by reducing the taxes available to his local rivals, they also reduced the overlord's income;

therefore there was a limit on the amount of tax the overlord polity was willing to forego. On the other hand, the local community's acceptance of the
terms of a royal sima was also their acknowledgment of the monarch's legitimate right to this collection.

Let us consider several examples of sima concessions. One comes from the
905 inscription in which King Balitung granted special trading concessions
and sima status to benefit two lords (rakrayan) in connection with the construction of an aqueduct and as a reward or boon (anugraha) because of their
success in an earlier royal military expedition against neighboring Bali (Barrett Jones: 1984, 168–71). The sima thus rewarded the two lords' initiative in
supporting wet-rice cultivation in their area, while also providing material
reciprocity for their political support. This sima initiative came from priests
who were acting in collaboration with local villagers. Elders from the village,
other individuals who had been involved in the construction of the aqueduct,
and various witnesses all received gifts to recognize their participation in the
sima initiation ritual (Barrett Jones: 1984, 166–77). According to the inscription, the two lords who were the recipients (i.e., supervisors) of the grant were
made heads of the residences in the assigned territory, "to look after the
offerings of each 'producer,'" meaning that the lords would make certain that
the resident producers made good on their contracted annual payments to the
temple.

In another early tenth-century example also from Balitung's reign, two
high priests rather than two secular lords were the designated sima administrators. This inscription documents the increasing importance of trade in the
Javanese realm, as it stresses King Balitung's desire to protect merchants and
other travelers from bandits and other dangers. The goal in this case was not
to extend wet-rice cultivation for its own sake, but the inscription provides an
extended commentary on how cultivated land rather than uncultivated frontier was more likely to support secure local marketplaces and the more efficient movement of traders. This sima charter's implicit suggestion is twofold:
that frontier lands were more likely to pose a threat of banditry against traders
and settled cultivators alike, and that cultivated lands would provide a stable
source of agricultural surplus and consumers, benefiting trade and traders.

Sima "freeholds" came about at the same time as the introduction of copper-
plate charters (Barrett Jones: 1984, 7–12; Hunter: 1996; Casparis: 1975). As
mentioned in chapter 4, the inscribed charters themselves were treated with
awe and reverence, not only as sacred relics, but also as a royal and thus
divine validation of the established system of rights and obligations. That
sima investitures had great local meaning is shown by the broad community
participation in chartering rituals. A Sangguran inscription of 928 specified
that "everyone attended, according to their rank, all the . . . representatives

of the neighboring villages; the aged and the young, men and women, from all classes without exception, all attended and partook of the ceremonial food" (Sarkar: 1972, 234).

With prominent local witnesses and ranking officials present to demonstrate their approval and support for the grant, the foundation ceremonies were preceded by gift giving to those officially taking part. In instances of royal involvement, the gifts were termed "customary ample measure" (*pasek-pasek/pasak-pasak*, variant spellings; each pair indicates the plural). Individuals with the most prominent positions were presented with gifts first, usually the objects of greatest value. Gold, silver, and cloth are the most commonly referenced pasek-pasek gifts. Accepting a gift was as important as the gift itself since it signaled the acceptance of one's position relative to the giver, and, together with its wider societal and political overtones, symbolically compensated for any loss of revenue (Wicks: 1992, 260–72; Sarkar: 1971, 139–40, 199). Next came the ceremony of land investiture. This portion of the ritual addressed the transfer of tax obligations from specific corporate entities, such as the king, to a religious institution. This involved the calling of witnesses, especially those who were directly affected and were there to certify the validity of the transaction. Ceremonial feasting followed completion of this business.

The ritual feast is frequently described in infinite detail. The Taji copperplate inscription of 901 lists the various dishes offered for the meal, including the precise number of *lontar* palm leaves distributed to each group of people, upon which they could place their food (Sarkar: 1971, 223; 1972, 4–8, 37). First the food was offered to the appropriate "participating" deities, and then all the ceremonial participants ate, including the members of the local community regardless of their social stature. Entertainment of various kinds followed. Dancing, gambling, cockfights, drama performances by masked players, music and singing, puppet (*wayang*) performances, and recitals of the *Ramayana* were the high point of the ritual feasting. These activities were seen as performances for the pleasure of the deities, and the blood of cockfights was a symbolic sacrifice, perhaps to guard against evil spirits trying to interfere with the consecration ritual that followed the entertainment (Setten van der Meer: 1979, 122, 126–30).

The final portion of the investiture ceremony consisted of the reciting of a solemn consecration formula. In the early inscriptions this involved an oath in which the recipient pledged fidelity. This portion of the ritual dealt with a linked transfer, specifying what the income from the freehold would finance—the construction of and/or maintenance of a temple, the creation of and placement of an icon, the periodic performance of ritual, or the support of noted holy men. A stone inscription or copper-plate charter was often the focal point of this consecration. For example:

> [All the participants] sat on the ground in a circle, with their faces turned to the officiating priest and the "sacred foundation stone," which was placed under the canopy in the middle. (Sarkar: 1972, 28)

> When all were seated the officiating priest uttered the oath formula, cut off the head of a hen, which was crushed on the sacred foundation stone, and (then) threw eggs on the *watu sima* and uttered oaths. (Sarkar: 1972, 95)

In one instance, the inscribed stone itself was symbolically presented with four sets of ceremonial cloth (i.e., cloth that when wrapped around the stone would empower it, as icons were in theory brought to life when wrapped in ritual cloth—the point here is that the inscribed stone, ritually consecrated and wrapped in empowering cloth, was itself a spiritually endowed religious artifact) (Wisseman Christie: 1993) and four weights of gold (Sarkar: 1972, 4–8).

The ending of the investiture ritual included a common plea that the grant should be maintained as originally intended. Sima charters from the late eighth century are the last to invoke future kings "by these words on the stone that will last forever, to protect the domains and the institutions [established herein] for posterity" (Sarkar: 1971, 31–48). While the later inscriptions and their curses still address disloyalty to the ruler who validates the sima tax transfer, topically their focus shifts from future kings' likely unauthorized incursions into the locality to the potential immorality and illegal actions of locals (Veerdonk: 2001). Typically in these post-eighth-century inscriptions there was a curse uttered by a villager or by a religious official that threatened those present who would transgress against the freehold and thus demonstrate disloyalty to the monarch. An elaborate example from the eleventh century was characteristically designed to strike terror in the hearts of potential transgressors.

> Who disturbs the village . . . he may be brought to destruction . . . he may be killed by all the gods in such a way that he may not (find time to) turn behind, he may not (find time to) look behind; he may be pushed in the front-side; struck on the left-side, his mouth may be struck, his forehead may be battered, his belly may be ripped open, his intestines may be rooted out, his entrails may be drawn out, his heart may be plucked out, his flesh may be eaten, his blood may be drunk up, then he may be trampled upon, lastly he may be killed! (Sarkar: 1972, 241)

By the eleventh century, the charters' omission of the dreadful curses and their focus instead on the elaborate fiscal terms entailed by the sima obligations implies that the contemporary monarchs had less need to intimidate by citing reciprocal divine intervention. The following selection from an eleventh-century inscription demonstrates the greater confidence of the monarchy at the time of Airlangga.

> This dam was built in order to bring about benefits for the world and the revival of all the holy religious foundations. . . . This was brought about through the command of His Majesty [Airlangga], who has his capital at Kahuripa, because he visibly showers upon the world the elixir of life that is his affection, causing a rain of merit. By this construction he will serve to perfect all the holy temple (*dharma*) foundations for the benefit of all his subjects, old and young, who dwell in the sanctified realm (*mandala*) of the island of Java. His reason for causing the source of devotion to spread is to provide a shining example for all the world, and also to add to the splendor (of the realm). This is his reason for conducting himself as a universal monarch (*chakravartin*) as he has in undertaking this construction which will bring about daily well-being for the world, thus providing a sign to the world that His Majesty is not interested solely in his own advantage. (Wisseman Christie: 1982, 499–500)

This outpouring of religious fervor is followed by very specific reference in monetary terms (coinage, produce, and cloth) to the taxes due to the kings from each of the communities that was to benefit from the development project (Wicks: 1992, 281; Hall: 1985, 129–35).

STRUCTURAL CHANGE IN THE KADIRI PERIOD, CA. 1100–1222

In 1044, at the end of his reign, Airlangga is said to have divided his kingdom between his two sons, creating the two independent and often unfriendly rival states of Janggala (later known as Singhasari), based in the more eastern Malang Plateau region in the Brantas River upstream, and Panjalu/Pangjalu, in the more west-central Brantas River downstream. The latter is known alternatively as Kadiri/Kediri (Boechari: 1968). The Kadiri-based kings were especially aggressive in their efforts to close the implied if not real societal space between the court and its countryside. They also worked to define better the distance between those who were residents and allies of their court and those who were not. Earlier maharajas had asserted that they were detached human intercessionaries, indulging in the luxury of their courts and passively mediating between the realm of the gods and that of humankind. In contrast, in a tradition established by Airlangga, the Kadiri kings stressed their aggressive pursuit of the betterment of humankind, both by their actions in the world and also, if necessary, through their appeals to the Divine on humankind's behalf.

Kadiri kings also created the tradition of building the realm around a continuous sanctified court rather than a focal temple complex. The Kadiri-era inscriptions included the first assertions of a continuous court-centered Javanese state (*bhumi*), and it was the royal court, rather than a central temple complex, that was portrayed as the ritual center of this bhumi—an earthbound space foundational to an inclusive Javanese community (Zoetmulder: 1982, 272). The court, its residential elite, and those who had the privilege of participating in its rituals set the social and moral standards for their society. The heightened focus on the court was also accompanied by a further elevation of the monarch's status. Airlangga had been the first Javanese monarch to assume the title "universal monarch" (*ratu chakravartin*, compounding the local reference to "king" and the Indic/Buddhist notion of universal spiritually empowered secular authority, as traditionally attributed to the initiation of the Mauryan emperor Asoka in the third century CE and similarly asserted by the kings of other Indic-inspired Southeast Asian monarchies). This increased stature was marked by other usages as well (Wisseman Christie: 1986, 74–75; Kulke: 1991, 17). For example, earlier the monarch had been addressed in inscriptions as a person: His Majesty the King. But Kadiri kings were spoken of in awed reverence, with the inscriptions referring not to the king's person but to "the Dust of His Majesty's Sandals," which expressed the notion of the earthbound bhumi of humanity blessed by the footsteps of an empowered monarch, as the monarch's feet were traditionally symbolic of his divine powers. The earlier phrasing had suggested that the king was the greatest among equals. This new wording reflected the perceptual social, ritual, and developing political distance between the king and his subjects (Casparis: 1986, 16).

The high point of the Kadiri court was reached in the reign of King Jayabhaya (1135–1157), who ordered the writing of the *Bharatayuddha kakawin*, which was completed around the time of his death (Zoetmulder: 1974, 129, 256–83). This court text develops a Javanese version of the *Mahabharata* classical Indian Sanskrit text, a moral tale about the forces of good and evil centered in the epic war between the Pandawas and the Korawas, here presented from the perspective of and consistent with the interests of the Kadiri court elite. In this *kakawin* (Old Javanese court poetic) text the source of conflict is the duality of power in the past—allegorically the legacy of Airlangga's ritual division of his realm in the mid-eleventh century—and the inherent desire for unity between the two competing clans of kinsmen. In the *Bharatayuddha kakawin* version, there is greater concern for the distinctions between male and female than in the Indic original, in keeping with local tradition. The monarch is the agent of the Indic warrior and male-dominant (*kasatriya*) civilization, and he represents the power that comes from male leadership. In contrast, female associations symbolize local civilization, which initially rejects the notion of state polity. The old feminine order is characterized by sexual desire and family loyalties, which must now submit to the king's disciplined masculine order. For the broader benefit of society, local communities now needed to resist self- and family-centered domestic passions if they were to overcome debilitating conflict and subsequent societal stagnation. That is, Javanese society needed to define where the realm of the court ended and that of the local community began.

As appropriate to their new self-proclaimed stature, Kadiri kings attempted to adjust the center-hinterland relationship to strengthen the position of their court (kraton) relative to its dependent countryside. As discussed in chapter 4, in its earliest days the state had been built on natural eco-regions, or watak, which had served as centers of rakrayan power, and relations between village elders and the king's court had been negotiated on a personal basis. By the time of the Kadiri state, however, settled village communities (*thani*) were widely categorized as "collections of hamlets" (*paraduwan*), which was more representative of their true nature, but in reality was nothing more than a change in terminology (Sedyawati: 1994, 202; Wisseman Christie, 1994) as represented in figure 5.1. The thani villages were grouped into new *wisaya* regional administrative divisions that redefined and replaced the old designation of eco-regions as watak. These new regional wisaya featured royal administrators whose roles superseded the prior conventions of personal negotiations implicit in the old order. These new royal agents were referred to as *sopana*, or intermediaries, who might bypass other officials to negotiate directly with the king to request favor for the local community (Boechari: 1967–1968). In essence, the line between sopana and the *rama* represented the "border" between state officialdom and local elite. The village elders (rama) still held substantial hereditary income rights to cultivated property. Among the collective clusters of villages in the wisaya, one central village cluster (*dalam thani*), designated as the "original" village settled by the rama, served as the center of wisaya district authority. The state's designated agent (sopana) interacted with the other village clusters at the dalam thani, where local interests continued to be represented by the rama, as designated agents of the rural communities of the district in negotiations with the state.

Accompanying these regional administrative changes, long-standing rakrayan titles of regional power were finally removed from the countryside and those who had held these old titles now became the court-based delegated regional agents—thus becoming accountable to the court rather than having inherent hereditary power as regional aristocracy (Kulke: 1991, 18). In reality there was really little change of personnel, but in theory the regional authorities now held their positions at the will of the king rather than by hereditary right or by local acknowledgments of their power.

As noted above, the conceptual bhumi of the Kadiri era centered on the king's court (*rajya*, with emphasis on the court as an administrative center rather than the traditional use of *kraton*, which is referential to the place of royal residency), with its regionally subordinate wisaya (outlying regions) and their clustered paraduwan/thani communities, organized conceptually into an encircling mandala divided into regions. Figure 5.1 illustrates these concepts.

Here we see the center, in this case the rajya (capital) at Pangjalu/Kadiri, surrounded by a set of regions, or districts, each organized around a dalem thani central village that acted as regional authority for networked local villages (thani).

These regional collectives were treated more as areas of influence over population clusters than as units of administered territory. As in earlier times, nonfarmers were still incorporated into and subordinated to the agrarian order. Paraduwan/thani (the groupings of hamlets) were broadly defined as including resident artisans (*kalang*), small local religious establishments and

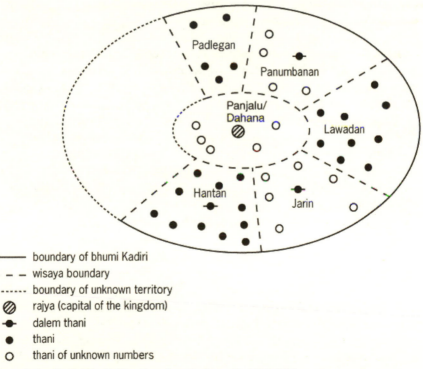

—— boundary of bhumi Kadiri
— — — wisaya boundary
········ boundary of unknown territory
⊘ rajya (capital of the kingdom)
—●— dalem thani
● thani
○ thani of unknown numbers

Figure 5.1.   Kadiri-Era Polity. Based on Sedyawati: 1994, 204

their personnel (*kalagyan*), and merchants (*kabanyagan*) (Wisseman Christie: 1991, 36). The specific reference to the residents of religious establishments among this group of restricted professionals may have been reflective of the need to negate the rise of powerful local religious centers and their clergy, who might rival those patronized by the state, whether as independent agents or as instruments of particular elite factions (Hefner: 1990, 36n4).

Throughout Java's early history, Indic temples had functioned as cultural brokers. As documented in chapter 4, elites who could patronize or control strategic religious centers were in a favorable position to administer wealth and exercise significant influence over their subject populations. Under the Kadiri kings, effective state administration still did not depend on an intricately managed court-based bureaucracy. Rather, it was the consequence of the ruler's network-building activities, which included his political patronage and reciprocal relations (including marriage alliances) with a variety of subordinate local lords, as well as religious initiatives that incorporated local temples and shrines into a hierarchical ritual network that centered on the court and its sacred temple sites. Therefore, the potential rise of competing centers remained a concern. In sum, these royal initiatives are indicative of the reality that local elites of various sorts might challenge not only royal despotism but, more broadly, royal authority.

Throughout this period relations between the court and its component parts were fragile and often in a state of flux. Local elites retained strategic importance in the Kadiri polity, as nobles and lords with direct access to the workforce and provincial products were in a strong position to check or challenge royal despotism. Since regional elites simultaneously functioned as managers of the component parts of the state's administrative infrastructure, they could determine any realignments of loyalties or resources that occurred whenever a center of monarchical authority diminished and other potential claimants competed to assume the maharaja title. For example, a Kadiri-era inscription dated 1194 details that "when the king was forced out of the Katangkatang *kraton*," named individuals with local ties who remained loyal were justly rewarded (Brandes: 1913, lxxiii). This inscription suggests that rivalry among different branches of the royal family was beneficial to the local elite (and similarly to local temples), who could reap rewards for their loyalty to one or another court faction.

THE DEVELOPMENT OF THE JAVANESE MARKETPLACE
AND THE CHANGING USES OF CASH

This is a good place to review the history of the Javanese markets and their coinage. The earliest Southeast Asian source that lists foreign traders (*vani-*

grama/banigrama) is the Kalirungan Sanskrit inscription dated 883, from Kedu in central Java. Its list includes merchants from Campa (Champa), Remman (Ramanyadesa in lower Burma), Kmira (Khmer/Cambodia), Kling (Kalinga, India's southeast coast), Aryya (Aryapura/Ayyavole, west-coast India), Pandikara (Karnataka), and Singhala (Sri Lanka) (Wisseman Christie: 1998a, 244; Sarkar: 1972, 217). A 1021 inscription from Cane in the Brantas River delta lists Kling, Aryya, Singhala, Pandikira (Pandyas), Drawida (Cholas), Campa (Champa), Remman, and Kmir; inscriptions from the 1040s and 1050s change Drawida to Colika, replace Pandikira with Karnataka, and add Malyala (Malayalam-speaking seafarers from the Malabar Coast) to this list (Brandes: 1913, lvii, lix; Barrett Jones: 1984, 178–94; Wisseman Christie, 1998a, 245–46).

Java is perhaps unique among its early Southeast Asia contemporaries in that it incorporated members of these communities into its political system. By the late thirteenth century members of these trade communities served as tax farmers (*wargga kilalan*), who as individuals were recruited to act as the Java rulers' revenue agents. Among these were said to be Kling, Aryya, Singhala, Karnataka, Cina (Chinese), Campa, Mandisa(?), Caremin (Ramanyadesa), and Kmir (Poerbatjarak: 1936, 378; Wisseman Christie: 1998a, 246ff). Notably, the various south Indian merchants were by then collectively categorized as Karnataka, if they came from the Tamil-speaking regions, or as Kling (Kalinga), if they came from the east-coast regions further north. Perhaps the greatest change is the inclusion of Chinese (Cina) merchants, which would have important implications for the coinage used in Java's economy.

In Java's epigraphy, there are frequent references to the utilization of money (or the weights of precious metals relative to monetary equivalents) in payments of taxes or the purchase of land. Evidence of the use of locally minted coinage begins in the eighth century. Inscriptions from then until the thirteenth century consistently include monetary terms such as *atak* (?), *pirak* (a general term for silver), and *mas* (a general term for gold). References to both silver and gold coins include monetary units such as the *kupang* (0.60 grams), the *masa* (equal to four kupang and weighing 2.40 grams), the *suvarna* (equal to sixteen masa or sixty-four kupang), the *karsapana* (equal to one suvarna), and the *ka/kati* (equal to sixteen suvarna). Coin hoards support these calculations and demonstrate the existence of a standardized weight system in which precious metals were the medium of exchange and value, and a standard of deferred payment (Wicks: 1986, 47).

Epigraphic evidence documents the gradual adoption of smaller units of weight and value. This pattern suggests that the silver and gold coins were initially used for redistributive or hoarding purposes rather than for marketplace transactions. The early epigraphic records support this conclusion, as they unanimously report large metallic values, as appropriate to temple donations and feasts of redistribution. These are often the transactions or obligations of entire villages rather than those of individuals. Later smaller coinage units would seem to have resulted from the region's greater involvement in the Indian Ocean trade and subsequent increases in marketplace transactions, which called for the use of smaller-denomination coinage by the eleventh century.

The distribution of coinage finds indicates that before the thirteenth century money use was restricted to the two core population centers in central and east Java. Central Java produced the most varied of the earliest coinage, perhaps due to the generally weak degree of administrative integration among the central Java eco-regions. In the Kedu plain there was a preference for silver, while in the sites to the east and west gold coins predominated. Areas to the west were in contact with the Sumatra-based Srivijaya realm and its legendary treasury of gold, while east Java similarly had a more substantial external commercial, political, and economic focus (Wicks: 1992, 219–99; Guillot, et al.: 1994).

Irregular, stamped silver ingots and silver sandalwood flower coins are concentrated in the Kedu Plain region of central Java. The 1225 text by Zhao Rugua, superintendent of maritime trade at the China-coast port of Quanzhou, described them as follows.

> [The central Javanese] cut up leaves of silver to make coins for business purposes, one coin of which is exchanged by the government for one *hu* and two *tou* [approximately twelve bushels] of rice. The people of central Java use as a medium of trade pieces of alloyed silver cut into bits like dice and bearing the seal of the Fan Guan [a foreign trade official] stamped on it. Six of these counters are worth one tael of trade gold, and each one may be exchanged for from thirty or forty up to one hundred *shong* [pecks] of rice. For all their other trading they use [this money] which is called '*shobo kin*' ["Java money"]. (Hirth and Rockhill: 1911, 81–83)

In this passage Zhao Rugua identifies two coinage sorts, silver coinage for local exchange and gold coinage for external trade. He goes on to say that most local officials were paid in local produce (perishables), while commanders of troops, who had to take their belongings with them, were paid in more mobile gold. Most local crimes that resulted in fines were also payable in gold coinage (only robbers and thieves received death sentences). According to this overview of the Javanese economy during the early thirteenth century, monetization affected commercial activity and military and fiscal administration, although local transactions were still largely exchanges of produce.

Sandalwood flower currency was not unique to central Java. Such currency, struck in silver, gold, and electrum (a goldlike mineral), is preeminent among the earliest coin finds. Gold sandalwood flower currency was issued roughly from 800 to 1300, initially from sites on the coast of Sumatra and the peninsular Thailand area of Nakhon Sri Tammarat/Suratthani that were known to be connected to the southeastern Sumatra–based Srivijayan realm, though slightly smaller and less finely engraved versions of the gold sandalwood flower currency were also being issued in Java by the ninth century (Wicks: 1986, 51). Javanese silver coinage duplicated the gold currency, although the obverse of the four-petaled Javanese sandalwood flower coin contains the letter *ma* (*masa*)—generally the reverse of Java's early coins is blank. The earliest examples of Javanese silver currency are flat and thick; later coins are broader, with a noticeable convexity.

A gold bullet- or disc-like coin began to circulate in Java and the Philippines during the ninth to the twelfth centuries. Modern Filipino scholars call these Piloncito coins, since they are in the shape of the unrefined sugar cones commonly sold in Philippine marketplaces. These coins circulated in central and east Java sites, while the gold and sandalwood flower coins are concentrated in central and west Java sites. The Javanese coins are distinguished from those minted in the Philippines by their rounded or angular square incuse with two beads (shaped like the seed of the sesamum plant) and a central line between them in relief. These are wide at the bottom and taper to a point; the reverse is inscribed with the single Sanskrit character *ta* (Wicks: 1992, 289).

Chinese copper cash minted in China was used in Java at least as early as the late twelfth century, and it replaced gold and silver coinage by roughly 1300. Zhao Rugua's 1225 text mentions that by this date Chinese merchants were already "in the habit of smuggling copper cash out of China for bartering for pepper in Java" (Hirth and Rockhill, 1911, 78). He characterized Java as a magnet for copper, gold, and silver, which was exchanged for pepper, cloves, and nutmeg. Hence there was an influx of Chinese coinage into Java, as well as Western currencies from both the Middle East and India (Hirth and Rockhill: 1911, 1–39). It is unclear from his account whether the copper was being used as a commodity or as a currency; his reference to the barter for pepper suggests the latter was the case at that time. The influx of Chinese coinage brought changes in the way goods were valued and fines calculated. The latest inscriptions in old Javanese script with the traditional *ku, ka, su*, and *ma* units are dated to 1294 and 1296, and by 1350 inscriptions use *picis/ pasis* in reference to Chinese copper cash currency (Poerbatjarak: 1940; Pigeaud: 1960–1963, 1:104–7, 3:151–55).

This currency transition was due partly to changes in China. By the twelfth century, the financially hard-pressed Song court no longer restricted the overseas activities of China's merchant community. Instead the Song court encouraged Chinese merchants to pursue foreign trade rather than wait for goods to arrive at China's ports on foreign ships and at the initiative of non-Chinese. In the minds of the Song rulers the resulting increase in trade volume would be a major source of vital tax revenues (Hartwell: 1967, 284–85; Wheatley: 1959, 37–38, 100–1, 113, 115; Vogel: 1993, 309–53). Due to this change the Chinese soon displaced South Asia merchants as the most numerous group of foreign traders in Southeast Asia (Reid: 1999b, 56–84; Manguin: 1994; Heng: 2008).

The adoption of Chinese cash was the result of the increasing role played by Java as a major international trading center during the thirteenth century. Yet it was also the culmination of a broad developmental process extending over several centuries. As described in chapter 4, in the eighth and ninth centuries, when Javanese civilization was based in central Java, ritualized transactions had been the norm. At that time gold and silver coinage was primarily used in ceremonial redistributions related to temple endowments and public feasts and had only a secondary role in commercial transactions (Wisseman Christie: 1993, 1996). Minted in relatively large denominations, coins were used in large-scale endowments to temples made by a limited number of wealthy donors who were primarily members of the political elite, or by entire villages (Barrett Jones: 1984, 59–90).

By the late twelfth century, low-denomination, locally minted gold and silver coinage had been introduced in the more externally focused east Java–based polities that were then culturally dominant. These smaller denominations of pre-Chinese coins supported a developing socioeconomy in which coinage had become a vital element. By the fourteenth century, when Chinese copper cash came to be widely used for all varieties of economic purposes, and not just as a commodity for barter exchange, definitive evidence substantiates that coinage was functioning at all levels of an evolving and complex Javanese polity (Aelast: 1995).

In their reflections on recent archeological recoveries in Java and its Straits of Melaka neighbors, scholars argue that the use of copper coinage in Java (and elsewhere in Southeast Asia) was initially for local market exchanges. The court elite, they reason, received precious imports via diplomatic exchanges, or used higher-value gold and silver coinage or bullion in their "administered" transactions with commercial outsiders. Tribute and fines were annually collected from villages in kind rather than in cash. Thus, the court had little initial need for coinage—the court did not need to create coinage simply to re-collect it. Nor did Java's kings use coins to promote their own image. Java-minted coins, as noted above, did not incorporate a king's portrait or name, in contrast to contemporary currency in South Asia that prominently displayed the images of kings as a statement of legitimacy. Proof that there was a local need for coinage, to acquire imported commodities if not to facilitate a wider range of local material consumption, is provided by the heavy concentrations of ceramics imported to South Asia from Yuan and Ming China, and also from neighboring Thailand, Champa, and Vietnam (Miksic: 2010b). Conversion to the use of copper coinage by the Java court was in part due to the court's incorporation of local initiative; Java's courts did not impose coinage use from the top down, but it was a consequence of the profusion of new local marketplaces, and the need for coinage in their marketplace transactions.

6

The Temple-Based Mainland Political Economies of Angkor Cambodia and Pagan Burma, ca. 889–1300

While the last two chapters introduced the evidence of an evolution in east Java from the eighth through the fourteenth centuries, this chapter studies the roughly parallel transformations in Khmer and Burmese civilizations that came to be based in Angkor Cambodia and Pagan Burma, at their height from the ninth through the thirteenth centuries. The introduction to this book criticized scholarship that measured Southeast Asian states by the number of stone temple complexes they left—the more impressive the archeological remains, the more prosperous and accomplished the state, or so the reasoning goes. Thus, the massive court temple complexes of Angkor Cambodia and Pagan Burma suggest that accomplished political systems were responsible for their construction, through a central administration that mobilized a realm's wealth and manpower to create these architectural wonders. But historians are now coming to find that the expected broad levels of social, economic, and political integration were not necessary for such construction, and that the building of impressive religious edifices does not necessarily demonstrate the political accomplishments of each society.

Chapter 3 demonstrated that Cham civilization's impressive temple complex remains did not correspond to expected levels of political integration; in common with other early island world riverine and coastal states, Champa was never more than a succession of regional Indic kingdoms that were based in one or another of the Cham realm's networked regional upstream-downstream Indic kingdoms, which never converged into a continuously centralized polity. Likewise chapter 4's discussion of the central Java polities is sensitive to the early Java elite's inability to forge a functional unity, as there were at least two alliance-backed competing networked lines of Hindu and Buddhist patronizing kings that laid the foundations for the greater centralization of Java monarchy from the ninth century. But when the center of Javanese polity shifted to east Java, large temple complexes were replaced by impressive courts. In the cases of Cambodian and Burmese civilizations, the legacies of lesser centralized predecessor polities were continued under eleventh- to thirteenth-century Angkor and Pagan Hindu and Buddhist kings, whose coincidental court and temple constructions were indicative of their temple-centered polities.

THE KHMER EMPIRE IN HISTORICAL OVERVIEW

The Angkor kingdom (802–1432 CE), based in what is now Cambodia, once included the adjacent regions of lowland Thailand and Laos. Historians use the name Angkor ("city") to refer to both the ancient capital city and the ancient kingdom. The boundaries of the realm were never clearly defined, and Angkor is best understood as a growing confederation of populations willing to submit to a central authority (Vickery: 1986).

Angkor was the successor to previous Khmer regional states centered in the middle Mekong River basin. These states began to leave inscriptions in the sixth century CE. Whether due to the limits on local agricultural production in the south, due to the vulnerability of the south to Cham raids, or to have a more strategic position in relation to the variety of communication channels of the mainland, Angkor recentered on the northern edge of Cambodia's Great Lake (Tonle Sap) in the ninth century. Its productive wet-rice agriculture system depended on the annual monsoon rainy season that flooded Khmer fields. Several rulers constructed enormous reservoirs (*baray*) and a network of canals around their capital city to provide a secure source of irrigation that would significantly increase their realm's agricultural productivity, and to reinforce the ritual symbolism of their capital.

The Angkor state was founded by King Jayavarman II (r. 802–834), who established the state *devaraja* (god-king) cult that celebrated the unity of the Khmer people under the favor of the Hindu god Siva. Jayavarman's capital was at Hariharalaya, southeast of Angkor. Angkor became the realm's continuing capital under Yasovarman I (r. 889–910), and was named Yasodharapura in his honor. Suryavarman I (r. 1002–1050) extended the Angkor state's territory in all directions and consolidated its political authority. Suryavarman II (r. 1113–1150) defended Angkor against its Champa neighbors based in central and southern Vietnam, and also sponsored the construction of the Angkor Wat temple complex, dedicated to the Hindu god Visnu.

In 1177, Champa forces raided Angkor, desecrated its temples, and carried off the state's wealth and significant numbers of its people. Jayavarman VII (r. 1181–1218) restored order through a series of military victories against regional opponents, then successfully defended his realm against the Chams. He also built a new capital city adjacent to Angkor Wat at Angkor Thom, which he centered on the Bayon Mahayana Buddhist shrine.

Following the death of Jayavarman VII, the Angkor state gradually declined, evidenced by the decreased number of inscriptions recording state activities. When the Chinese envoy Zhou Daguan visited Angkor in 1295–1296, he described a royal city in decay, which he attributed to a series of exhausting wars against Thai armies.

The armies of the region of Thai Ayudhya, based in former Angkor territories in the north and west, sacked the Angkor capital in 1431 and carried Angkor's royal regalia back to the Thai capital, where it remains to this day as the symbolic source of Thai political authority. After 1432, Cambodian rulers continued to rule from Angkor until the Khmer capital shifted to Phnom Penh on the Mekong River at the end of the fifteenth century (Vickery: 1977).

The Khmer Political Economy

Angkor's temples and their associated epigraphy provide an example of the eventual linkage of a temple-centered polity, suggesting that, at least at first, Angkor had been able to found itself on an elaborate network of temples without developing an equally elaborate secular administration. At the beginning of the Angkor age, Khmer temples were centers of redistribution in the continuous movement of products within the Khmer countryside. Khmer temples collected and ultimately returned to the countryside a significant portion of the local output, which was redistributed according to the wealth, power, or prestige of the recipients. However, with the temple network as its base, Khmer society eventually went beyond primary redistributive integration and reached a higher level of centralized economic control. The massive public-works projects directed by Khmer monarchs, highlighted by Suryavarman II's construction of Angkor Wat in the early twelfth century and the equally impressive Angkor Thom built by Jayavarman VII at the end of the same century, required a degree of economic and social integration high enough to provide the economic resources and service relationships necessary to fund and carry out these projects. They could not be supplied by a simple redistributive economy. Rather, goods and services from the Khmer agrarian system had to be channeled into the hands of those representatives of the state who were responsible for the achievement of broadly political goals. They in turn used these resources to create an integrated state polity.

Although separate mechanisms of administration developed in each temple, Khmer temples were never autonomous from Khmer society and its stratified political order. At the primary level, Khmer temples were subject to the authority of the elite and were an instrument through which the elite reinforced their economic and political control. Members of elite families were often members of the temple's staff, and the staff of a local temple was frequently supervised by members of the local landholding elite who had entered the clergy or by priests who owed their positions and prosperity to patronage by that elite. Normally, construction of a temple legitimized and accompanied the consolidation of the elite's land rights into an estate, and income from specified estate lands supported the temple's activities. Collections, gifts, and offerings flowed in to the temple as part of the cycle of economic redistribution. They flowed back outward in the form of support for construction and ritual performances and in so doing reinforced the prowess of the elite as patrons of the temple deity and as the source of prosperity.

By the height of the Angkor era, from roughly 1000 to 1200, local temples and their cults were linked in a statewide network of temples that was ultimately tied to the king's central temple at the royal capital. Priests from local temples participated in rituals at major royal temples that were constructed at strategic points throughout the state. The priests and their aristocratic patrons derived legitimacy from this participation, while helping to finance the activities of the royal temples by assigning to them a portion of the local temples' annual collections. Thus, under the guise of religion, Khmer monarchs, in partnership with the royal temples and their staffs, could draw part of their realm's wealth into the royal capital without employing an elaborate secular administration to collect revenues in the state's name. As suggested by inscriptions of the period, the development of the temple network ran parallel to the emergence of early Khmer sovereignty, and the temples consistently served as centers for the collection of economic resources (Mabbett: 1978; Higham: 2001).

Thus, temples were the centers of and the means for redistributing economic and symbolic capital, as well as providing the spiritual motivations behind the donations and the economic consequences thereof, thereby enabling the temple network to integrate the Khmer realm in two ways. On the one hand, temples linked disparate agricultural regions horizontally into an ever-expanding economic network whose wealth fueled the Khmer state. On the other hand, temples were also the locus for the manipulation of cultural symbols that vertically integrated the various levels of Khmer society. As institutions embedded within the traditional socioeconomy, temples assumed the leading role of, as one scholar describes it, "limiting and dis-guising the play of economic interests and calculations" (Bourdieu: 1977, 172). While this chapter is substantially focused on these economic calcula-tions and treats temples and donations as materialistic, we cannot downplay the spiritual/religious significance of all these resources flowing into the tem-ples. The importance of a common Khmer spiritual bond was critical to Jaya-varman VII's (r. 1181–1218) restoration of the Angkor realm following a dynastic crisis and devastating Cham raids, which will be examined at the end of this chapter.

To understand better the role of temples, we begin by examining the role of Khmer religion in the years preceding the reign of Jayavarman II (r. 802–834), which would be a watershed in the development of the Khmer religious system.

Temples and Statecraft in Pre-Angkor Society

The principal concern of the leaders of early Khmer society, as reflected in their epigraphy, was the establishment and endowment of local temples, for which they accrued religious merit and economic return. Key figures in the foundation of these early temples were the consensual leaders of local soci-ety, rather than persons claiming royal authority. Inscriptions recording such activities emphasize the religious prowess rather than the physical might of the local elites who were establishing the temples. Regional leaders (*pon*) emerged who held official titles assigned by those claiming royal sovereignty. However, those claiming the supreme authority to rule over the Khmer people essentially legitimized their sovereignty by bestowing titles on preexisting rural leaders, giving them "new" authority as district officers (*mratan*) in the state administration. In such a way dominant landholders, and the preexisting local economic, social, and political leadership, became members of a devel-oping state system.

The emerging aristocracy also worshipped local and state divinities to "acquire merit" and to "exhibit devotion" (Coedes: *IC*, 2:135). Inscriptions celebrated the presentation of temple gifts by local leaders as part of their worship, applauding the wealth of those making the gifts through the records of their carefully calculated donations. The elite sponsors of this epigraphy emphasized that their gifts to temples were their foremost means to ensure the continued prosperity of their dependent society.

The literacy of the temples' patrons was also acclaimed in the inscriptions recording gifts, as if this literacy, in addition to the merit they acquired as temple benefactors, legitimized the donors' status as the leaders of society. Gifts were normally provided not by single officials but by several officials, members of the aristocracy, who made endowments as a group rather than as individuals, denoting the existence of familial bonds among the Khmer aristocracy, who may or may not have been blood relatives. The landed elites' patronage of temples as a communal group, thus, may be seen as in some way formalizing their political alliances. For example, a man who could not afford to build and endow a temple by himself might take up a collection from those who would benefit by the gift.

The Khmer aristocracy concentrated economic resources under a temple's administration, whether to acquire the spiritual merit associated with such donations, allow for a more efficient management of elite resources, or avoid the revenue demands of those political authorities claiming rights to a share of the local authority's possessions. Temple beneficence was a means to consolidate political, economic, and ritual authority by transferring income rights to land to temples. Boundaries of donated lands were clearly defined in the inscriptions, usually by reference to places such as a village, an estate, a pond, or the riceland of another landholder. Past and present holders of income rights to the assigned lands were enumerated, along with the mode of the property's acquisition and its price if acquired by purchase (Coedes: 1937–1966, 6:32); the land's productivity (rice yield) was even estimated. Inscriptions reporting assignments of populated land gave the parcel's current occupants and spelled out what portion of the occupants' production was assigned to the temple. Unpopulated land received an assigned labor force to bring the land under cultivation, to the temple's benefit. The variety of laborers—males, females, females with children—and their ethnic identity (e.g., Mon or Khmer) were counted and recorded (Coedes: *IC*, 5:7).

It is not uncommon to discover that the relatives of the donors of such land endowments were members of the priesthood servicing the local temple, who became managers of the assigned property (Coedes: *IC*, 3:180–92; 5:143–46; 7:104–19). In many instances the donor family rather than the temple staff managed family land assigned to a temple, the temple receiving only a designated share of the income. What donors transferred was not ownership of the land, but the right to income from the land. As explained in chapter 1, control over manpower and production rather than ownership of land was critical for the development of early Southeast Asian states. To Khmer elites, "landholding" meant rights to the production and labor service of the inhabitants of a parcel of land rather than absolute possession of it. In land donations to temples, only certain rights over the land were transferred; while inhabitants of the assigned land normally continued to farm the land, the recipient temple collected much or all of their production. Donated property was usually subject to a combination of claims, those of the temple receiving the donation as well as those of the donor's family, who retained certain personal rights to the property—for example, the right to a share of the land's production as well as administrative or political rights over the inhabitants.

The economic diversity of local temples is reflected in the variety of donations "for the service of the property" assigned: domesticated animals, goats, buffalo, cattle, coconut palms, fruit trees, areca nuts, betel leaves, clothing, and a threshing floor, plus numerous individual objects, are examples (Coedes: *IC*, 2:21–23, 37, 123, 135, 154, 200, 5:39; 6:47, 49, 62). The type and size of gifts to temples indicate not only economic specialization within early Khmer society in order to create such wealth, but also the developing institutional capacity to utilize and administer this production. An economic system was emerging, centered in the temple. The assignments of land and its production by Khmer aristocrats turned temples into local storage centers; goods deposited in temple storehouses were a source of social and economic power, reinforcing the prestige of the temples' primary benefactors, the locally powerful, who influenced the redistribution of the temples' stores in support of their followers (including those working for the temple).

The concentration in temples of the authority to manage local resources had a significant impact on the process of political integration. The implication of such centralization for economic control is reflected in epigraphic references to the "joining together for the enjoyment of the gods," whereby a single or several landholders shifted a share of the income (goods and services) destined to one god or temple to that of another, or amalgamated the administration of one temple's lands with that of another (Coedes: *IC*, 2:23, 200; 5:15, 87; 6:49). This joining together or joint usufruct is termed *samparibhoga* or *misrabhoga* (Ricklefs: 1967). Regional temple networks came to be sustained and controlled by secular elite with landholding rights, who transferred some of these income rights to the productivity of their lands or donated material goods (local produce) and services to temples in the network.

During the Angkor era *misrabhoga* amalgamation arrangements were normally not undertaken without the approval of the king himself, but in pre-Angkor society private holders of land rights and not a royal authority dominated the concentration of economic resources and the amalgamation of temple administration. Prior to the ninth century Khmer monarchs were concerned only with recruiting as their allies the local elites who held land rights, who had initiated such transfers and consolidations, confirming the transactions rather than challenging them. Royal edicts, although expressing concern for land, never claim that the monarchy's authority over land supersedes that of the local landed elites (Coedes: *IC*, 2:12, 39, 45, 117, 121, 199; 3:145; 5:25, 30; Barth and Bergaigne: 1885–1893, 42, 44, 46, 51, 60).

Within the Khmer realm networked religious foundations (i.e., temples) of powerful local families, who held official titles in the Khmer state's administration, were a means of integrating the land and its production into the structure of the state (Sedov: 1963, 73–81). Family temples and their properties became networked subordinates to central temples placed strategically throughout the realm. A portion of the production collected by private temples was channeled to the state temples. In return, the priests of local family temples received validation through periodic participation in the rituals of the central temples. Local family cults also became legitimized via their worship by Khmer monarchs and their subordination to royal cults. In these times temples were not just religious centers but important links in the state's economic and political network. Religion supplied an ideology and a structure that could organize the populace to produce while enabling the state to tap this production and secure a region's political subordination without the aid of separate secular economic or political institutions.

The Integration of Indian and Local Religion in Pre-Angkor Society

While their foremost essence was spiritual, in early Cambodia temples and temple ceremony not only played an important role in the management of local resources, but also legitimized political (and by implication economic) integration through localized Hindu forms of religion, especially Saivite religion, which reinforced existing indigenous symbols of authority relationships. Since Siva was known in the Indic tradition as the Lord of the Mountain, proprietors of early temples were able to connect the worship of Siva to local beliefs in the sanctity of mountains, which were believed to be the abode of ancestor spirits responsible for the prosperity of the living and the fertility of the land. These fertility spirits were represented in early Cambodia by a stone or metal phallus usually inserted upright in a circular "vulva." Technically speaking, these traditional ritual objects became a male linga inserted in a female yoni once associated specifically with Siva. As was the case in neighboring Champa, as discussed in chapter 3, Khmer linga became the focal ritual objects in early temples in a localization of Siva, the Indic god of fertility, and traditional fertility spirits.

These linga cults also promoted the chief's prowess, and indeed early Khmer epigraphy glorified rulers in terms of their personal and spiritual achievements and their consequent ability to reward their subjects with prosperity in this life and the next. The nature of the relationship of cult to politics is indicated by the reign of Jayavarman I (657–681), who was based in northern Cambodia and northeastern Thailand (a region the Chinese knew as Zhenla). As Jayavarman I extended his authority over local communities, he did so in part by bestowing legitimacy on local temples, as he awarded *mra-tan* titles to submissive local elites (Higham: 2001, 39–52). Jayavarman I's inscriptions document his attempt to play a role in validating regional land rights as these specifically related to property endowments made to temples, though he clearly did not have the authority to block such land transactions. What is significant here is the local acknowledgment of his rightful participation and his referential role as the means of asserting the transaction's validity.

The nature of Jayavarman's integration of the local and Hindu religious traditions is revealed in a seventh-century inscription in which Jayavarman ordered bondsmen to be brought to a prominent chief and then allocated them as resources among the monarch's sanctuaries in a certain area (Coedes: *IC*, 2:117; Aeusrivongse: 1976, 115). In this inscription "Hindu" gods shared the "domain" of a tree spirit (this spirit is also named in a 611 inscription that recorded the merging of arrangements for maintaining a "Hindu" god's cult with those in honor of a sacred tree) (Coedes: *IC*, 2:21–23). In these two instances, the local tree spirit acquired a direct relationship with a political overlord (Jayavarman) as well as with "Hindu" gods. The local spirit was thereby provided a place in the "Hindu" pantheon and also in the network of social and political relationships that defined seventh-century Khmer society in that early period of overlordship. The familiar local spirit became identified with the more abstract and universal Indian deities and was thus upgraded to an entity with greater distinction than was previously the case. Throughout Khmer history no single Khmer chief or monarch monopolized the "Hindu" materials. Khmer elites/chiefs as a whole were involved as early religious and political relationships overlapped. Seventh-century Khmer chiefs did, however, refer to themselves as worshippers (*bhakta*) of their overlords (Wolters: 1979b; Vickery: 1998). They explained this homage as being due to their overlord's special spiritual relationship with Siva, which brought rewards to those who served him. Subordinate chiefs, with their own devotional cults, offered Siva gifts as tokens of their devotion to powerful political overlords such as Jayavarman. The "Hindu" cults in honor of Siva heightened the political subordinate's devotion to Siva and thereby called attention to a network of relationships in early Khmer society. All this was important background to the devaraja cult that would be established by Jayavarman II, a cult that would form an important watershed in the development of the Khmer state.

The Devaraja Cult of Jayavarman II

During the reign of Jayavarman II (r. 802–ca. 834) the above arrangements were formalized in the devaraja cult, which focused the integration of Indian and local conceptions in the person of the king, while also refocusing the sacred power and resource control away from the local and toward the state. The institution of the devaraja cult was therefore an important step in strengthening the Khmer monarchy, and for this reason Jayavarman II's reign marks the beginning of the Angkor era proper.

Jayavarman's invocation ritual was important as much for where he performed it as for the content of the ritual itself. The devaraja cult was based on a mountaintop at the center of the royal capital that became the site of the realm's principal temple (Wolters: 1973, 29–30). It drew on both local and Indian conceptions. In the Brahmanical concept of the universe, seven oceans and continents surrounded a circular central continent, Jambudvipa. The sun, the moon, and the stars revolved around Mount Meru, which arose at the center of this continent. On Meru's summit was the city of the gods, where Indra, the Lord of Heaven, reigned. The Buddhist concept was somewhat different as Mount Meru was the center of seven seas and seven mountain ranges, with four continents strategically situated in an ocean beyond these seven mountain ranges; Jambudvipa was the southernmost of these. Guardians of the World resided in the lowest of paradises (Lokapala), located at the base of Mount Meru. Cambodia's capital was a local realization of this realm. Jayavarman II accordingly centered his cult of the devaraja at his capital city of Hariharalaya, south of Angkor on the edge of the Great Lake (Tonle Sap) in central Cambodia, on the summit of Mount Mahendra (Great Indra), the Khmer equivalent of Mount Meru, although he had initiated the cult at Phnom Kulen, a small mountain located some thirty miles (fifty kilometers) northeast (upstream) of the site that would become known as Angkor. Yasovarman I (r. 889–910) moved the capital and the "mountain" to Yasodhapura, the site of present-day Angkor. However, because the complexes at this site continue the patterns initiated by Jayavarman II, the Angkor period is considered to begin with Jayavarman II's reign.

Like his predecessors in the pre-Angkor period, Jayavarman II built his Khmer state through a combination of conquest and the formation of networks of personal alliances. However, the devaraja cult was an important additional tool of political integration, for it consolidated the worship of regional deities into the worship of the royal devaraja, Jayavarman II (Kulke: 1978). As it did so, the cult incorporated local veneration for mountains, subordinated local ancestor spirits to the worship of Siva, and then proclaimed Jayavarman II to be Siva's representative on earth. By associating himself with Siva and the royal mountain, the king symbolized his ability to guarantee the flow of life-power from the spirit realm to his subjects. His establishment of the devaraja cult also tied Jayavarman spiritually to his supporters. More importantly, the cult became an emblem of the unification of the Khmer realm. Henceforth, although there were struggles for power within the royal domain, struggles for local independence lacked religious sanction (Wolters: 1973). From Jayavarman II's time onward, the Khmer monarch could monopolize temporal power within his realm, power that was justified by a royal cult in which the king alone could represent the supreme Indian deity at the pinnacle (often Siva or Visnu). In theory, the Lord of the Heavens (the supreme Indian deity) protected the royal capital and its realm, while the king, his representative on earth, was the Lord of the Mountains, the guardian of law and order, the protector of religion, the defender of his land against external foes, the source of fertility, and the sum of all authority on earth. Thus, from the summit of Mount Mahendra (Mount Meru, the center of the universe), the devaraja entered into a ritual partnership with the divine world.

The most important aspect of Jayavarman's devaraja cult was its incorporation of local deities and indigenous ancestor worship into the state's religious ceremony. While earlier Khmer monarchs had to some extent brought together the local and Indic gods, the native and universal divine had always been worshipped separately. The indigenous belief system of Cambodia held that at death the spirit passed into the realm of the ancestors, and death rites ushered the spirit into this world of the dead. However, this entry into the realm of the dead was not terminal. In return for faithful worship of the dead, the ancestors granted a certain life-power to the living. These ancestral spirits were also traditionally important as protectors of the local realm. In local belief a chief was the repository of their prowess and could activate their powers on his subjects' behalf. To proclaim their legitimacy, Jayavarman II and subsequent Khmer monarchs merged these beliefs with worship of Indic deities such as Siva, Visnu, and the Buddha. Beginning with the reign of Jayavarman II, Khmer monarchs did not build temples or invoke the cults of past monarchs just to honor their ancestors. Rather, they also installed the traditional spiritual protectors of their ancestors and past kings in their central temple compound as a means of symbolically and physically invoking the king's authority over his lesser elite. In addition, the icons and lingas of gods placed in the central and subordinate temples of the Khmer realm were respectively portraits and symbols of kings, whose names fused the monarchs' personal titles with the names of the gods.

It should be noted that the devaraja cult and the Khmer royal cults that were created in its image exalted but did not deify the reigning monarch. At their deaths, however, the Khmer monarchs became divine. The royal temple was dedicated to the living monarch, but it also became the mausoleum of the god-king when he died, enabling the reigning king to draw on the deceased king's superhuman powers. Thus, for example, Jayavarman's successor, Indravarman I (r. 877–889), constructed a stone temple to shelter the royal Siva-linga Indresvara in which resided the devaraja, the deceased Jaya-varman. The immortal Jayavarman, who was known posthumously as the divine Paramesvara, thus empowered the new Indresvara linga (Barth and Bergaigne: 1885–1893, 370; Jacques: 1978, 1997).

The specific Indian deity at the pinnacle of the system varied over time. Although initially Khmer kings such as Jayavarman II and Indravarman I were identified with Siva, in the early twelfth century Suryavarman II assumed a similarly intimate relationship with Visnu and built Angkor Wat to honor this union. At the end of the same century, as will be discussed below, Jayavarman VII became in his own lifetime the earthly embodiment of the bodhisattva Lokesvara, who decorated the faces of Angkor Thom's Bayon temple complex and was honored in a new Buddharaja royal cult. Whether identified with Siva, Visnu, or the Buddha, the Khmer king was the intermediary between humankind and the divinity, the upholder of the estab-lished order (dharma) handed down by his ancestors, the intercessor with the spirit world for the fertility and prosperity of his realm. His capital city, with his focal royal temple at its center, was constructed in the image of the uni-verse interpreted in terms of the Indic Mount Meru (Briggs: 1951).

The key religious elite of the Khmer realm were not legalistic Brahmins but devotional Brahmin (*bhakti*) ascetics, "wayward Brahmins" who were not interested in Vedic ritual sacrifices and preferred to stress Siva's grace rather than the laws of orthodox Hinduism (Wolters: 1979b). Gifts to Siva or to any other Indic or local deity linked to him brought one merit and the hope of a superior death status (Coedes: *IC*, 1:15; 2:151; 3:163; 4:326; 8; see chap-ter 3). In this system it was not a Brahmin priest as in Vedic India, but a political overlord, an aristocrat with landholding rights who conceptually par-took of divinity, who had the foremost spiritual influence on his followers' lives and their hopes for salvation. While Brahmins appear in the epigraphy over the long term as the custodians of ritual, secular landholding elite per-formed customary ritual roles, which provided the opportunity for those of lesser spiritual prowess (*sakti*) to enhance their prospects after death. Political allegiance, expressed by personal loyalty, was based in indigenous attitudes about death and spiritual prowess. As acts of homage, and in theory to secure the favor of their overlord, subordinates offered presents to temples or erected icons or lingas in honor of the divinely empowered king (Coedes: *IC*, 5:29). Lesser landholding elites saw subordination to an overlord as providing fur-ther means of earning merit, thereby satisfying their wishes for a successful transition to the afterlife, and also enhancing their secular power (Coedes: *IC*, 2:27–28, 1124; 5:37–38). Direct gifts to ritual priests (Brahmins) were rare. Merit was earned by personal achievement, by one's donation of land rights or material objects to temples, rather than by honoring Brahmins. Temple priests were not honored because of the rituals they performed; they benefited instead through their superintendence of the temples.

Thus, Jayavarman's devaraja cult was a watershed in the history of Khmer religion. It synthesized Indian and local cults, and it enhanced the role of the king. Even though Khmer kings after Jayavarman II formulated their own royal cults, they continued to venerate his devaraja cult. Although his devaraja cult was like other previous linga cults that promoted a chief's prowess, Jayavarman's spectacular achievements guaranteed his status as an "ancestor of note" among Khmer kings who followed. His reign established new criteria for accomplishment; not only were his military victories impressive, but his religious rites employed new sacred vocabulary to proclaim his glory and abilities. He also appropriated the new secular vocabulary initiated by his predecessor Jayavarman I, replacing the old Khmer titles of regional authority *pon* (chieftains) that dated to the pre-Angkor period with new mratan titles, which also dated to pre-Angkor times, but now designated regional lords holding territories of greater significance (Vickery: 1998, 203; O'Reilly: 2006, 117–20). Furthermore, after Jayavarman's reign, succession disputes ended with the victor reaffirming his ties to the devaraja. This was more than a simple claim of royal ancestry, for it also was a claim to possess sacred power. With the backing of his divine ancestors, the new king could assure his subjects that, in return for their loyalty, he would be able to bestow upon them the magical powers embodied in the devaraja cult (Coedes and Dupont: 1943–1946; Kulke: 1978). On a practical level, loyal followers were rewarded with grants of land and court titles, duties, and symbols of status (e.g., the right to walk with a white parasol over one's head), which became the basis of continuing claims to estates and privileges by their ancestors (Higham: 2001, 51). This centralization of power was a significant development, and it would be strengthened further in the early eleventh-century reign of Suryavarman I.

Temples and Temple Networks in the Angkor Era under Suryavarman I

The reign of Suryavarman I (r. 1002–1050) marked a critical transition in the nature of Cambodian kingship. His reign was founded in warfare, as he fought his way to the throne against others with better credentials (Finot: 1904b; Coedes: 1911; Briggs: 1951, 149). Once in power, Suryavarman expanded the realm, waged periodic war with his neighbors (such as the Chams to the east), stabilized his external boundaries, and extended his resource base (Higham: 2001, 91–101). He initiated substantial territorial expansion into what is now Thailand in the west and the north and commissioned a number of diplomatic initiatives to solicit foreign trade, which enhanced his realm's commercial economy (Bourg: 1970; Mabbett and Chandler: 1995, 180–82). Most of his initiatives to construct new state temples were on the edges of his realm; these strategically placed monuments on his realm's periphery were a means of integrating regional populations into the royal domain (Briggs: 1951, 144–68).

Suryavarman I initiated a number of reforms that further concentrated administrative and symbolic power. For example, he revised the hereditary rights of the Khmer priesthood and landed elite, forcing the aristocratic families who administered royal cults and who had sided with his rivals to relinquish their prior hereditary rights and to accept buyouts or revisions in the terms of their service. Furthermore, even elite families who supported him had to be willing to subordinate their own interests to those of the king, as they were gradually incorporated into the royal administrative order. This centralization was not absolute, however, and as an act of conciliation he sustained the reconstruction of family temples that had been desecrated in the war of succession. As a result of this activity, at least sixteen major inscriptions recording the histories of aristocratic families were issued between 1002 and 1080 (i.e., from the reign of Suryavarman to the death of Harshavarman III) (Bourge: 1970; Sahai: 1970; 1977; Vickery: 1985; Coedes: *IC*, 7:164–89).

Meanwhile, at Angkor, Suryavarman redesigned the royal city by expanding and refocusing the old city of Yasodharapura, where the capital had been moved during the reign of Yasovarman I (r. 889–910). Formerly centered on the Phnom Bakheng hill temple, it was now recentered on the king's royal residence and its adjacent royal temple and associated public spaces. Suryavarman is also believed to have initiated the construction of Angkor's West Baray (reservoir), which was significantly larger than the East Baray that had been constructed by Yasovarman I, and thus made a substantive statement relative to his new ritual Mount Mahendra (see below).

Suryavarman's reign was marked by substantial population growth, generalized prosperity, and increased urbanization. There were at least forty-seven "cities" (*pura*, the Sanskrit word that was added as a suffix to designate an urban center) in his realm, twenty of which appear for the first time in this period (Bourge: 1970, 308). Suryavarman encouraged the development of new lands in order to increase production that could be shared between aristocratic officials and the state (Vickery: 1985, 232ff). He sent royal inspectors to the sites of land transfers to validate transactions and to determine if the land for development was free of any competing claims from aristocratic families. Indeed, in some cases villagers were already occupying lands, and the king reassigned the rights to their production and labor to the families receiving his favor. Notably, the villagers came under the administration (*cat camnat*) of the family's temple. After conquering a territory with his armies, Suryavarman was particularly adept at incorporating the leaderships on the outer edges of his personal domain as district chiefs (*khlon visaya*), with little change in their status (Coedes: *IC*, 7:124–26; 1961, 13–18; Osborne: 1966).

Early historiography on the Khmer realm envisioned Angkor-era society as a social pyramid with the king and his elite sitting on top and little contact between them and the people below (Heine-Geldern: 1942). In Suryavarman I's realm, however, there was more interaction between the king's representatives and the local populations. The Khmer polity protected regional interests by incorporating the local concept of a status quo (i.e., the local peasantry reporting to the local aristocracy) into its formal structure instead of replacing

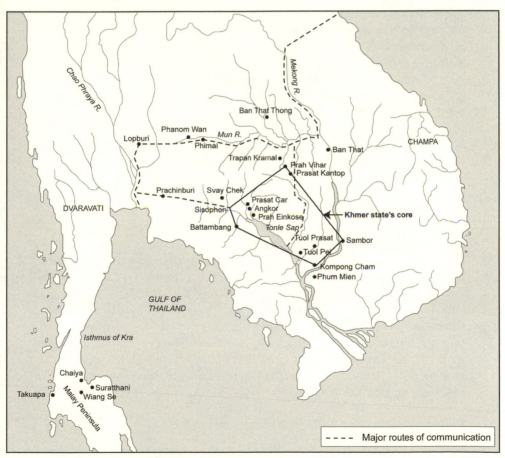

Map 6.1. Angkor in the Eleventh Century

the major local landed families with officials sent out from the capital. It further benefited local communities by making its army an umbrella available to stand guard, maintaining order in the regions under state control and protecting the domain from invasions. Unlike pre-Angkor inscriptions, which denote a limited presence of court officials at the local level, Suryavarman's inscriptions indicate the physical presence of royal officials (*tamrvac*) to act as the king's eyes and ears, administer the transfer of land, and directly collect revenues due to the king. The inscriptions also mention local visits made by the royal retinue (*kamsten*). The latter was a mobile body of state administrators who traveled from place to place within the realm. Holding religious rather than secular titles, the kamsten settled disputes that could not be solved locally and also sat in judgment on affairs that were considered to be within the state's sphere of interest (Coedes: *IC*, 3:57–64; 4:140–50; 6:225–37).

Suryavarman's reign thus represents a critical phase in the development of an integrated Khmer polity. The Khmer temple network assumed a major role in this process. Although the prosperity of elite families in the Khmer realm—prosperity based on control over the production of land and manpower—came to depend more and more on royal favor, it also drew on the economic and ritual services of royal or family temples. During Suryavarman's reign the proportion of inscriptions emanating from royalty increased, yet by far the majority of temple construction was still inaugurated by families subordinate to the king. Though this construction often had royal encouragement, the most impressive new temple construction of that period was attributed to named officials and not viewed as being due to the king's direct initiative. This does not demonstrate any weakness at the center, but instead came about through the intensified integration of the regional aristocracy into the Khmer polity. As noted, these regionally powerful men were given official administrative titles, their authority over land and manpower was recognized, and they were charged with responsibility for the expansion of the Khmer state's economic and ritual base. Along with this recognition, however, went the responsibility of sharing their land's production with the state. Land transferred to aristocratic families was assigned specifically for the benefit of family temples, whose staffs, including members of the families, assumed responsibility for supervising their development. But because they were subordinated to royal temples, these family temples had to share the local production with the central temples and thus with the Khmer kings who had made the original assignment.

Temples and Politics under Suryavarman I

What developed through this pattern of land assignment and development was a network of private and temple landholding rights that was subject to the supervision of the monarchy. The king held the power to maintain elites with patronage and at the same time needed to prevent or neutralize the emergence of rival power centers. Elites were linked to the royal court through the Khmer temple network, if not through the bestowal of royal favor. In addition, Angkor's rulers were capable of reducing local power centers to subordinate provinces of their government. At the same time, however, "ownership" of land was embedded in a system of rights held by related people. The king in theory held the final authority to validate rights to income from land, although this authority was not normally exercised (Suryavarman I's initiatives were unusual). In theory, then, the Khmer monarch assumed the role of patron placing land under the "exclusive" control of favored families and their temples. The aristocracy, drawing their livelihood from the land, theoretically owed their continued prosperity directly or indirectly to royal favor.

Despite the appearance created by these arrangements, the Khmer state system was not highly centralized or "bureaucratic," nor was it a "feudal" order in which the king assigned administrative duties to a landed elite who derived their landholding rights and status as a consequence of the king's favor. Records of land assignments to families and their temples during the Angkor era reflect constant friction between the center and its periphery and provide evidence about the nature of the relationship between the Khmer monarch and his regional elites (Mabbett: 1977b, 1978). Even so, the king had considerable resources at his disposal. Exercising his theoretical land rights, Suryavarman dealt directly with the aristocratic families constantly opposed to his interest by dictating that henceforth their lands were to be controlled by the Khmer king's administrators and their resources merged with those of the king's temples (Coedes: *IC*, 6:254–72). However, this was not a total seizure of family lands, as aristocratic rights were not reassigned to other families.

An example of how this worked in practice is provided by the Sdok Kak Thom inscription dated 1052 (Coedes and Dupont: 1943; Briggs: 1951, 150–51, 163). In the account given in this inscription, one of the foremost families of royal officials with hereditary responsibility for the devaraja cult claimed land and rights over land administered by a family temple. These rights had been granted by a series of kings dating to Jayavarman II. New settlements (*sruk*), provisions, and manpower had been endowed to equip the temple and to guarantee the growth of the community around it. In the turmoil associated with Suryavarman I's rise to the throne, however, most of this priest/administrator landholding family had sided against Suryavarman, and this raised the problem of how to deal with the family.

After gaining authority over areas where this family held land, the newly victorious king did not confiscate this family's property and reassign its land rights to his direct supporters, as he certainly could have done as punishment for their opposition. Instead, Suryavarman forced a temple priest related to the family, who was responsible for the temple's property management, to leave the temple staff and to marry a younger sister of Suryavarman's first queen. Some of the original family's land rights were then reassigned, but in return the family was compensated with new rights over land in an area beyond the royal core where they would seemingly be less of a threat to royal interests and where their presence could have helped consolidate the royal hold on the newly conquered regions. Udayadityavarman II (1050–1066), Suryavarman's successor, renewed the endowment in the 1052 inscription, which allowed the now reconstituted family of officials to clear land overgrown by forests, consecrate temple icons, and rebuild their wealth. The inscription details the royal permissions, the titles and bondsmen granted, and the work done by each of the parties. It also notes that two lingas were placed, one by the head of the family and the other by the king in the family's honor. Also established here at this time were icons of the royal ancestors (founders of the cult of the devaraja). All this activity seems to have been a compensatory buyout of the Sivakaivalya family, whose worship of and exclusive right of guardianship over the devaraja cult had been taken away by Suryavarman.

Overall, the epigraphic records reveal two strategies used by Khmer monarchs in the land endowments of local temples: on the one hand they intervened where possible to limit the power of potential rivals, and on the other hand they rewarded and enhanced the economic strength of their supporters. After having made the endowment, Khmer kings rarely intervened in local temple affairs unless there was a direct threat to royal interests. Nevertheless, the assignment of temple endowments could be a powerful tool. Landholding rights to unpopulated and overgrown land could be reassigned, as could the land rights of extinct lineages, and we have already seen how land rights could be used to manage the delicate relationships with elite families. The point was to utilize temple land endowments as political rewards that would ensure the well-being of the king's allies, while also making use of these local elite and their familial temples as agents to enhance the Khmer realm's economic productivity, as well as its political stability. However, the temple lands were more than just tools of political reward and punishment. They were also important centers of social, political, and economic organization.

Khmer Urban and Commercial Expansion under Suryavarman I

As noted, by the beginning of the eleventh century the Khmer realm experienced a considerable upturn in its overall welfare. This prosperity was reflected in the development of concentrated population clusters in the tenth and eleventh centuries. This concentrated clustering first becomes noticeable in the epigraphy associated with the reign of Rajendravarman II (944–968), continued under Jayavarman V (968–1001), and reached its fullness under Suryavarman I (1002–1050). For example, during the reign of Jayavarman IV (928–942), the epigraphy mentioned only twelve urban areas whose place names ended in -pura (a Sanskrit term traditionally used to identify urban areas). But the number rose to twenty-four in the period of Rajendravarman II and twenty under Jayavarman V. In the reign of Suryavarman I, the number jumps again to forty-seven, more than double the number mentioned in the time of his immediate predecessors, and nearly four times the number mentioned in the time of Jayavarman IV (Bourge: 1970, 308).

The expansion of the Khmer agricultural core in this period was an important dynamic infrastructure for these developments. In part, by providing the food needed by these population clusters, expansion of the state's agricultural base allowed dramatic extension of the state's sphere of influence. From the middle of the tenth century to the middle of the eleventh, the Mon-populated upper Malay Peninsula and Chaophraya River regions, collectively known by historians as the centers of Dvaravati-civilization archeological sites, were absorbed by the Khmer (Shorto: 1961; O'Reilly: 2007, 65–86), and in the same period the Khmer realm made its first extended forays into the area around Lopburi in the middle Chaophraya River basin and the upper Mun River valley, both northwest of the Dangrek mountain range. In the first half of the eleventh century, Suryavarman expanded the Khmer state's administrative control definitively to include Lopburi and Phimai, northwest of the old Khmer core territory, and also expanded west beyond the Chaophraya valley of present-day Thailand and down toward the Isthmus of Kra on the Malay Peninsula. As noted, Suryavarman I's reign was a political watershed. Despite his predecessors' initial moves toward the west and northwest, tenth-century Angkor's political interests had been directed primarily toward the eastern portion of the traditional Khmer realm (Vickery: 1998, 71–138). Suryavarman I reversed this pattern with his activities in the west (Higham: 2001, 84–86, 91–101) and before long, despite continued monumental development in the Angkor area, the newly acquired northwestern territories would effectively become the political bases of most of the next several monarchs. Suryavarman's extension of Khmer authority into the Lopburi region had strong economic implications as well, for Lopburi became the Khmer center for control of the former lower Chaophraya Dvaravati regions, which provided access to international commerce at Tambralinga, in the Chaiya-Suratthani area of southern Thailand, and thus gave the Khmers a more direct contact with the international trade routes than had previously been the case. As noted in chapter 2, the lower Chaophraya had been a longstanding participant in the international maritime trade, and Khmer incorporation of these regions provided the Angkor realm with its first direct access to the Bay of Bengal maritime trade networks across the upper Malay Peninsula and specifically the Isthmus of Kra.

Inscriptions from Suryavarman's reign show that the new commercial opportunities available from the extension of Khmer administrative control into the region north of the Dangrek mountain range and into central Thailand in the west resulted in the development of new commercial networks (Wicks: 1992, 66–218). Although Khmer civilization was primarily centered in an inland wet-rice state, anything useful to the economic strengthening of the realm was encouraged. There are few direct inscriptional references to markets and trade generally in the Angkor-era records. However, Khmer epigraphic accounts of tenth- and early eleventh-century land and "slave" (*knum*) purchases reveal a number of commercial items used in these transactions, including cloth; cattle and buffalo; silver, gold, and various other metals; paddy; spittoons for betel; elephants; and (in the case of slave purchase) wax and other slaves. There was also occasional use of copper, oil, salt, and horses (Wicks: 1992, 197–98). Other Khmer inscriptions referring to commerce include one from the Ta Prohm temple that enumerated the goods in the temple's possession during the late twelfth century; it reports a quantity of honey and lead, two female slaves, and two elephants that had been acquired in an unspecified marketplace exchange (Coedes: 1906, 76). In addition, a 1191 Prah Khan temple inscription, also from the reign of Jayavarman VII, specifies that 7,848 units (*kharika*) of rice came from markets rather than from temple lands (Coedes: 1941, 297, 299n1).

There are few direct references to merchants in Angkor-era epigraphy, but the few we have suggest they played valued roles. For example, according to an inscription from Ban That Thong (922) in modern-day northeast Thailand, when the district chief of the Dharmapura region was required to collect gold, silver, and "precious objects of all sorts" to be offered to members of the royal family, he obtained them from four or five commercial specialists who were residents of his district (Coedes: *IC*, 7:94–98). Similarly, the inscription of Tuol Pei (992) from western Cambodia stipulates that the noble (mratan) to which it is addressed should procure certain specified goods for the royal family from the merchant Vap China (Aymonier: 1900–1904, 1:443; Hirth and Rockhill: 1911, 37, 53; Sahai: 1977, 127–28n39). In other instances the Khmer monarchs used their court agents (kamsten) as intermediaries, as in a late tenth-century inscription from Prasat Car, when several members of the kamsten interacted with the local marketplace to complete the sale of land rights, for which the buyer paid a quantity of money (silver and other precious objects) and clothing (Coedes: *IC*, 4:140–50).

There is no inscriptional evidence of merchants being directly taxed (Coedes: 1937–1966, 3:16–24). Nevertheless, the monarchs benefited from a taxation-like set of reciprocal expectations. Strong kings such as Suryavarman I, for example, supported merchants' activity by establishing and enforcing standards of weights and measures (Coedes: *IC*, 3:16–24, 5:133–42). In return, Khmer kings expected certain services, in reality a form of taxation, such as those performed by the marketplace agents mentioned above (Wicks: 1992, 201–2). For example, "donations" to temples by royal subordinates were expected (Bourge: 1970, 307). Worship services at central temples, in which the state took a particular interest, required that scented woods, spices, gold and silver, and cloth goods be presented to the deity. As indicated in the epigraphy, these were acquired from Khmer marketplaces; in return the market agents were reimbursed with land, buffaloes, rice, jewelry, and "slaves"—as previously discussed, there are different interpretations of what "slave" meant in the context of early Cambodian and Southeast Asian history (Coedes: *IC*, 5:133–42). This service relationship between Khmer marketplaces and kings is clarified in the late tenth-century Prasat Car inscription, in which the local population, in receiving their payment of silver, cloth goods, and salt in exchange for land that they had been asked to sell, declared to the royal judge who sanctioned the transactions that "all these goods that we receive allow us to perform our royal service. The rest serves for our sustenance" (Coedes: *IC*, 4:149–50). The emphasis here is on service and not on pious gifting.

In addition to these service requirements, the Khmer state under Suryavarman developed administrative mechanisms for the extraction of revenues (Bourge: 1970). Inscriptions focus on the role of marketplaces in facilitating the flow of goods to an elite's or king's center of authority, or as intermediaries in endowments to temples and the source of items used in the temple ceremonies so critical to royal legitimacy. Further, marketplaces were essential as the suppliers of goods to the king's kamsten (royal agents) when they made their periodic treks to the subordinate centers of power to tend to the king's affairs there.

Suryavarman I would seem to have been especially perceptive of the contributions that commerce and the activities of the marketplace made to the economic well-being of his state. The growth of the Khmer commercial economy during Suryavarman's reign can be examined by mapping the distribution of Khmer inscriptions that refer to marketing activity (Lajonquiere: 1911; Winichakul: 1994). The center of Khmer administration during the tenth and eleventh centuries can be indicated by using Battambang, Sisophon,

Prah Vihar, Sambor, and Kompong Cham as the points for the construction of a pentagon that contained the Khmer heartland around the Tonle Sap as represented in map 6.1 (Bourge: 1970, 297). As we have seen, Suryavarman's reign brought the extension of Khmer administration west of this core area to the region of Lopburi, north of present-day Bangkok in the Chaophraya River basin (the area between the core and Lopburi region was already under constant Khmer occupation) (Bourge: 1970, 298). Both archeological and epigraphic evidence indicate that the initial penetration of the Khmers into the Lopburi region occurred by the reign of Rajendravarman II (944–968), if not before (Wyatt: 1984, 20–30; Coedes: *IC*, 5:97–104). Whether or not there was an ongoing relationship with this area prior to his reign, inscriptions indicate that Suryavarman I consolidated the earlier contacts by incorporating this western territory under the administrative structure of the Khmer empire and also intensifying commercial communications with it (Coedes: 1961, 13–15).

Commercial communication at this time generally followed the river systems of the Khmer domain (see map 6.1). The main routes radiated out from the Khmer core around the Tonle Sap. In the eastern part of the realm a major commercial route followed the Sen River north to Prah Vihar (Bourge: 1970, 291; Briggs: 1951, 111). From this point goods were carried across the Dangrek range to commercial centers in the area of a Ban That Thong inscription (Coedes: *IC*, 7:94–98). Another route was the Mekong communication network. The zone in which the Ban That Thong inscription is located had contacts with this network as well, as an inscription from Ban That Thong dating to the reign of Jayavarman VI (1080–1107) references "barges" that used the Mekong (Finot: 1912, 2). In addition, Vietnamese traders such as the Yuan of Kamvan Tadin mentioned in a Phum Mien inscription (987) likely used a Mekong River route to enter Cambodia, coming from the Vietnam Nghe An region through the Ha Trai pass and then down the Mekong (Coedes: *IC*, 6:183–86; Maspero: 1918). On to the north, the Nghe An terminus of this route had contact with commercial developments in the Red River delta and with the Vietnamese capital at Thang Long (Hanoi). Proceeding southward along the Mekong, an overland route connected Ban That to Prasat Kantop, thereby avoiding the Khong rapids south of Ban That and also allowing a more direct access to the Khmer core. Sambor (Sambupura), located below the Khong rapids, was connected to an even more easterly route, serving as a center for Khmer contact with hill peoples to the east who provided "slaves," deer skins, and forest products to the Khmers, and beyond to the realm of the Chams and their South China Sea coastline connection to the international trade passageway (Osborne: 1966, 447; see chapters 3 and 7).

Elsewhere during the time of Suryavarman there also developed an east-west route north of the Dangrek mountain range that followed the Mun River system through Phnom Wan and then continued westward through Phimai and Lopburi. These northern areas were incorporated into the Khmer empire under Suryavarman I; the route flourished commercially. Inscriptions from the Phnom Wan and Phimai areas that date to the last ten years of Suryavarman's reign (1040–1050) indicate that goods from China as well as many other commercial items were available in local markets there (Coedes: *IC*, 7:63–70; Briggs: 1951, 178–82). Phimai, whose temple was founded about this time, was of especial importance commercially and administratively. Ranking with Lopburi in its value to the Khmer at that time, Phimai was the center for regional government in the Mun River valley. With the administrative integration of Phimai and Lopburi into the Khmer empire under Suryavarman, overland communication between these two western centers became desirable not only for its economic potential but also for its political strategic role. The development of such communication and exchange networks aided Suryavarman's efforts to integrate these outlying territories into his domain (Kennedy: 1970; Briggs: 1951, 178–79).

Another east-west route extended from the core area through Battambang and Svay Chek to Lopburi and the west. Epigraphy from these areas, particularly at Wat Baset (in Battambang) and Bantay Prav (in Svay Chek) documents commerce passing through this region to Lopburi and the west. These two areas developed into major commercial centers in the reign of Suryavarman I, and they apparently sat on the main route from the Khmer heartland to the west—it is no coincidence that the modern roads from the Tonle Sap region west follow this same route via Battambang and Sisophon to Thailand. Six of the seven known Angkor-era inscriptions that have evidence of the Khmer realm's commerce are from the Wat Baset and Bantay Prav temples, and date to Suryavarman's reign. The Wat Baset inscriptions record the bestowal of honors upon the "chief of royal artisans," who was responsible for the construction of that temple under Suryavarman (Coedes: *IC*, 3:3–11; Briggs: 1951, 160). At least eighteen commercial specialists are identified in two inscriptions dated 1042; there is also reference to government supervision of weights and measures and recognition of royal agents who were surveying local commercial activity (Coedes: *IC*, 3:11–24). Cloth goods (including silk) and spices were among the goods being traded there.

As we have just noted, during the reign of Suryavarman I western trade routes assumed an especially important economic position in the Khmer state. Although inscriptions report the incorporation of Lopburi into the administrative structure of the state during Suryavarman's reign, they provide little information on the economic interchange between Lopburi and the Khmer core (Coedes: 1961, 10–15). However, control of Lopburi and the area to its south gave the Khmers direct access to the trade routes of the Isthmus of Kra. The Chaiya-Suratthani area, which was known regionally as Tambralinga, rendered Tanliumei in Chinese sources (Wolters: 1958), was an important commercial center on the peninsula. At Chaiya, archeologists have recovered Mahayana Buddhist votive tablets dating to the tenth and eleventh centuries of a style similar to those at Lopburi, indicating likely communication between the two areas, though the nature and degree of contact between the two places is not clear (Lamb: 1961; Wolters: 1958, 593–94, 600; Hirth and Rockhill: 1911, 31–33). Nevertheless, the remains on the upper Malay Peninsula show continued contacts with both Indian and Arab-Persian traders to the west. Though the area's relative importance in international trade routes was not as great as it had been during the Funan period, its trade contacts may have been among the primary reasons for the Khmer interest in securing a foothold there (O'Connor: 1972, 60–62, fig. 34; Lamb: 1961; Jacq-Hergoualc'h: 2002).

The Khmer acquisition of the Chaophraya delta, the upper Malay Peninsula, and the region around Lopburi and Phimai brought a rerouting of trade goods from China, and evidence from the period shows that the northwestern acquisitions acquired near-immediate cultural and political importance (Coedes: *IC*, 7:63–70). Epigraphy suggests that prior to Suryavarman's reign, goods of Chinese origin had entered the Khmer core through the eastern part of the domain, as the inscriptions concentrate on commercial activities in that direction (Coedes: *IC*, 6: 183–86; Aymonier: 1900–1904, 443). Inscriptions from Suryavarman's reign reverse this eastern focus, being concentrated in the western region. While the proliferation of inscriptions in the newly integrated areas is a reflection of the period's administrative expansion, there are strong commercial implications as well. Once the Khmer had established control in Lopburi and areas to the south, goods brought from China to, say, Phanom Wan no longer needed to cross the mountains to the east. Instead, they could reach Lopburi and Phanom Wan via the Chaophraya River system, the same route being used for goods that were coming from India, Persia, and Arabia via Tambralinga. Such a direct interaction with the international routes no doubt was viewed as an asset to the internal development of the Khmer economy in Suryavarman's time.

At the same time that Chinese goods were being rerouted, Suryavarman attempted to establish regular commercial networking with both the south Indian Chola state to the west and the Ly state that was based in the northern edge of the Red River delta of Vietnam (Hall: 1978). Suryavarman appears to have been especially intent upon encouraging a flow of trade from south Indian ports to the Southeast Asian mainland via the Isthmus of Kra and Suratthani area. Goods could then have been transported north from the isthmus to Lopburi, where they would have followed the two exchange networks that evolved in Suryavarman's reign. As described above, the first entered the royal heartland in the Sisophon area, while the second serviced the region north of the Dangrek mountain range, with a link to the core at Prah Vihar and a likely connection to the Mekong River in the east (see map 6.1), and beyond was a vital new connection between the Khmer realm and Vietnam, using the upper Mekong to transit goods rather than the indirect way of the Mekong Delta and Cham coastline.

Under Suryavarman's rule the commercial economy of the Khmer state achieved such importance that the upper Malay Peninsula receded from the patterns of power and trade in the island world and was drawn into those of the mainland. Thereafter, the contacts of this area came to lie not with the international trade route but with a more regional route that went across the Bay of Bengal to south India and Sri Lanka that had its roots several centuries earlier, but became even more prominent in the eleventh century (Kulke: 1999; Gommans and Leider: 2002). Angkor's commercial and diplomatic contact with its Vietnam and Cham neighbors to its north and east were the source of a variety of trade goods as well as intermittent military conflict that continued through the remainder of the Angkor era. These developments and their consequences are addressed in the next chapter.

Despite these outward-looking commercial developments, the Khmer state soon withdrew inward following Suryavarman's reign, as in the middle of the eleventh century Khmer rulers began to be occupied with internal political strife while also being pressured by external forces. Around 1050, for example, Angkor's relationship with the Isthmus of Kra was challenged as the Burmese expanded into the Malay Peninsula (see chapter 8); as they did so, the Khmer state offered little resistance (Luce: 1969–1970, 1:21–23, 26). About this same year Cham raids sacked Sambupura on the Mekong (see below). This was also the year that Suryavarman died, for reasons unrelated to the Cham attacks, and shortly thereafter the center of political authority shifted north into the Mun River Valley beyond the Dangrek mountain range. Khmer inscriptions reflect little court interest in further commercial developments from then until the late twelfth century.

Although the evidence discussed above indicates a more than casual involvement in commercial affairs, at least under Suryavarman I, even during his reign the Khmer state's participation in the international commercial routes was a secondary concern. Khmer rulers were primarily committed to developing their agrarian base around Angkor and to overcoming Cambodia's peripheral position, geographically speaking, relative to the major east-west maritime routes. Thus, Suryavarman expanded his economic base by encouraging his subordinates to bring unused land under cultivation, extending his political hegemony from his core domain, and then making diplomatic overtures to the Cholas and the Ly state in Vietnam. With Suryavarman's death his successors chose to internalize the political focus of the Khmer polity rather than promote a stronger international presence, in contrast to their eastern Champa and Vietnam neighbors as described in chapters 2 and 3.

THE ROLE OF TEMPLES IN SOCIAL AND ECONOMIC LIFE: FAMILY AND CENTRAL TEMPLES AS ECONOMIC CENTERS

The extension of agriculture into previously uncultivated lands, necessary to facilitate the production of rice surpluses, was central to the development schemes of Khmer kings and their subordinates. Local temples played an important role in this process. Earlier works, such as Karl Wittfogel's *Oriental Despotism*, suggested that the hydraulic agricultural networks of the Angkor period demanded centralized control by the state (Wittfogel: 1957). However, we now know that the extension of wet-rice cultivation in this time was affected through the development of regional hydroagricultural networks. The construction and operation of these regional irrigational networks occurred under the supervision of regional communities and their temples, as was illustrated in the Sdok Kak Thom inscription. As in that instance, the heads of a family and its branches acted—through their family temple—as managers of land, clearing forests, erecting dwellings for new inhabitants, building dikes and reservoirs, and setting "slaves" to work on land assigned for development.

Khmer temples fulfilled three economic functions in this process. First, they were centers of investment ("banks"), the source of investment capital and management, as donors' gifts were redistributed to individuals or to groups of peasant and bondsman cultivators. These donations functioned as capital investments (e.g., seeds, livestock, and land to be cultivated) that stimulated the agrarian sector. Second, temples were repositories of technological information and knowledge, directly or indirectly supporting scholars, astrologers, and artisans whose expertise and literacy cultivators could draw upon. Third, Khmer temples were supervisory agencies that involved agricultural laborers in the development process, offering sufficient returns to encourage them to remain on the land.

As has been noted, lands assigned to temples for development were often unpopulated, requiring the assignment of a labor force (the men, women, and children enumerated in the inscriptions) with no previous claim to the land's production. These people might be war captives, or they might be moved from elsewhere into the state's core domain (Ricklefs: 1967, 411–20). The temples incorporated these laborers into the local economic and social system. Peasant families could not easily have borne alone the economic burdens of the inevitable shortfalls in production as they brought new land into production or implemented the agricultural technology associated with the construction of irrigation projects. Also, recently enslaved laborers would have been unlikely to understand the technical requirements of the new irrigation system and would have had to learn when and how to execute, considering the fluctuating environmental conditions, the variety of tasks necessary in a wet-rice system. Temples, however, could mobilize their storage and redistributive mechanisms to meet the subsistence needs of the laborers in such an event, drawing from material resources assigned for this purpose by kings or regional elites. Temples were also in charge of agricultural development, engaging diggers, scribes, managers, and other specialists, combining the technical expertise and human resources necessary for the extension of agriculture (Coedes: *IC*, 3:180–92; 5:143–46; 7:104–19). Furthermore, temples offered laborers emotional security; workers not only sought personal economic profit but also worked for the spiritual gain derived from service to a temple's deity (Sahai: 1977, 130; Bourdieu: 1977, 171–83).

Lands assigned to family temples were in some cases divided among the temple personnel or in other instances were considered together as "fields of the cult"; the temple personnel received shares of the "sacrificial rice" from the fields of the cult. The temple knum ("junior lineages" or bondsmen) who worked the land had "fields of sustenance" apportioned to them by the temple staff for cultivation (see figure 6.1). They were allowed to retain a portion of their production from their assigned land or were given a share of the har-

Temple of Trapaeng Don On: Redistribution of Temple Land Production

(X = redistributed shares of land's production)

Temple staff and temple residents fed from temple lands	Lands held by temple			
	"common fields of the cult"	"fields of the servants of the cult"	"fields of the chief priests"	"fields of sustenance"
Temple priests	X	X	X	
Temple officiants	X	X		
Temple assistants	X	X		
Hermits (residents of *asrama*)	X			
Temple laborers				X

Figure 6.1.   Khmer Temple Agricultural Economics

vest from the produce collections belonging to the entire temple. Family temple lands also had specific obligations to the state, except when there was a royal decree relieving the temple of these responsibilities (Coedes: *IC*, 4:107). Land assigned to temples was free of direct revenue obligations to the state; especially forbidden were collections by royal officials, who normally derived a portion of their income from making assessments for revenue demands (Sahai: 1977, 123–38).

Local temples were commonly expected to contribute misrabhoga duties to a royal temple in the form of goods and services. However, these were not tremendously large payments, and they appear to have had more political and social than economic importance. Royal interest in local temples, aside from guaranteeing the financial well-being of allies and limiting the economic resources of potential rivals, focused primarily on ensuring that a local temple's ritual was in harmony with that of royal temples rather than on making a local temple economically subordinate to a royal temple. The misrabhoga payments were therefore more symbolic than economically critical to the central temple's existence. For instance, a typical local temple in Suryavarman I's reign received an income of 55,000 pounds (25,000 kilograms) of hulled rice annually but shared only 20 pounds (90 kilograms of it with a designated central temple (Coedes: *IC*, 6:228–33).

From the perspective of the royal temples, the payments were more important, but still a minor proportion of income. For example, the Ta Prohm temple's rice needs during the reign of Jayavarman VII (1181–1218) were said to be 14,500 pounds (6,589 kilograms) daily for cooking and a total of 5,527,300 pounds (2,512,406 kilograms) annually (Coedes: 1906). This rice fed a total of 12,640 people who lived within the walls of the temple compound, including 18 high priests, 2,740 officiants, and 2,632 assistants (the latter included 615 female dancers, 439 learned hermits who lived in the temple monastery [*asrama*], and 970 students). Of the 5,527,300 pounds (2,512,406 kilograms) needed, only 806,960 pounds (366,800 kilograms) were delivered by villages assigned to the temple and 92,745 pounds (42,157 kilograms) from royal storehouses; together this was less than one-fifth of the temple's rice consumption (Sedov: 1963). Therefore, the central temple's primary source of income was the temple's own assigned lands worked by knum at the behest of Khmer monarchs and other state elite. State-level central temples thus functioned economically in a fashion similar to that of the local family temples, but on a much larger scale. That scale was certainly significant. For example, the Ta Prohm inscription's enumeration of the temple's stores includes a set of golden dishes weighing more than 1100 pounds (500 kilograms); a silver service of equal size; 35 diamonds; 40,620 pearls; 4,540 gems; 523 parasols; 512 sets of silk bedding; 876 Chinese veils; a huge quantity of rice, molasses, oil, seeds, wax, sandalwood, and camphor; and 2,387 changes of clothing for the adornment of temple icons.

Endowments to temples at both the state and local levels represented the mobilization, organization, and pooling of economic resources (capital, land, labor, and so forth) to support portions of the overall ritual process of the temple—for example, the financing of a single event in the temple's religious calendar of ritual, the construction of a building in the temple compound, clothing for a temple image, or a subsidy for a temple priest. While this redistribution of economic capital was central to a temple's existence, the mobilization of "symbolic capital" was also critical, as temple endowments generated one or more ritual contexts in which honors rather than material returns were distributed to and received by donors. In this way economic capital was converted to culturally symbolic capital, honors that enhanced the stature of the donor in the minds of his kin and clients (see figure 6.2).

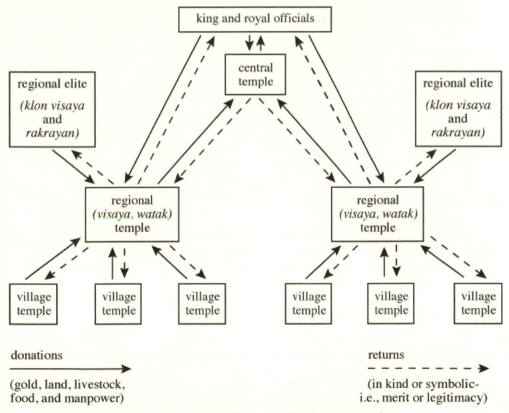

Figure 6.2.   Cambodia and Java Temple-Centered Exchange Networks

An endowment permitted the entry and incorporation of Khmer corporate units (e.g., families and kings) into a temple as temple servants (priests, assistants, and so on) or as donors. The donor represented a social, economic, or political unit, and the gift was a means by which the group or its leader could formally and publicly receive recognition. While an endowment supported the deity, and often returned some material advantage to the donor, perhaps more important were the symbolic returns of the "donation." Rulers—regional elites or Khmer monarchs—were patrons and protectors of temples, ensuring the continuance of temples' services, resources, and rules. They were not "rulers" of temples, however, but were instead servants of the temple's deity, human agents of the lord of the temple—a stone image that could not arbitrate in the real world on its own behalf—who protected and served the deity.

In the Indian tradition a ruler's relationship with a temple represented a symbolic division of sovereignty, whereby the ruler became the greatest servant of the temple's lord, his patronage of the temple's deity sustaining and displaying his rule over humankind (Appadurai and Breckenridge: 1976, 206–7). Indeed, identification with a deity seems to have been essential to legitimize rule. Yet kings and others who claimed political authority were subject to challenges by those who perceived their shares and rights in the local temple to be independently derived from the sovereign deity. The issue of who was the ultimate servant of the temple's lord had political significance and explains the attempts by Angkor's monarchs to subordinate local temples to royal ones. This subordination involved not only misrabhoga payments but also attempts to subordinate the deities of local temples to those of royal temples, thereby integrating these local deities into royal cults. In one example, a local deity of Sambupura was placed under the protection of the central shrine of Jayavarman VII's realm at Angkor's Bayon (Osborne: 1966, 446). In another example from the same locale, in the early ninth century a linga to Siva was erected in the temple of Amratakesvara, a local family god of Sambupura, by a queen of Jayavarman II (Coedes: *IC*, 1:31–35, 2:83, 87, 3:170–71; Osborne: 1966, 436–39, 445–46).

Thus temple donations had both economic and political implications. In the Khmer realm, temples never became independent of those in political authority, whether at the local or the state level. There was never a shift of socioeconomic power away from the secular authorities to a religious order. However, Khmer monarchs were limited by the very nature of their policy of utilizing temples and temple networks as a means of integrating their domains economically and politically. The Khmer realm did not develop a centralized administrative order, depending instead upon the assignments of land rights and impressive titles to those in royal favor to elicit the loyalty of semiautonomous regionally based landed elites. Yet there does not appear to have been a lack of ability to finance major royal projects. In the absence of an administrative system for collecting large amounts of income for the state's treasury, temples were viewed as important centers of economic accumulation that could be tapped to finance the king's patronage of religion. Most conspicuous were temple construction and elaborate temple ceremonies and festivals, which provided a pretext under which the state's economic and social resources could be mobilized to achieve the state's political goals. These goals mainly focused on the construction and strengthening of a court-dominated political system, and temples assumed major roles in this process.

The Khmer state's central temple complex thus related land and population to the king and his symbolic capital city. Temples controlled land, the labor on the land, and the land's productive output. Religious development was therefore viewed as an aid to the state's economic development. The extension of cultivated land in the tenth and eleventh centuries was thereby connected to the endowment of religious establishments. Rich temples formed economic bases that were tapped for construction projects, the development of irrigation, rice production, and so on—projects which were healthy for the economy as a whole and which the central government could not always cover. More importantly, the process of supporting the development of local temples was also a process of tying the periphery to the center and of enhancing the legitimacy of the king's rule.

THE NATURE AND SIGNIFICANCE OF ANGKOR'S WATER MANAGEMENT SYSTEM

The hydraulic systems at the Angkor complexes deserve special comment, as they also played a role in enhancing the king's legitimate rule. As has been noted, the traditional conviction among the Khmer was that their monarch was the source of his subjects' material welfare. Symbolizing the king's magical capacity to fulfill his obligation, the naga, the water spirit, was widely portrayed in Khmer art and was a central figure of popular religion (Jacques: 1997; 2006). Zhou Daguan, Mongol envoy to Angkor in 1296, reported that the Khmer people believed that their ruler slept with a naga princess, and that the result of their union was the country's prosperity (Paul: 1967/1992, 31). This report implies that the Khmer monarch enjoyed a ritual relationship with this traditional spirit of the soil and water, the source of the fertility that guaranteed the earth's productivity. In this same tradition Yasovarman I (r. 889–910) constructed an artificial lake (baray) named Yasodharatataka (also known as the east baray) northeast of his new capital city of Yasodharapura

(Angkor) at the end of the ninth century. According to the inscription reporting this event, the king wished to "facilitate an outlet for his abundant glory
in the direction of the underworld" (Barth and Bergaigne: 1885–1893, 407).
This underworld, also depicted as the place from which Khmer monarchs
judged the dead, was the abode of the nagas, as well as also the source of
fertility from which Angkor's kings "spread everywhere and ceaselessly the
amrita (ambrosia) of this immaculate glory" (Barth and Bergaigne: 1885–
1893, 426, 473, 502; Wolters: 1982, 85–92). This was the first of two lakes
that would be constructed at Angkor. The other, the west baray, was probably
initiated by Suryavarman I in the eleventh century.

Scholars have debated whether the barays were a critical source of water
for the Angkor region's agricultural production in a technical sense. Archeologists had assumed that water seeped through the dike base of Yasovarman's
lake (which measured 4 miles long by 1 mile wide—6.5 kilometers long by
1.5 kilometers wide) into collector channels outside the dike, which subsequently carried the water to surrounding fields. Similarly, it was speculated
that the baray begun by Suryavarman I at least doubled the potential cultivated land in the Angkor region, thereby providing the economic wealth to
fund the dramatic expansion of the Khmer state during his reign (Groslier:
1979b, 108–12, 179). French scholars viewed the resulting economic prosperity as responsible for the impressive urban development, recorded in
Khmer inscriptions, which took place in the tenth and eleventh centuries
(Bourge: 1970, 308).

However, reevaluations of the Angkor era water management system questioned whether these lakes were actually used for traditional irrigation agriculture, though, as the focus of Khmer religion, they were important
symbolically in the Khmer system of "theocratic hydraulics" (Higham: 2001,
155–61). Studies conducted in the late 1970s noted that Angkor-era agriculture was based not on centralized irrigation systems but on bunded-field
transplanted wet-rice cultivation. This system allowed the planting of approximately fifty million fields covering twelve and a half million acres/five million hectares (Liere: 1980). In the Angkor region floodwaters would slowly
rise from the Great Lake, the Tonle Sap, to its tributaries, but would rapidly
recede after the rainy season. In part, this rainy season flooding at Angkor
was the consequence of the Mekong River. As is still the case today, when
the Mekong River fills with rainy season water it has so much force that it
seals off the river that flows southeast from the Tonle Sap and intersects with
the Mekong at modern-day Phnom Penh. When this river network backs up,
it causes vast flooding upstream. When the Mekong recedes, the impact on
Angkor is like removing the stopper from the sink; water in Angkor's fields
swiftly drains into the Mekong River.

In the Angkor era a network of dams and bunds diverted and retained the receding floodwaters of the Tonle Sap after the rainy season. Though the Khmer lacked the technology to build large-scale dams, they depended instead on a network of earthworks on regional streams to retard and spread floodwaters into clay-based ponds during the rainy season, which stored the water for later use. Earthworks were concentrated downriver from Angkor on the edge of the Tonle Sap, to retain the floodwaters (Liere: 1980, 277). The most recent studies have mapped a vast water management network that extends 386 square miles (1000 square kilometers), which allowed Angkor to remain agriculturally productive in the nonrainy season by producing multiple rice crops a year. To sustain additional resident urban populations there were periodic new extensions dating from the ninth to the fourteenth century. The system tapped water from successive natural rivers flowing from Angkor's northeast to the southwest; north-south channels eventually delivered water to the baray reservoirs and temple moats, which were connected by channels that managed a water flow from northwest to southeast (across the slope of the land), to eventually drain into the Tonle Sap (Fletcher, et al.: 2008; Kummu: 2009).

The waterworks also conveyed important symbolic messages. We saw one set of these messages in the baray of Yasovarman. Others were built into the complexes that supplied the barays. The Phnom Kulen "mountain," which was located upriver from Yasovarman's lake some thirty miles (fifty kilometers) northwest of Angkor, near the headwaters of the Siem Reap, was one source of the Angkor ritual complex's water supply, which in turn flowed from Angkor to the Tonle Sap. A network of small earth dams regulated the flow of water downstream from Phnom Kulen to Angkor, where this water filled the collection of reservoirs that surrounded the court's temples. Throughout the Angkor region Khmer temples were constructed at the intersection of moats and roads that were oriented east-west and north-south; this was done purposely to project the image of a mandala, a geometric sacred space intended to symbolize the universe, that had been initiated by Khmer monarchs (map 6.2). In addition to being constructed in a manner consistent with the Indian and Khmer cosmological focus on east-west and north-south orientation, the water management network was consecrated with traditional symbols of fertility. A number of naga and linga phallic symbols were carved in the rocky riverbed at the Phnom Kulen mountain source, mutually denoting the sanctity of the water that flowed from the mountain region to Angkor using traditional and Hindu fertility symbols (Paul: 1967/1992, 31).

Notably, it was at Phnom Kulen that Jayavarman II had consecrated his devaraja cult (the emblem of the unification of the Khmer realm), making it the original Mount Mahendra, the center of the heaven on earth, prior to the establishment of his new capital downriver at Hariharalaya and the subsequent consecration of a new symbolic Mount Mahendra temple mountain there. This mountain consisted of the king's sacred focal temple complex, surrounded by a cosmic ocean, that is, the various baray reservoirs that reinforced the intended message that the king's paramount temple was indeed a heaven on earth (Coedes: 1968, 100–3). The original Mount Mahendra at Phnom Kulen was thus not only a source of legitimacy for later monarchs who drew upon the protective powers of Jayavarman's devaraja cult, but was also seen quite correctly as the source of the sacred waters that filled Angkor's surrounding baray. Together, this ritual/court complex symbolically enhanced the possibilities for success among the monarch's loyal subjects.

THE MAHAYANA BUDDHIST CULT AT ANGKOR DURING THE REIGN OF JAYAVARMAN VII: 1181–1218 CE

As described above, for the most part Angkor-based monarchs from the ninth to the twelfth century were successful in their promotion of state-focused and Hindu-inspired ritual performance that, together with its accompanying ideology, enabled that state to organize and tap into the populace's economic production. So effective was this ideological-ritual complex that it allowed the state to secure a region's political subordination without the aid of separate, secular economic or political institutions. However, the Khmer state also contained inherent stresses, and when these strains became sufficient in the late twelfth century, they led to the rise of state forms drawing on Mahayana Buddhism.

As noted, in the Angkor state wealth and prerogative were based on landholding rights and local control over temple administration. Though these arrangements were periodically reviewed by the state, competition among the elite and would-be elite for these resources and their associated titles could lead to dynastic instability. Successful candidates for the Angkor throne manipulated these status competitions among their regionally based aristocrats by focusing the elites' collective loyalty on the king's temple mountain (Mabbett: 1978). However, when elements of the regional elite bonded with rival claimants to the Khmer throne, as often happened at times of succession, a crisis would ensue. In the middle of the twelfth century, this upheaval became especially significant. Cyclical competitions for wealth, status, and power culminated in a civil war and a Champa intervention that included a water-borne raid on the royal complex at Angkor in 1177. The future King Jayavarman VII (1181–1218) responded to the crisis by rallying the Khmers

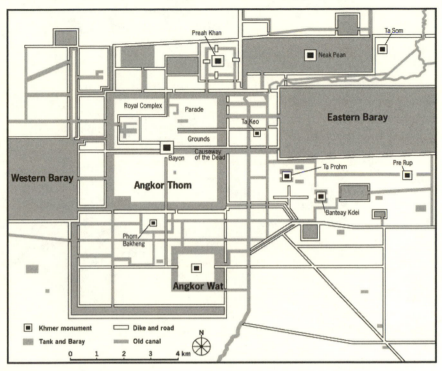

Map 6.2. Angkor, ca. 1300

and leading them to victory against his dynastic rivals and the Chams in 1178–1181 (Maspero: 1928, 164).

Against the earlier view that Champa was Jayavarman's and Angkor's true rival, current revisionist thought is that Jayavarman's intervention was not to depose the Chams, but to defeat his rivals *with* Cham assistance, and subsequently Champa was less Angkor's rival than Jayavarman's ritual ally in a mutually profitable era of trade and Buddhist religious exchanges. The earlier view, now refuted, was that Jayavarman defeated the Chams in a 1190s war of retribution for Champa's 1177 sack of Angkor, and thereafter Champa became a province of the Angkor-based state for the next twenty years. Now art historians especially point to the iconography on the outer walls of the Angkor Thom Baray, wherein Chams are portrayed as Jayavarman's allies in a war against his dynastic rivals (Lockhart and Phuong: 2010; Schweyer: 2007; Jacques: 2007).

Unlike his predecessors, Jayavarman was a Buddhist, having been raised by a deeply devout Buddhist royal prince. Consequent to a dynastic crisis, he

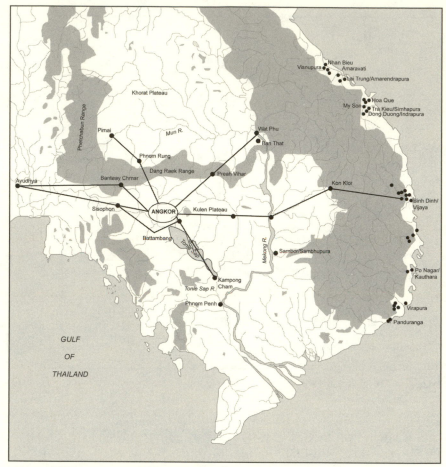

Map 6.3.   Angkor under Jayavarmam VII

spent a prolonged period of exile in Champa (1160–ca. 1165), during which
he diligently studied Mahayana teachings (Maxwell: 2007; Schweyer: 2007;
Sharrock: 2007). Following this Champa expatriation he resided for fifteen
years at the eastern edge of Khmer territories in the vicinity of the Prah Khan
temple complex at Kompong Svay, roughly forty-five miles (seventy-seven
kilometers) northeast of Angkor, where bas-reliefs were erected proclaiming
his succession to the throne following his victories against his dynastic rivals
in 1181 (Coedes: 1960).

   In contrast to his predecessors, Jayavarman was not a devotee of a particular Hindu divinity, nor was he drawn to the status of divinity at death. Rather,
he was personally committed to Buddhist teachings and the performance of

meritorious acts such as were appropriate to a Buddhist monarch (Boisselier: 1952; Mus, 1937). He made no attempt to convert his Khmer subjects to Buddhism or to challenge their local religious practices, yet he devoted a good deal of energy to the construction of new Buddhist temples. These temples were highly eclectic, sometimes even incorporating the Hindu temples of Jayavarman's predecessors into the new and enlarged Buddhist temple compounds. He also incorporated Hindu and local deities and their priests into inclusive state rituals (Groslier: 1973, 118). The new king also reconsecrated ancestral temples that had been polluted and desecrated by the Chams, thereby in theory reviving their authority. Yet despite his respect for the past, his allegiance to Buddhism was also a significant departure toward the future. In this time of chaos, Buddhism was an important resource in Jayavarman's attempt to reintegrate the centrality of his Khmer state.

Consistent with the Buddhist ideal of kingship, Jayavarman's inscriptions emphasized his efforts to establish a more direct relationship with his subjects, who became the objects of his religious compassion. This compassion was expressed through his merit making and temple building, which also made his subjects participants in what was described as his personal redemption (Chandler: 1992, 58). Surveying his new realm, he reportedly found it "plunged into a sea of misfortune" and "heavy in crime," and he felt it essential as king to play a role in its deliverance. He was also said to have "suffered from the illness of his subjects more than his own; the pain that afflicted men's bodies was for him a spiritual pain, and thus more piercing" (Finot: 1903a; Coedes: 1940a, 344). One of his wives later stated his protective concerns in highly symbolic terms: "in the previous reign the land, though shaded by many parasols [symbols of authority], suffered from extremes of heat; under [Jayavarman] there remained but one parasol, and yet the land, remarkedly, was delivered from suffering" (Coedes: *IC*, 2:171–75).

As a Buddhist monarch, Jayavarman asserted that he was otherworldly in his thoughts, and early statues portray him as a man of ascetic meditation. But he was also very much of this world in his actions. The bas-reliefs and inscriptions at Jayavarman's early temples, and also the lower-level bas-reliefs at his Angkor Thom temple mountain, portray the suffering of the Khmer people in the aftermath of the illicit seizure of the throne by Jayavarman's dynastic rivals, followed by the Cham invasion, along with the vengeance Jayavarman exacted against his rivals (Coedes: 1960). These bas-reliefs proclaim Jayavarman's leadership capacity and his victories in battle. Jayavarman's later inscriptions also refer to both military and moral conquests. Even as they record Khmer historical "fact," these epigraphic records also convey Jayavarman's expressions of deep sympathy, as appropriate for

Buddhist monarchs. These expressions are often highly symbolic, as military victories created opportunities for generosity.

> To the multitude of his warriors, he gave the capitals of enemy kings, with their shining palaces, to the beasts roaming the forests of the enemy; to prisoners of war, he gave his own forests [i.e., he resettled them as "slaves," who in turn brought newly conquered lands to the north and west of Angkor into cultivation], thus manifesting generosity and justice. (Coedes: 1906; Chandler: 1992, 61)

In his own mind, Jayavarman saved his subjects from subsequent suffering not only through his military efforts but also through his religious ones. Consequently, prior to his victory over his rivals he swore this oath for the good of the world: "All the beings who are plunged in the ocean of existence, may I draw them out by virtue of this good work. And may the kings of Cambodia who come after me, attached to goodness . . . attain with their wives, dignitaries, and friends the place of deliverance where there is no more illness" (Coedes: 1941; Chandler: 1992, 62).

As king, Jayavarman combined traditional and Buddhist symbols of legitimacy. Most significantly, he repeated the sequential steps to legitimacy common among his predecessors: he initiated public works, built temples to honor his parents, and then constructed his own temple mountain (Stern: 1965; Auboyer: 1977; Woodward: 1975). He devoted his initial administrative efforts as king to the clarification of his realm's status networks; numerous epigraphic records issued in his name report the reconfirmation of landholding and income rights or their transfer to others (Mabbett and Chandler: 1995, 204–17). Under Jayavarman construction works had a specifically Buddhist cast, although they also included Hindu elements. For example, his Ta Prohm inscription (1186) reports that he instituted a health care network that consisted of 102 regional "hospitals" that were dedicated to Bhaishajyagura, the Indic god of healing. Inscriptions such as this one also document a contemporary road network that Jayavarman improved to allow pilgrims easy circulation among the great Buddhist shrines—they were also of strategic importance, as most were intended to improve networking between Angkor and the west and northwest regions annexed by Suryavarman I in the eleventh century (Coedes: 1940a). Along these roads he built 121 rest houses, which were placed every ten miles (sixteen kilometers). Over fifty of these were built on a road connecting Angkor to the Cham region of Vijaya on the central Vietnam coastline (see chapter 7), seventeen were on the northwest road between Angkor and Pimai, and forty-four were on the southern Angkor-Suryaparvata (site of the ritually significant Phnom Chisor "Mountain of the Sun God" temple complex) circuit (Coedes: 1940b, 1941).

He also built ancestral temples to his mother and father. The first of these, at Ta Prohm (1186), associated his mother with Prajnaparamita, goddess of wisdom and mother of all buddhas, who was Jayavarman's Buddhist spiritual mentor. The latter, at Preah Khan (1191), held a statue of his father, Dharan-indravarman, who was associated with Lokesvara (Avalokitesvara), the bodhisattva of compassion. These two temples pointed to the third, the Angkor Thom temple mountain, which was the centerpiece of the reconstruction and reintegration of the Angkor (Yasodharapura) court complex. This complex was his crowning achievement. The central image on the Bayon at Angkor Thom is thought to present Jayavarman VII himself as Lokesvara (Woodward: 1981). Jayavarman's religious constructions did not end here, for his inscriptions say that he also distributed twenty-three Jayabuddhamahanatha images (proclamations of his bodhisattva stature) among regional religious centers (see below). Furthermore, the 1191 Prah Khan inscription proclaims that, as a consequence of the Angkor-era expansion during Jayavarman's reign, 13,500 villages now supported 20,400 religious images (Coedes: 1941).

The construction projects of Jayavarman's reign required massive commitments of resources. Thousands of his Khmer subjects were mobilized to erect and maintain the new state temples, roads, bridges, and hospitals. For example, the Ta Prohm inscription states that the 102 hospitals, which maintained staffs of roughly 100 each, were sustained by the labor and rice of 838 villages and their 80,000 inhabitants (Coedes: 1906; Chandler: 1992, 24). The construction seems to have been done with urgency. Though Jayavarman's roads were sturdy (Angkor-era stone bridges on the old Phimai road in northwest Cambodia are still incorporated into the major highway there), the buildings seem to have been hastily constructed. The Angkor Thom walls, for example, are roughly piled up. There are false columns and blind windows that imply the goal of magnitude, and the immediate impression of size and grandeur, in contrast to the refined artistic detail of Angkor Wat (Mannikka: 2000). Historians commonly assert that the haste with which Jayavarman's buildings seem to have been constructed reflect his own race against time—he assumed the Khmer throne at the age of sixty, and although he would retain the throne for over thirty years, Jayavarman had no assurance that he would live to complete his personal redemption (Boisselier: 1952).

Jayavarman's temples to his parents illustrate both the size and the eclecticism of his construction projects. According to inscriptions, the temple at Ta Prohm (1186), honoring his mother as Prajnaparamita, surrounded her with 600 dependent gods and bodhisattvas, though none of these associated icons has been found. Buddhism, Hinduism, and the local divinities coexisted in this site; while the temple ostensibly addressed the Buddha, it also presumably housed icons and priests associated with Hindu and local sects. Saivite and Vaisnava ascetics had cells on the temple grounds, where they meditated alongside Buddhist monks and other scholars. As previously reported, a grand total of 12,640 people were entitled to reside at the temple: 400 men, 18 high priests, 2,740 other priests, and 2,232 assistants, including 615 female dancers. An additional 66,625 men and women from 5,300 villages supplied rice and performed other services for the gods. A total of 13,500 villages, with populations totaling 300,000, were said to have derived benefit from this temple.

Yet, despite their eclecticism, the ancestral temples also displayed carefully considered Buddhist symbolism, especially in their relationship to Angkor Thom. The temples at Ta Prohm (representing his mother), Prah Khan (his father), and Angkor Thom (representing himself as the bodhisattva) formed a triad illustrating Prajnaparamita (wisdom), Lokesvara (compassion), and the Buddha (enlightenment), respectively. Adding to the triadic symbolism was that Ta Prohm was built to the southeast and Prah Khan to the northeast of the city of Yasodharapura, which was centered on the soon-to-be-completed Bayon at Angkor Thom. Symbolically, therefore, wisdom and compassion gave birth to enlightenment (Jayavarman), who stood at the center of the Bayon as the four-faced omniscient bodhisattva who looked down on his subjects with a half smile and a benignly powerful glance from half-closed eyes (Sharrock: 2007).

Also expressing the Buddhist symbolism at the center of Jayavarman VII's statecraft was the Neak Pean temple, which forms an island in the middle of the Jayatataka (north baray) that lies adjacent to the Prah Khan temple. This temple provides the fourth foundation for Jayavarman's Buddhist message, for the island temple, constructed in a lotus pattern, is the symbol of paradise floating on the primal ocean, the miraculous and mythical Lake Anavatapata in the Himalayas that was sacred to Buddhists (Boisselier: 1970). In Buddhist tradition Lake Anavatapata was sacred not just to Buddhists in general but especially to Buddhist rulers (*chakravartin*), who magically drew water from the lake to enhance their purity and power and to cure disease among their subjects. Thus the waters surrounding the Neak Pean temple flow forth to sanctify and bring prosperity to the Khmer people. This is consistent with the temple's description in the Prah Khan inscription (1191).

> The king has placed the Jayatataka [the north baray] like a lucky mirror, colored by stones, gold, and garlands. In the middle, there is an island, drawing its charm from separate basins, washing the mud of sin from those coming in contact with it, serving as a boat in which they can cross the ocean of existence [i.e., to salvation]. (Finot and Goloubew: 1923; Goloubew: 1927)

Above the water of the central pool is a white horse, which in Buddhist lore symbolically snatched shipwrecked merchants from fearful death. It bounds over the Ocean of Torments with men clinging to it, just as Jayavarman tried to snatch his people from death with his superhuman effort. This small temple may also have housed Jayavarman's sacred regalia, as the Prah Khan inscription refers to the Rajasri, "the royal regalia," in association with Neak Pean, which was carried back to Ayudhya by Thai invaders in 1431—in the Thai view, their destruction of Neak Pean negated the legitimacy of the universal kingship instituted by Jayavarman VII, and thus transferred it to the Thai monarchy (Wyatt: 1984, 70, 101–3).

Another important piece of symbolism is the unique Causeway of Giants, which leads into the walled city of Angkor Thom. Its walls represent a ring of mountains surrounding Mount Meru (heaven), which is also Jayavarman's sacred temple city (the center of the universe). Each causeway leads to one of five gateways—one each for the four points of the compass; the fifth, the Gateway of Victories, faces eastward from the earlier palace of Ta Keo to proclaim Jayavarman's triumphal victory over his rivals. This also configures the Buddhist notion of four realms centered by the Buddha. Giants (*asura*) and angels (*devata*) on the causeways participate in a tug-of-war, grasping two enormous serpentine nagas—thereby "churning the creative sea of ambrosia/milk" ("the waters of life and wealth") centered at the Bayon. The asuras may represent the Chams and the devatas the Khmer, embodying the underworld and the divine respectively, and the struggle between them on the causeways and in the bas-relief at the Bayon symbolizes the struggle that brought birth to the newly reconstituted Khmer polity. This causeway also represents Indra's rainbow, leading humans out of their secular world into the Angkor Thom world of the gods, and is therefore symbolic of humanity's ascent to heaven, or their crossing over the river of *samsara* (rebirth) into the afterlife (Mus: 1937; Moron: 1977; Groslier: 1973, 162; Woodward: 1981, 63).

The Bayon was the inclusive home of all gods, embodying the totality of spiritual energy. It was the sum of both local and royal prowess. All other cults were transformed into a single cult centered in a compassionate bodhisattva (i.e., Jayavarman), who had the ability inclusively to assume all forms of life-power. The Bayon ritual center embraces, illustrates, and perhaps contributes magically to ensuring the universality of the king's power.

Jayavarman was thus an innovator in an age of potential decay who sought a new form of thought and organization that would allow Angkor civilization to reintegrate to survive. However, his reign was ultimately followed by widespread conversions to Theravada Buddhism (Vickery: 1977; Jacques: 2007). Theravada offered an institutional and structural alternative to the traditional Khmer state, which depended on the willingness of regional lords to submit to the ruler's cult center, rather than on their incorporation into a bureaucratic hierarchy (Tambiah: 1976).

The appeal of the Theravada tradition was likely heightened by the Mon-
and Thai-speaking peoples who participated in Jayavarman's state, as they
were associated with the Theravada tradition in neighboring regions of the
Chaophraya River basin and the Malay Peninsula. While Jayavarman's
Mahayana cult centered in the Bayon did not have a lasting influence on
Khmer civilization, his Buddhist-inspired initiatives lay the groundwork for
the transitions that would lead to a future in which Theravada Buddhism was
the common source of Khmer identity (Vickery: 1977; Jacques: 2007).

THE THERAVADA BUDDHIST SANGHA AND
STATE POWER IN PAGAN BURMA

Among the new mainland Buddhist civilizations described in past chapters,
the one in Burma faced the greatest variety of societal and geographical

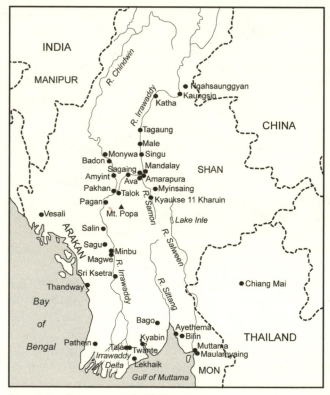

Map 6.4.   Pagan, ca. 900–1300

options. The culminating early polity, based at Pagan (Bagan) on the Irrawaddy River, was formed in the early ninth century when the leaders of the Burmese speakers based in north central and northern Burma took control of the territory that had formerly been dominated by the Pyus (in south central Burma/Myanmar) (Hudson, et al.: 2001). Then, in the mid-eleventh century, under the Burmese monarch Anawrahta (Aniruddha, ca. 1044–1077), Pagan extended into the coastal regions in the south and their populations. Aniruddha "pacified" the Lower Burma region of the Irrawaddy and Salween river deltas, which had direct links to the Bay of Bengal coast.

The resulting kingdom of Pagan, which reached its height under Aniruddha's successor Narapatisithu (r. 1173–1210), nearly corresponding to the core of present-day Myanmar, posed a number of political and economic challenges to its rulers. It was now necessary to blend several languages and their speakers (some remnants of the Pyu, possibly a small Mon elite, and the Burmese majority). At the outset, different economies (the trading centers of the monsoon coasts, the ricelands of the dry zone in the north, and the swidden cultivation of the uplands) and various enclaves of power (with challenges coming from both the mountains and the sea) also had to be accommodated (Kasetsiri: 1976; Aung Thwin: 2002; Lieberman: 2003, 89–112; Wyatt: 2003). There was also a variety of localized and eclectic India-derived Buddhism and Hinduism, practiced by the Pyus of south central Burma and the people of the coasts, with wider networked cultural and economic communication with the regions of modern Thailand, an eclecticism that continued for centuries after the Burmese kings chose to patronize Sri Lanka–based Theravada Buddhism. Consequently, Pagan had considerable contact with the outside world, especially South Asia, with which Burma had more direct and earlier contact than did the other mainland states of Southeast Asia. Not only was there an overland passage to the west to Bengal and the north Indian heartland as early as the fourth century CE, there was also regular maritime contact with India's east coast and Sri Lanka to the south (Frasch: 1998). The kingdom of Pagan also had direct overland links with the Yunnan region of southern China to its northeast (Bin: 2004), and also with its Mon, Thai, and Khmer mainland neighbors to its east (Richard O'Connor: 1995; Wyatt: 1984, 21–25, 28, 32, 50, 83).

From the start, Pagan's political organization had some important differences from that of Angkorian Cambodia, due largely to Pagan's associations with Theravada Buddhism. As described above, Angkor-era Khmer culture centered on successful monarchs, who had forged personal partnerships with powerful celestial Indic gods on their subjects' behalf. Conversely, the statecraft of Pagan and subsequent Burmese monarchies placed greater stress on the rulers' moral actions and meritorious demonstrations than on divine intervention as reasons for local submission to a universal secular monarchy. Thus Buddhism provided the economic and conceptual bases on which the sovereignty of Pagan's monarchs was built (Aung Thwin: 1985, 1991). Burmese statecraft also drew on non-Buddhist local traditions. Among the earliest pre-Pagan societies, leaders had represented their communities in rituals that linked the living elite to local patron gods. At their death, these men of prowess would go to join their ancestors in the spiritual realm—in the Pagan era this would be at Mount Popa—the abode of the *nats* (or spirits) where they would unite with the supreme earth goddess. A local tree or mound served as the point of contact between the human and celestial realms of existence. As the new Burmese rulers localized these previous animistic traditions with Theravada Buddhism, the burial mounds of prominent ancestors became Buddhist stupas, and local spirits (nats), especially those associated with spiritually endowed trees, came to be considered *sotapan*, followers of the Buddhist teachings who were well along the pathway to salvation (Shorto: 1967; Spiro: 1967). Through this localization process, the traditional cults of the nat spirits in Burma acquired official status and were sanctioned by Buddhist orthodoxy (Aung Thwin: 1987).

We now believe that these processes were well underway in central Burma even before the rise of Pagan. In the seventh century two Chinese pilgrims, Xuanzang and I Qing, visited the Pyu kingdom of Sri Ksetra, which was centered on the Irrawaddy River near Prome in central Myanmar. They described it as having a hundred Buddhist monasteries that were densely populated by local monks (Luce: 1937, 249ff; Wheatley: 1983, 165–98). The Pyu polity, which had its ritual centers at what is known today as Thayekhittaya (Sri Ksetra), Old Prome, Beikthano near modern Taungdwingyi, and the Mu Valley town of Halin, represents the earliest Southeast Asian evidence of widespread commitment to Theravada Buddhism (Aung Thwin: 2002, 2005). There is also archeological evidence of Sarvarstivadin (Theravada sects that wrote in Sanskrit) and Mahayana influences in Pyu society, as well as of elite worship of Visnu and of his consort Laksmi, goddess of royal majesty and of fortune, and these relatively marginal traditions would continue well into the Pagan period. In the Pagan era, Kyanzittha (r. 1084–ca. 1120) considered himself an earthly incarnation of Visnu, proclaimed to be the "heavenly king of the universe" in a temple built by the king (Luce: 1969–1970, 1:216).

The revisionist attention recently given to the Pyu rather than to the Mon by Michael Aung-Thwin contrasts with earlier treatments by scholars, who had assumed that there was in Lower Burma a Mon Theravada Buddhist kingdom called Ramannadesa that became the foundations of Upper Burma, Pagan civilization, and its development of Theravada Buddhism. The association of the Mons with Theravada Buddhism in Thailand is certainly strong but there is no evidence of the same in Lower Burma until much later. The alleged early Mon civilization of Lower Burma, seen as an extended member of the networked Dvaravati Mon civilizations discussed above, which were centered in the upper Malay Peninsula, the lower Chaophraya valley, and the Chiangmai region in northern Thailand, may have produced early Buddha images said to be in the "Dvaravati" style, although virtually identical to the Amaravati style of north India as well, as discussed in chapter 2 (Coedes: 1966a, 112–16; Wheatley: 1983, 199–230). According to convention, by the eleventh century the alleged Mon centers at Thaton and Mergui in Lower Burma were drawing their inspiration from their maritime contacts with Sri Lanka and south India. Tradition asserts that in 1057, Thaton and its Mon culture were absorbed into the Pagan realm following its alleged invasion by the Burmese monarch Anawrahta (Aniruddha, ca. 1044–1077). After this mythical "conquest," King Anawrahta was said to have introduced Sri Lankan Theravada Buddhism in Pagan. Conventionally, then, early historians had portrayed Anawrahta as having imported Theravada Buddhism from "Mon" Thaton of Lower Burma to Upper Burma.

More recently, however, Aung-Thwin has shown that "the Mon paradigm" is a myth. Based on old as well as new archeological evidence and a reevaluation of existing epigraphic sources, Aung-Thwin has demonstrated that no such city called Thaton and no kingdom called Ramannadesa existed in Lower Burma. Indeed, these two names do not appear in original epigraphy until the late fifteenth century. Thus, the alleged connection conventionally made between a Mon Lower Burma and the civilizing of Pagan cannot be supported by the evidence. Instead, the focus should be on the importance of the Pyu and their traditional ritual centers as critical foundations for Pagan's expansive eleventh-century monarchy (Hudson, et al.: 2001). This new historiography, drawing on Pyu-related sources, highlights Anawrahta's promotion of Theravada Buddhism by means of land endowments to religious institutions, similar to the "sacred sovereignty" policies used by his contemporaries in Angkor, Champa, Vietnam, and Java, as a means to consolidate his monarchy. At the heart of Pagan Buddhism was merit making. This was accomplished by spiritual as well as economic acts, which were in turn conceived to be the source of spiritual reward as material capital was transformed into spiritual capital, as described above.

Buddhist monasteries and temples received strategic allocations of land and permanent or temporary rights to resettled labor, and in turn they asserted leadership in the development of new irrigation networks in support of the wet-rice agriculture needed by the flourishing state (Aung Thwin: 1990). In the new eleventh-century Pagan Buddhist state established by Anawrahta, "revenue" from local sources "flowed" to the new Pagan administrative center, where it was redistributed as rights to those revenues that the monarch conferred on his administrators and the Sangha. While some revenue physically moved to the capital, most remained where it was produced and would not have reached the king or his court. Instead, while some was "diverted" to provincial administrators, much also found its way to the local Buddhist institutions or individual monks in lieu of tax payments for the upkeep of the monastic order (Sangha). It also financed assorted economic development projects that were coordinated by the Sangha, as workers were hired to farm temple fields, build and maintain temples, and service the Sangha. Temple endowment funds also paid the expenses of monks through returns on investments in new wells, water storage tanks, irrigation canals, palm trees, and gardens. Festivals, feasts, and various performances by theatrical and dance troupes were also financed by yearly income derived from the revenue assigned to temples by the king. Thus, linked transfers of this royal entitlement to local income provided jobs, extended cultivated lands, and financed religion and entertainment (Aung Thwin: 1985, 1990).

In this period, status was defined more by how much one gave to the Buddhist church than by the wealth one accumulated. Consequently, donations by royalty were considerable. Burmese kings and queens were themselves responsible for over 20 percent of the total donative expenditures on some nearly 3,000 Buddhist temples in the Pagan core, 4,000 throughout the kingdom, doing so as acts of merit-spreading piety. These public donations were done within the framework of the alternative paths of Theravada Buddhism: one might pursue meritorious good works that improved the performer's or donor's potential next life, as opposed to a strictly monastic path to enlightenment and thereby nirvana (Spiro: 1967). From a Burmese perspective, the intellectual quest for salvation was most appropriate for those who were already very devout, while "merit making" was more practical for the average layman. What made these royal actions significant was that the fruits of merit making could not only be accumulated to oneself but also could be transferred or shared. The merit of one person could enhance the merit of another (usually deceased) person. A person's merit could also be redistributed, for example when a rich man such as a king built a temple that would bring merit to those who could not afford to do so. Kings and other wealthy patrons shared merit directly through the act of building, and the temple subsequently provided fields of merit in which others could practice.

The Pagan monarch's concern that his gifts should bring spiritual benefits to others is reflected in an inscription, dated 1141, by King Alaungsithu (r. 1112–1187), who reigned when the Pagan kingdom was on its ascendancy. In this inscription he expresses a desire, through his gifts, to give up worldly wealth in order to draw near to the religion and to draw others along with him. In an extended passage, he says, in part,

> By this my gift, . . .
> I would build a causeway sheer athwart
> The river of Samsara, and all folk
> Would speed across thereby until they reach
> The Blessed City. I myself would cross
> And drag the drowning over. (Luce: 1920)

Yet despite this expressed willingness to forsake all in devotion to the religion, the pure form of this impulse was not the practice for those who wished to continue ruling. Indeed, a Pagan king's greatest dilemma was actually whether to accumulate material or symbolic capital (Aung Thwin: 1979, 1985; Lieberman: 1980, 2003, 120–21). In other words, should he withdraw from worldly pursuits into a monastic existence, giving his personal assets away to achieve nirvana by spiritual enlightenment, or focus on maintaining and increasing the financial resources of his kingdom? As the Theravada Buddhist kings of the Pagan era considered these issues, the pull in favor of strategic donations was shaped by pursuit of the following three potentials: (1) salvation achieved through good works and the sharing of merit; (2) religious endowments as a practical means of achieving religious as well as social and political goals; and (3) assorted redistributions of material wealth, most of which involved reassignments to the Buddhist Sangha, upon which the political economy depended (Aung Thwin: 1983). Despite Alaungsithu's focus in the above inscription on his spiritual quest that would enable all his subjects to achieve nirvana (speeding across the sea of samsara to reach the blessed city of salvation), the mode of his assistance was ultimately grounded in his merit-making efforts that required actual monetary and material donations.

Though the Burmese kings generously supported Buddhist institutions, their relations with the Sangha were marked by periodic tensions stemming from this very generosity. Though support of Buddhism enhanced the legitimacy of Pagan's kings, the merit-making style of kingship had significant pitfalls that weakened the state in turn. As Michael Aung-Thwin has shown, because of the traditional tax-free status of the Sangha's economic resources, generosity toward the Sangha gradually made it the major land owner with access to much of the state's land and labor resources. In such situations the Pagan king faced the dilemma of whether or not to directly challenge the Sangha's control over the state's economic resources. If done as an overt grab of power, this would negate his image as the Sangha's leading benefactor. The monarch's only viable recourse against the Sangha's wealth and power was therefore to act as its benefactor in another sense, through the periodic ritual purification of the religious order. Kings derived their legitimacy from Buddhist tradition, yet the Buddhist institutions also depended on the king's leadership: periodic purifications of the religious order were expected since monks were human, not divine, and therefore vulnerable to material corruption. Since the monastic order's ideal was austerity and asceticism, purifying the Sangha was considered an act of kingly piety (Aung Thwin: 1976b, 1979).

The reform/purification process in Burma, as elsewhere, was a carefully calibrated one. Pagan monarchs would initiate the process by publicly denouncing the Sangha as being corrupt, lazy, and worldly, and thus impure as evident by its wealth. Burmese rulers would then begin the process of purification by sending selected monks to Sri Lanka, considered the center of Theravada Buddhist piety in that era, so that these monks could be purified through reordination. While the selected monks were gone, the king built a special hall for the reordination ceremony. First the ground was ritually cleansed to remove the spiritual ties of the local nat spirits that might pollute the ceremony. Then a moat was dug around the hall, so that the water in the moat could insulate the ordination hall grounds from impurities. All trees whose branches hung over the ritual site were trimmed to prevent their contamination of the grounds. When the monks returned, they would in turn lead the reordination/purification of all the other Burmese monks. There was considerable incentive to submit to these reordinations, for monks who refused to be reordained risked being cut off from state and public funding. In addition, reordination strengthened royal power by recalibrating the status rankings within the Buddhist monkhood. Even in normal times seniority depended upon the order of ordination.

Furthermore, according to Buddhist tradition, the quality of one's merit was linked to the piety of the monks the worshipper supported. In times of purification the status rankings were established anew in order of reordination; detailed accounts were kept of the precise minute the ordination/reordination took place, in order to allow monks to demonstrate their relative superiority over others. Furthermore, since the newly purified Burmese monks, patronized by the king, had the greatest status, in theory they possessed the greatest ability to attract support.

The purifications strengthened royal control in several additional ways. For example, the king had carefully decided which monks to send for reordination in Sri Lanka and on their return he could also determine the order of reordination, based on his perception of monks' personal loyalty (though the monks' applications for reordination were channeled through a reordination committee). At the same time, the purifications functioned to increase the state's material resources, as previous tax-free lands returned to the public domain. To be worthy of reordination, monks had to give up their worldly possessions—cattle, land, and manpower. Rights to these possessions could not be transferred to a layman; they could only pass to the state, which in theory represented the interests of the wider public. Those monks who chose not to give up their material, worldly possessions were required to assume layman status, and their property immediately became subject to state tax assessments.

Thus, the purifications became a means of regaining state wealth and returning manpower from the Sangha to the state. The purifications squeezed a temple's resources indirectly; although the temples were not forced to relinquish their own endowed lands, temple-based monks who held income rights as a consequence of meritorious assignments were, and numbers of these monks who did not relinquish their income rights chose to leave the temples to return to the secular world. Over time, however, the Pagan state became less capable of instituting these purifications (Aung Thwin: 1979, 1985; Lieberman: 1980; 2003, 120–21).

In Michael Aung-Thwin's view, by the thirteenth century, the Sangha's hand had been strengthened by the emergence of a new landed elite whose interests coincided with those of the "impure" Sangha. Many of them belonged to the artisan class, which had become wealthy due to its members' work on the numerous temple construction projects that had been financed by the state and its secular subordinates. As they grew wealthy, these artisans had reinvested their wages in land. Furthermore, over time the Sangha itself had become increasingly large and wealthy, to the point that it had more wealth to redistribute than did the state—especially to the artisans who were responsible for the construction of temples and monasteries. Thus the combined economic power of the Sangha and this newly landed artisan class came to conflict with the economic and political power of the state. Furthermore, where there might once have been public sentiment in favor of purification, there was now little public sympathy for the state's attempts to curb the power of the Sangha, for the economic interests of the Sangha had become closer to that of lay society, while the Sangha had increasingly become its patron, providing an alternative to the state (Harvey: 1925; Aung Thwin: 1985).

By the thirteenth century, therefore, the Buddhist church was openly disputing the state's claims to ownership of glebe lands, opposing it in court publicly. The Sangha also bought and sold land and sponsored public feasts to celebrate those transactions. The Sangha could oppose the state openly in part because Pagan's thirteenth-century rulers no longer monopolized state wealth and were unable to control the Sangha as they had done theretofore. With the continued devolution of land and labor to the Sangha, regional socioeconomic units came to act against an integrated kingdom. It was not until the mid-fourteenth century that growing public disfavor with an overly "impure" and materialistic Sangha enabled Burmese rulers of a new Ava dynasty to once more institute Sangha-wide purifications. But following the new purification the state once again was compelled to make donations of land and labor to the Sangha, for its legitimacy was directly tied to the patronage and well-being of the Sangha. But the "purer" the Sangha was, the more they received donations, for the quality of one's merit was directly linked to the purity of the monk one donated to. This instituted a new cycle of Sangha-state competition for "fixed" agrarian resources.

At one time it was widely thought that Mongol raids in the 1280s were the end of Pagan, but recent research by Michael Aung-Thwin has shown that the Mongols never reached the city of Pagan, and that the end of Pagan civilization was the result of a complex variety of factors, not the least the slow and continuous migration of the Shan hill tribesmen from Burma's northern highlands into the Irrawaddy River valley; they began to stage raids against agricultural settlements during the period 1359–1368 (Aung Thwin: 1998). New waves of migrants and raiders poured into Burma from the north, and rival regional successor polities struggled against each other for control. A new Burmese dynasty eventually emerged in the mid-fourteenth century at Ava in Upper Burma, while on the coasts the first Mon kingdom in Burma appeared by the mid-fourteenth century, first at Martaban and subsequently at Pegu/Begu (Aung Thwin: 2011). The new dynasty clearly capitalized on the burgeoning of trade and commerce in the maritime regions of Lower Burma and the rest of Southeast Asia at the time. Consequently, and for the first time, a center of Burma political authority was focused on the coasts, in much the same way that the Khmer political center relocated at Phnom Penh on the upper edge of the Mekong Delta in the same era, as a downstream location provided better access to the prosperous international trade on the coastlines (Lieberman: 2003, 123–54).

THE KHMER AND BURMESE REALMS IN COMPARATIVE SOUTHEAST ASIAN PERSPECTIVE

This chapter and the previous one have described the societal reorganizations that were documented in local epigraphic records as Java, Cambodia, and Burma moved beyond the old village-based reciprocity networks. In these processes individuals and families became members of a court-centered order. Local associations were still acknowledged, but were increasingly superseded by judgments emanating from royal courts or the actions of those empowered by courts. In both cases, these legal decisions related to landholding rights, aristocratic privileges, and symbols of aristocratic status (Hoadley: 1971). Symbolic gifting remained a vital activity in the process of societal definition, but its consequence was now increasingly material (Hall: 1996b). Royal inscriptions, in contrast to local epigraphic fragments, no longer emphasized the abstract potential for immortality that resulted from local loyalties to the court, as had been the case in the initial inscriptions. Instead they addressed the affairs of this world that were the consequence of orderly and interventionist court leadership, which was in partnership with families who held titles of distinction. Individual expressions of self and family were becoming less based in the local community (Day: 2002). Now they were members of a larger societal entity that included those who identified with a common ethnicity and its heritage, and those who viewed themselves as sharing residency under the protection of a royal court to which they were submissive.

In the Khmer and Burmese realms temples remained important as centers of state political and economic initiative. Khmer inscriptions largely report royal interventions that brought order to new economic opportunities deriving from a stable royal order, which was centered in the traditionally meaningful networking of Khmer temples that culminated in the king's temple complex at his sanctified Angkor court (e.g., Angkor Wat and Angkor Thom). This legacy would be the basis of Jayavarman VII's successful restoration of Khmer sovereignty in the late twelfth century. When Jayavarman VII restored order to the Khmer realm following the war of succession and a devastating Cham raid of the royal complex at Angkor in the 1170s, he did so by focusing his energies on rebuilding the Khmer temple network, centered in his new Angkor Thom temple complex. Meanwhile, as we have already seen, the polities based in eastern Java were moving in a different direction. In part because of their greater involvement in the international trade routes, east Javanese polities were going beyond temple-based economics to develop ritual networks centered on and in the sanctity of the court itself, while in the Angkor and Burmese Pagan polities the temples remained important sources of authority and bases of social organization as separate institutional entities. But this notion of Angkor and Pagan as exclusively temple-based economies should not be taken too far, as commerce was important in the Khmer and Pagan realms as well. It was even more important in the neighboring mainland evolving polities of Thailand and Vietnam.

Transitions in the Southeast Asian Mainland Commercial Realm, ca. 900–1500

NEW MARITIME PATTERNS
AND SHIP TECHNOLOGY

Through the ninth and tenth centuries, when the Tang state was slowly collapsing and China was splintering into numerous regional political entities, international trade did not fall off to any great degree, due to the efforts of the Southern Han and Min dynasties based respectively at Guangzhou and Fuzhou (Wolters: 1970, 42; Schafer: 1954, 75–78; Wang: 1968a, 47, 296n27). New pressures were building up along the sea routes in South and Southeast Asia. Where previously the political development of these regions was such that there had been little conflict among major regional powers, the tenth century saw the beginnings of disturbances, particularly with the rise of maritime power in east Java and on the Tamil section of the east coast of India (Hall: 2010b, 2010c). Added to this interregional competition was the major upsurge in trade that followed the reunification of China under the Song dynasty (960–1279) and its efforts to enhance China's communications with the Southern Seas (Nanyang), which reached their peak in the twelfth century.

The hundred years following the upsurge along the trade route from the final third of the tenth century forward saw a serious weakening of Sivijaya's dominant emporium position in the Straits of Melaka region (see chapter 4), as political and economic strains proved too great for it. The Srivijayan rulers first sought to consolidate their position with diplomatic maneuvers in the direction of India and Sri Lanka and then followed by attacking Java's coast-

Map 7.1.   Southeast Asia, ca. 1000–1500

line, which by that time had become a threat to Srivijaya's dominance over the regional maritime trade (*ARE*: 1956–1957, 161, 164, 166; *EI*: 22, 213–81). The Javanese counterattacked in 992 but in 1016 suffered the retaliatory devastating raid from their enemies that allowed the Srivijayan ruler to proclaim himself the "king of the ocean lands" when he sent a richly laden mission to China the following year (Wolters: 1970, 1, 14; Coedes: 1968, 130, 142, 144). Yet, within a decade, the Chola navy of India's Coromandel Coast had sacked the legendary riches of the Srivijayan capital and for the next fifty years was to play a role in the politics of the straits and west Java Sea area (Spencer: 1983). The attack of 1025 disrupted the concentration of the international route through the Srivijayan ports along the Straits, and by the last quarter of the eleventh century the trading pattern had become more diffuse. No longer did the primary focus of the route center on the southeastern Sumatra coast and its control of the Straits of Melaka. In 1178, Chinese sources stated: "Of all the wealthy foreign lands which have great store of precious and varied goods, none surpasses the realm of *Dashi* (the Middle East). Next to them comes the *Shepo* (Java), while *Sanfozhi* (Srivijaya) is third; many others come in the next rank" (Wheatley: 1961, 63; Wolters: 1967, 251).

In addition to facilitating the rise of east Java, the 1025 Chola expedition was critical to the Southeast Asian mainland as well. By removing Srivijaya's presence from the ports of the upper Malay Peninsula, the Cholas cleared the way for the expanding mainland polities to fill the resulting power vacuum (*SII*: 2, 105–9; Nilakanta Sastri: 1949, 80; Kulke: 1999). As we will see below, immediately after this raid, first the Khmer Empire of Suryavarman I and then the Burmese empire of Anawrahta, and still later the Thai, all established their influence in this area.

With the weakening of the old international trade system, different types of foreign traders, notably Muslims and Chinese, in increasing numbers pursued Southeast Asian goods more directly into Southeast Asia itself. With new ports on the southeastern coast of China (Fuzhou and Quanzhou supplementing the older port of Guangzhou) (Chaffee: 2008), and the increasing commercial strength of southern India, multiethnic sojourning traders not only continued to transport the goods of East and West but wished to acquire Southeast Asian commodities more directly themselves (Hall: 1980; Ptak: 1999; Heng: 2008). While increasing numbers of maritime diaspora were well received on the coasts of the Philippines, northern Borneo, Vietnam, the Gulf of Thailand, and north and west Sumatra, they dealt still with intermediaries, notably Java-based traders, in obtaining the increased flow of spices from the eastern Indonesian archipelago via the Java Sea. These sojourning traders also began to penetrate the downstream areas of the lowland empires on the mainland, though most appear to have gone no farther inland (Gommans and Leider: 2002; Heng: 2009).

The rise of China-based trade brought yet another shift in the ethnicity of the area's maritime traders. In the early tenth century, Middle Eastern traders based in the Red Sea and the Persian Gulf regions were prominent in Southeast Asia and were supplementing Malay crews as carriers of international cargoes between India and China. A significant increase in Middle Eastern demand for Asian products had spurred an increased volume of trade (as opposed to the limited volume of the earlier luxury trade). During the twelfth and thirteenth centuries there was another shift as the role of Middle East–based sojourners in Southeast Asian trade diminished (Tibbetts: 1979). In part this was due to the greater volume of trade, which made it more efficient for regionally based merchants to specialize in one segment of the international route. This decreasing Middle Eastern role in Southeast Asian trade was also due to the direct entry of China-based traders into Southeast Asian markets during this era, as well as to the continuing instability of the Persian Gulf political realm since the demise of the Abbasid dynasty in the mid-tenth century. Middle Eastern trade was especially strong following the rise of Fatimid rulers in Egypt in the late tenth century. During this period the Red Sea served as the new western terminus for the Asian maritime route. Red Sea ports focused their commercial contacts on the Indian and Sri Lankan coasts, as Red Sea–based merchants rarely ventured beyond South Asia into Southeast Asian waters (Goitein: 1974). For the rest of the eastern route, the Western traders depended on contacts with a multiethnic group of traders (including ethnic Middle Easterners who had taken up residency in South and Southeast Asia) who worked the India-to-Southeast Asia leg of the international maritime route to acquire Southeast Asian and Chinese merchandise (Lambourn: 2008b).

During Song times southern Chinese interest was once again exclusively directed to the sea, since the fall of Kaifeng in 1127 brought the closing of the overland caravan routes across the Central Asian steppes. After that date, all tribute with trade that came to the Chinese capital at Hangzhou came by sea, while before that date approximately 35 percent of the tribute missions had come by land (Lo: 1955, 497). In addition, for the first time a Chinese dynasty encouraged China-based traders to trade directly with the south rather than depending on the import of goods through the tributary trade network. The Song government looked to the sea not only as a valued source of tax revenue on imports, but also as a market for exported (and still taxable) products such as silk, a variety of ceramics, and tea, and it also began to integrate the sea into China's defense strategy. In support of these initiatives, a Chinese navy became the foundation for later Mongol and Ming naval expeditions (Heng: 2009).

Although the entry of Chinese private merchants into Southeast Asia had already begun during the ninth and early tenth centuries, in the Song era this activity intensified. At first, Chinese merchants boarded Southeast Asia–based ships for trade in the Southern Seas, but soon Chinese junks also appeared in the Nanyang. Initially working out of the North China Sea, junks from the Chinese commercial fleet were voyaging as far to the west as Lamuri on the northern coast of Sumatra before the end of the twelfth century. By the mid-thirteenth century Chinese junks and traders were also active in the

Indian Ocean and competed against indigenous craft and their multiethnic crews (Wolters: 1970, 42; Wheatley: 1959, 24–25). The Arab traveler Ibn Battuta described with amazement the size of the Chinese junks he found in India during the early fourteenth century; he boarded one of them and voyaged to the northern Sumatra coast and said of the Sea of China (which probably meant the stretch of water from India eastward to the Chinese coast) that "traveling is done in Chinese ships only" (Gibb: 1929/1957, 235–36).

Ibn Battuta's account that Chinese junks were in control of the passageway has been corrected based upon recent analysis of shipwrecks and other archeological evidence dating to this era, which document that Southeast Asian *jong* (as they were referenced in retrospective sixteenth-century Portuguese accounts, as their linguistic variation of their references to the Chinese *junk*) were equivalent to the Chinese junks and were indeed their models, and thus Ibn Battuta's portrayal of a Chinese monopoly over that era's transport trade is incorrect (Manguin: 1994; Charney: 1997; Heng: 2008). The Chinese junk itself was of remarkable craftsmanship. It was larger than and superior to the Arab lateen; its sails were also superior, and it was able to tack in a headwind with remarkable ease. Ibn Battuta states that a single junk could carry a thousand men and that Chinese junks were built only in Quanzhou and Guangzhou, from which they sailed southward (Gibb: 1957, 235).

That era's vessels were an advance over earlier ship designs found in the South China Sea and Melaka Strait shipwreck sites associated with the first-millennium Southeast Asia polities discussed in chapter 2 (Flecker: 2009). While the later ships were fitted with wooden dowel pegs (rather than nailed), these earlier ships, which are portrayed in Borobudur's bas-relief, had planks and frames fastened together with vegetal fibers. Their hulls were built by raising planks on each side of a center keel and were held together by vegetal stitches or lashings (the fiber of sugar palms) (Li: 1979, 90). There were two kinds of these traditional ships. "Sewn plank" ships had stitches of vegetal fiber passing through holes drilled near the plank edges within seams. "Lashed lug" ships had the insides of their planks cut out, so that the planks could be lashed to the ship frame. In either case, the frame was not watertight, for the rope fibers expanded as water passed over them.

These sewn and lashed ships were adequate for the luxury trade of the pre-1000 era, but the increased volume of the maritime trade route in the Song era made this technology inadequate. By the thirteenth and fourteenth centuries they were replaced by new dowel-fitted ships (jong), which provided greater rigidity for ocean crossings by larger boats. These new Southeast Asian jong ships were held together by wooden dowel fittings inserted into the seams. Normally these new ships, like the Chinese junks, had multiple layers of hull planks (two to three layers was typical) so that if the outer layer was damaged the inner layers would maintain the ship's buoyancy. By this time Chinese junks were keel-less and flat-bottomed, and had watertight compartments in their holds as a further precaution to prevent the ship from sinking in a heavy storm. Southeast Asian jong, which had rounded hulls and did not have watertight compartments, were made of durable teak from Burma, Java, and Borneo, where they were built, and used double, lateral quarter-rudders as opposed to a single, axial stern-post rudder, as was common among Chinese and European ships of that era. Both the Southeast Asian jong and the contemporary Chinese junk had multiple masts, two to four, plus a bowsprit, which held sails made of vegetal matting (Manguin: 1980; Brown and Sjostrand: 2000).

A new Indian Ocean ship design technology also developed in the 1000–1500 era (Manguin: 1994). Neither exclusively Southeast Asian nor Chinese, the newly constructed ship, referenced in the early fifteenth-century Portuguese accounts as a *junco*, had planking that was fastened to the frame by iron nails, but which was also dowelled together by wooden pegs. Some had a single, axial rudder, in the Chinese tradition; others had quarter-rudders in the Southeast Asian style, as well as rounded hulls. Like Chinese vessels, these new seacraft had holds that were separated by bulkheads. But, unlike their Chinese counterparts, they were like Southeast Asian ships and did not have watertight holds. These new vessels, as well as the similarity between the Southeast Asian jong and the Chinese junk, demonstrate the interactive nature of the Indian Ocean maritime realm, where there was regular exchange of ideas and technology coincidental to the transaction of trade.

By the thirteenth century new commercial patterns were in place that would persist into the sixteenth century. Throughout this period, despite political upheavals that gave rise to shifting configurations of states on the island, Java was the dominant commercial power, due to its control of the spice trade that depended on its strategic location, wet-rice productivity, and political stability, and its dominance influenced much that was going on around it (see chapters 4 and 8). From the thirteenth century Java held ultimate power over southern Sumatra and surrounding island ports in the Straits of Melaka until the early fifteenth century, resisting even the intrusions of the newly formed Ming dynasty (1368–1644) in China (Hall: 2006; Heng: 2008). In fact, the substantial Chinese shipping that had developed in the eastern Indian Ocean disappeared in the early fifteenth century, due to the changing stance relative to commerce by Ming rulers from the 1430s, when they began to restrict the transit of China-based ships into the southern oceans, as well as certain Chinese products—above all Chinese ceramics. In this period through the sixteenth century, Chinese junks and numbers of south China merchants withdrew to the South China Sea, where they concentrated their activities as maritime diaspora based in ports on the Vietnam coastline, the Gulf of Thailand, Java, Borneo, and the Philippines, which was their base from which to sail eastward to the Spice Islands (see chapter 9). The Ming restriction on China-based overseas commerce, together with a substantial growth in Western demand for Asian goods, opened the way to expanded multiethnic Muslim shipping out of Indian ports, while ships from farther west also began covering the Middle East to Southeast Asia portion of the Indian Ocean maritime route (Schreike: 1955–1957; Lombard and Aubin: 1988/2000). The remainder of this chapter explores the variety of developments in the Southeast Asian mainland as they relate to the sea trade in general, beginning with the competitive conflicts on the Malay Peninsula and in the Melaka Straits regions from the early eleventh century as they relate to the Burma, Thailand, and Cambodian realms and the inclusive Vietnam coastline in the ca. 1200–1500 era.

ELEVENTH-CENTURY BURMESE EXPANSION ON THE MALAY ISTHMUS

As we have seen in chapter 6, by the first half of the eleventh century the Khmers of Cambodia had pushed their control westward into the Chaophraya valley of present-day Thailand. From there they temporarily directed their attention southward toward the Isthmus of Kra. Under Suryavarman I (1002–1050) Khmer administration was formally extended into the Lopburi region, with strong economic implications for the area to the south. Control of the lower Chaophraya River provided access to international commerce at Tambralinga on the Chaiya-Suratthani coast of southern Thailand, giving the Khmers a more direct contact with the international trade routes than had previously been the case in their eastern overland networking with the Cham and Dai Viet coastlines (see maps 6.3 and 7.1). After the Chola raids of 1024–1025 eliminated Srivijaya's power over the isthmus, the Khmers established their own influence over Tambralinga. As a consequence, a realm whose commercial interests had formerly been directed toward the eastern portions of its land was now reoriented to the west.

Khmer control of the area would be short-lived, for the Burmese to the northwest were also pushing south. As we have seen in chapter 6, the Burmese established their base at Pagan in the tenth century. Then, in 1057, the Burmese annexed the population centers at Thaton and Mergui in Lower Burma and thereby established control over the ports of trade in the upper Bay of Bengal (*SII*: 2, 105–9; Nilakanta Sastri: 1949, 80; Hergoualc'h: 2002; Aung Thwin: 2002; Abraham: 1988; Chutintaranond: 2002). Still in the late

1050s, the Pagan-based regime was expanding into the Malay Peninsula. As they did so, they encountered little resistance from the Khmers, who were suffering significant external and internal pressures (Luce: 1922; 1969–1970, 1: 21–23, 26). The Chams were applying pressure on the eastern Khmer border, and Suryavarman had died in 1050. After his death the center of Khmer political power temporarily shifted northeast into the Mun River valley beyond the Dangrek mountain range in what is today eastern Thailand. There the Khmer realm remained internally focused until the late twelfth century, effectively leaving the isthmus to the Burmese (Osborne: 1966, 447; Wyatt: 1994).

The Burmese move south was motivated by developments in the southern Yunnan region the Chinese knew as the Nanzhao kingdom, which lay north of the Burmese, Khmer, and Vietnamese realms. Previously, Burma had served as a center of exchange between northern India and Yunnan and onward to China proper, and overland trade to Burma via Arakan had been of major economic importance to the Burmese heartland (Yang: 2004). However, disorder with the collapse of the Tang and in the Nanzhao realm in the tenth century appears to have blocked the overland commercial networks connecting the Irrawaddy plains and China, forcing the Burmese to turn southward, where commercial centers on the Malay Peninsula provided an alternative source of foreign commodities for the India trade (Stargardt: 1971). Southern Burma commercial centers at Bassein (Kusumi) and Tala (a port near Pegu) became high-priority administrative centers under Pagan rule. Important ministers were allowed "to eat" (*ca*) a percentage of the revenues (trade revenues?) of these commercial centers. In 1058, Anawrahta (1044–1077) erected a statue of Gavaruputi (Gavampati) after his alleged 1057 sack of Thaton. This guardian deity of cities was originally that of Pagan and Sri Ksetra in the Irrawaddy River upstream, whose patrons were merchants and seamen. Subsequently, by the fifteenth century, it became the tutelary deity of the Mons in Lower Burma (Aung Thwin: 2005). As for points farther south, the isthmus port of Takuapa was located well within the range of Lower Burma coastal shipping, and it would soon pass under Burmese control as well. Around 1057, King Anawrahta followed his conquest of the coasts by moving his armies south to Mergui, and from Mergui the Burmese forces may have crossed the isthmus and extended their control south to Takuapa (Luce: 1966, 59).

Burmese military success in this direction is reflected in a request by King Vijayabahu I (1055–1110) of Sri Lanka for aid against the Cholas, to which the Burmese king ("the king of Ramanna") responded with "peninsular products," which were used to pay Vijayabahu's soldiers (Luce: 1965, 270). The Cholas did not look favorably upon this show of support. In 1067, they launched an expedition against "Kadaram" (Takuapa), in "aid of its ruler," who had been forced to flee his country and had sought Chola assistance in regaining the realm. The raid was of no lasting value to the Cholas, who by 1069–1070 had abandoned Sri Lanka to the victorious Vijayabahu I. The ultimate beneficiary may have been Pagan. Though a Chola inscription claims to have restored Takuapa to its ruler (*SII*: 3, 84; *ARE*: 1 of 1937–1938; *EI*: 25, 241–66), Takuapa actually never recovered, as the archeological evidence from the Takuapa area terminates at about this time (Lamb: 1961; Hergoualc'h: 2002). Meanwhile, the *Culavamsa*, the Sri Lankan Buddhist chronicle, records that in 1070, after he had consolidated his new Sri Lanka state, Vijayabahu I sent many costly treasures to the Pagan king. Then, in 1075, he invited Buddhist priests from Burma to Sri Lanka to purify the monastic order (Geiger: 1930, 58:8–9; Luce: 1969–1970, 1:40; Bandaranayake, et al.: 1990; Gunawardana: 2001).

The 1067 raid was but the final step in Takuapa's decline, for the entrepôt had already been weakened by the restructuring of trade routes since 1025. As noted above, the Chola raid of 1025 had resulted in loosening Srivijaya-Palembang's control of commerce in the strait region. These changes had moved trade away from Takuapa as well. By the late eleventh century the northern Sumatra coast was becoming an important commercial alternative to Srivijaya (Guillot: 1998; McKinnon: 2006), and the Kedah coast directly across the strait was more strategically located for contact with these centers than was Takuapa. Archeological remains at Kedah reflect a dramatic increase during the second half of the eleventh century, and they also show architectural similarities with northern Sumatra temples constructed in this period (Lamb: 1961; Peacock: 1974; Wisseman Christie: 1998a). In addition to Takuapa's inability to compete with Kedah's geographical location and cultural ties, it was also becoming clear that Takuapa was no longer a port that could offer security to foreign merchants. The Burmese military presence at Takuapa, followed by the second Chola raid, sealed Takuapa's fate and reinforced Kedah's attractiveness (Tibbetts: 1979: 118–28). Meanwhile, in 1070 the eastern Isthmus of Kra "kingdom" of Tambralinga presented its first tribute to the Chinese court since 1016 (Wolters: 1958, 595). This mission, which was its last, may have been meant to reassure the Chinese that their status as the east coast terminus was unchanged despite the Burmese inroads and the western terminus's shift from Takuapa to Kedah.

More importantly, the Pagan realm was emerging as a focal point of regional commerce (Gommans and Leider: 2002). South Indian merchants who were formerly active at Takuapa moved their activities either south to Kedah or north to the regional commercial centers of the Burma coast. Pagan itself was moving to establish commercial ties with northern and southern

India. An inscription (1105–1106) from Bodhgaya in Bengal recorded that ships laden with large quantities of jewels had been sent by the Burmese ruler to finance the restoration and the endowment of the Buddhist monument there (*EI*: 2, 119). The fact that this mission was sent by sea is indicative of Pagan's new status as a participant in the regional trade of the Bay of Bengal.

The Shwesandaw Pagoda inscription in Pagan (1093) records another mission that Kyanzittha sent to either south India or Sri Lanka.

> Then the king wrote of the grace of the Buddharatna, Dhammaratna, and Sangharatna (upon a leaf of gold with vermilion ink). The king sent it to the Choli prince. The Choli prince with all his array, hearing of the grace of the Buddha, the Law and the Sangha, from King Sri Tribhuwanadityadhammaraja's mission . . . he cast off his adherence to fake doctrines, and he adhered straight away to the true doctrine. (Duroiselle: 1960, I, viii, 165)

The last line of the inscription states that the Choli prince showed his gratitude by presenting to Kyanzittha "a virgin daughter of his, full of beauty," together with other presents (Luce: 1969–1970, 1:63).

Although stated in religious terms, there are strong economic implications in this second account. This prince may have been the Chola king Kulottunga I (1070–1122) who in 1090, though a significant patron of Hinduism in his south Indian realm, renewed an endowment of village revenues to the Buddhist *vihara* at Nagapattinam on the Coromandel Coast (*EI*: 22, 267–81; Spencer: 1983, 149–50). This was both an act of religious eclecticism and derived direct benefits, as this temple was also patronized by Chinese diaspora seafarers who were presumably based at Nagapattinam, then the most prominent port of trade in the Chola realm. By the early twelfth century the Nagapattinam vihara would come under the control of the Theravada school of Buddhism, which had become dominant in Burma as well (Paranavitana: 1944; Gunawardana: 2001).

At this time there continued to be a close but possibly conflicted relationship between the Chola realm and Srivijaya, despite the devastating Chola raid on the latter in 1025. Srivijaya's rulers had endowed the Buddhist temple (vihara) at Nagapattinam on the Coromandel Coast in the early eleventh century (*EI*: 22, 213–66; Spencer: 1983, 134–35). Later that same century a stone tablet inscription dated 1079, which was discovered in a Taoist monastery temple in Guangzhou, states that the temple's benefactor was the Chola king (Ti Hua Ka Lo), who was also called the "lord of the land of *Sanfozhi*" (i.e., Srivijaya) (Seong: 1964). The Chinese themselves were not quite sure of the relationship between the two realms, and some Chinese chronicles even represent the Cholas as being subordinate to Srivijaya (Seong: 1964, 21). Some twentieth-century Indian historians assumed that the Cholas exercised considerable control over Srivijaya's government on a continuing basis during the eleventh century (Majumdar: 1937, 182–90). While the latter is unlikely, it is nevertheless true that the Cholas were favorably remembered in the Malay historical traditions; noting that Chola monarchs were incorporated as ancestors of fifteenth-century Melaka monarchs in the sixteenth-century court chronicle *Sejarah Melayu* (Alexander the Great is also included in this lineage, as are the Srivijayan monarchs), George W. Spencer's detailed study of the evidence concludes: "What seems significant is that the Malay chronicler-genealogists of the fifteenth century and later were so impressed by Malay memories of the Cholas that they regarded an ancestral connection with them to be worth bragging about" (Spencer: 1983, 148–49).

This background adds significance to the possible diplomatic connections between the Chola king Kulottunga and the Burmese king Kyanzittha. It is difficult to resist the conclusion that these efforts were economic in motive, even though they were clothed in religious garb. Closer economic ties by sea to south India and Sri Lanka would have provided new economic potential for Pagan, and, as Kyanzittha's inscription indicates, royal patronage was granted to efforts to open these new channels of communication. Given these contacts, it is not surprising to find evidence of the south Indian maritime diaspora at Pagan itself. A thirteenth-century Pagan inscription documents such a presence, recording that a native of India's Malabar Coast made a donation to a *nanadesi* temple at Pagan (*EI*: 7, 197–98). The nanadesi was one among several organizations of south Indian itinerant merchants in existence during the Chola period. These merchants' activities also took them to the Barus region of the northern Sumatra coast in the late eleventh century (Nilakanta Sastri: 1932; Subbarayalu: 1998–2003). The thirteenth-century Pagan inscription indicates that the merchants' temple had been present there for some time; the recorded gift provided for the construction of a new shrine (*mandapa*) for the temple compound, which was also dedicated to Visnu. Further evidence of a continuing economic relationship between Pagan and south India is demonstrated in an 1178 Chinese note on the Cholas: "Some say that one can go there by way of the kingdom of P'u-kan [Pagan]" (Hirth and Rockhill: 1911, 94, 98; Guy: 1993–1994; 2001).

THE UPPER MALAY PENINSULA AND THAI
REGIONS IN THE TWELFTH CENTURY

Burma's rise to commercial prominence shattered further the old dominance that Srivijaya had enjoyed over international trade along the Straits of Melaka. While Java and the northern Sumatra ports drew the major international route south and west, the Burmese drew the regional route of the Bay of Bengal north, and the Isthmus of Kra came to exist essentially as a transition area to the mainland states. In the following decades, the upper Malay Peninsula became the center of a multipartite interaction among the Singhalese of Sri Lanka, the Burmese, and the Khmers. Based on his study of Buddhist votive tablets and other evidence, historian G. H. Luce believed that Pagan controlled the isthmus from 1060 until roughly 1200 (Luce: 1959). However, Burma may not actually have exercised direct control of the upper peninsula during this period, especially not during the second half of the twelfth century. The Tambralinga realm, for example, sent an independent embassy to China in 1170 (Wolters: 1958, 600). There is evidence that just prior to this Sri Lanka exercised some kind of suzerainty over Tambralinga (Wyatt: 1994, 1975, 26–28, 38–39, 42, 59, 66–71, 72–79; Aung Thwin: 1985). As for Burma itself, later chronicles indicate that during the reign of King Alaung-sitthu (1113–1169) the lower Burma provinces were in a state of "anarchy" and "rebellion" (Aung Thwin: 1998). Though King Narapatisithu of Pagan (r. 1174–1211) reportedly reconquered the area to the south, at the end of the twelfth century he claimed control only over the peninsula ports at Tavoy (an urban center near Mergui), Tenasserim, and Takuapa, all on the west coast, though extending well down the peninsula. Furthermore, archeological evidence documenting Pagan's control in this period has not been found south of Mergui (Luce: 1965, 276).

During this period, Tambralinga itself became an important center of the Theravada Buddhist school. Pali literature from Sri Lanka regarded Tambralinga (Tamalingamu) as an important twelfth-century center of Buddhist scholarship (Wyatt: 1994). Indeed, a Polonnaruva inscription from the reign of the Singhalese king Vikkamabahu I (1111–1132) may even record the "conversion" of Tambralinga to the Mahavihara Theravada school of Sri Lanka (Paranavitana: 1966, 80). This inscription honors a great elder (*thera*) of the Sri Lanka *sangha* named Ananda who was instrumental in purifying the order in that land (*EZ*: 4:66–72; Paranavitana: 1944, 24). Also, Tambralinga continued to be recognized in international records as an important source of forest products in the trade with China and elsewhere (Wheatley: 1961, 67, 77; Heng 2009). The commentary of Zhou Qufei writing in 1178 asserted that the upper peninsula produced some of the best incense available.

Beyond the seas the *Teng-liu-mei* gharuwood ranks next to that of Hainan [where the price of incense had become too high]. It is first rate. Its trees are a thousand years old. . . . It is something belonging to the immortals. Light one stick and the whole house is filled with a fragrant mist which is still there after three days. It is priceless and rarely to be seen in this world. Many of the families of the officials in

Guangdong and Guangxi [provinces] and families of the great ones use it. (Wolters: 1958, 600)

Though the isthmus had become less significant as a stop in the trade route between the West and China, it continued to be important in secondary Bay of Bengal regional trade networking among Sri Lanka, Burma, and the Khmer Empire. Keeping the route open was especially important to Sri Lanka, potentially motivating an early twelfth-century Singhalese intervention at Tambralinga that was recorded in the subsequent regional chronicles of Nakhon Si Thammarat (Wyatt: 1994). Similar concerns sparked a major raid of lower Burma in 1165 that is reported in the *Culavamsa* chronicle of Sri Lanka (Geiger: 1930, 76:10–75). According to the chronicle, in the 1160s the Burmese (most likely one of the governors of southern Burma) somehow either refused or monopolized the trade in elephants and blocked the way across the peninsula to Angkor, and the Singhalese responded with a retaliatory raid. Five ships from Sri Lanka, led by a certain Kitti Nagaragiri, arrived at the port of *Kusimiya* (Bassein) in Ramanna (Lower Burma). A sixth ship commanded by a government treasurer reached Papphala, the Lower Burma port mentioned in the 1030 Tanjavur inscription of the south Indian Cholas. These Singhalese troops fought their way into the country's interior to the city of Ukkama and killed the monarch of Ramanna, bringing the kingdom under Sri Lanka's influence. The people of Ramanna granted concessions to the Singhalese and sent envoys to the community of monks based on the island, with the result that the Theravada monks interceded with the Sri Lankan king on the behalf of the Ramanna population (Geiger: 1930, 76:59–75).

The *Culavamsa*'s account of the 1165 raid has received considerable attention. Historians used to believe that the Singhalese raid penetrated to Pagan, that the death of King Narathu (r. 1167–1170) coincided with this raid, and that the 1160s were furthermore a period of general disorder in Burmese history. However, inscriptions published in the 1970s indicate that Alaungsitthu ruled until 1169, four years after the date of the Singhalese raid (Burma Archeological Department: 1972, 33–37; Aung Thwin: 1976a, 53–54). Furthermore, Michael Aung-Thwin's revisionist research, based on his translations of this new epigraphic data, shows that this era was a time of general and increasing prosperity, with normal affairs of state continuing rather than declining, at least in the Pagan core region. It seems most likely, therefore, especially given the small number of ships, that the Sri Lankan expedition was at most a naval raid against Lower Burma.

As noted above, later Burmese chronicles record that during Alaungsitthu's reign the lower Burma provinces were in a state of "anarchy" and "rebellion," suggesting that a local governor had become quite powerful and may have attempted to assert his independence from Pagan. Though the location of Ukkama is not known, it may have been a commercial and administrative center in Lower Burma, possibly Martaban, a later capital of the area. (Aung Thwin: 1998, 7–32). Pagan "governors" in Lower Burma derived considerable income from trade revenues generated by the regional commercial networks, and by obstructing Sri Lankan commerce with Angkor this governor would have established personal control over this lucrative trade.

Similarly, the *Culavamsa* notes that one of the Sri Lankan attack ships was led by a Singhalese treasurer, who like the Lower Burma governor would have had much to gain personally from an increase in trade revenues. This interpretation of the expedition as an economically motivated raid fits the evidence in an inscription from the twelfth year of the Singhalese king Parakramabahu I (1165), which records a land grant to a certain Kit Nuvaragal (i.e., Kitti Nagaragiri) as a reward for carrying out a successful expedition against Aramana (Ramanna), perhaps this very same raid, where he is said to have sacked Kusumiya (Bassein) (*EZ*: 3:321, no. 34). The reward was not for the military achievement itself, but for inspiring the people of Aramana to send envoys to conclude a treaty—evidence that the primary aim was not conquest but the restoration of trade. Whatever the specific circumstances, the raid by the Singhalese on Lower Burma was the high point of the twelfth-century competition for control of the isthmus, and in 1186 Parakramabahu's successor Vijayabahu II concluded a final treaty of peace with Burma that left the way to Cambodia open through the rest of the century (Geiger: 1930, 80:6–8).

Around this same time, the peninsula appears to have once again become important to the Khmer as well. Though they had withdrawn from the isthmus after the 1050s, by the twelfth century Chinese authors of the Song period saw the upper east coast of the peninsula as being within the Cambodian sphere of influence (Wheatley: 1961, 65–66, 299–300). We lack specifics on the twelfth-century relationship between Sri Lanka and the Khmer state, despite its evident importance to the Singhalese. The upper peninsula was a significant intermediary of economic and cultural contacts between Sri Lanka and Angkor. It was for this reason that Sri Lanka was willing to risk war with the Burmese to preserve access. Furthermore, a late twelfth-century inscription from Sri Lanka specifically states that friendly relations with Cambodia were maintained (*EZ*: 2, no. 17), while another twelfth-century inscription references one of the city gates at Polonnaruva as Kambojavasala, reflecting a possible Cambodian settlement in the city (*EZ*: 2, no. 74). In addition, the *Culavamsa* documents the Burmese interception of a betrothed Singhalese princess en route to Kamboja, allegedly one of the events leading to the 1160s war (Geiger: 1930, 76:35). Marriage alliances with the Khmers may have been a common tool of the Singhalese royal house. The cross-cousin marriage patterns of the Singhalese royalty favored continuing relationships (Trautmann: 1973), and such an alliance with Cambodia would perhaps have been seen as providing long-range benefits to Sri Lanka's court, especially a military alliance against the Burmese, since the Khmer Angkor realm that was at that time Pagan's neighbor was widely acknowledged as a significant power on the continent.

Cambodian interaction with the peninsula is evinced in the relationship between the Khmer realm and Tambralinga on the east coast of the Isthmus of Kra. The last recorded embassy of the latter to the Chinese court took place in 1070, while Cambodia sent embassies in 1116, 1120, 1128–1129, and 1131 (Wolters: 1958, 605). Though it might be argued from this that the Khmers came to dominate the upper coast between 1070 and 1130, it is more likely, given Cambodia's internal political problems in the late eleventh and early twelfth centuries as described in chapter 6, that Tambralinga was a neutral polity (albeit of reduced significance) and that the Khmer embassies were meant to reassure the Chinese that the disorders being experienced in the Khmer realm would not interrupt the flow of southern commerce. As noted earlier, the Tambralinga realm was long recognized as an important source of forest products. In the twelfth century Chinese merchants were dealing directly with the sources of supply—on the peninsula and in Sumatra and Java—rather than with middleman entrepôts of the Srivijaya type, and Tambralinga would not have needed to send embassies to advertise its products. Meanwhile, the Khmer realm was struggling to maintain its control even closer to home. In 1155, for example, the Chinese record a gift of elephants from the western Zhenla state (*Zhenla* was used consistently by the Chinese to designate the Khmer realm from earliest times) of Lohu (Lavo/Lopburi), an indication that the Chaophraya valley (Lohu) was then free from Khmer control (Wolters: 1958, 605).

Despite the mid-century loss of their westernmost realms, the Khmer appear to have maintained ongoing relations with the Isthmus of Kra. The Prah Khan inscription of 1191 in the time of Jayavarman VII (see chapter 6) includes a reference to localities in the northern access zone to the peninsula, including Ratburi and Phetburi, though there is no record of any specific relationship between Angkor and the Isthmus of Kra (Coedes: 1941; Wyatt: 2001, 15–22). A Cham inscription from central Vietnam reportedly refers to a campaign by Jayavarman VII on the peninsula in 1195, which would indicate an attempt to restore a formal relationship (Aymonier: 1900–1904, 3:528; Woodward: 1975, 91–102; Dupont: 1942; Casparis: 1967; Coedes: 1937–1966, 7:124–26). Clay Buddhist votive tablets dating to that era scattered between the Bay of Bandon and Nakhon Si Thammarat provide further evidence of communication between the isthmus and Angkor. These twelfth-century tablets are linked to the multiple focal figures of Angkor Thom and are a departure from earlier Mahayana-style tablets of the eleventh century, having more affinity to Theravada Buddhism than to the Mahayana tradition that was favored by Jayavarman VII. But they are consistent with other evidence that suggests that Jayavarman's Mahayana Buddhism was eclectic and was highly influenced by the contemporary Tantric traditions that were common to the Bay of Bengal Buddhist community (O'Connor: 1968; Wyatt: 2001, 47–52; Woodward: 1981). Thus, a networked Theravada Buddhist religious community was spreading along the communication routes shared by Pagan, Sri Lanka, and Angkor Cambodia. As noted earlier, by the mid-twelfth century, Tambralinga had also become a center of Theravada Buddhist scholarship, and Cambodia's contacts with the peninsula would have facilitated the spread of the Theravada school from this source as well. Furthermore, according to Burmese legend, when Pagan's monks were reordained in the line of the Singhalese school of Theravada Buddhism at the end of the twelfth century, one of the five monks who returned from Sri Lanka to begin this purification was supposedly the son of a Khmer king, probably Jayavarman VII (Ko: 1892, 53). In addition, art historians believe that the Preah Palilay temple at Angkor Thom, constructed during Jayavarman VII's reign, exhibits a Theravada Buddhist style that was introduced from Burma via the Chaophraya valley (Boisselier: 1966, 94, 275–76; Woodward: 1975, 104–7).

As noted, these networked cultural exchanges happened at a time when the Khmer were likely losing control over their westernmost territories of Lavo, centered at Lopburi, and the wider Chaophraya valley (Wyatt: 2001, 25–47). These losses correspond in time to the increasing number of military expeditions that the Khmer monarchs waged against their eastern Vietnamese and Cham neighbors. Such expeditions assume an important role in Khmer history from the late eleventh century on. Khmer and Cham inscriptions imply that the Khmer, Cham, and Vietnamese were competing for manpower and resources to finance their courts, as the inscriptions eulogize successful expeditions of royal conquest and consequent redistributions of material and human plunder to Khmer and Cham temples (see chapter 6). The increasing importance of trade revenues and trade-derived material resources as sources of state revenue and ritualized redistributions demonstrates the inability or unwillingness of Khmer monarchs to increase the state's direct revenue collections from its agrarian base. As explained in chapter 6, the Khmer state's ritualistic statecraft depended on endowing temple networks with revenue assignments rather than on creating an elaborate administration that could tap the realm's agricultural production. Until the eleventh century, this system had been successful, as Khmer inscriptions document widespread prosperity, general stability, and continuous expansion of the state's agrarian base despite periodic wars of succession and invasions by the Vietnamese and Chams. However, the warfare that dominated Khmer history from the eleventh century on must have placed additional financial burdens on the Angkor-based state.

The earlier expansion of commerce during the reign of Suryavarman I (1002–1050), as described in chapter 6, solicited local and international trade that he might tap through collection of taxes and/or the formalization of service relationships with merchants, as was done by other contemporary regional rulers. But his commercial initiatives were not adequately maintained by his successors, who relinquished control of the economically important western sector to emerging Thai polities.

Trade remained important in the time of Suryavarman II (1113–1150), who built the Angkor Wat temple complex and is said to have become personally involved in trade relations with China and to have possessed his own fleet (Wolters: 1958, 598–606). During his reign Chinese traders visited Cambodia with cargoes of silk goods and porcelain. In 1147, the Chinese conferred "specific favors" upon the Khmer state. Song porcelain has been excavated at Angkor, but after Suryavarman II's reign there is a noticeable gap in epigraphic references to commercial relations that extends until the reign of Jayavarman VII (1181–1218), when the inscriptions of Ta Prohm (1186) and Prah Khan (1191) account Chinese articles in their inventories of temple property. An inscription from the Phimanakas palace temple at Angkor Thom, also from the time of Jayavarman VII, references a flag made of colored Chinese silk (Coedes: 1937–1966, 2:178).

Even more important than the ties with China were Angkor's links with Sri Lanka and Burma, as it was from these countries, mediated by the polities on the Isthmus of Kra, that the Khmer realm acquired the Theravada Buddhism that predominates there to this day. Earlier historians have speculated that one or another of these three powers must have politically dominated the Isthmus of Kra at various times in the century. But the evidence cited above indicates that while the contemporary Burma, Angkor, and Sri Lankan polities each had a real interest in the peninsula, Sri Lanka's interest was of a more commercial nature, while Pagan and Angkor did have ambitions of territorial expansion. Thus for Sri Lanka attempts to dominate the peninsula politically were unnecessary and perhaps undesirable, and the Singhalese raid on Lower Burma in the 1160s, for example, is best understood as an attempt to clear obstacles to trade rather than an effort to incorporate this distant region politically. Partly through these efforts, by the end of the twelfth century the way across Lower Burma and the isthmus was again open and serving as a path for the spread of Theravada Buddhism to the western and central sections of the Southeast Asian mainland (Sumio: 2004). Thereby a net-worked cultural relationship of great significance for later centuries began. Meanwhile, as we have seen, the old Isthmus of Kra emporia had declined in importance. The same was true of the entrepôts on southeastern Sumatra that were associated with the old state of Srivijaya.

THE DECAY OF SOUTHEASTERN SUMATRA
RIVERINE SYSTEM EMPORIA

The location and type of commodities involved in the Song maritime trade demonstrate what areas the Chinese were familiar with as well as those they did not know (Wheatley: 1959, 16–17; Heng: 2009). Zhao Rugua, superin-tendent of maritime trade at the China coast port of Quanzhou, reconstructed the world he knew in a 1225 work on maritime trading patterns that derived much of its information directly from the seamen and traders themselves (Wheatley: 1959, 5–8; Hirth and Rockhill: 1911, 35–39). He divided South-east Asia into an Upper Shore (Shang An), including the mainland and the Malay Peninsula, a region with which the Chinese had had contact in prior centuries; and a Lower Shore (Hsia An), covering Sumatra and the Java Sea, whose trading network had been in former times controlled by the Srivijaya state. On the former were Champa, the Khmer state, and the east coast of the peninsula; the latter included the old favored coast of southern Sumatra, the ports of Java, and the south coast of Borneo. Two areas are conspicuously missing from this Chinese view in any geographical detail: the hinterland of the isthmus and the eastern islands beyond the Java Sea. Yet where the latter, merely referred to en masse as the Ocean Islands (Hai Tao), were concerned, the Chinese still had an idea of the types of goods that the area produced and that it took in exchange (Wheatley: 1959, 45, 61, 73, 83, 98, 100, 119, 124; Heng: 2009).

In the twelfth century Southeast Asia's spices had become popular in an increasingly wealthy Europe and China, not only as consumables, but also as cures for all sorts of ailments, which were treated by mixtures of pepper, gin-ger, cinnamon, sugar, cloves, and especially nutmeg. Southeast Asian spices were also incorporated into European diets as flavoring for meats, coincident with Europeans eating much more meat year-round than previously (Bautier: 1971, 142–44, 205–9, 217–19). By the thirteenth century Western European demand had greatly enhanced the commercial importance of Southeast Asia. The name Java became synonymous in the West with spices, and to satisfy this demand there came to Java's ports a multiethnic community of traders whose bases were spread throughout southern India, Sri Lanka, and Southeast Asia (Yule: 1913–1916, 1:88–89; Tibbetts: 1979, 179–82).

During this time merchants based on the Java coast carried on two kinds of external trade. The first was a trade in spices and other luxury goods directed outside the archipelago toward both the East and the West (primarily with India and China and from India on to Europe). The second was a trade within the archipelago in which Javanese rice and Indian and Javanese cloth were exchanged for such things as Maluku spices, Balinese cloth, and Sumatran pepper. Many of these imported goods were then reexported from Java by seasonally resident Chinese and other multiethnic Java-based sojourners to China and India. Chinese goods exchanged for the archipelago's products included porcelain, musk, "gold-flecked hemp silks," beads, yarns, gold, silver, iron, and copper coins; those from the West included Indian textiles and Middle Eastern glass and frankincense. All these also found their way to western and eastern archipelago spice centers (Mills: 1970, 97; Meilink-Roelofsz: 1962, 83–84, 93–100, 105–15). The Chinese were already importing Southeast Asian spices in quantity from Java by the twelfth century. Pepper produced in northern Sumatra was particularly in demand and was also obtained through Java (Wheatley: 1959, 100; Ptak: 1993; Schottenhammer: 1999; Clark: 1995). Although Chinese consumers regarded Sumatra's pepper to be of lower grade than that produced along India's Malabar Coast, it was cheaper, especially as a result of the high demand for India's pepper among new Western consumers, and was more directly available to the Chinese. Monarchs based in east Java fostered this trade as well, but no single port dominated Java's trade (Wisseman Christie: 1999). At the end of the thirteenth century the most dominant were Tuban on the north coast and Surabaya at the mouth of the Brantas River (see chapter 8). Both ports were adjacent to major rice-producing regions; Surabaya traded with its hinterland via the river, while Tuban was linked to its hinterland by a road network. Along these networks, rice was brought to the coast from internal market centers, which in return were supplied with spices and foreign luxury goods. Ships then sailed from both Tuban and Surabaya to the spice-producing regions.

Java's place as intermediary of the international spice trade was based on a mutual dependency that had developed between Java and the islands of the eastern archipelago. The great international demand for spices made it economically expedient for the eastern archipelago's populations to concentrate their energies on spice production rather than on subsistence agriculture. Java on the other hand had the ability to produce a surplus of rice, while also being strategically positioned next to the international maritime route. Thus, when Marco Polo visited Java on his return voyage to Europe from China at the end

of the thirteenth century, he encountered a tremendous array of riches, reporting that "Java . . . is of surpassing wealth, producing . . . all . . . kinds of
spices, . . . frequented by a vast amount of shipping, and by merchants who
buy and sell costly goods from which they reap great profit. Indeed, the treasure of this island is so great as to be past telling" (Polo: 1958, 247–48).

Most of the goods he listed were actually items the Java-based traders had
obtained on the intra-insular trade route. Polo's list of Java's trade goods
included diamonds and sapanwood (used in making red dye) from western
Borneo, white sandalwood incense from Timor, nutmeg from Banda and the
Malukus, and pepper from north and east coast Sumatra ports.

As Java's commercial stature grew, the role of the Straits of Melaka ports
diminished. In addition to the commercial and military competition from
Java, there was a new threat from the north as the Thai extended their reach
southward. The unsettled nature of the Straits realm in the thirteenth century
is demonstrated in local chronicles that report Thai incursions into the region
during the latter part of the century. In the late thirteenth century a Thai
muang regional center of political power was evolving in the Chaophraya rice
plain in the region between the declining Angkor realm to the east and the
Burmese domain of Pagan to the west. This emerging Thai civilization was
based on the fertile wet-rice lands of central Thailand, but its leaders derived
their primary income from control over the trading of rice rather than from
revenues directly assessed on landholders (Kasetsiri: 1976; Lieberman: 2003,
242–74; Wyatt: 2001). Consequently, the early Thai polities developed a
direct interest in commerce, especially in the direction of the main international maritime route to the south (Wyatt: 2001, 19–25).

Ramkhamhaeng, who reigned over the emergent Sukhothai state from
1279–1298, asserted that his power extended to the sea in the south (Griswold and Nagara: 1971; Chamberlain: 1991; Wyatt: 1984, 45–50). Whether
or not Ramkhamhaeng's own realm actually extended that far is generally
discounted by most scholars, as his was but one of several competing Thai
muang in that period, albeit one that claimed to dominate most of the Thai
cultural realm (Chamberlain: 1991). The notion of Thai political and military
activity in the Malay world is validated in a Chinese source relating that
around 1295 the Thai were ordered by the Chinese not to wage war again
with "Malayu," the remnant of the Srivijaya realm then based at Jambi on
the southeastern Sumatra coast (Coedes: 1968, 205; Pelliot: 1904, 398). Did
the lower Chaophraya River basin Thai settlements indeed undertake a naval
expedition against the southeastern Sumatra coast at this time? While we lack
direct epigraphic evidence, oral traditions suggest that they actually did so.

Early nineteenth-century ethnographers recording local oral tradition in the
Jambi region of Sumatra found several legends of wars with the Thai; one
legend holds that Jambi was devastated by a Thai army led by a Jambi prince

(Schnitger: 1939, 21). In addition, the *Hikayat Raja-Raja Pasai*, the court chronicle of the contemporary Samudra-Pasai pepper entrepôt in northern Sumatra, proudly reports that ports in that area were able to repulse undated Thai attacks, a detail that adds credence to the notion that Thai were active in the Straits region during the late thirteenth or early fourteenth century (Hill: 1960, 128–29). Furthermore, Chinese sources report that Singapore Island (Tumasek) in the Straits region was intermittently subject to alternating Thai and Javanese interests from the late thirteenth to the early fifteenth century, when this area came under the recently established Melaka emporium's authority (Wolters: 1970, 78–79, 108–9, 115–17; Coedes: 1968, 243, 245; Miksic: 1994; Heng: 2008).

Java's late fourteenth-century *Nagarakertagama* court chronicle likewise references the Thai as direct neighbors, saying that the Thai sphere of influence on the Malay Peninsula bordered on that of the Javanese kingdom of Majapahit. It was likely speaking of the kingdom of Ayudhya, which by this time had consolidated its hold over the Thai heartland as the politically dominant Thai polity. However, unlike the Chinese and Arab sources, which ascribed the area to the Thai at least part of the time, the Javanese claimed the southern Malay Peninsula entirely for themselves; according to the *Nagarakertagama* chronicle, the east coast Malay-speaking regions of Patani (Langkasuka), Kelantan (Kalanten), and Trengganu (Tringgano) were dependencies of Majapahit, with only regions to the north being Thai (*syangka*) (Robson: 1997).

A potential source of support for a Thai maritime presence were the overseas Chinese commercial communities resident in the Thai coastal region, whom Thai chronicles acknowledge as participants in the consolidation of the thirteenth- and fourteenth-century Thai state (Wade: 2000; Kasetsiri: 1992). Thai sources even credit a member of a Chinese merchant household with the founding of the Ayudhya realm in 1351. According to the Thai chronicles:

> The [previous] king [of Lopburi?] passed away and no member of the royal family could be found to succeed him. So all the people praised Prince U Thong, who was the son of [the leader of the Chinese merchant community; he was also well connected to two powerful Thai clan networks in Suphanburi and Lopburi], to be anointed as king and govern the kingdom [in due course he settled his people in the new capital city of Ayudhaya in 1351]. (Paul: 1967, 37).

THE RISE OF THAI AYUDHYA

Centers of early Thai (Siamese) political development culminated in the establishment of the Ayudhya court (1351–1767 CE). The new Thai political realm included most of the Chaophraya River basin in western and central Thailand, parts of the Malay Peninsula to its south, and the Mun River basin to its east. Ayudhya's core initially developed as the western edge of the Angkor realm in the early eleventh century CE. As reported above, Lopburi in the central Chaophraya River basin was an early Thai center. During the late thirteenth century, Lopburi's northern neighbor and rival, Suphanburi, was the urban center of a network of the remaining Khmer territories on the western edge of the Chaophraya valley.

In the famous Ramkhamhaeng Inscription cited above, the Sukhothai king Ramkhamhaeng (r. 1279–1298) claimed to have supported the development of a common Thai culture. At this time, however, the Thai realm was still split into networked political factions of regional chiefdoms (muang), the two most prominent centered in Sukhothai and in Lopburi. Although the Thai absorbed new ideas and techniques from their neighbors, these initially failed to trigger any large-scale integration of the Thai people. This changed in the first half of the fourteenth century, when development of commercial links with Sri Lanka supported Thai conversions to Theravada Buddhism. Thai kings supported the aggressive and patronizing Theravada Sangha, which evolved into a hierarchical network of monastic communities that provided a linked infrastructure for the Thai realm. The close relationship between Thai secular and religious leaders culminated in a central monastic and temple complex that was either coincident to or directly linked to the royal court. Ayudhya's political network, which depended on fragile personal alliances, was reinforced by the stable inclusive institutional structure of the Sangha as well as Buddhism's universal moral code, in contrast to neighboring Burmese states where there was ongoing political competition between the Burmese Buddhist Sangha and monarchs from the Pagan age (Lieberman: 2003, 119–48, 271–74). Thai Buddhism was always subordinate to the Thai monarchy.

In the mid-fourteenth century, U Thong (Ramathibodi, r. 1351–1369), supported by his southern Lopburi-based alliance, defeated the northern Suphanburi-based muang alliance network, united the two major Thai factions, and proceeded to annex many other Thai muang and stabilize his northern border against the rival Chiangmai-centered Lan Na realm (Lieberman: 2003, 267–68). He subsequently founded Ayudhya, which was the name of his new capital city on the northern edge of the Chaophraya Delta.

There are two Thai historical traditions relative to Thai monarchy (Kasetsiri: 1976; Wyatt: 2003). The *phongsawadan* "court tradition" focuses on dynastic chronology as the source of legitimacy, while the earlier *tamman* "Buddhist tradition" addresses Thai development in terms of the universal spread of the Buddhist faith. U Thong was the legitimate founder of Ayudhya in the tamman tradition because of his spiritual morality as a *phumibon* (one who has merit), as the son of a *setthi* (a rich man), and as the founder of a new center of Buddhism. His genealogical heritage was irrelevant. In contrast, the phongsawadan tradition addresses his secular legitimacy as the direct descendant of an old Thai ruling house from the north and says that he migrated to the south where he intermarried with two powerful families. The fifteenth-century Thai poem *Yuan Phai* reflects the blending of the Theravada tradition with earlier Hindu and Mahayana Buddhist beliefs. Speaking of King Trailok's (r. 1431–1488) intellectual virtues, the *Yuan Phai* refers to the reigning monarch as being well versed in the three gems of Buddhism (the Buddha, the Dhamma/Law, and the Sangha) as well as the Vedic texts (see chapters 1 and 6). Further, he was the reincarnation of eleven Hindu gods—Brahma, Visnu, Siva, Indra, Yama, Marut (god of wind), Varuna (god of rain), Agni (god of fire), Upendra (Krana), the Sun, and the Moon. Ayudhya kingship was thus ritually defined by a merging of the Theravada and the Hindu/Mahayana conceptual systems.

U Thong's new polity drew upon three sources of strength: Thai manpower and military skills from the western Suphanburi portion of his realm, Khmer and Mon prestige and administrative capacities from the Lopburi and eastern regions, and the wealth and the commercial skills of the Chinese and other Asian commercial communities that were based in his lower Chaophraya port capital. Political conflict centered on succession to the throne, which passed between the Suphanburi and Lopburi branches of the royal family until the early fifteenth century, when the Suphanburi faction prevailed.

King Trailok (Borommatrailokanat) annexed the remnants of the Sukhothai network in 1431, followed by sacking Angkor and seizing the Khmer kings' royal regalia as a statement of Thai independence. Ayudhya's kings were henceforth consecrated in the *indrabhiseka* ritual that had been the traditional ceremony of investiture performed on the behalf of Angkor's monarchs. This ritual, which symbolized the omnipotent power of the Ayudhya monarch, presented the myth of the Churning of the Ocean that was the thematic basis for the construction of Angkor Wat and Thom (see chapter 6). Herein the monarch sat on top of an artificial Mount Meru, the abode of the gods, just like Angkor's former kings, and was thereby empowered by the Indic deistic tradition.

In securing his realm, Trailok set in motion a Thai social/political system that would endure into the nineteenth century. Above all, Trailok's creation contrasts with the Malay maritime states to its south, as these had limited adjacent or upstream hinterlands and were thus highly vulnerable to the fluctuations of the international sea trade. Ayudhya derived from its southern maritime roots, a series of well-established downstream and Malay Peninsula population centers populated by mixed ethnicities (as the Thai chronicles, as cited above, acknowledged that U Thong was of likely Chinese ancestry), foundational to the conquest of an upstream mix of migrant highland Thai tribal and clustered pre-Thai wet-rice plain settlements scattered among the hills, valleys, and riverine plains (Ishii: 1978; O'Connor: 1995).

Thus Thai Ayudhya differed from its Burmese neighbors to its west. The pre-1500 Burmese polities similarly derived from a series of north-to-south tribal migrations from highland seminomadic to productive permanently settled river-valley settlements, but in Burma the internally focused northern agricultural and tribal factions periodically prevailed over those of the Bay of Bengal networked downstream, or there were multiple and/or separate upstream and downstream polities. In Burma, the fall of Pagan in the late thirteenth century was followed by the fragmentation of the old Pagan realm into an upstream-based Ava realm, which consisted of a series of networked "governorships" (*myosaship*) in the Shan highlands and the rich agricultural lands that had been at Pagan's center, and the downstream Pegu and Arakan polities that depended on Bay of Bengal maritime commerce. During their fourteenth- and fifteenth-century height, the Pegu and Ava polities were linked by their need for each other—as a source of upstream products and as the upstream's international marketplace—and by the unity of the Burmese Sangha, as a strong Theravada Buddhist Sangha provided the institutional umbrella for societal stability instead of a continuous and inclusive monarchy (Aung Thwin: 2011).

Trailok's initiatives institutionalized the continuing importance of the Ayudhya monarchy's maritime trade engagements, but its upstream gave it added stability against the periodic fluctuations in the sea trade as he incorporated his productive Chaophraya River upstream wet-rice civilization. Thus, as many Thai scholars now argue, Ayudhya was at first a maritime state on the edge of a productive hinterland, which evolved into a territorial power with positive consequence (Baker: 2003). In contrast, neighboring Burma and Khmer polities never moved from their limitations as upstream territorial powers to fully embrace the potentials of international trade, and Ayudhya's southern neighbors in maritime Southeast Asia that were limited to their coastlines and multiple riverine system geography lacked sufficient agriculturally productive upstream ricelands (with the exception of east Java as we shall see in chapter 8) to sustain diverse economic options.

The new Ayudhya polity reorganized its existing port and upstream population clusters into a unified administration based in a hierarchy of fortified urban centers ranging from the inner cities and outer cities, to tributaries. The old tradition of appointing royal princes to govern muang population centers ceased (since it had always led to clashes at the time of succession), and was replaced by a check-and-balance paired administration of military and civil officials. Separate civil officials (*mahattha*, organized into administrative agencies: interior, capital, finance/foreign trade, agriculture, palace, and justice) and military officials (kalahom) received distinctive ranks in a hierarchy of nobility, rewarded with delegated assigned income rights to productive land (*sakdina*/"field power").

The king had unlimited land (rai) income rights (2.3 rai equaled 1 acre of income); the uparat (crown prince/heir), 100,000; the chief minister, 10,000; minor department heads, 400. Among the sakdina, 400 and up began the bureaucratic nobility or the *khunnang*; below were the commoner petty officials, 50–400; craftsmen, 50; peasant freemen, 25; and slaves and beggars, 5. Differentiated societal grades were paired with pervasive decimal-based-system labor taxes, which were payable in a variety of labor assignments and military service. Men were obligated to provide six months of labor each year to the king and could be employed on public works or military campaigns. Their work was coordinated by *mun nai*, the court's territorial bureaucrats. The court's administrative authority over manpower replaced the prior flexible service relationships that existed between the freemen and their personal patrons. Those who escaped this bureaucratic control either attached themselves as personal clients to powerful officials, fled into the wilderness, or sold themselves into debt bondage.

The nobility were the inclusive patrons and local overseers of Buddhist temples and monasteries, and the conspicuous participants in secular spectacles. Feasts, game days, and civil commemorative holidays (e.g., the king's birthday) were state celebrations that paralleled religious ritual cycles, to reinforce the celebration of a Thai civil society in which Buddhism was foundational to the social ethos. Instead of the Buddhist Sangha and the court being concentrated in the new capital city, Sukothai initially remained the religious center of the realm. Trailok promulgated the Ayudhayan Law in 1458, which made the entire society subject to a series of written law codes in a palatine legal system (*kot manthianban*) in which the monarch was the ultimate lawgiver, but noblemen exercised certain delegated royal powers within their own domains.

By the 1460s, Ayudhaya dominated the affairs of the upper Malay Peninsula. It shared in the regionwide prosperity that followed the establishment of the Melaka sultanate at the beginning of the fifteenth century. Ayudhya annexed the Tenasserim (1460s) and Tavoy (1488) regions on the northwestern Malay Peninsula, which provided it with direct access to the international trade of the Bay of Bengal and Indian Ocean.

Ceramics were a vital new source of Thai prosperity from the fourteenth century, as recent regional archeological excavations and recovery of contemporary shipwrecks demonstrate that Thai ceramic production was widely marketed throughout the regions of the international maritime trade. Thai, Cham, and Dai Viet kilns challenged the early Chinese monopoly of ceramic exports from the late fourteenth century to the mid-sixteenth century, and dominated the marketplace coincident to the Ming dynasty's new restrictions on the export of Chinese blue-and-white porcelain from the 1430s (see below). Thai kilns at Sisatchanalai appear to have started production of underglazed black decorated ware in the fourteenth century under the influence of resident Chinese diaspora. Nearby Sukhothai started producing at around this time, and may have been the first to export their wares. The later introduction of celadon at Sisatchanalai seems to have been influenced by a second infusion of technological know-how, and subsequently Sisatchanalai overtook the export market from the Sukhothai kilns. Underglazed decorated and celadon plates were their main product until the mid-sixteenth century, when they ceased production after high-grade Chinese blue-and-white porcelain became immensely popular in Asian and European markets (Spinks: 1956; Roxanna Brown: 2008a, 2008b; Miksic: 2010a).

TRANSITIONS IN THE MELAKA STRAITS

Despite their interests in the south, the Thai states of the thirteenth through fifteenth centuries were not able to take on the role of direct commercial successors to Srivijaya, because the system of economics upon which the Srivijaya era was based had passed. By the thirteenth century the southeastern Sumatra coast was no longer the point of primary access to the goods from the Java Sea, having been replaced by Java ports. Sumatra coast centers did not regain their previous commercial stature until rising demand for Sumatran pepper elevated the commercial centers of the Sumatra northern coast to first-order status in the late fourteenth century (Salmon: 2002; So: 1998; L. Andaya: 2008, 146–72, 191–201, 222–34).

During this pre-1400 era, Java extended its authority not only over southern Malaya but also over southeastern Sumatra's ports. The latter development occurred during the thirteenth-century reign of Kertanagara (1268–1292), a period critical to Java's commercial expansion. Chinese dynastic records report the last mission from Palembang to China in 1277, and by 1286 Javanese power had reached Jambi (Wolters: 1970, 45). An inscription with the same 1286 date is found on a Buddha icon recovered from the Batang Hari River in the Jambi River basin; the inscription proclaims the installation of the Buddha by four Javanese officials under the authority of Kertanagara "for the joy of all the subjects of the country of Malayu" (Coedes: 1968, 201; Nilakanta Sastri: 1949, 96). How far north the power of

Kertanagara extended is unknown. The Javanese were not interested in re-establishing Srivijaya's old empire nor were they able to. Rather, they were intent upon destroying potential rivals in the lucrative trade, while also serving notice to the Straits region, which had by that time lapsed into a state of competitive disorder, that they would intervene, if necessary, to negate the widespread piracy that was endangering shipping passing through the Straits, and thus facilitate the passage of trade ships through to Java's ports.

However, as it imposed its authority over the Straits, Java found that its interests ran counter to those of the Chinese, who were themselves assuming a new aggressive role in Southeast Asian commerce. The old Tang and Song tributary system had passed; by contrast, both the Yuan (the Mongol dynasty) and the Ming were concerned with Southeast Asian affairs and were willing to take direct action in Southeast Asia if necessary to guarantee the flow of goods to Chinese ports (Hucker: 1975, 187–92; Heng: 2008). This interest is reflected in the reported Yuan warnings in the late thirteenth century that future Thai incursions into the Straits would not be tolerated. The Javanese were similarly perceived to be challenging what the Yuan conceived to be China's authority to supervise commerce in the Straits, and for this reason the Yuan mounted a naval expedition in 1292 against the Javanese, ostensibly to assert their dominance over Southeast Asia's sea channels. Piracy in the Straits was a major issue in bringing on this confrontation. The Chinese may also have been motivated by the memory of Srivijaya, for the Chinese still looked to Malayu/Jambi as their designated authority over the straits commercial realm. By the late thirteenth century it is doubtful whether the Jambi region held any commercial prominence. Nevertheless, when the Yuan court called for tributary missions from the Straits in this period, it was in essence trying to draw from would-be Straits tributary port-polities guarantees of security for the maritime trade route, while also trying to limit Java's role in the region.

The response of the old straits polities was meager. From Palembang, there was initially no response at all, likely a sign that it was subordinated to Jambi or Java at this time. From Malayu/Jambi, Yuan dynastic records report a tributary mission led by two Muslim envoys in 1281. Shortly afterward, in 1286, Javanese power under Kertanagara reached Jambi (as we saw above), and the 1292 Yuan expedition against Java followed shortly after this development. In 1293, the leader of the expedition notified the Yuan court that Malayu/Jambi had been issued imperial orders to show its submission to the throne by sending sons or brothers of the rulers to the Chinese capital, which they did in 1294 (Pelliot: 1904, 326). Then, in 1295, came the Yuan warning (mentioned above) that the Thai should stop their own attacks against Jambi, and this was followed by another tribute mission from Jambi in 1301.

Nevertheless, the region was becoming more internally focused, and Jambi continued to decline politically; a 1347 inscription from a ruined Jambi temple reports that at that time Adityavarman, ruler over the upstream highlands, held authority over Jambi (L. Andaya: 2008, 88–89). As for Palembang, not until the early Ming period in the late fourteenth century did this port seem to regain some degree of independence. In response to an imperial command presented to Palembang in 1370, a mission was sent to the Ming court in 1371, and subsequent missions were sent in 1373, 1374, 1375, and 1377 (Groeneveldt: 1887, 192–93) O. W. Wolters interpreted this frequency as an attempt by Palembang's rulers to recapture the old position of Srivijaya in the China trade (Wolters: 1970: 49–76; 187–90). If so, they failed. Retrospective Ming histories viewed Palembang as a minor commercial center, attributing its poverty to the Javanese conquest and the fact that thereafter "few trading vessels [went] there." To underline the point, it was referred to as the Old Harbor (Groeneveldt: 1887, 197; Heng: 2009).

Thus, by the fourteenth century the southeastern Sumatra coast had become insignificant in the international trade. Even on Sumatra itself, the southeast was now overshadowed by the developing pepper production and port centers clustered along Sumatra's northern coast. While southeastern Sumatra did not disappear entirely from the politico-economic map (tribute to China continued intermittently through the fourteenth century, coming first from Jambi and later from Palembang), commercial prominence had passed to the north. Even so, in the late thirteenth century only two ports on the northern Sumatra coast were invited by the Yuan to send tribute missions to China. One was Lamuli (Lamuri/Ramni), a port on the northern tip of the island (the future Aceh) frequented by Middle East traders since at least the tenth century (Tibbetts: 1979, 138–40). The second was Sumutula (Samudra), which during the thirteenth through the fifteenth centuries came to dominate north coast trade, as will be discussed in chapter 9.

CHAM AND VIETNAM COMPETITION FOR THE VIETNAMESE COASTLINE, 1200–1471

While the Thai and Javanese prospered and southeast Sumatra declined, the Champa realm was enjoying a period of relative strength, albeit one that would come to a sudden end in the fifteenth century. The theme of cultural and religious restoration is center stage in Cham inscriptions dating from the 1220s and 1230s, as they followed an era of Khmer dominance over the Cham realm that had dated to Jayavarman VII's late twelfth- and early-thirteenth century reign (as described in chapter 6). A Cham inscription from

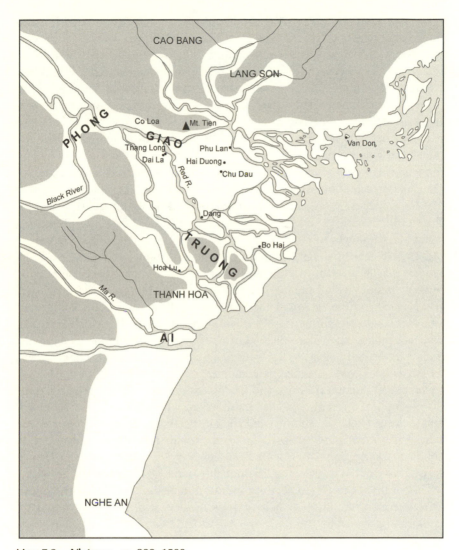

Map 7.2.   Vietnam, ca. 800–1500

this era reports that restoration efforts were necessary because Jayavarman had "carried away all the *lingas*" (Majumdar: 1927/1985, no. 85). The new Cham ruler, based in Vijaya, reconsecrated and purified temples, reactivated regional cults, and restored damaged temples. This new construction paralleled the style of Jayavarman VII described in the last chapter. As with Jayavarman's Khmer predecessors, the earlier temple architecture in the Cham realm had been refined in style, while the new thirteenth-century style was more imperial in content, monumental in size, and imposing in scale and subject matter, as the new rulers substantiated their legitimacy in a new age in which the Vijaya-centered Cham coastline became the centerpiece of a new Vietnam–to–south China networked trading community (see below).

As with the Bayon, new Cham temples were constructed with large plain blocks; the resulting temples were imposing in their massive bulk, in contrast to the earlier care for aesthetics and effort to maximize the decorative elements on temple walls. The point was to generate awe at a distance. This monumental style was especially evident in the case of the fortified citadel at the Cha Ban center of Vijaya, that era's dominant court. It was also visible at Thi Nai (modern Qui Nhon), its nearby port (Doanh: 2002), as well as in the Silver and Golden towers in the Binh Dinh Province, the Ivory Towers at Thap Mam (thought to be Vijaya's ritual center), and the Copper Towers in the Thua Thien Province. Commonly in the inscriptions dating 1224–1234, the new Cham ruler, Jaya Paramesvaravarman IV (1226–ca. 1243) based in Vijaya, "reinstalled all the *lingas* of the south, [viz.] those of Yan Pu nagara [Po Nagar], and the *lingas* of the north, [viz.] those of Srisanabhadresvara [the focal deity of Mi Son] . . . [following his coronation]," which is significant since these dates mark the end of Khmer dominance in the Cham realm during the reign of Jayavarman VII (Majumdar: 1927, 3:87, 88, 89, 91, 92). These temples were assigned new supplies of manpower—Khmer, Chinese, Syam (Thai), Pukam (Pagan), and Cham—to restore temples physically and also to work the temples' lands. As a consequence of these restorations, it was expected that the realm would again become strong and prosperous, because the proper worship of the gods could flourish. A late eleventh-century (1060) Cham inscription from neighboring Mi Son is of interest in its overview of the fragmented Cham realm that the Vijaya-based ruler faced; its list of threats to Cham security included the "Cambodians, Vietnamese, Vijaya, Amaravati, and all the countries of the north; Panduranga and the countries of the south; the Rade, the Mada, and other barbarous tribes in the regions of the west" (Majumdar: 1927, 3:76).

The inclusive Cham realm flourished from the early thirteenth century while Angkor and Pagan were declining, due in part to their temporary upstream isolation from the developing international maritime trade. Champa, by contrast, prospered in its response to new trade opportunities afforded by the growing maritime transit between Java and China. At the principal Cham port at Thi Nai (Qui Nhon), Chinese porcelain and silk were exchanged for Champa's highland forest products, especially aloewood, native cloth, rhinoceros horns, and elephant tusks (Shiro: 1998b, 1999). Cham (Zhanzheng) rice, produced in intensively cultivated upstream hinterlands, provisioned increasing numbers of sojourners who made stopovers in the Cham ports. Regularized contact between the Vijaya lowlands and the central highlands is documented by late fourteenth-century Hindu icons that have been recovered throughout the Central Plateau, as well as temple towers and stelae with Sanskrit inscriptions. As discussed in chapter 3, the early thirteenth century was the era in which the Cham rulers began to formalize their relationship with highland chiefs by bestowing royal titles on them (Hickey: 1982).

During the thirteenth century both local inscriptions and foreign accounts focus on the Cham ruler's personal wealth. According to the contemporary early thirteenth-century record of the Chinese portmaster Zhao Rugua (1225), the Cham ruler reigned from a spacious brick palace, attended by his subordinate princes. All of these possessed vast quantities of gold and jewels, as the royal and noble paraphernalia and symbols of authority included diadems, waistbands, necklaces, and earrings (Rockhill: 1917, 87–88). The Cham elite's focus on personal wealth and conspicuous consumption is not unlike the similar obsession with personal status markers elsewhere in the region, which reflects the local impact of the era's international trade boom (Hall: 2000). Chinese accounts link Champa's heightened trade and subsequent prosperity to Java, and according to the Chinese sources Cham ports (notably Vijaya's port of Thi Nai) passed Java's spices along to China, adding their own rich forest products from the Cham highlands (Rockhill: 1915, 26; Coedes: 1968, 229–30). By the end of the thirteenth century Cham ports were major players in the international trade, as demonstrated by the 1283–1285 Mongol (Yuan) raids against these ports when the Cham monarch refused to respond to the Yuan dynasty's demands for tribute (Coedes: 1968, 192–93).

Some historians suggest that Champa's commercial ties with Java may have been supplemented by political ones. During the early fourteenth century the Cham monarch Jayasinhavarman III (r. 1288–1307?) is thought to have married a Javanese princess, Tapasi. In the Vietnam chronicles' version of the events, Jayasinhavarman III was also said to have married a Vietnamese princess (Che Chi), whom he had received in exchange for relinquishing his rights to certain territories in the north that were contested by Dai Viet and Champa. The Vietnamese sources chronicle persistent rebellions against Vietnamese rule in these ceded territories, which forced the monarch Tran Anh Tong to send troops in 1312, when they also captured the Cham monarch and took him back to the Dai Viet capital, where he died in 1313. The Vietnamese emperor placed the deceased Cham king's brother Che Nang on the Cham throne as "feudatory prince of the second rank." But when Anh Tong became senior ruler and his son Minh Tong assumed executive authority in

1314, Che Nang asserted his independence and invaded the northern territories, which brought a Vietnamese reprisal in 1318; defeated, Che Nang fled to Java (some historians have proposed that he was the son of the Java princess) (Maspero: 1928, 189–205; Coedes: 1968, 217, 229–30). The Dai Viet emperor then placed a military chief Che Annan on the Cham throne. He proceeded to ally with the Mongols, and with their assistance he declared his independence in 1326. When Che Annan died in 1342, his son-in-law Tra Hoa Bo De seized the throne following a ten-year succession war against the legitimate heir Che Mo. The date of Tra Hoa Bo De's death is unknown. There is also the Javanese legend of Dvaravati, sister of a Cham king, who married the fourteenth-century ruler of Majapahit and subsequently encouraged the spread of Islam in Java (Maspero: 1928, 189). Cham representatives participated each year in Java's annual Caitra festival, which celebrated the sovereignty of the late fourteenth-century Majapahit monarchy (Robson: 1995, 34), where they shared in the Saivite-Buddhist rituals of their trade partners to the south.

Champa's links with Java were not the only important ones at this time. Newly recovered shipwreck cargoes in the Philippines demonstrate that by the fourteenth century there were also new links between Champa and the Philippines and from thence along a newly developing eastern maritime route via the Sulu Sea to Indonesia's Spice Islands (see chapter 9) (Ptak: 1992, 1998a). Champa's connections to the north were consequent to a developing new regional network that included China's southern coast, the west coast of Hainan Island, the eastern delta of Dai Viet and its port of Van Don, and the Cham coastline, as discussed below. In the late 1360s the Cham court developed an especially favorable relationship with the new Ming dynasty in China, at the expense of Dai Viet, which would last for several decades. Champa's extensive trade links, together with Dai Viet's dynastic confusion during the later fourteenth century (eventually including a two-decade Ming occupation [1407–1428]), enabled Thi Nai to become the primary intermediary stopover between Melaka and Java and south China's ports (Whitmore: 1985, 19–20; Li: 2006).

Fourteenth-century Vijaya's interest in securing its northern borderlands as a more stable resource base for the future paired with the prior Cham obsession with raiding Dai Viet to secure additional manpower for its slave market and to supplement its longstanding population deficiency (Whitmore: 2010b). However, Victor Lieberman's revisionist perspective is that fourteenth-century Champa faced a population surplus rather than a manpower deficiency, which was compounded by poor weather conditions (Lieberman: 2003, 385–93). Lieberman argues that an inevitable food crisis forced Champa to find new means to sustain its then-high standard of living, and this meant recovering northern lands that were starting to be settled by expansive Vietnamese.

In contrast to earlier periods, when Champa seems to have been considered a realm prone to piracy, Ming sources report that in the late fourteenth century the Chams won the early Ming court's support for military expeditions by sending lavish tribute missions and characterizing their Vietnamese neighbors to the north as the constant aggressors. During the 1380s, for example, Cham tribute missions lavished the Ming emperor with two hundred elephant tusks in 1384, fifty-four elephants in 1388; and fifty-one elephants in 1389, in response to which it was reported that "the Emperor was pleased with their sincerity" (Wade: 2010; Whitmore: 1985, 23). By contrast, the sources make repeated references to the Ming emperor's displeasure with Dai Viet, including a 1382 refusal to receive a Vietnamese tribute mission due to Dai Viet's "guile." In addition, Ming records note the immense pleasure of the Ming emperor in 1373 when the Chams convinced the Chinese monarch that they had seized pirates who were operating off the Cham coast, thereby pacifying the seas to China's south. Together, these efforts went a long way toward legitimating Cham preemptive strikes against Dai Viet (Whitmore: 1985).

There were at least two Cham military incursions in the 1370s and 1380s that reached all the way to Dai Viet's capital at Thang Long. Their 1376 sacking of the capital was the result of a trap sprung on retaliating Vietnamese forces in which the Chams destroyed the Vietnamese military, killed the Dai Viet junior monarch who had led his troops against Champa, and captured a Vietnamese prince (Whitmore: 1985, 12–18). The once-hostage prince subsequently married the Cham king's daughter and later successfully led Cham forces against the Vietnamese on the behalf of his Cham father-in-law, who the Vietnamese chronicles call Che Bong Nga (Jaya Simhavarman) (Whitmore: 2010b). The Vietnamese chronicles concede that in that era "many" of the locals in the southern regions chose to serve the Cham "false mandate," that is, the Mandate of Heaven, the favor of the gods that was in Chinese tradition vital to a polity's success, although there are no records of any Cham administrators just to the north in the Thanh Nghe region, which was culturally and ethnically Vietnamese.

In addition to its successes toward the north during this late fourteenth-century era, Vijaya controlled Khmer access to China's marketplace and profited accordingly (see above and below). As the Ming chronicles relate, "When *Zhen La* [the Khmer realm] submits tribute, the king of Champa exacts one quarter of it" (Wade: 2010). The Khmer would complain to the Chinese court about this and other issues in their tributary missions of 1408 and 1414.

Champa's late fourteenth-century military supremacy over Vietnam proved temporary. The Vietnamese were finally able to regroup and in 1390 they successfully defended Thang Long from another raid by invading Cham forces. The Vietnamese chronicles highlight the victory of Dai Viet troops against overwhelming odds as they killed Che Bong Nga, and the subsequent dissension among the Chams. According to the account, the Vietnamese prince who had previously sided with the Chams had taken the head of the dead Cham king, Che Bong Nga, and returned to Vietnam with it as his trophy. A Cham general now returned to Champa with his remaining forces, seized the Cham throne, deposed the previous king's heirs, and established a new Vijaya-based Cham political order that would remain stable until the 1470s (Whitmore: 1985, 28–31; 2010b). The Ming chronicles generally concur with this account, though with some crucial differences in detail. The Chinese chronicles report that in the aftermath of the battle the Cham king was killed not by the Vietnamese but by one of his own ministers. Considering the Chams had not honored rightful succession, the Ming now became reluctant to favor the Chams, and for a while they even refused Cham attempts to present tribute at the Chinese court.

Following up on this 1390 success, the Thang Long rulers now took the opportunity to assert their authority in the contested south. Between 1400 and 1403, the usurping monarch Ho Quy Ly (r. 1400–1407) led four successful Vietnamese raids against the Chams, penetrating beyond the Hai Van Pass, despite Chinese warships defending Champa. Before the Ming retaliatory invasion of Vietnam in 1407 ended his brief reign, Quy Ly initiated the first aggressive settlement of the southern borderlands, sending landless Vietnamese peasants to populate and defend the newly conquered regions. He encouraged Cham leaders to defect, honoring them as legitimate competitors and potential allies, giving them Vietnamese names, and appointing them to regional bureaucratic posts. Subsequently, when the Ming instituted their two-decade occupation of Vietnam (1407–1428), they stabilized the southern edge of Dai Viet by maintaining the existing Viet borders and kept the Chams out.

THE JIAOZHI OCEAN NETWORK, ca. 1200–1471

Revisionist research since the 1990s, reactive to new archeological discoveries that have mandated the need to reread the written sources, has significantly enhanced the vision of pre-1500 Vietnam economic history. The most recent research has focused on the thirteenth- to fifteenth-century Jiaozhi Yang ("Ocean") Network that effectively linked the Cham and Vietnamese coastlines from the Mekong Delta in the south to Hainan Island in the north and beyond to south China ports (Li: 2006; Whitmore: 2006; Shiro: 1998a). Prior to the ninth century, as explained in chapter 3, the Cham coastline was the major maritime route stopover for ships going to or from south China's ports, as ships sailed directly from this collective commercial area to Hainan Island rather than calling at ports in the Gulf of Tonkin region to the northwest. This was in part because it was more efficient to sail directly north from Cham ports to China, but was also because there were huge hidden rocks along the Gulf of Tonkin passage, not removed by a Tang dynasty's governor until the ninth century, which made this passageway so treacherous that large ships would not chance the voyage, but would instead offload their cargoes in Cham ports.

From there trade commodities traveled north on smaller boats, or were more often transported overland by foot via the central highlands, connecting to the upper Mekong River and from there north via Khmer and Lao (Lu Zhenla) regions to the Nanzhou/Yunnan upstream south China borderlands into Vietnam (Jiaozhi). An early terminus of this overland route was via the Ha Trai pass to Nghe An and from there to the Red River delta and Jiaozhi. Early merchants, pilgrims, and envoys all landed in the central Vietnam Cham region prior to making this overland passage or to move up the coastline to Jiaozhi (the Chinese name for the Red River–centered northern region of Vietnam prior to its independence from Chinese rule as the Dai Viet state in the tenth century). The overland route was also the source of Jiaozhi's most desired highland trade products: gold, silver, aromatics, rhinoceros horn, and elephant tusks. As reported in chapter 6, the route also served as the Angkor-era realm's primary access to the South China Sea, whether to Cham ports to the east or to Dai Viet in the north. Khmer kings thus sent tribute to the Dai Viet court nineteen times in the 960–1279 Song era, in contrast to only five tributes sent to the previous Tang China court (Shiro: 1998a, 11–15).

The *Zhufanzhi* 1226 report of the sea trade filed by Zhao Rugua, the commissioner of foreign trade at Quanzhou, the principal south China port terminus of the international maritime route at that time, provides the following description of his networked port's trade partner Qinzhou (in the modern-day Guangxi Province, then the Song prefecture bordering the Gulf of Tonkin north of Dai Viet) and its contemporary marketplace activities, incorporating the late twelfth-century account of Zhou Qufei:

> All of Jiaozhi's everyday wares depend on Qinzhou, thus ships constantly go back and forth between the two. The *boyi* [trade] field is East of the river outside the town. Those who come with sea products to exchange for rice and cotton fabric in small quantities are called the *Dan of Jiaozhi* [people known as *Dan* in Guangdong]. Those rich merchants who come are from [Dai Viet's] border area of Vinh Tuyen

prefecture to Qinzhou, these are called "small present" (*xiaogang*). The "large quantity present" (*dagang*) refers to the envoys sent by the court [of Dai Viet] to trade here. The goods they trade are gold, silver, copper coins, aloeswood, varieties of fragrant wood, pearls, elephant tusks and rhinoceros horn. The small traders from our side who come to exchange paper, writing brushes, rice and cotton with the people of Jiaozhi do not deserve much mention; but there are rich merchants who brought brocades from Shu [Sichuan] to Qinzhou to trade for perfume once a year, often involving thousands of *quan* of cash. Those merchants haggle over prices for hours before reaching an agreement. Once it is agreed, no one is allowed to negotiate with other merchants. When the talk has just started the gap between the asking price and the offer is often as huge as between heaven and earth. Our [Han Chinese] rich merchants send their servants to buy things to sustain their daily life and even build temporary residences and stay there, in order to frustrate the [Jiaozhi] merchants. Their rich merchants stay calm, and also use perseverance as a weapon. When the two merchants see each other, they drink together; and as time passes, they get along. Those smooth-talking ones cut or add a few [*quan*] so the prices from the two sides become closer and closer. [When the deal is made], the officers [at the markets] weigh the perfume and deliver the brocade for both sides to finish the deal. At the trading site the [Song] officers only levy taxes on the merchants of our side. (Li: 2006, 93)

The Jiaozhi Ocean system was a product of the twelfth century, when during the decline and interregnum of the Song dynasty (960–1279) and the consolidation of Yuan authority (1279–1368) numbers of Chinese and other maritime diaspora active in south China ports, many of them Muslim, established alternate bases in the region (Heng: 2009). During the twelfth century the more northern port of Van Don, strategically located near the Bach Dang River (at that time the main branch of the Red River), replaced the Nghe An region as the focal downstream access to the Dai Viet heartland (Shiro: 1998a, 12). Van Don was populated by Fujian Chinese, Cham, and multiethnic Muslim merchants dispersed among several island harbors northeast of the Red River delta in the Gulf of Tonkin (Whitmore: 2011a; *TT*, 4, 6b, 12, 41a). In the contemporary Cham realm, confirming the Cham evidence cited above, trade came to be centered in the Vijaya port of Thi Nai, the "New Harbor" (Xinzhou) in contemporary Chinese records, although there were secondary ports further south in Kauthara and Panduranga. Like its Cham predecessors, the Thi Nai port of trade (today's Qui Nhon) of the Vijaya realm was linked to the Central Highlands via an overland connection and, most critically, the Go Sanh ceramic production site was nearby (Aoyagi and Hasebe: 2002).

The details of fifteenth-century commercial transitions in the inclusive Vietnam realm are played out in Chinese dynastic records, the Vietnam chronicles, and archeological artifacts. Collectively these substantiate a burst of economic energy in the Cham and Dai Viet realms from the 1430s, responsive to the opportunities afforded when the Ming dynasty began to restrict the overseas activities of Chinese private traders and, above all, the export of Chinese ceramics in what scholars call the "Ming gap." In this era the Burmese, Thai, Chams, and Vietnamese responded to market opportunities by increasing their production of ceramics to fill the international marketplace demand. While the Ming were effective in decreasing China's ceramics exports, there was an expansive international market that Southeast Asia–based production and shipping filled for over a century.

Recovered artifacts from late fifteenth-century shipwrecks in the southern Philippines and at Hoi An on the central Vietnam coast provide the critical new evidence. Thai, Cham, and Vietnamese ceramics dominate the cargoes of other fifteenth-century regional wrecks, as earlier Chinese ceramics had (Roxanna Brown: 2008b, 2010; Diem, 1998–2001, 1999, 2001, 2010). Specific to the history of the Vietnam coastline, the ca. 1450–1470 Pandanan shipwreck is believed to have begun its voyage on the Cham coastline, and sank off the southern coast of Palawan Island in the southern Philippines on its passage between a Brunei Borneo coast stopover and a Sulu Sea destination (see chapter 9). Its cargo was 70 percent Cham ceramics, green-glazed monochrome dishes for daily use produced at the Go Sanh kilns near the fortified capital city of Vijaya (Cha Ban), upstream from the port of Thi Nai (Cayron: 2006; Tingley: 2009; Roxanna Brown: 1988; Stevenson and Guy: 1997). In contrast, the Hoi An (Cu Lao Cham) wreck off the central Vietnam coastline, dating ca. 1490, consistent with other regional shipwreck cargoes from the later fifteenth- and early sixteenth-century era, has little evidence of Cham ceramics, but is almost exclusively composed of Dai Viet blue-and-white stoneware. These ceramics were influenced by the Ming-era China Jingdezhen kiln patterns in blue-and-white porcelain, but with notable inclusions of Vietnamese elements (e.g., birds) and representations and production specific to the Java marketplace (garuda patterns and ceremonial kendi, ceramic spouted water vessels) (Roomy: 2003) fired at the Dai Viet kiln site of Chu Dau in the lower Red River delta, near Dai Viet's Van Don port (Guy: 2000).

These shipwreck ceramics and accompanying excavations of the Cham and Dai Viet ceramics production sites relate to the recurrent Cham and Vietnamese borderlands warfare detailed above. Vietnam scholars have reevaluated their past views of fifteenth-century Vietnam. John K. Whitmore, like other Vietnam historians, had previously concluded that in his initiatives to restructure the Dai Viet realm, Le Thanh Tong (r. 1460–1497) took an unfavorable stance toward international trade, and instead internalized the Dai Viet economy in the name of achieving the "well-being" of his subjects, by emphasizing the need to develop a self-sustaining Dai Viet agricultural economy over promoting marketplace commerce (Whitmore: 1999, 222–26, 230–32). Whitmore and other scholars had accepted the retrospective Vietnamese chronicle representation of Le Thanh Tong's reign, as the written account is focused on his work with literati advisors to establish a contemporary Ming pattern of bureaucratic administration. These past studies depict Thang Tong's reign as focused on widespread aristocratic and administrative restructuring intent on strengthening the Thang Long court against its regionally entrenched aristocratic rivals.

In a 1461 edict, Thanh Tong ordered provincial officials, "Do not cast aside the roots [agriculture] and pursue the insignificant [trade/commerce]" to ensure internal welfare and restrict outsiders from entering Dai Viet provinces (*TT*, 12, 7b; Whitmore: 2010b; Li Tana: 2010). He followed this in 1465 by demanding that every six years villages had to submit written records of their human and material resources to demonstrate that they were effectively productive (*TT*, 12, 19a; Whitmore: 2010b). A new court agency managed these records, and to increase their productivity villages were specifically charged to promote the construction and proper management of local dikes. In the name of the well-being of the people (in contrast to the promotion of trade) he imposed a marketplaces code of conduct and standardized weights and measures (*TT*, 12, 40 a-b; 13, 9a, 12a; Whitmore: 1999, 232–33). Against banditry in the mountain regions and piracy in the Gulf of Tonkin (and thereby to stabilize his borders against another potential Ming intervention), in 1469 he declared gunpowder weapons a state monopoly, promised promotions to any officials who captured pirates, and followed in 1470 by sending a naval expedition against pirates in the Gulf of Tonkin (*TT* 12, 37 a-b, 41a, 50a, 52b, 53b–54a; Whitmore: 2005). Combining his aggressive stance relative to protecting sea transit in the Gulf and his efforts to promote agriculture (by supplying additional agricultural labor), he had thirteen men shipwrecked on the Dai Viet coastline while in transit from Hainan Island to Qinzhou sent to agricultural colonies (Shin: 2007, 91–92, 99–100).

All of these foundational centralizing initiatives culminated in the Dai Viet attack on Champa in 1471, as Thanh Tong sent massive land and sea forces south against the Cham realm to destroy Vijaya (Whitmore: 2004, 127–30). In theory, according to the Vietnamese chronicles the invasion was intended to secure Dai Viet's southern borderlands against repeated Cham raids and eliminate the ongoing threats of this "uncivilized" society, and not to repeat the patterns of the past, for example, to conquer, loot, seize manpower, and return home with the spoils of war. In the end Thanh Tong annexed the Vijaya northern borderlands and immediately implemented provincial administrations in the new Dai Viet Quang Nam Province. Despite his lofty ambitions, Thanh Tong took back significant numbers of Chams and forced them to take

Vietnamese-style names and "embrace sinic morality" (*TT* 12, 73b; Whitmore: 2011b). That Champa was still functional after 1471, but with consequences, is demonstrated in two items from 1485. A report from the new southern province officials to the Thang Long court asserted that it was difficult for them to remit tax collections to the court because there were not sufficient ships available, while new regulations for the reception of foreign envoys at the Dai Viet court listed Champa among other regional polities, notably Laos, Ayudhya, Java, and Melaka, who were welcome at the court (*TT*, 12, 44b–45a, 48a; Whitmore: 2011b).

That same year, Thanh Tong complained to the Ming court that seagoing links between Champa and the Ryukyu Islands had resulted in a raid on the southern Dai Viet coastline. That he was proactive in his regional maritime initiatives following his capture of the Jiazhi ocean network is illustrated by several complaints to the Ming court: one from Melaka in 1481 asserted that Dai Viet had interfered with their embassy to the Ming court (Wade: 1994, 1691–92, 1730, 1784–87, 1797–99, 1837–41). In 1487, 1489, and 1495, Kauthara and Panduranga used their remaining connections to Guangzhou to promote a Ming intervention against Dai Viet, which the Ming court refused, citing that this "involved merchants and the vast maritime region," as this was counter to the post-1430s Ming restrictions on China's Southern Seas (Nanyang) engagements (L. Andaya: 2008, 46). In 1497, following Le Thanh Tong's death, Champa tried once more to gain the Ming court's support for the restitution of the Vijaya region, by arguing that "Xinzhou [Thi Nai] is our country that has long been occupied by Annan [Dai Viet]," and asked for recognition "so that in future days [the king's son] can protect the area of Xinzhou port" (Wade: 1994, 1857–58).

Against collective written evidence that the 1471 Dai Viet invasion was the culmination of the centuries-old endgame competition between the Cham and Dai Viet polities over the control of their borderlands, but with diplomatic fallout, the new shipwreck and archeological evidence negates the prior conclusion that Le Thanh Tong's aggression went beyond a "traditional" victory only in his failure to relinquish the newly gained Cham–Dai Viet borderlands. The more innovative addendum to this 1471 victory was Thanh Tong's subsequent monopolistic control of foreign trade in the Gulf of Tonkin, as the new archeological evidence substantiates that he also consolidated Thi Nai's trade and ceramics production into a special commercial zone centered on the Van Don port and its linked Chu Dau artisan community.

Roxanna Brown, the recently deceased Asian trade ceramics scholar, suggested the significance of the Cu Lao Cham wreck's (ca. 1490) cargo, which consisted of substantial numbers of Vietnamese ceramic ware, including a new Cham-style bowl. Pairing Thanh Tong's purposeful destruction of the

Go Sanh kilns in 1471 with the archeological evidence that there was subsequent expansion of Dai Viet ceramics production at Chu Dau and other new ceramics centers in the Red River upstream, Brown concluded that the collective documentation attested that Le Thanh Tong had taken Champa's ceramics producers back to Dai Viet with him. Brown saw the concentration of ceramics production in the Van Don hinterland as foundational to Dai Viet's substantial increase in ceramics production in competition with Thai and Burmese wares to meet the increasing East-West maritime ceramics route demand (Roxanna Brown: 2008a). Thus rather than suppressing foreign trade subsequent to his 1471 victory, Le Thanh Tong, by effectively reformulating the longstanding fluid Jiaozhi Ocean networked community by his conquest of Vijaya, followed with the consolidation of regional ceramics production in Dai Viet, and made Van Don the central node in a new regionally networked maritime trade community.

John Whitmore follows on Brown's ceramics research in his retrospective on the Vietnamese chronicles by agreeing that Thanh Tong's post-1471 actions had significant commercial implications. But Whitmore adds that these implications were ultimately supportive of Thanh Tong's celebrated political ambition to establish a Ming-style Vietnamese monarchy, as they were beneficial to societal well-being. Thus Dai Viet's newly achieved dominance over the regional maritime trade and its ceramics production were profitable opportunities that provided government revenues as well as quality ceramics and other consumer goods, to the benefit of his society, yet there were regional attempts to find a compromise between agriculture and commerce within the Ming governmental model (Zhao: 2008, 92–97, 100, 102).

In the aftermath of 1471, a new commercial system began to form on the Vietnam coastline. Li Tana asserts that the Hai Duong area became a diverse downstream production center in the aftermath, as it was networked with the Van Don port, and had foundational links to the Thirty-Six Streets (36 Pho Phuong, or commercial "Old Quarter") in Thang Long. There were concentrated settlements of metalworkers, builders, carpenters, dyers, leather shoemakers, and woodcarvers, all of these also foundational to the initial development of a Dai Viet print industry. Li also suggests that the ruins of seven fifteenth- and sixteenth-century Buddhist temples at Van Don reflects the likely contribution of these temple communities to the development of the new special economic zone, as the temples were employers, consumers of the variety of trade and artisan commodities, and centers of a redistributive economic system that would have supported the wider development of downstream marketplace economics. All of these foundational developments became the basis for the rise of the Mac monarchs "from the sea" in the sixteenth century, which is Whitmore's conclusion (Li: 2006, 95–102;

Whitmore: 2008). In the sixteenth century, a new port at Hoi An rose at the site of the Jiuzhou ("Old District") port of the former Cham Amaravati realm (marking a return from the Vijaya "New Harbor"/Xinzhou in Chinese sources), as the center of the rising alternative Nguyen Vietnamese polity on Dai Viet's southern border (Wheeler: 2006). In the south, the remaining Champa polities at Kauthara and Panduranga remained a factor in the coastal trade, as new regional sacred centers represented by the Po Klong Garai and Po Rome temple complexes document the continuing vitality of the southern Cham culture.

THE POST-1471 DAI VIET AGRICULTURAL ECONOMY

The final victory against the Chams in 1471 stabilized the Dai Viet state's political economy. Victory not only removed the financial drain of the perpetual southern wars, but also supplied prime territory for agricultural expansion. A nineteenth-century Vietnamese document explains that after this final victory, the Emperor Le Thanh Tong (1460–1497) resettled the Cham coastal plain with Vietnamese settlers (Khoi: 1981, 243). Both before and after his 1471 victory, Le Thanh Tong sent prisoners and convicted criminals to the remote parts of Quang Binh Province in the south to clear and cultivate the newly conquered lands. After 1471, he banned large landholdings in the region to avoid the creation of potentially troublesome large aristocratic estates and had local fortifications built to protect newly developed paddy fields. Military officers strategically posted in the southern outposts received plots of land to provide their income source, which would not revert to the state at their death. Newly organized administrations supervised the digging of dikes and canals. Assigned state representatives provided information that would improve animal husbandry and the cultivation of mulberry trees. After two years of colonized settlement, court officials arrived to establish appropriate taxes and promote the new patriarchal-family-focused sinic moral code that was believed to be critical to the establishment of Vietnamese authority.

One factor that helped decide the long-standing Cham and Vietnamese rivalry was fifteenth-century Vietnam's access to guns paired with the implementation of administrative patterns acquired from Ming China. The Chams were particularly vulnerable to gun warfare, as they had no alternative source of supply. Both Vietnamese and Chinese records highlight the role of Chinese guns in the conquest of Champa. As early as 1390, Vietnamese gunmen helped to secure Vietnam's victory over a larger Cham army intended to seize

Thang Long; it was a gunshot wound that killed the notable Cham monarch Che Bong Nga and stopped the campaign.

Dai Viet military perfected their training in gun warfare during the early fifteenth-century era of Ming occupation. In that time the Vietnamese began to smuggle copper down the Red River from the Yunnan north and used it to improve the quality of their local production of handguns and cannons (Laichen: 2003; Parker: 1988, 83–84, 136–37; Charney: 1997; B. Andaya: 2003, 139–42). In addition, in 1466 the Vietnamese court reorganized its army along Ming lines to better utilize Ming handgun and artillery technology. Early in the next century the Portuguese scribe Tomé Pires offered his view that Dai Viet had "countless musketeers and small bombards" and consumed "a very great deal of powder" in war (Cortesao: 1944, 115).

The Vietnamese victory of 1471 went beyond acknowledging this technological advantage, as it was based even more on the successful Neoconfucian reforms instituted by the emperor Le Thanh Tong when he implemented Chinese administrative and social techniques, including new tax registers, codes, gazetteers, and bureaucratic examinations. These administrative tools became the basis for a degree of uniformity that penetrated into the local level. Previously, the state had depended on oaths of personal loyalty to the monarch by a relatively autonomous landed aristocracy. Now, the state was based on new institutional obligations that enforced loyalty to the emperor's court (Whitmore: 1997). Combined with the military reforms, these administrative advances gave the Vietnamese advantages that the Chams could not match. And though the southward expansion would be primarily agricultural in intent, the southward movement also enabled the Vietnamese to take over the commercial role that the Chams had been playing among the intensifying networks of international trade. The victory over Champa put the Vietnamese in a position to monopolize the coastal access to the highland products most desired by international traders. Although highlanders still had the option of trading overland with their Khmer neighbors to the west, by the early sixteenth century the highlands were loosely incorporated into the Vietnamese state. The Vietnamese not only seized Champa's profitable trade with China, but also forged a tributary trade system with the remaining southern Cham port-polities (Shiro: 1999; Whitmore: 1983, 369–70).

8

Maritime Trade and Community Development in Fourteenth- and Fifteenth-Century Java

The emergence in the thirteenth century of the Javanese court at Majapahit in eastern Java marked the beginning of new levels of internal and external political and economic integration throughout Southeast Asia. Although Airlangga had united central and eastern Java after 1025 CE, the division of the kingdom between his two sons in 1044 had recreated the two independent and often unfriendly rival states of Janggala and Pangjalu, the latter also being known as Kadiri (see chapter 5). The process of unification began anew some two centuries later, when Rajasa (also known as Ken Angrok) founded a dynasty based at Singhasari that would eventually subjugate Kadiri. Singhasari was succeeded by Majapahit, through a process soon to be described. By the time Kertarajasa had established this successor kingdom at the turn of the fourteenth century, Java's rulers claimed to reign over a far-flung maritime empire that included ports on Sumatra, the Malay Peninsula, Borneo, and the spice-producing islands of the eastern portion of the Indonesian archipelago. This maritime empire was patrolled by a Javanese "navy" made up of a multiethnic seafaring people resident in north Java coast ports whose loyalty to the empire was directly proportional to the Majapahit monarch's ability to deliver to them a substantial cut from the profits of the region's spice trade. No doubt, Majapahit's domination of these overseas ports was more economic than political, yet there is no question that its control over eastern and central Java was political as well (Colless: 1975a, 1975b).

The roots of Majapahit and its ambitions were in Singhasari (1222–1292). The Singhasari rulers had subordinated the rival Kadiri court and thereby became the preeminent political authority in east Java until 1292. It was Ker-

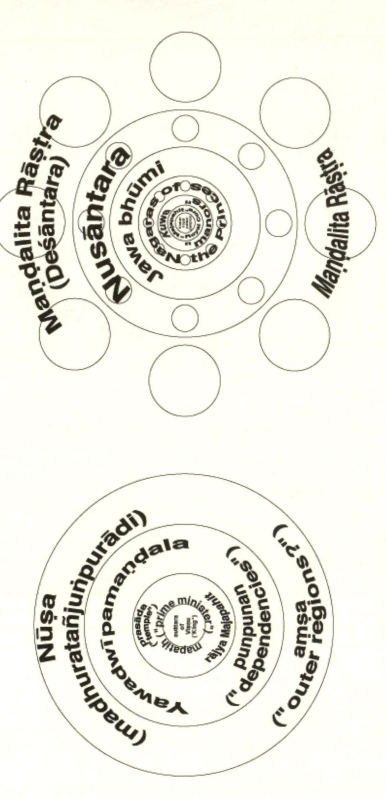

The Concept of the Majapahit Polity
according to the Tuhañarn Inscription (1326)

The Concept of the Majapahit Polity
according to the Nāgarakertāgama (1365)

Figure 8.1.   Majapahit Java Mandala State (adapted from an unpublished original by Hermann Kulke)

tanagara (r. 1268–1292), the last of the Singhasari kings, who laid the foundations for Majapahit. Indeed, the *Nagarakertagama,* an epic poem and chronicle of the Majapahit kingdom composed in 1365 by the Buddhist monk Prapanca under the patronage of Majapahit's rulers, begins its story not with the founding of Majapahit, but with the reign of this mysterious and highly controversial Singhasari king. Among other things, Kertanagara claimed to have been initiated into secret Tantric rites that gave him extraordinary powers against demonic forces. In order to maintain these powers, he was obliged to bring on his own ecstasy through Tantric rituals. Although a later fifteenth-century chronicler hostile to Tantric rituals characterized him as a drunkard who was brought to ruin by his lust, the *Nagarakertagama* described him as a saint and ascetic, free of all passion.

To end despair (and the difficulties that Airlangga's legendary division of the realm seems to have caused), Kertanagara erected a statue depicting himself as Aksubhya, the meditative Buddha, on the spot where Bharada, the ascetic blamed for the partition of the meditating Airlangga's kingdom, had lived. He also confirmed his father Visnuvardhana's (r. 1248–1268) patronage and synthesis of the multiple Javanese religious traditions: Hindu, Buddhist, and animistic. Kertanagara divided his cremated father's ashes between two shrines; at one he was worshipped as an incarnation of Siva, while at the second he was revered as Amoghapasa, the Bodhisattva of Compassion. The *Nagarakertagama* viewed Kertanagara's religious purification of Java as the cause of his and his descendants' glory as divine kings and reuniters of the realm.

Kertanagara would need all the powers he could summon, for he, and then his son-in-law, would face the Mongols, the Central Asian conquerors whose steppe cavalries had overrun much of the continents of Asia and Europe. By the time that Kertanagara came to power in 1268, southern China and mainland Southeast Asia had already begun to suffer the invasion of these armies. Nanchao, an independent kingdom in what is now China's southern Yunnan Province, had been invaded in 1253 (see chapter 9). The Mongols followed up their occupation of Nanzhao with an unsuccessful invasion of Vietnam in 1257, the first round of a pattern of aggression that the Vietnamese combated for some thirty-one years. The last attack was in 1288, when the Mongols were defeated once and for all.

In 1267, the year before Kertanagara came to power, Khubilai Khan made a direct attack on the Southern Song strongholds. He followed with an invasion of Burma in 1271, to block the retreat of Song refugees, and sporadic fighting between Mongol and Burmese forces continued until 1300 (Aung Thwin: 1998, 33–92). In 1276 the Southern Song capital, Hangzhou, fell to his armies, and in the aftermath in 1279 Khubilai Khan established the Mongol version of a Chinese dynasty, the Yuan. While these campaigns were still underway, the expansive Mongols took to the seas in 1274 and launched the first of their ill-fated naval attacks against Japan. With the establishment of the Yuan dynasty, would-be preferred port-polities on the Sumatra coast lost no time in applying to the new Yuan dynasty for recognition, hoping to fill the intermediary role previously assumed by Srivijaya's ports of trade. In 1277 Palembang, in 1281 Jambi-Malayu, and in 1282 Samudra-Pasai (a pepper depot on the northern tip of the island whose foundation is described in the next chapter) sent tributary envoys to Khubilai's capital.

It was in this unsettled context, perhaps motivated by concern about political destabilization in the Melaka Straits, that Kertanagara conducted his own overseas expansion. In 1275 he sent an expedition to temporarily occupy Jambi-Malayu, the old Sumatran port that had recently been the center of the Srivijaya Straits polity. This initial Javanese presence was temporary, or at best indirect, since in 1281 Jambi sent a mission to the Yuan court seeking recognition as an independent tributary. But in 1286, Kertanagara erected an icon with a dated inscription honoring his deified father in the Batang Hari River upstream (Coedes: 1968, 201; Robson: 1995, 54; Slametmuljana: 1976, 26). Up to this point in time, there is no record of an east Javanese presence in the Straits region; at most, the east Java–based polities' only concern had been to keep the Straits of Melaka open so that international shipping could reach Java's north coast ports. After this initial move into the Straits, Kertanagara shifted his attention eastward, subjugating Bali in 1284. He then again sent his armies westward, and by 1286 he had established Javanese hegemony over the Straits region. It was in that year that he erected a statue of his father at Jambi-Malayu. Khubilai Khan was apparently displeased with this new Javanese hegemony in the Straits. In 1289 he sent envoys to Kertanagara to confront him and demand that Javanese tribute missions be sent to his court. Kertanagara replied by disfiguring and tattooing the faces of the Mongol envoys and sent them back in this disgraced fashion. His impudence so enraged Khubilai Khan that the Mongol ruler sent one thousand warships to chastise Java.

Before the fleet arrived, Kertanagara's previously subordinated ruler of Kadiri defeated Singhasari in 1292 and, during the final attack on the royal residence of Singhasari, King Kertanagara died in the assault. After this crisis in the last months of 1292 or early 1293, Kertanagara's son-in-law Raden Vijaya, leading the remnants of Singhasari's forces, cleared a new capital site from the downstream forest and named it Majapahit. This royal city, which gave its name to the realm, was located about thirty miles upriver from Surabaya on the coast. When the Mongol warships arrived, the son-in-law managed to persuade them that the Singhasari kingdom was gone and that, since

Kertanagara had died, this was punishment enough. He proposed that the Mongols should instead help him chastise Kadiri's usurping vassal, since the new Yuan rulers, in common with their dynastic predecessors, should officially disapprove of coups and other illegitimate successions. After he had destroyed his rivals and enemies with the help of the Mongol expeditionary army, Raden Vijaya turned on the Mongols and forced them to evacuate from Java. He then declared himself Java's new king, taking the reign title Kertarajasa (1294–1309).

Kertarajasa's 1293 victory resulted in a peace agreement with the Mongols, who then reconfirmed Java's special commercial and tributary relationship with China, the Mongols' intent from the beginning. The agreement also recognized Java's commercial connections to the west, which gave Java access to the expanding and increasingly significant market of Western Europe. Java's marketing network benefited from the growth in international demand, from the internal peace and security provided by Majapahit's hegemony, and from its kings' efforts to remove obstacles between hinterland producers and ports. Majapahit would itself be transformed by these developments, as the underlying relatively loose system of tributary relationships was gradually molded into a more centralized state.

Kertarajasa's reign was followed by that of his son Jayanagara (1309–1328). When Jayanagara died without an heir, he was succeeded by his mother the Rajapatni (1329–1350), great-granddaughter of Kertanagara, and eventually by the queen's daughter's son, who reigned as king Rajasanagara or Hayam Wuruk (1350–1389). Behind these intricate successions stood the legendary state minister Gajah Mada (*mahapatih*/prime minister 1329–ca. 1369), who handled day-to-day administrative affairs (Robson: 1995, 26–27, 58–59, 69, 71, 73, 76–77).

Jayanagara's reign was largely marked by local resistance to his consolidations, as the new king tried to maintain regional loyalties to the Majapahit state. After Jayanagara's death in 1328, Gajah Mada, acting in the name of the new queen, restored order in eastern Java as well as the island of Madura by 1331. Royal relatives and (in a few cases) deserving members of the court took charge of each of these provinces, while the queen maintained firm control at the center, backed by her chief minister. By 1343 Bali had been annexed, and in 1347 the ports and regions to Majapahit's north and west on Java came under the court's authority. From the Javanese perspective of Java's court scribes, this expansion under Gajah Mada's leadership extended Majapahit's ritual hegemony over the Java Sea regions as well as the Straits of Melaka (see chapter 9).

Despite its vigorous expansion elsewhere, through much of the fourteenth century Majapahit was apparently content with the situation in the straits region. Although it had on occasion punished local rulers who became too ambitious, such as the west Java–based Sunda Strait ruler in 1357 (McKinnon: 1985), Majapahit's forces do not seem to have made any attempt to establish a formal presence in the straits until 1377. Exactly what prompted Majapahit to move then is not clear, but it may have been the threat of a new alliance between those ports and the new dynasty in China. In 1368 the Ming had expelled the Mongols and established their dynasty. In 1371 the Ming court sent an imperial invitation to Palembang, whose rulers responded with a tribute mission to China. Whether Majapahit's aggression was motivated by this or by something else, Majapahit's 1377 expedition was apparently successful, for soon the ports in the straits were sending representatives to participate in Majapahit's tributary rituals (Robson: 1995, 33–34, 85).

Thus, by 1377 Majapahit's claimed networked ports and their hinterlands extended from the furthest tip of Sumatra in the west to New Guinea in the east and as far north as the southern islands of the Philippines, a far-flung realm that Javanese records called Nusantara. The "navy" with which it exercised its suzerainty was based in ports on Java's north coast, and its monarchs paid the multiethnic resident sailors who constituted this force for their good behavior and their transportation services. These maritime populations were essentially mercenaries of trade as well as of maritime security, and they served Majapahit only so long as it provided the most profitable opportunities (Lombard: 1990).

JAVA IN THE FOURTEENTH CENTURY

Throughout the fourteenth century the power of the Majapahit court continued to develop, ultimately leading to a most significant transition. This change in political structure was to be a hallmark for the future of the entire Southeast Asian region, for the developments that were clearly discernible in Majapahit Java from 1294 on would subsequently appear as features generally characteristic of Southeast Asian statecraft in the fourteenth through sixteenth centuries. Java was one of the first states to begin to make the transition from a pattern of statecraft in which the wealth of the realm gravitated toward the center through a network of ceremonially defined tributary relationships to one in which the royal house came to rely on more direct collection of local specialties and surpluses (though they were sometimes initially justified as direct contributions to exclusively royal ceremonies). It is not simply because Java was first that it can stand as a paradigm for an age. Equally important are the availability of material on the characteristics of pre-1300 Southeast Asian states and highly revealing sources that illuminate important features of the fourteenth-century change. As this chapter will demonstrate, external demand for Southeast Asian products, domestic integration in both the political and economic arenas, and regional control of the spice trade were all part of a complex dynamic in which each of the three elements both acted upon and reinforced the others.

As discussed in chapter 5, Java first began to blossom as a commercial power and center of international trade in the eleventh century. Increasing commercial interaction between the populations of the Javanese hinterland and port areas on Java's north coast was reflected in the inscriptions of east Java–based monarchs; indeed, the largest percentage of royal charters issued during the tenth through the twelfth centuries concerned port or coastal settlements in the Brantas Delta region of eastern Java (Barrett Jones: 1984; Wisseman Christie: 1998b). Royal strategies for producing revenue from the trade included taxation and price fixing (see chapter 5). These strategies also functioned to control the trade and traders by mediating the foreigners' contact with the Javanese rice-producing hinterland and encouraging the development of commercial contacts beyond Java. Inscriptions from this period provide the first references to foreigners attached to the royal court, and overseas trade took on increasing importance to the Javanese ruler as a source of revenue. However, this international linkage seems to have had little direct impact on village-level market trade (Hall: 2010b)

Although a number of inland sites have produced a considerable quantity of tenth- and eleventh-century Chinese ceramic sherds, and though contemporary Chinese references to the volume of trade with this area imply a reasonable level of consumption of Chinese trade items outside Javanese court circles, local inscriptions make no mention of foreign merchants (Wisseman Christie: 1992, 1998b, 1999). Foreigners, at least, could well have been absent from the local market, for trade was not the only mechanism by which goods found their way into the countryside. This was especially the case with luxury goods. Though foreign luxury goods are also not mentioned in the inscriptions, it is believed from archeological evidence that Javanese kings acquired prestigious foreign goods, notably metallic objects, glazed ceramics, and textiles, and especially iron, from overseas traders in Java's coastal ports (Hall: 2010b). The kings then redistributed these luxury items throughout the realm, including the hinterland, through alliance making or the presentation of gifts. Such redistributions assumed a major role in shoring up the Javanese ruler's hegemony. As for nonprestige goods of foreign origin, specifically metals and dyes, these do appear in local market lists and undoubtedly reached the local markets via indigenous exchange networks. The Javanese traders who took these goods into the hinterland obtained them in the east Java ports and then traded them in the hinterland for local products, especially rice, which were marketed in the coastal ports (Wisseman Christie: 1998b). From the ports this rice was sent with Indian cloth to the eastern archipelago islands, where it was exchanged for the spices. As reported in chapter 1, these spices were brought to Java on the return voyage and exchanged for foreign products brought by Eastern and Western merchants. The foreign products were again taken inland, thus completing the triangular trade pattern.

Within Java, the demand for exported rice promoted the continued evolution of networks uniting the interior markets with Java's coastal ports. By the Majapahit era there had developed a realmwide road system that served as a supplement to Java's river systems. In the fourteenth century all roads were said to lead to the Majapahit court, connecting important regions that lacked a river route to the capital (Schrieke: 1957, 103ff). In the *Nagarakertagama*, the fourteenth-century court chronicle poem mentioned above, the crossroads near the royal court were described as being "south of the market place, that is the crossroads, sacred, imposing" (Pigeaud: 1960–1963, 3:9). The poem's sanctification of the road system and the intersection near the court reflected the Majapahit monarchs' view of the network's great importance to the realm as a whole. The network's value was both economic and political. The ruler and his retinue periodically traveled along this road network, making what the *Nagarakertagama* described as "royal progressions" to receive the personal homage of the various royal subordinates and to confirm royal authority over distant areas that the king did not directly administer (Pigeaud: 1960–1963, 3:24, 4:55; Robson: 1995, 42).

The roads were also a means for transporting rice and other trade goods, though the bulk of the trade was carried by river. The *Nagarakertagama* speaks of "caravans of carts" along Java's roads and of crowded royal highways (Pigeaud: 1960–1963, 3:23, 4:497; Robson: 1995, 38). Special reference is made to tradesmen who accompanied the royal progressions and who camped in open fields near the court's lodging at the conclusion of each day's journey (Robson: 1995, 60; Pigeaud: 1960–1963, 3:25). These carts and tradesmen are also well represented in the Majapahit era's temple reliefs. But use of the road network was seasonal because of the monsoons, and movement on the road network was concentrated in the dry season from March to September. The *Nagarakertagama* describes road travel in the wet season.

The road . . . over its whole length was rough and narrow;
On top of this it rained, so that the steep places became slippery,
And some of the carriages came loose and collided with each other. (Robson: 1995, 42)

Because of the difficulty of transporting commodities along these roads, the bulk of Javanese rice was conveyed by river from the hinterland to the coast, and foreign goods moved upriver in return.

The Canggu Ferry Charter of 1358 sheds additional light on the movement of goods and traders (*akalang*) to and from the royal court (Pigeaud: 1960–1963, 1:108–12, 3:156–62, 4:399–411). Canggu was an important commercial center located near the Majapahit capital, as documented by Ma Huan's account of Zheng He's early fifteenth-century naval expedition to Java that reports that the marketplace of Canggu was twenty-five miles (forty-two kilometers) upriver on the Brantas River from Surabaya on the coast, and from there was a half-day walk to the Majapahit court (Mills: 1970, 91); the late fifteenth-century Javanese *Pararaton* prose chronicle describes Canggu as the point of collection for goods passing between the coast and the capital (Hardjowardojo: 1965, 43, 58). The context of the charter's comments indicates that traders transported cartloads of goods over Majapahit's roads and that ferryboats at critical river crossings in the road network were at least large enough to carry the traders' carts. Some seventy-nine ferry crossing districts are enumerated in the charter.

SHIFTS IN JAVANESE TRADE AND STATECRAFT IN THE EARLY MAJAPAHIT ERA

Several Majapahit inscriptions dating to the second half of the fourteenth century register modifications in the way the state collected taxes from east Java commercial communities. Previously, the state had extended its authority to local communities by means of networked reciprocity-based relationships with local elites. Despite the centralizing moves of the tenth century and later, these personal relations remained important. By the early fourteenth century, local landed elites remained in semiautonomous positions between the state and the localities, surrendering a portion of the taxes they collected, yet staying somewhat supreme in their own realms as the empowered intermediaries between the Majapahit state and its regions. Add to this the fact that there had been a disinclination to recognize local commercial communities as significant elements of the polity, despite the importance accorded to them in the coastal centers, and one has the context in which these inscriptions were issued.

In the middle fourteenth century, at the height of the state's authority, the changes recorded in inscriptions displaced some of the local elites while also granting new recognition and greater communal independence to upriver commercial communities. Collectively, these inscriptions show the local landed elites being displaced in favor of more direct involvement by the royal court, while the sphere of independence for local merchant communities, which were becoming increasingly important in the monarch's eyes, was increased. In addition, these inscriptions show a growing standardization of the Javanese state's revenue collections. Furthermore, the taxes that had previously been collected by tax farmers (merchants or local landed elites who collected local taxes and turned a portion over to the state) were now increasingly delivered directly to the state, to revenue agents who were not dependent on or subject to local authority. In addition to increasing the state's presence both symbolically and administratively, the taxes may also have ensured that the state would receive a larger share of such locally collected cesses.

The Canggu Ferry Charter of 1358 was the first of these important inscriptions. The charter recorded a change in the status of ferrymen based in Canggu and Terung, located on opposite banks of the Brantas River. As noted in the previous section, the Canggu crossing was on a major road network that connected assorted hinterland population centers to the Majapahit court. Canggu was also an important trade center for Brantas River traffic, as goods transported to the court from the coast passed through Canggu. The inscription's principal concern was the replacement of an old system of state tax collections with a new one. The old type of cesses, known as *derwaya haji*, were collected by tax farmers who were assigned the right to collect local revenues (derwaya haji) on the state's behalf on their guarantee that the state would receive a share of the collection. East Java–based monarchs had first begun to implement this revenue assessment process in the tenth century, and these tax farmers are known as *mangilala derwaya haji* in inscriptions dating from the same period. Initially, the assorted individuals who collected these revenues seemingly had no local loyalties, and they often included merchants and other "foreigners," whose presence was most notable during the early years of east Java supremacy (Sarkar: 1972, 215–19; Wisseman Christie: 1999). But for the most part, over time these taxes came to be collected by local landed elites or their agents on the state's behalf.

The Canggu Ferry inscription displaced the authority that had accrued to the local collectors of the derwaya haji, restored the independence of one of the local commercial communities, and replaced the derwaya haji with a new tax, the *pamuja*, whose use was directed toward the support of ceremonies that wedded the local community to the court while highlighting the court's symbolic supremacy. It did so by means of several specific provisions. First, the charter freed the local ferrymen from their former responsibility to make payments of derwaya haji to the local landed elite. Second, the inscription provided that the ferrymen could thereafter assume a status socially and politically independent from the local agricultural community and could, as a consequence, begin to interact directly with the royal court rather than through the agency of the landed elite. Third, the ferrymen were granted a place in the king's ceremonial cycle. This new social and ritual status was signaled by their mandated participation in two specific ceremonies, both of which involved partial payments of the new pamuja tax. The first of these involved participation as individuals or as a group in a new local festival honoring the Majapahit monarch. In support of this festival and as repayment for their recognition by the king, the ferrymen provided pamuja payments in the form of flowers and cash. The second granted the privilege of presence at the Caitra festival marking the renewal of the agricultural cycle that took place annually at the royal capital and in other locations near it (Pigeaud: 1960–1963, 3:160–62; 4:109). At this festival the remainder of the pamuja tax was due, and in the Canggu case this payment included unspecified textiles.

The new social, political, and religious status of the ferrymen as revealed in the Ferry Charter is of particular importance as evidence of the emergence of a supralocal nonagrarian commercial community within the Java hinterland population. Moreover, the charter's assignment of tax receipts to the support of local and court ceremonies was consistent with the practice not only throughout Majapahit but also in contemporary ritualized monarchies elsewhere in Southeast Asia, for in these institutions the ruler depended on sacred ceremonies and other religious donations to legitimize his rule. In this context, the conversion of revenue payments into the symbolic capital of the ceremonies bestowed merit on the ruler as a patron of religion, while the ritual itself, as in the Caitra festival, presented the ruler as the source of his subjects' prosperity (Bourdieu: 1977, 172ff). The granting of separate ritual recognition to the ferrymen, who had previously been grouped with the local agrarian population as commoners subject to the authority of the landed elite, revised the old pattern of polity whereby their contact with the state had been, at best, indirect and completely dependent on the local agrarian community and its elite, who had represented them.

There are several explanations for the special attention given to the Canggu ferrymen at this time. The fact that the ferry crossing between Canggu and Terung was critical in facilitating the flow to the court of hinterland goods as well as goods of foreign origin may partially explain the desire of the Majapahit monarch to establish a more direct relationship with this particular community. At the same time the new relationship undercut the authority of the local landed aristocracy. This revision of local relations involved more than a change in taxation system. For example, plates 9 and 10 of the Ferry Charter list among the privileges granted to the ferrymen exemption from legal rules that might have interfered with the efficient performance of their work. They were also allowed to organize cockfights and other gambling activities— activities that the *Nagarakertagama* deemed appropriate to commercial centers—and to have the music of gamelan gong orchestras played at their worship services, as appropriate to their new religious status (Pigeaud: 1960–1963, 4:400). The reason for issuing the charter at this particular time may well have related to events of the previous year, when a naval expedition led by a west Java–based commercial rival of Majapahit had penetrated up the Brantas River to the Canggu area. That the inscription explicitly mentions this event demonstrates Canggu's strategic position on the riverine commercial route from the Majapahit court to the coast.

Also of interest is that the ferrymen's partial payment of the pamuja tax included cash and textiles. Both were related to the local effects of international trade. On the one hand, the cash payment documents the growing monetarization of the Javanese economy that accompanied Java's emergence as a major center of international trade (Wicks: 1992, 290–97; Wisseman Christie: 1996). On the other hand, the cess in textiles was also consistent with earlier patterns of Javanese statecraft whereby Javanese monarchs exercised control over goods acquired from and dispensed to the international trade route. As noted earlier, Java's monarchs traditionally shared foreign-produced luxury goods, notably imported textiles and metal objects, with those they favored in ceremonies of redistribution, thus reinforcing the alliances that sustained their sovereignty (Robson: 1995, 88).

A second source of information on this period is a group of three letters addressed by the Majapahit court to the occupants of Biluluk and Tanggulu-nan, two neighboring communities located northwest of Majapahit and inland from the coast. Inscribed on metal plates dating 1366–1395, these three letters comprise the Biluluk Charters (Pigeaud: 1960–1963, 1:115–17, 3:166–68; Damais: 1952–1954, 105; 1955, 238). The letters depict a prosperous area that depended on nonagrarian production for its income. Among the residents of the local community were

1. salt dealers
2. palm-sugar dealers
3. butchers (meat packers of salt-cured and spiced meats; *dendeng*, salted water buffalo meat, was a particular luxury in that era)
4. bleachers of textile
5. indigo dyers
6. millers of oil (*jarak*, a ricinus oil)
7. makers of vermicelli (*laksa*, a luxury), and
8. lime burners (lime was burned in the making of cloth).

The first letter, dated 1366, reminded the aristocratic families of the area that visitors attending an annual festival were exempt during that time from the dues the elite normally collected from those commoners (*adapur*) who purchased or gathered salt in the salt lands. Instead, these commoners were to pay pamuja—the same royal festival tax imposed on the Canggu area in the Ferry Charter—as well as a cess on salt collections (*pagagarem*). The state was not challenging the local right to collect revenues on local production, but was using this opportunity to assert the assessment of a new state festival tax as the alternative (Hall, 1996b). The aristocratic families of Biluluk and Tanggulunan still held income rights to the saline spring where locals and people from other areas came to buy salt or to make salt themselves; indeed, the charter reaffirmed the local elite's rights to this privilege. The 1366 charter specified that those who came to make salt during the local festival should henceforth first make a payment of three hundred cash as pamuja, and that thereafter they were subject to a monthly salt duty (pagagarem) of seven *ku* payable to the elite.

Unlike the Ferry Charter's total withdrawal of the collection privileges held by the local elite over the commercial affairs at Canggu, the Biluluk Charter confirmed the revenue collection privileges of the elites of Biluluk and Tanggulunan on the local salt production and marketing and even went so far as to put an extended curse on those commoners who would cause physical harm to local elite (implying that there was considerable pressure on the traditional elite in this age of rapid economic change).

> He shall meet misfortune . . . when he crosses a field he will be bitten by a poisonous snake, when he goes to the forest he shall be felled by a tiger, or he shall be bitten by an alligator . . . when he passes a high-road he shall become exhausted and dizzy, when it rains he shall be struck by lightning, and when he is in his house fire will fall upon him without any rain, he shall be consumed by the holy Fire, he shall be turned to ashes together with his possessions. (Pigeaud: 1960–1963, 3:166–67)

The two later letters of the Biluluk Charters, dated 1393 and 1395, further document the local consequence of these economic transitions and their social implications. Although the two following charters were addressed to the traditional landed elite, they both concern the local artisans (*parawangsa*)—who are still distinguished as commoners, in marked contrast to the addressed landed aristocrats. These charters reflect the increased autonomy of the local marketing community from the interventions of the traditional landed elite, the increased separation of marketplace activities from those of the traditional agricultural community since the initial 1366 charter, and the consequent threat to traditional order implicit in these changes. The 1393 letter concerns the local commercial elite, the "chiefs of trade" (seemingly the heads of the marketplace), who were by then entitled to *titiban* ("what drops in the lap"), compulsory payments and purchases by the local merchants and artisans who participated in the eight commercial trades.

Like the trade specialists in commercial centers near the royal capital, local merchants and artisans were required to buy lots (*tiban*) at fixed prices set by the chiefs of trade (Pigeaud: 1960–1963, 4:426). In the Biluluk area these payments had formerly included ironware, earthenware dishes (Chinese and other ceramics), rattan, cotton cloth, and the obligation to buy four kinds of spices (these were likely used in the preparation of meats). These were all trade goods acquired from other places in exchange for local products. Titiban also referred to the compulsory relinquishing to the chiefs of trade part of the stocks created and accumulated by local artisans. The 1393 letter revealed that messengers from the royal court normally "came down" to collect its share of local titiban lots from the chiefs of trade, and these state revenue collectors were paid for their efforts an additional fee (*tahil padugi*) that was collected from local tradesmen on the state's behalf by the chiefs of trade. The court's right to a share of the titiban collections guaranteed the flow of locally produced trade commodities (salt, sugar, salted meats, cloth, and oil) and a share of goods acquired in exchange for these products to the court or its designee.

The 1393 letter stipulated that a new fixed head tax payable to the court called *pamihos* was to replace a list of prior marketplace cesses payable to the chiefs of trade, as well as numerous other social assessments collectively known as *arikpurih* that had formerly been payable by local merchants and artisans to the chiefs of trade. These dues had been payable on thirteen different instances or occasions, each of which was a privilege normally reserved for Majapahit elite in this era, but these privileges were now being performed by the locally wealthy as assertions of their new elite status (Hall: 2000). Five of the assessments were expected payments for the privilege of performing certain family rituals, such as elaborate birth, marriage, and death ceremonies. Seven others concerned household rights and duties such as the obligation to entertain the elite's guests, as well as rights concerning distinctive houses, such as the privilege of building a house made of brick, adorning a house with special roof decorations, and surrounding a house with a hedge.

As with the Ferry Charter, the new arrangements in the 1366 and 1393 Biluluk Charters demonstrate a more direct exercise of royal authority. These sources commonly imply significant social change taking place in the second half of the fourteenth century, including a closer relationship between the royal court and its elite and nonelite subjects. This is especially evident in the second Biluluk Charter's documentation that by 1393 the local "chiefs of trade" had assumed the stature of local elite, declaring themselves worthy of income privileges that they believed themselves entitled to collect as the marketplace authorities, backed by the stable Majapahit political economy— the chiefs of trade had thus become landed elite of sorts. Yet in both the 1366 and 1393 charters, the local Biluluk traditional elite retained their role as the court's ultimate local agents, as was also the case in the court's continuing dependency on the skills of the traditional aristocracy in Canggu to secure local collections on the state's behalf. In both cases more local productivity was being designated directly to the court rather than being retained locally, to the potential detriment of the traditional elite; in other ways, the elite were accorded greater trust than before. This is notable in the Biluluk Charters, wherein the earlier practice of sending officials out from the court to receive royal shares of local revenue collections was superseded by the local landed elite's assurance that these new revenue transfers were made to the court, a role, we should note, that the Ferry Charter did *not* grant to the *landed* elite in Canggu.

In 1395 a third letter was sent from the Majapahit court to Biluluk, this time regarding assessments on the local sugar palm tappers. This charter seems to have responded to an even greater challenge to the authority of the traditional elite by the local marketplace community, as it confirmed the right to make local collections on local sugar palm production as belonging to the traditional landholders, instead of the chiefs of trade, who had apparently taken control over the local production from the sugar palms from the landed elite, and were thus receiving one-half of the sugar collected by the tapper (apparently the tapper was allowed to retain the remaining half share). The normal flow of this payment was to the traditional elite who claimed hereditary income rights over this property. In reaffirming the local elite's privilege to these fees instead of the chiefs of trade, the inscription further stipulated that from this one-half share the elite were required to make specified payments to the state.

The Charter of Karang Bogem, dated 1384, involves another royal intervention to assess the court's pamuja ritual tax on commercial specialists, in this case to the detriment of local elite. Karang Bogem was on the north Java coast in the western part of the Majapahit state's territories. This inscription concerns a royal debt-bondsman (*kawula*) (Pigeaud: 1960–1963, 3:173, 4:449ff). The bondsman had initially been a freeborn fisherman active in a nearby coastal center, but a royal court judge had fined him 120,000 cash as punishment for an alleged crime. Unable to pay the debt, the fisherman was forced to become a debt-bondsman of the king and was assigned the task of developing a fishery on seven acres (one jung) of wasteland at Karang Bogem, some to be terraced (*pasawahan*), and one *kikil* (half jung) of clearings. The royal court received one part of the fishery's production as repayment of the fine and another part as payment of interest on the money invested by the court in the fishery. A further return on this economic initiative by the Majapahit court came in the form of a consignment of fish to the

state at the time of the court's Caitra festival (Hall: 1996b). The Charter of
Karang Bogem also imposed the pamuja festival tax—which was likely payable at the Caitra festival as well—on local traders, fishermen, and sugar palm
tappers, while exempting them from old *arik purih* dues that had been previously paid to the landed elite (who held estates and bondsmen) of that area.
These elite were considered to be members of the royal family, due to their
alliance through marriage with the court, so to appease them for their loss of
their old arik purih income rights their own pamuja tax cess was reduced by
one-half. Thus the local elite's authority over commercial activity—an
authority wielded by the extended family of the monarch no less—was displaced in favor of both the court and the local commercial community, and
the independence of the local commercial community relative to previously
dominant local political institutions was established, similar to the case in the
Canggu charter.

Collectively these royal charters portray an evolving standardization of the
Javanese state's revenue collections. In each inscription the Majapahit court
replaced tax assessments of earlier times—notably derwaya haji and arikpurih—with new state cesses, pamuja and pamihos respectively, that were
ultimately payable to the state, through the agency of local or court assigned
intermediaries. In all cases, payments of the annual pamuja ritual tax assessments afforded local commercial communities a place in the annual royal
ritual calendar, both through the reproduction of the required payments to
sustain those rituals in the local setting and in the linked invitation to send
local representatives to the royal festivals themselves. Overall, local elites
were subordinated to the center a bit more, while local commoners were elevated to more direct participation in the king's rituals, with subsequent consequences relative to their enhanced ritual stature in Majapahit-era society, and
the networked effect extended the monarch's reach a bit more deeply into
the countryside. The case can be made that the upwardly mobile commercial
communities were content at this point in time to achieve royal recognition
of their valid ritual stature, and thus negate their general negative public
image, as the first step in their achievement of other sociopolitical recogni-
tions (Robson: 1995, 84; Hall: 2000).

The new royal relationship with these three communities is most strikingly
shown in the Canggu Ferry Charter's curtailment of the political rights of the
landed elite. In this case the ferrymen were granted an independent political
and social status, and their elevation reinforced the emergence of Canggu as
a commercial center. In Biluluk and Karang Bogem the effects are not as
clear. On the one hand, the new revenue collection policy diminished the
political rights of the local elite relative to the state, but on the other the Biluluk traditional elite and the landed elite of Karang Bogem retained consider-

able rights, possibly because they held local political authority that the monarch chose not to (or lacked the power to) challenge, or perhaps, in the case of Karang Bogem, because of the local elite's marriage alliance with the court.

THE JAVANESE ECONOMY UNDER
THE MAJAPAHIT STATE

Beyond the political implications of the new revenue settlements, the Majapahit government's new tax collection policies had positive implications for the Javanese economy. The replacement of the derwaya haji and arikpurih collection systems with fixed yearly fees collected more directly from the producer would have theoretically allowed the producer more personal control over his surplus production. The previous arrangements appear to have allowed local landed elites to assume control over the peasants' surplus. So long as they made the required payments to the state, there appears to have been no upper limit to what these "revenue collectors" could extract from producers, and they undoubtedly kept for themselves as much as they could.

In the Angkor realm, peasants often had retained only about 30 percent of what they produced on their lands, the remainder being due to elites or institutions (especially temples) that held rights to income from property (see chapter 6). Loss of control over surplus did not mean poverty for the peasant, however. In Angkor, the percentage of local production due to those elites who held income rights to land was fixed, so increased productivity benefited both the producer and those holding income rights to his land. In Java, by contrast, there had been no upper limit to what could be collected, as was the case in each of the Majapahit-era charters discussed above.

In Java, the state collected revenue in three forms, cash, produce, and labor, with the latter two being the most common. In the fourteenth century, rice was the principal means of payment, although cash settlements were becoming more common, especially among the nonagrarian population. Rice payments due to the Majapahit government were collected by state ministers (*patih*) and were often stored until needed by the state (Pigeaud: 1960–1963, 4:386).

Payments of rice are mentioned in several sources. For example, another late fourteenth-century inscription, the Charter of Katiden (1395), mentions a rice tax of *takerturun* ("a bundle of rice in the blade for every compound gate") (Pigeaud: 1960–1963, 3:174, 4:456). The rice was likely collected from the fields at harvesttime, as the *Nagarakertagama* mentions *prabherti*, the "first fruits of the harvest" that were payable to the government for use

in the Caitra festival (Robson: 1995, 85, 140). A hundred years earlier, writing in 1225, Zhao Rugua, the commissioner of foreign trade at the China
coast port of Quanzhou, noted that the Javanese paid a "tithe-rent" rice tax.
Javanese government officials of the Singhasari period who supervised cities,
the state's treasury, and the state's granaries received rice from this payment
as their salaries (Hirth and Rockhill: 1911, 76–77, 83). A similar arrangement
is implied in the Biluluk Charters discussed above, in which the state's revenue officials received a share of their fee collections on the court's behalf.

As in earlier times as discussed in chapter 5, revenue collections from
lands that were not considered subject to the king's personal and direct landholding rights do not seem to have been important to the state's existence; in
most cases the king's income rights to lands that were not his own were likely
subject to sima revenue grants, including transfers of the king's income rights
to sustain favored court officials, who were then themselves responsible for
that revenue's collection. Rather than confront the local elites with direct
demands for a set share of local production, the Majapahit state instead
depended on the income rights on lands directly subject to the king to sustain
most of the court's expenses and its centralization ambitions. These were
supplemented by the king's tax collections on commercial transactions as
noted above, which were beyond the old order's income rights to a share of
a land's harvest, and direct collections that the king received in his various
royal progressions and at the annual state festivals held in the vicinity of the
court.

Most of the new revenue settlements discussed above were consistent with
this principle. They generally required that the royal revenues from local producers meet the costs not of state administration but of local religious ceremonies that honored the monarch. Much of the remainder of these revenues
financed court rituals, by which representatives of the community were
required to contribute and in which they had to participate. As for cesses
collected in trade goods such as textiles, these luxuries were reassigned to
royal allies as part of redistribution arrangements that continued to be important to the Javanese monarch's sovereignty. In addition, the inclusion of nonelite (common) folk in the royal ritual realm promoted the state's authority
relative to local elites and encouraged ritual at the local level that emulated
that of the royal court (Kulke: 1980; Hall: 1996b).

In addition to promoting the symbolic presence of the court, the fourteenth-
century reassignments of royal revenue assessments would have stimulated
production by giving the producer greater control of his produce. Eliminating
the dues collected by tax farmers would have allowed local producers to keep
a larger share of their production surplus and profit from its sale. This in turn
would have given the community an incentive to increase its rice output. In

the charters discussed above, for example, the imposition of fixed head taxes and regular assessments on local producers that replaced the multitude of local assessments must have had a positive impact on local productivity by encouraging local production rather than discouraging it, as would be the case if these royal assessments were based on local productivity instead. That is, increased productivity would now benefit the local producer (or, more precisely, the individuals holding land income rights) rather than the state.

The state, however, was also the beneficiary in these revenue settlements, since it was more likely to derive additional revenues from the subsequent increased market activity. Another key factor that is also demonstrated in the Biluluk Charters is the importance of local material consumption and conspicuous display of an assortment of consumer goods that could only be secured by increased local productivity. Thus any reduction of taxes that might have diminished local productivity (because less productive effort was needed for survival) was countered by local desire for consumption, not just by an elite who because of their landholding rights directly benefited from increased rural productivity, but increasingly by the Java rural public. The extended era of internal peace and security in the last half of the fourteenth century provided by the Majapahit state and the development of a realmwide road network also contributed to increased productivity. These infrastructural arrangements fostered the expansion of the marketing network and a growing concentration of nonagrarian populations (merchants, artisans, and government officials) across the countryside. These internal developments overlapped with the increase in international demand for eastern archipelago spices and the need for Java's rice to feed the seasonal maritime trade that brought the spices westward. Java's peasants accordingly increased their production in response to the rising demand in both hinterland and coastal market centers, as well as in response to consequent opportunities to consume.

Improved marketing possibilities provided ample opportunity for an ambitious peasant to increase his family's income, as signaled by the increasingly widespread consumption of foreign and luxury goods (Miksic: 1994). The heavy concentration of Chinese ceramics in a wide array of Majapahit-era archeological sites, the literary and epigraphic references to local consumption of commercial products of nonlocal origin, written records of monetarized exchange at all levels of the Javanese economy, and archeological evidence substantiating those records all suggest that the desire and ability to consume imported or luxury goods was spreading beyond the elite (Miksic and Soekatno: 1995; Hall: 2000). Given the importance of religious ritual in Javanese society at this time, the royal focus on enhancing religious and civil rituals and ceremonies must have provided additional incentives for public accumulations of surplus, as increased incomes enabled nonelites to sponsor and participate in Hindu and Buddhist religious ceremonies for the first time. Indeed, in the three charters discussed above the king explicitly solicits the participation of the nonelite in state ritual. Using surplus income in this manner, especially for ceremonies directly associated with the king, would have reciprocated merit for the donor and enhanced the donor's ritual status (Moertono: 1968, 14–26; Hall: 1996b).

Not only was the countryside increasingly prosperous, but the economy was increasingly monetized. The fact that the new pamihos cess collected in Biluluk as well as the pamuja tax due from the Canggu ferrymen were payable in cash rather than in kind illustrates the growing monetization, a consequence of Java's commercial prosperity as a major international center of trade. Not only was the economy increasingly monetized, but the medium of exchange had recently shifted away from gold and silver in favor of Chinese copper coinage known as *pasis*, which greatly facilitated smaller-denomination market transactions (Aelast: 1995; Wisseman Christie: 1996).

Gold and silver remained important, but they were now bulk commodities and merchandise for the market, not units of currency. On the other hand, gold and silver "Java money" (*shepo kin)* was widely used in the transitional tenth to twelfth centuries as the standard of exchange in regional ports, as reported in Chinese and Arab sources (Aelast: 1995, 367; Tibbetts: 1979, 53; Hirth and Rockhill: 1911, 78, 82, 156, 160). Precious metals were still received in trade for the spices of the eastern archipelago islands, where, as will be discussed in chapter 9, there was a commodity trade rather than a monetary trade, and merchants based in Java's ports received considerable amounts of copper, gold, and silver as intermediaries in exchanges for the eastern archipelago's pepper, cloves, and nutmeg. The spice trade exchanges were major components not only in the flow of copper cash out of China, but also in the flow of specie out of the West. As the European demand for spices increased in the thirteenth century, a corresponding increased flow of Western gold and silver currency moved through the Middle East and India to Java, where it stayed (Mills: 1970, 45–47, 88, 96–97, 102, 107, 129–30, 141, 151, 153). As early as the end of the thirteenth century, as previously cited, Marco Polo had considered Java the wealthiest place on earth (Yule: 1903, 2:272–74). The movement of gold into Java had a lot to do with his perceptions.

However, as we have just seen, in Java itself gold and silver no longer played the role in local exchanges that they once did. Ninth- and tenth-century charters in Java had referenced gold and silver payments by weight. But in the thirteenth- and fourteenth-century charters there is rarely mention of gold, due to the transition to copper coins as the standard unit of exchange. The local awareness of this transition can be seen in the previously referenced

1350 Majapahit-era sima copper-plate inscription, which relates that in an earlier generation a certain transaction had been made in silver, because "at that time this land of Java did not possess the means of the *pasis* [copper coins]" (Pigeaud: 1960–1963, 3:154; Wicks: 1992, 291–92). The implication was that the pasis was then in everyday use. Additional evidence appears in Old Javanese–language texts that were originally translated from Sanskrit and in which Indian monetary values (*pana*) were initially converted into local nomenclature. The Majapahit-era translations append references to pasis, or Chinese cash, as appropriate to the revised and universal system of economic valuation. Also of interest among the Majapahit-era numismatic evidence are terra-cotta "piggy banks," which are found with Chinese coins still remaining inside them (Wicks: 1992).

Zhao Rugua, the commissioner of foreign trade at the China coast port of Quanzhou, had already been impressed by the use of precious metals in early thirteenth-century Java. There, according to him, people were using copper coins alloyed with mixtures of silver, tin, and lead, similar to the ones in China. Sixty small metal coins with holes in their centers were strung on a string. A string of sixty was equal to one *tael* of gold and thirty-two equaled a half tael of gold (Hirth and Rockhill: 1911, 78, 82–83). It is not clear whether Java was simply using Chinese coins or was also making its own (Aelast: 1995, 367ff). Nevertheless, Zhao Rugua also reports that the Chinese were buying so much spice (especially pepper) from eastern Java ports that copper coinage was flowing out of the country at an alarming rate, and in an effort to protect its currency the Chinese government eventually banned trade with Java altogether (Hirth and Rockhill: 1911, 78, 81–82n16). The ban likely had little effect, as Java-based traders circumvented it by referring to their country as Sukadana (Su-ki-tan), a name they apparently made up. By the early fifteenth century, if not before, Chinese records report that the countries located in eastern Java (Majapahit) and southern and northern Sumatra (Palembang and Lamuri/Ramni, respectively) reportedly used copper cash extensively (Wade: 2010). Thus, whether they were recirculating coins from China or minting their own copper cash, by the fifteenth century the countries in the Straits of Melaka and Java Sea region had come to prefer copper or copper-tin-lead blend "Javanese pasis" as the basis for their own monetary system (Aelast: 1995, 387–88; Wisseman Christie: 1996; Whitmore: 1983; Hall: 1999).

Due to the transition to a more monetized economy, Java's taxes were collected in both cash and in kind, as documented above. Profits made on the tridirectional exchange in Java's coastal ports of Javanese rice for eastern archipelago spices and of these for the goods and metals of the East and West were subject to royal taxes. From the international trade passing through east

Javanese ports, Java's monarchs received significant income that helped finance the expanded domestic activities of the Majapahit court. In addition to these cesses from the coastal ports, market merchants active near the court were obliged to relinquish part of their stocks to the "chiefs of trade," as in the Biluluk inscription discussed above, who shared this collection (titiban) with the court. The government's reliance on income from commerce was sometimes quite explicit. Zhao Rugua reports that soldiers and troop commanders received their salaries in gold rather than copper pisis, while high government officials periodically received a supply of native produce to supplement their monthly salaries (Hirth and Rockhill: 1911, 76). In addition, the commander in chief of Majapahit's forces was said to have received eight thousand cash per diem directly from markets (Pigeaud: 1960–1963, 4:426). Some of these sources considered the Java-based merchants in the international spice trade to be the monarch's trade agents. The *Nagarakertagama* (canto 16) similarly implies that at least some of the traders, as religious specialists based in Java, were under royal patent (Robson: 1995, 35).

To provision the key export-import sector with local products, especially rice, royal policy encouraged the participation of local productive units in the higher levels of the market economy (see chapter 1). Recognition of the rights of Biluluk's artisan community relative to their chiefs of trade and the increased independence of commercial communities at Canggu and Karang Bogem were examples of this aspect of the Majapahit state's economic policy. As discussed above, the new charters with these communities would not have immediately added substantial income to the royal treasury, yet the new tax policies encouraged the production of local surpluses and the flow of these surpluses via the expanding marketing network to the coast, where their exchange for foreign goods was directly taxed by the state.

While they enhanced the freedoms and improved the production incentives of local commercial communities, the Majapahit rulers were also careful not to infringe too much on the traditional local elites in the court's centralization initiatives, because kings continued to depend on the personal alliances forged with these elites. Rather than encroaching further upon the rights and powers of these entrenched elites, Majapahit's monarchs instead encouraged the development of the Javanese nonagricultural economy and promoted the cause of merchants and artisans who could best assist in facilitating the flow of goods to and from Java's north coast ports. Zhao Rugua reports that traders making stopovers in east Java ports stayed in visitors' lodges, where food and drink was supplied, and were otherwise generously treated and yet were not charged for harborage or board. Instead the Java monarch received a return on foreign traders' exchange of gold, silver, and other metals and produce for Java's spices (Hirth and Rockhill: 1911, 77, 83). The considerable income potential of the commercial sector of the Javanese economy meant that Majapahit's monarchs did not have to enhance their income directly from the lands controlled by local elites, and their consolidation policies avoided political confrontation that might immerse the state in widespread conflict, which would have benefited no group.

The entire system depended on income from the coastal ports. When in the fifteenth century Majapahit's authority was challenged by coastal commercial elites who broke away from the state's authority, the state ceased to exist in its most politically dominant form, to be revived only in the late sixteenth and early seventeenth centuries when the new Mataram monarchy, recentered back to central Java, again secured a share of the international trade profits (Moertono: 1968; Ricklefs: 1998). At the moment, however, the system appeared to create mutual benefits to all parties, as revealed in the following passage from the *Nagarakertagama*, which, as noted earlier, was composed in the time of King Hayam Wuruk (ca. 1365).

> If the peasants' cultivated lands are destroyed, then the court too will be short of sustenance [i.e., if rice were produced, then the court, which consumed and also benefited from the sale of rice, would also suffer]. If there is not retinue [i.e., the king's retinue, his administrative corps and especially his military] in evidence and no subjects inhabiting the land, there will be foreign islands coming to attack. Therefore equally let them be cared for so that both will be stable. (Pigeaud: 1960–1963, 3:105)

The state thus provided the physical protection necessary to promote the realm's economic prosperity and protect it from outsiders. With protection provided by the state military and proper administration, the land would be populated and peasants could produce the rice that sustained the entire realm (Pigeaud: 1960–1963, 4:93–94, 103, 257).

Another indication of the importance of trade in the middle fourteenth century is in the *Nagarakertagama*'s references to Bubat, a substantial commercial center located on the Brantas River in the hinterland. Bubat was surrounded on three sides by large buildings (*bhawanas*). Its population resided in ethnically segregated neighborhoods (*mapanta*), of which the Indian and Chinese quarters received special mention (Pigeaud: 1960–1963, 4:291; Robson: 1995, 85, 87–88). The poem makes it clear that Bubat was frequented by foreign traders and was also the site of royal symbolism. Here traders from India, Cambodia, China, Champa, Ayudhya, and other places gathered to pay homage to and provision the Majapahit monarch. The *Nagarakertagama* gave Bubat special prominence as the first center for the celebration of the Caitra festival. As has been noted earlier, the Caitra festival celebrated both the Majapahit monarch's successful leadership and the beginning of a new year in the agricultural cycle (cantos 86–91). During the first seven days of the festival the Majapahit court "came down" to Bubat to participate in public amusements in a fair atmosphere. The celebrations began with public activities intermixed with speeches at gatherings of the royal family and its allies, and culminated with a community meal and dancing and singing performances in the royal compound. Here games and gambling were permitted in a place more appropriate for such actions than the sanctified court. It was here in Bubat that the king received various collections in kind due to him from assorted commercial communities, for example the pamuja payments described in the charters mentioned above.

Not only did domestic tradesmen bring tribute to the king at the annual Caitra festival ceremonies, but representatives from China, India, Cambodia, Champa, and Ayudhya also paid their respects to the king. Foreign Buddhist monks and Brahmans also participated in the Caitra festival (canto 93.1). The foreigners came to Java on merchant ships (it is unclear whose), arriving by the western monsoon before the beginning of the festival (February or March) and returning to the Asian mainland on the eastern monsoon. An external contemporary view of the Majapahit festivities is provided in the following passage from the *Hikayat Raja-Raja Pasai*, which is discussed at greater length at the beginning of the next chapter.

> From places inland right down to the shores of the Southern Ocean the people all came for an audience with the Emperor, bringing tribute and offerings. . . . Everywhere one went there were gongs and drums being beaten, people dancing to the strains of all kinds of loud music, entertainments of many kinds like the living theatre, the shadow play, masked-plays, step-dancing and musical dramas. These were the commonest sights and went on day and night in the land. (Hill: 1960, 161)

Also on the banks of the Brantas River the king on another occasion celebrated the "passing-over ceremony" that marked the coming of the Javanese new year. This act emphasized the life-bringing powers of the Brantas, which was the source of the eastern Java–based state's prosperity. The Brantas supplied the water necessary for eastern Java's wet-rice agriculture and also provided contact with the outside world, whence came luxury goods and revenues.

More information comes from the *Pararaton*, a chronicle in prose form composed outside the court in the late fifteenth century (Phalgunadi: 1996). While the mid-fourteenth-century *Nagarakertagama* refers to the state's commercial activities only occasionally and in the context of state ceremonies, the *Pararaton* offers much more (Hall: 2003). It records the retrospective of the coming to power of the "founder" of the thirteenth-century Singasari court, Ken Angrok (Rajasa, r. 1222–1227), but also traces the affairs of the

Majapahit dynasty through the early fifteenth century. It also provides a much longer list of centers of trade and commercial affairs than does the *Nagara-kertagama*. Tuban was said to be the Majapahit realm's most prosperous port; although it benefited from royal favor it held no royal monopoly and there was ample trade at other enumerated north Java coast ports. In one episode the *Pararaton* reports a maritime expedition that had been launched against Majapahit by the ruler of the Sunda Strait region in 1357 (one year previous to the Ferry Charter of Canggu). Even though the expedition had been able to sail all the way up the Brantas by way of Canggu to Bubat, Majapahit's military still defeated the Sunda forces. According to the *Pararaton*, the Sundanese king had escorted his daughter to Majapahit with a large retinue of ships in order to present her in marriage and thereby seal a formal alliance with the Majapahit king. When the Majapahit court refused to recognize her as a suitable queen of equal rank to the king, the offended Sundanese ruler retaliated by returning with his navy and waging battle at Bubat. This maritime raid by the Sunda ruler is consistent with the patterns of riverine system competition common to the island realm in early Southeast Asian history, as variously described in earlier chapters. In this instance the Sunda Strait ruler—who appears to have been in control of the riverine systems on both sides of the strait and who from this strategic location could have been a serious rival to Majapahit's commercial interests in the western Indonesian archipelago—sent a naval expedition up the Brantas River intent upon eliminating a rival and enhancing his commercial interests. But the Sundanese king had initially sought to enact an alliance with his powerful neighbor and natural opponent, and his failed attempt to eliminate his rival was reactive and consequential to the straits realm.

With Majapahit's victory, the Sunda Strait ruler's subordinates in the riverine systems of western Java and southern Sumatra became vulnerable to the Majapahit state's ambitions, although there is no evidence of an immediate Majapahit raid into that area. Twenty years later, in 1377, Majapahit sent a punitive expedition against Palembang, another competitor in this Melaka and Sunda straits region (Wolters: 1970, 113–14; 1983, 60n54). Conflict among rivals for commercial hegemony in the archipelago trade network had been a common occurrence in the pre-Majapahit era. True to this tradition, Majapahit's rulers' repulse of the reactive invasion attempt by their competitor, the Sunda Strait ruler, confirmed Majapahit's stature as the archipelago's leading maritime power. Whether this rivalry with the Sunda realm actually threatened Majapahit's authority or not, the potential symbolism of this event was not lost on the *Pararaton*'s author, who used this victory to confirm Majapahit's subsequent commercial leadership over the maritime realm, fulfilling the legacy and unfulfilled ambitions of Kertanagara in the late thirteenth century.

To summarize, the establishment of Majapahit culminated the evolution of royal power in Java. The time before was marked by expanding and contracting royal authority over the Javanese countryside, and the fourteenth-century accomplishments were followed by another contraction in the fifteenth century. As we have seen in previous chapters, from the tenth to the early fourteenth century royal administration had already been making inroads into the state's regions. Now, in the height of the Majapahit period, post-1350, the growing political, economic, and social integration of the realm produced a truly Javanese cultural form that is most conspicuous in the era's literature, art, and architecture (Kinney: 2003). The Majapahit era was the peak of the cultural synthesis of Siva worship and Buddhist Tantrism, an era of the "Indonesianization" of classical forms in art, literature, and music. In this period the Javanese *wayang* (puppet theater) and *gamelan* (orchestra) developed in the Majapahit court and were imitated throughout the realm (Holt: 1967, 72; Hall: 2005).

Economically, the rice economy of eastern Java as well as the older region of central Java prospered. Because of the increased external demand for Javanese rice, there emerged a hierarchical market network that united communities of local exchange with Java's coastal ports. Yet at the topmost levels of this marketing system there was a conscious separation of political and commercial function. Ports of trade were not political centers, and the state's political center was not a major commercial center. Majapahit's capital was located well in the interior up the Brantas River from the coast, where it was less likely to have been subject to direct contact with outsiders. The Majapahit court consciously located its own marketplace on the periphery of the state's ritual center to make sure that the commercial activities that took place there would not pollute the royal court's aristocratic residents (Pigeaud: 1960–1963, 5, insert; Hall: 1996b). According to the *Nagarakertagama*, the court's major commercial affairs and contact with foreigners were transacted at Bubat, some distance from the court, as the Canggu Ferry Charter also demonstrates relative to the Canggu Brantas River ferry crossing, which does not receive mention in the *Nagarakertagama*. The commercial leadership of the Javanese state was thus downplayed in the *Nagarakertagama*, wherein Majapahit's rulers followed the Javanese tradition of wet-rice statecraft that traced its history to early central Java. Thus while the Majapahit monarch ruled both a wet-rice and maritime realm, it was his association with the Javanese wet-rice state tradition that was the most critical to his expression of legitimacy, in the mind of the *Nagarakertagama*'s court-based author.

Politically, Majapahit monarchs assumed greater leadership and also enhanced their status as the source of cultural identity. At the same time, like earlier Javanese political centers, Majapahit was the focus of a chain of patron-client relationships, with the state-level center attempting to maintain itself economically and politically against the centrifugal forces of local-level alliance networks. To combat the divisive tendencies of the past, Majapahit's monarchs substantiated their legitimacy by fabricating links to eras of past glory. For example, the *Nagarakertagama* claimed that Majapahit's rulers were the legitimate successors to a line of monarchs who had ruled Java since the origin of the Javanese polity in the sixth century (see chapter 5).

The kings of Majapahit also patronized a Tantric Siva-Buddhist religion in which indigenous Javanese religious values dominated, yet which proclaimed the supremacy of the king as the earthly representative of the divine. Drawing on Hindu and Buddhist references, the *Nagarakertagama* describes the royal family as being above mortals and the king as an innately divine incarnation of a god (Pigeaud: 1960–1963, 3:3–4, 4:468; Johns: 1964, 93). The king was also the divinely ordained head of society, with the function of giving human life its appropriate place in the cosmic order (Pigeaud: 1960–1963, 4:528). Consistent with the patterns of Indianized statecraft practiced in earlier Javanese states, the *Nagarakertagama* idealized the Majapahit court and its kingdom as being created in the image of the universe as a whole. The Majapahit monarch provided for his subjects' well-being by maintaining order in his realm. It was his task to enlarge his miniature cosmos as he created a heaven on earth (mandala) (Moertono: 1968, 1).

The accomplishments of Majapahit's fourteenth-century monarchs provided a standard of achievement that resonated not only for their successors in Java but also among the Malay populations of the Indonesian archipelago (Supomo: 1976). The *Nagarakertagama* and Majapahit's inscriptions report a state that impressively administered the whole "land of Java" (Javabhumi), that held sovereignty over "other islands" (*nusantara/dvipantara*), and whose authority was also recognized by all "other countries" (*desantara*) (Kulke: 1991). The state's monarchs justly ruled and protected their subject population, were well informed of the affairs of their state, and stimulated their state's development.

However, Majapahit's monarchs did not hold absolute authority over their domain in the modern sense (Schrieke: 1957, 25–70). As already shown, against the royal initiatives toward centralization, inscriptions of the period demonstrate that Majapahit's state system still depended on a network of patron-client relationships with regional elites who were normally linked to the reigning monarch by blood or marriage. The inscriptions of the period make it clear that the local elites acted in the name of their Majapahit overlord, but they also document that these elites were effectively semiautonomous. The *Nagarakertagama* highlights another centrifugal force. During the reign of Hayam Wuruk (1350–1389), the most powerful among the chronicle poem's monarchs, the king shared power with his father Kertawardhana and with his uncle Vijayarajasa. The former was known as the Prince of Singhasari. The latter was known as the Prince of Wengker and had administrative responsibilities in the eastern Java region. Essentially, this arrangement reproduced the old division between Singhasari and Kadiri, with both presumably being subordinated to Majapahit.

The Prince of Singhasari title associated Hayam Wuruk's father with the previous rulers of Singhasari, while the Prince of Wengker title associated Vijayarajasa with the previous rulers of Kadiri (he was also married to the Princess of Kadiri). The Wengker region was near Madiun, west of Kadiri on the upper eastern branch of the Solo River, and Vijayarajasa's administrative duties included responsibility for eastern Java and Bali, which had been conquered by Majapahit in 1343 (Noorduyn: 1975). Both princes were depicted in the *Nagarakertagama* as organizing the compilation of descriptions of the districts that were under royal authority and as stimulating the upkeep of roads, public buildings, and temples—all activities associated with the kings themselves in earlier times (Pigeaud: 1960–1963, 4:540–46). Additionally, the Prince of Wengker maintained independent diplomatic contact with the Chinese court, personally sending envoys in 1377 and 1379, and these contacts led the Ming court to assume that the Javanese realm was politically divided (Noorduyn: 1975, 481–82).

MAJAPAHIT'S FIFTEENTH-CENTURY "DEMISE"

While Majapahit inscriptions and other indigenous sources do not support the Ming view that the Majapahit population divided its loyalty between two sovereigns in the fourteenth century, they do demonstrate that there were rival branches of the royal family (Pigeaud: 1960–1963, 4:537–46). Majapahit's monarchs tolerated the semiautonomy of their Wengker kinsmen until 1406, when, apparently in response to the increasingly offensive actions of these relatives, it became necessary for the Majapahit monarchy to confirm its supremacy over eastern Java. Chinese envoys were present when the Majapahit monarch of "western Java" (the Prince of Wengker) invaded and ravaged this "eastern capital" (of the Prince of Singhasari) in 1406, and 170 Chinese residents were reported to have been accidentally killed in the fighting (Colless: 1975b).

Modern historians have theorized about the demise of the Majapahit state following the 1406 action (Coedes: 1968, 239–242; Krom: 1931, 427–32).

At this time the north coast ports were dominated by commercial populations who were converting to Islam and breaking away from Majapahit's political authority. Conventionally, this drive for independence by the north coast commercial enclaves has been viewed as severely weakening the Majapahit political system. Loss of control over the north coast trade deprived Majapahit's monarchs of the trade revenues that had supported their statecraft. In response, they depended increasingly on revenue collections from the land. This refocusing of state revenue demands brought a backlash from regional landed elites, who were already suspicious of the recent concentration of power in royal hands. Thus, as the north coast broke away, the various other subordinate regions also sought to reestablish their semiautonomy, either by shifting their support among various factions of the royal family or by allying with one or another of the coastal commercial centers, who willingly supplied military assistance in return for a region's commitment to provision its benefactor. The result was a lessening of focus on the political center. This is suggested by the limited number of Majapahit realm inscriptional records in comparison to the number of inscriptions in the previous century. Those that exist focus on the flourishing rural economy and its Hindu-Javanese culture rather than continuing to highlight the state's efforts to centralize and extend Majapahit's political authority (Noorduyn: 1978).

The ports that were breaking away in the fifteenth century were ruled by Muslim sultans who were descended from foreign merchants or maritime diaspora, many of whom were of Chinese ethnicity, who had grown rich and powerful (Robson: 1981; Supomo: 1997). Only Tuban was ruled by a native Javanese family. All these ruling elites were now Muslim. Former sojourners who won the respect of the Majapahit court were allowed to build mosques and support the importation of religious teachers, or mullahs, whose presence attracted still other Muslims. Meanwhile, the Muslim elites began to assimilate to Javanese noble customs, at least in the ports dominated by longtime Southeast Asia resident populations, and the results of this process would be noted by the Portuguese scribe Tomé Pires in the early sixteenth century (Cortesao: 1944, 180–223). As they assimilated to the Majapahit legacy, these elites began to limit the numbers of Muslim traders who were allowed to enter the country, for fear that despite their independence they might unbalance the tenuous political network centered on the Majapahit court (Noorduyn: 1978, 244–53). Nevertheless, the ports were at least economically autonomous. Port elites known as orang kaya, "rich men," dominated trade by levying tolls and monopolizing the trade in specific staple products, and they took an active part in maritime activities such as ship ownership, piracy, and trading.

The coastal centers that were breaking away had gained their commercial

stature largely due to Majapahit's economic initiatives of the previous century. As we have seen, Majapahit's rulers had initially patronized trade and
traders. However, when the commercial populations began to challenge its
authority, the court appears to have deliberately withdrawn from the coast,
refocusing its statecraft on the ruler's spiritual rather than economic and
political leadership. In effect, the central court allowed the coast to develop
as a zone of international trade separate from the Java hinterland and its rural
traditions. Consequently, in this period the Majapahit monarch could no
longer guarantee that he could maintain the order necessary for his subjects'
physical and spiritual well-being—the most critical requirement of traditional
Javanese monarchs—except in Java's hinterland. Thus, statecraft legitimately
refocused on the miniature cosmos that the monarch continued to rule in Java's
interior. Overall, in the conventional view, Majapahit's supposed fifteenth-
century decline involved two related movements: (1) the growing political
autonomy of the formerly subordinate north coast ports and (2) the Majapahit
state's conscious "internalization" of its statecraft.

Chinese sources reflect this abandonment of the coast and extra-island
affairs. The Chinese report that at the beginning of the fifteenth century the
Javanese welcomed an enhanced Chinese role in the western archipelago, particularly in the Straits of Melaka region that Majapahit had previously
claimed as its own. When Chinese admiral Zheng He removed the pirate
chief of the Palembang coastal enclave in southeastern Sumatra in 1407, he
claimed to be acting in the name of the Majapahit monarch. His continued
actions in the Straits of Melaka region until the 1430s do not seem to have
been aimed at destroying Majapahit's authority but rather were increasingly
motivated by the understanding that by this time Majapahit's authority in the
region was in name only (Mills: 1970). The *Pararaton* likewise reflects the
transition, largely by ignoring the events of the fifteenth century (Hardjowardojo: 1965). The *Pararaton*'s focus on pre-fifteenth-century Java suggests
that the idealistic fourteenth-century image in the *Nagarakertagama* was no
longer valid; the *Pararaton* may thus have been a retrospective accounting
that explained why the Majapahit state was no longer what it had once been,
or in the hope of a restoration of the fourteenth-century age in the future,
consistent with Javanese beliefs that time was cyclically repetitive (Robson:
1979).

It is appropriate to say something here about the north coast's conversion
to Islam. Java's Muslim foundation myth focuses not on a specific secular
authority who is the source of this conversion, but on nine saints (*wali sanga*)
who, independent of one another, came to Java from various regions of the
world, bringing with them the new faith and initiating Islamic scholarship
and worship. Gradually, under the guidance of these saints, the rulers of well-

established Hindu-Buddhist courts accepted Islam. There is no citation of Divine intervention, nor of any distinctive signs of the conversion; rather, the wali sanga performed miracles that so impressed the court and local elite that they convinced the rulers to enter religious partnerships with the wali sanga. As a consequence of this founding myth, instead of basing their claims to power on political or religious descent from Mecca (as was done by the Sumatran kingdom of Sumadra-Pasai, on which more is said in chapter 9), Java's Islamic courts perceived themselves as successors to the legacy of centralized authority that in the Majapahit polity had been based in a partnership between kings and priests. Like Mecca in Arabia, Demak, one of the several coastal trading centers, would emerge from among its competitors to become the ritual center of Javanese Islam.

Demak's origin myth focuses on the personal history of Raden Patah, "the visitor," who was born in late fourteenth-century Palembang, the former center of the Srivijaya polity in Sumatra, to a Chinese woman with bloodlines to the Majapahit royal lineage. Raden Patah was thus descended not only from the Majapahit court but also from the Chinese Muslim merchant communities that resided in Java's north coast ports (Chang: 1991, 14, 16–18). Raden Patah emigrated to the north Java coast port of Gresik, which was largely populated by Chinese merchants, and then to Demak in the first quarter of the fifteenth century. He became immeasurably wealthy, and as an acknowledgment of his commercial and personal prowess, as well as because he had royal blood and had married a Majapahit princess, the Majapahit monarch appointed him Demak's governor. Reactive to Majapahit's fifteenth-century decline, he later declared his independence and established the Demak sultanate.

Yet even though Demak and the other north coast ports were becoming politically autonomous, they still needed the hinterland's produce—especially its rice. For their part, the hinterland elites still required external trade goods to reinforce their legitimacy. These facts necessitated continued exchanges between the Javanese coast and its hinterland, even after the ports had established their autonomy. For example, even after the north coast port of Tuban established its political sovereignty, with its elite subsequently converting to Islam, it retained its close exchange relationship with the Majapahit court. Tuban and Gresik were the most important of the fifteenth-century ports on Java's north coast, largely because of their trade alliances with the Javanese interior (where they secured rice), the eastern archipelago (where they exchanged Java's rice for spices), and Melaka (where they provisioned the port population with Java's rice and the eastern archipelago's spices; see chapter 9) (Meilink-Roelofsz: 1962, 103–15). And, as we have just seen, Demak's first sultan was of mixed Majapahit and Chinese bloodlines and had been a district governor serving Majapahit before he declared his independence.

Other fifteenth-century ports cultivated economic contact with Majapahit's regional subordinates, who were interested in securing military assistance against Majapahit and pledged their trade in return. In some instances the hinterlands were reluctant to make such commitments and had to be encouraged to do so by means of military force. Thus it was that Tomé Pires, retrospectively writing at the beginning of the sixteenth century, spoke of repeated late fifteenth-century wars between the Java coast ports and their hinterlands (Cortesao: 1944, 180–223). It might be thought that these were religiously motivated conflicts between the Muslim and non-Muslim parts of the island. However, the coastal-hinterland conflicts continued long after Java's indigenous populations began to convert to Islam, indicating that these conflicts were more likely to have been the consequence of competition over the flow of rice and other products between the interior and the coast (Damais: 1968; Ricklefs: 2006).

Whatever the case, Javanese culture continued to thrive in the hinterland, still under the at least nominal authority of the Majapahit monarchs. However, literary, epigraphic, and archeological sources from the period give the impression that the area's ritual observances had been considerably scaled down and decentralized. For example, in the *Tantu Panggelaran*, a literary product of the countryside rather than the court, lavish state temples were no longer the focus of attention. Instead, a profusion of familial shrines were being constructed and endowed in the rural communities, as the state encouraged or at least tolerated greater local self-expression. These can be seen as mirrors of the state's fourteenth-century temples that celebrated royal ancestors (Kinney: 2003; Hall: 2001b). They were centers for the performance of life-giving (water/*amrta*) and death (*sraddha*) rituals and meditations on a family ancestor's behalf, to ensure successful transition to the realm of the dead.

Similar family shrines were erected near the capital. While there was no impressive large-scale state temple construction during the fifteenth century, Mount Penanggunan, which rose above the Majapahit court, was considered to be the court's paramount ritual center. There familial groups who accepted their positions in the orbit of the court built small ancestral shrines. In doing so, these families and their ancestral deities symbolically submitted to the supremacy of the court (O'Brien: 1988). These were not acts of decentralization, but were representative of an evolution to a higher level of societal integration that would serve as the inspiration for post-Majapahit Java.

Yet though social and cultural integration remained strong, it seems that the fifteenth-century Majapahit state wanted less centralized grandeur, possibly to take some of the burden for the economic and spiritual well-being of its subjects off its own shoulders and place that burden, along with the economic rewards, on the shoulders of others who wanted this kind of prestige. This devolution could be read as a response to rising expectations that could not be fulfilled by the court, and perhaps as an expression of economic and cultural dislocation due to regular succession crises. But it could also be read as evidence that the state confidently encouraged greater local expression, as suggested by the family shrines and the existence of the Mount Penanggunan complex (Hall: 2001b).

In these and other ways, literary and archeological evidence from the fifteenth and sixteenth centuries reflects a locally articulated yet collective understanding of kingship, kinship, and respect for spirits and ancestors at all levels of Javanese society (Johns: 1967). Yet despite the greater regional self-assertion, Javanese society still needed a royal court to serve as a functional center that could intervene as a legal and spiritual mediator in local disputes and that could function as the acknowledged apex of the collective community's social and ritual networks. Majapahit's court did so by combining the granting of titles and other status symbols with a stress on the ruler's asceticism. And the Javanese cultural milieu reinforced all this by invoking the past glories.

Fourteenth-century Majapahit had perfected the notion of state-initiated hierarchy, emphasizing familial and personal rather than communal accomplishments. Success was acknowledged and rewarded by individual and familial titles and by associated symbols of status, such as material objects and especially the privileges of wearing or displaying cloth. This manner of empowerment was already different from earlier notions, which focused on societal success and access to life in the hereafter through the ruler's withdrawal from daily life to practice asceticism (Hall: 2005). In the late fourteenth- and fifteenth-century records, as for example in the Biluluk Charter inscriptions discussed above, there is even an increased focus on material prosperity in this world, consistent with the economic growth documented in contemporary inscriptions and external records. Now access to the next world was to be a consequence of individual and familial initiatives, made possible by the orderliness of the state polity and acknowledged in the ruler's validations of individual titles of status.

The issue of whether the Majapahit court actually held effective power in the late fifteenth century is impossible to resolve on the basis of available materials, but there is ample evidence from the literary, iconographic, and inscriptional sources of the era that Javanese populations rallied around the Majapahit court, or at least the memory of what it once had been, as it continued to be the source of common cultural reference. Local inscriptions, temple iconography, chronicles, *kakawin*, *kidung*, and other vernacular literature all articulate this sense of a commonly understood textual, cultural, and ideational community (Hall: 2005; O'Brien: 1998, 1990).

However, some scholars have pointed out that while the fifteenth-century Majapahit sources may express an ideal of societal unity, the reality may have been one of social division and competitive transition. For example, some argue that the increased volume of sea trade, both now and in earlier periods, destabilized "the rather loosely-structured Javanese states, whose administrations were poorly equipped to counter the centrifugal tendencies of very wealthy coastal enclaves" (Wisseman Christie: 1998a, 346). And, as noted above, even the hinterland regions became relatively autonomous as a result of their exchange relationships with the newly autonomous port-polities. Fragmentation is also suggested by the conversions to Islam in this period, which signaled that Javanese society was seeking a new psychological stability. Another view suggests that the cultural unity presented in the materials from the period was quite different than the reality of cultural and social divisions. Challenging the notion of a stable fifteenth-century Javanese community centered in a self-confident Majapahit court, the notable failure of the fourteenth- and fifteenth-century Majapahit literature and inscriptions even to acknowledge the existence of a resident Islamic community, let alone highlight the differences between Muslims and non-Muslims, is significant. Thus, the reflection of order conveyed in the fourteenth- and fifteenth-century sources must be factored against the potentials for disorder between Islamic and non-Islamic factions physically present within the court.

In any event, Majapahit would eventually be replaced by the new Islamic state of Mataram, which rose to power in the late sixteenth century. Like Majapahit, Mataram was dominated by landed elites based in the central Java rice basin. Mataram initially suppressed the commercial elite of the coastal ports in an attempt to reestablish the hinterland's control over coastal trade. But in the early seventeenth century it allowed the Dutch to dominate the coastal ports, while being content to rule the hinterland, guaranteeing the periodic delivery of Javanese rice and other hinterland products in exchange for foreign commodities supplied by the Dutch (Burger: 1956; Naerssen and Iongh: 1977, 102–4; Moertono: 1968). Mataram's rise effectively internalized Javanese commerce and ended the Javanese merchants' remaining control over the Java Sea trade. Henceforth the international trade would pass to others, not only to the Dutch but also to Southeast Asia–based maritime diaspora and other locally resident peoples (Hall: 2006; Reid: 1988, 1994).

9

Upstream and Downstream Unification and the Changing Sense of Community in Southeast Asia's Fifteenth-Century Maritime Port-Polities

This book has thus far addressed the variety of major early rice plain and riverine states and civilizations that developed in the regions of Southeast Asia to roughly 1500. The previous chapter specifically highlighted the culminating Majapahit realm based in Java, which had a wide regional presence in the fourteenth century, and ended with alternative views of what was taking place in Java during the fifteenth-century era of transition. There the fifteenth century was notable for the confrontations between Java's newly Islamic and highly multiethnic coastal ports and the sophisticated Hindu-Buddhist Javanese hinterland. There was a mutual dependency between the coast and the hinterland. Majapahit's productive rice farmers supplied the ports with substantial quantities of rice that were exported to Indonesia's eastern archipelago to acquire that region's spices. In return for the hinterland's rice, Java's prosperous fifteenth-century north coast ports satisfied the affluent Majapahit society's demand for exotic foreign goods. Because of their strategic position relative to the eastern archipelago navigation patterns and their access to Java's rice surplus, by the fourteenth century Java's ports were the foremost source of the eastern Indonesian archipelago spices among international traders from the West.

This chapter is concerned with the wider fifteenth-century developments in the Southeast Asian maritime region. It presents four representative case studies of new port-polities in maritime Southeast Asia that serviced the international trade: Samudra-Pasai and Melaka in the Straits of Melaka, Banda in the eastern Indonesian archipelago, and Cebu in the Philippines.

287

Samudra-Pasai on Sumatra's northeast Straits of Melaka coast was Southeast Asia's first Islamic state and became the favored thirteenth- and fourteenth-century international source of Sumatra's pepper, as well as that era's most respected regional center of Islamic scholarship. Regional conversions to Islam brought forth a rich cultural synthesis between local practice and Islamic tradition, as entry into Islam had both local and translocal implications. Locally, acceptance of Islam enabled rulers to supersede earlier tribalism or self-indulgent behavior due to the strong sense of communal responsibility promoted by Islam. Those who became Muslims accepted common laws of societal conduct, while those who did not withdrew to the periphery to avoid subjugation to the authority of Islam and its communities' leaders. Meanwhile, commitment to Islam offered opportunities for participation in the international Islamic political, cultural, and economic network, and in turn this participation enhanced local expressions of power.

Islamic historical records are often at odds with the needs of Western historians. They intentionally convey cultural values appropriate to Muslims and local values that are not "political" in the Western sense, and they contain ideas and symbolism that are not easily recognized by Western-oriented scholars. For example, Western studies of the origin of states conventionally emphasize the development of administrative capacity or the ability to collect revenues. In contrast, as represented variously in Southeast Asia, Islamic sources are more concerned with an elite's capacity to define and bestow social rank and sustain ritual performance, which in the local view was what unified a society. In this chapter the *Hikayat Raja-Raja Pasai*, the court chronicle of Samudra-Pasai, and the *Sejarah Melayu*, the court chronicle of the fifteenth-century Melaka state, are examples of this type of documentation, as they allow greater understanding and appreciation of Islamic ideas concerning the original Islamic polities.

This was a time when remembered ties to historical figures or places, as well as sacred objects derived from them, were an important source of distinctions in archipelago society, and they remain important today, for they define the community and who you are in a world marked by geographical diversity (Wolters: 1982/1999). In this area of numerous ethnicities, societies have often defined themselves not by shared language, custom, or birth, but by a common perception of historical experience, as was provided in both the focal chronicles (Wee: 1988; Creese: 1997; B. Andaya: 1993a, 8–13; Drakard: 1990; L. Andaya: 2008).

In the straits region, alliances were assertions of social rather than individual identity, being statements that either built upon or invalidated past tradition, or that rebelled against the contemporary traditions. The common thread among these political initiatives was the desire to preserve local society even in the case of rebellions against prevailing tradition. The primary criterion for societal hierarchy was not language or social manners, nor even purity of religious performance, but rather a conception of indigenousness. This conception allowed a community to claim superior status because of historical contacts with a locally respected person or center of perceived power. Locals normally felt no need to join a larger political entity, as such membership was not needed for local status. Furthermore, actual political or economic subordination was not sufficient basis for legitimate rule. Instead, local statements of legitimacy were typically based on ancestral ties, and these ties were often confirmed by marital exchanges, references to titles received, and titles and historical treasures bestowed by those of perceived power or from places associated with power, none of which were necessarily local. For example, Melaka, as discussed below, would claim the legacy of Srivijaya. In the case of Samudra-Pasai, its founder was said to have been associated with the royalty of an earlier neighboring realm; Pasai's royal regalia supposedly came from Mecca; the climax of Pasai's chronicle is an attempted marriage alliance with contemporary Majapahit; and (even in a later era, as we will see below) there was a tendency among populations originally from Sumatra who had migrated to western Malaya for leaders of coastal communities to claim to have received their titles from an upstream "head chief" (*batin*)—*batin* derives from *boat*, and thus implies "boat chief" as consistent with the migratory settlement of the Straits regions. A similar idea is referenced in Philippines riverine system *barangay*, "boat communities," as discussed below. Ancestors were important primarily because of the status they had held. The two chronicles demonstrate an ancestor's proximity to those who had held power earlier to validate a contemporary ruler's claim that he was himself worthy of status in the present.

Fifteenth-century Melaka became an Islamic sultanate, and as the preferred trade partner of China's Ming dynasty became the region's preeminent international emporium. Banda became one of the most important eastern Indonesian archipelago spice ports, and Cebu in the Philippines was a strategic intermediary port along the Sulu Sea spice-trade network that provided the China marketplace with an alternative connection with the eastern archipelago Spice Islands. These case studies collectively demonstrate the variety of local responses to similar coastal and multiple-river-system landscapes in the island world (as introduced in chapter 1), but in ways that were consistent with previously developed and commonly accepted societal patterns. The point here is that though in each case the international trade provided a potential "motor" for local development, local response depended on local initiatives rather than external interventions.

SOUTHEAST ASIA'S FIRST ISLAMIC POLITY

This chapter begins with a study of Samudra-Pasai, Southeast Asia's first Islamic polity. Much of what we know about Samudra-Pasai draws from the traditional Malay court text, the fifteenth-century *Hikayat Raja-Raja Pasai*, which, despite its high degree of mythical elements, still reveals much about local early Southeast Asia port-polities and the reasons for their acceptance of Islam (Hill: 1960; Braginsky: 2004). The Pasai chronicle is undoubtedly less than precise in its record of historical detail, and though it did not reach its final version until one to two centuries after the details it records, it clearly presents local values and common perceptions likely held at the time of the Islamic conversion, revealing what archipelago populations would call "the body beneath the cloth." In the chronicle's account, in the thirteenth and fourteenth century Samudra-Pasai's earliest rulers linked disparate northeast Sumatra upstream and downstream population clusters under the authority of their port-centered court, in ways that were appropriate to an Islamic society while also being consistent with local beliefs.

The Samudra-Pasai polity came into existence due to its access to northern Sumatra's pepper production and its strategic position in the Straits of Melaka, adjacent the major international sea route between India and China (Hall: 1981). As summarized in chapter 7, the thirteenth century saw an expansion in the East-West maritime trade, and Sumatra's pepper production was an important commodity in this expansive commerce. However, though the international trade was a potentially important motor encouraging local development, since the material rewards of international exchanges were substantial, the local societal networks that emerged at this time were also foundational to Samudra-Pasai's success. Islam was an important part of these local developments. Samudra-Pasai's leadership made a decided commitment to Islam, as Islam was vital in the local expressions of political legitimacy.

As revealed in the *Hikayat Raja-Raja Pasai*, the legitimations made by Pasai's monarchs drew on several themes. To begin with, would-be monarchs emphasized genealogy and a sense of magical empowerment, an empowerment that was in part ancestral, as well as the capacity to situate the community externally on at least an equal if not a superior diplomatic footing with its immediately neighboring port-polities on the Sumatra coast, and perhaps also with the major Asian civilizations in Java, China, and India. The magically endowed ruler was the source not only of the polity's welfare, but also of his subjects' spiritual, material, and societal well-being. This is symbolized in an early *Hikayat* episode in which the first monarch was said to be able miraculously to transform worms into gold. More likely this was symbolic of his role in the initiation of a local silk culture, where silk derived from local silkworms was exchanged for gold, although the Sumatra highlands were a source of gold in Srivijaya times (Bonatz: 2006, 322). The monarch's supposed capacity to bring his subjects material reward was reinforced by periodic rituals that highlighted symbolic redistributions of spiritual and material benefits. Both at the downstream court and in the upstream communities the effectiveness of these rituals grounded Samudra-Pasai's participation in the international trade. The *Hikayat* proclaimed these societal benefits to be the consequence of the ruler's successful initiatives, specifically those that brought the imported textiles that became the centerpiece of the monarch's ritualized redistributions.

A second form of legitimation was built on the ruler's ability to acquire these textiles through trade, warfare, or local production, combined with his distribution of them as rewards for service. These activities decisively reinforced his efforts to institute a stable, hierarchical, and court-centered social order, for in this age local populations began to use cloth in ways that they had not done previously (Reid: 1988, 83–96; Hall: 1996a). Imported cloth was exotic and expensive, and wearing it became associated with ceremonial rank and social status. The monarch personally bestowed ranks of ritualized status that coincided with the privilege of possessing and displaying particular kinds of cloth. In the local understanding of empowerment, this was more critical than any sense of administrative function. As Samudra-Pasai developed, cloth became more valuable than gold and silver, and its uses in display and exchange became the source of the society's vitality and well-being.

A third factor in the successful evolution of the Samudra-Pasai polity was the local creation of an Islamic-based monarchy, which combined political hegemony with religious authority. There is no evidence that the local populations were forced to convert, yet those who elected to participate in the new polity submitted to the sovereignty of rulers who happened to be Muslim, and this fact linked the previously opposed upstream and downstream population clusters into a new spiritual community situated within the broader Islamic world. Samudra-Pasai's Islamic rulers augmented local conceptions of authority by drawing upon concepts from the Islamic tradition. For example, as intermediary between Samudra-Pasai and the heavily Islamic international world, the ruler became the conduit for the economic, cultural, and intellectual benefits afforded by that region's participation in the growing international community of Islam. Among these elements, Samudra-Pasai's monarchs found the ideals of Sufi Islam especially appealing.

Building on traditional expectations of a ruler's spiritual empowerment, the Samudra-Pasai ruler became the equivalent of a Sufi saint. Indeed, the *Hikayat* claims that the ruler's new spiritual and intellectual prowess was so outstanding that both global travelers and neighboring monarchs commonly acknowledged his exceptional qualities, and as a consequence foreign diplomats and scholars often came to solicit his opinion on the interpretation of Islamic scripture. One might expect that these external dimensions of the monarch's proclamations of legitimacy would have distanced him from his subject population, but in the mind of the *Hikayat Raja-Raja Pasai*'s authors his conversion to Islam was actually the inspiration for a more inclusive society, as the peoples of the local riverine systems submitted to the common values understood to be appropriate to an Islamic polity. It is the internal dynamics that are most important here, for it was those dynamics that produced the need for a new and more inclusive source of legitimacy, and this in turn promoted a synthesis between the local and the external. Samudra-Pasai's successful localization of Islam would also have broader implications, for it would shape the assertions of legitimacy in its competitor and ultimate successor, Melaka, and would also have broad impact on other emerging Southeast Asian archipelago port-polities.

THE ORIGIN OF SAMUDRA-PASAI:
TRADITIONAL DEFINITIONS OF POWER

The *Hikayat* grounds the new Samudra-Pasai monarchy in both Islamic and Hindu-Buddhist antecedents. Not only is the ruler a Muslim, but the regalia of office are brought from Mecca by the caliph's designate, on the basis of a prophecy by Muhammad himself. The Samudra-Pasai sultan's assertion of legitimacy went beyond his local genealogical grounding, because the sultan also claimed that he was a descendent of the Prophet, who had personally converted him in a dream. There is also Hindu-Buddhist symbolism in the account of the rise of the king and his ancestors, as the father of the founding sultan was royalty himself; the future sultan was discovered by the royal family of a previous neighboring polity through the intervention of what appears to be an Indic sage. The two religious traditions combine symbolically in the account of the bringing of the regalia of office from Mecca. The ship makes a stopover in southern India, where the local ruler, due to Divine intervention, relinquishes his throne, becomes an Islamic mystic (fakir), and accompanies the expedition to Pasai, where he participates in the royal installation rituals and subsequently assumes a major role in teaching the local population the basics of the new religion (Hill: 1960, 117–20).

The *Hikayat Raja-Raja Pasai* goes on to recount that when the new Samudra-Pasai port-polity came into existence its rulers at first paid reciprocal homage to the traditional non-Muslim rulers of the Barus coastal enclave to their west. They followed this with a marriage alliance with the rulers of Perlak to their east, which had become Muslim even earlier (L. Andaya: 2008; McKinnon: 1984; Miksic and Yap: 1992; Drakard: 1982, 1989; Guillot: 1998–2003). Although these two neighboring port-polities were seen as the new society's most likely threats (or at least were Samudra-Pasai's relative equals in terms of economic and military power), Majapahit Java, China, and India were listed as commanding enough power to "surely prevail against [us]" (Hill: 1960, 120–23, 145). Among these, Majapahit in particular was acknowledged as still having an important presence in the Straits, and even as taking control of Pasai for a while in the middle of the fourteenth century. But Pasai regained its independence at the end of the story, an act symbolizing the final severing of Majapahit's interests in the Straits as well as foundational to the legitimacy of the subsequent Minangkabau authority in the Sumatra upstream (Hill: 1960, 167–71; Drakard: 1999; L. Andaya: 2008, 82–107).

There is a prolonged eulogy to the Majapahit court that proclaims Majapahit as a prosperous, orderly realm, a model for Pasai.

> [The Majapahit ruler] was famous for his love of justice. The empire grew prosperous. People in vast numbers thronged to [Majapahit]. At this time every kind of food was in great abundance. There was a ceaseless coming and going from the territories overseas that had submitted to the king, to say nothing of places inside Java itself. . . . [from] the places inland right down to the shores of the Southern Ocean the people came for an audience with the [Majapahit] emperor, bringing tribute and offerings. . . . The land of Majapahit was supporting a large population. . . . Food was in plentiful supply. (Hill: 1960, 161)

The Pasai chronicle does not directly claim that Pasai is Majapahit's political heir. Rather, its Majapahit references legitimize Pasai's claims to the northern Sumatra coast simply by demonstrating that Pasai's sovereigns were worthy of supplying marital partners to Majapahit's royalty. Despite a veneer of admiration, awe, and grudging respect for Majapahit's power, there is always the reminder that Pasai was more astute than Majapahit. Pasai was only in danger when threatened by larger fighting forces, or when made vulnerable by the Pasai ruler's corruption, never because of Majapahit's superior skills or courage—the *Hikayat*'s generally positive image of Majapahit, to substantiate its own legitimacy, contrasts with that of other early Islamic sources in Java, which universally denigrate Majapahit's legacy (Ricklefs: 1976, 333–36). Such themes became especially salient in the treatment of the mid-fourteenth century, when Majapahit became more assertive of its Straits interests, which the *Hikayat* attributes to the guidance of Majapahit's chief minister Gajah Mada (see chapter 8) (Hill: 1960, 153–65). Pasai's eventual (though temporary) acquiescence to Majapahit's interests is explained in the chronicle as resulting from the unpredictability, ego, lack of foresight, and political miscalculation of Pasai's Sultan Ahmad II (r. 1346–1383). Sultan Ahmad refused to welcome a Majapahit diplomatic mission with the expected and appropriate courtesy, and his jealousy of his own son led him to negate a marriage alliance with Majapahit by arranging his son's murder. Majapahit's monarch sent a retaliatory military expedition that forced Pasai into a tributary relationship with the Majapahit court. The generic references to Majapahit and its ruler contrast to references to the other polities with which Pasai regularly interacted, as the latter incorporate the personal names of the monarchs who ruled those polities. Significantly, a Pasai loss to any of these other polities would have been unthinkable, due to their relatively equal stature. In the minds of the Pasai chroniclers only Majapahit had enough historical legacy and stature to warrant an admission of a Pasai defeat.

Just as the Pasai ruler gained political, economic, and military legitimacy by his dealings with Majapahit, so he also reinforced his magically derived spiritual authority by his association with Islam. Here, too, the *Hikayat*'s emphasis is on a personal legacy. It links Pasai's monarchs to the Prophet himself, by stating that already in the early seventh century Muhammad had left word that Mecca's caliph should someday invest Pasai's ruler with the regalia of office.

> This is the story which has been handed down to us. Once upon a time, in the days when the Prophet Muhammad the Apostle . . . was still alive, he said to the elect of Mecca "In time to come, when I have passed away, there will rise in the east a city called Semudera. When you hear tell of this city make ready a ship to take to it all the regalia and panoply of royalty. Guide its people into the religion of Islam. Let them recite the words of the profession of faith. For in that city shall God . . . raise up saints in great number. . . ."
>
> Some time after the Prophet . . . had passed away from this world the elect of Mecca heard that there was a city in the east called Semudera. So the Caliph made ready a ship to take to Semudera all the regalia and panoply of royalty. (Hill: 1960, 116–17)

The Prophet also directly contributed to the sultan's conversion, which the chronicle relates as having happened when the Prophet visited the sultan in a dream and spit into his mouth, thus personally converting him to Islam. (This episode will be mentioned again below.) He awoke miraculously circumcised and with the ability to recite the *Quran*. Thus, the conversion of Pasai and its establishment as a royal center were direct gifts of the Prophet and endowed Pasai's monarch with a magical quality.

The ruler's magical and intellectual abilities were apparent not only to the local population, but also to outsiders. For example, the chronicle cites a Hindu yogi from India who arrived in Pasai subsequent to the Indian Muslim mystic who had accompanied the royal regalia to Pasai to compete with the sultan in the performance of miracles. Not only did he lose, but, "overcome by the sanctity of the Sultan's presence, the [yogi mystic] fell to the ground in a faint. The Sultan was amazed to see what had happened to him in spite of his deep knowledge of the magic arts" (Hill: 1960, 134). The visitor was so impressed by Pasai's ruler that he subsequently converted to Islam.

As suggested by passages such as this one, the *Hikayat*'s stress is on a ruler-centered, ritually bound community, rather than on the polity as simply a community of the faithful Muslims (*umma*) governed by law (sharia), consistent with the Persian concept of Islamic kingship in which the ruler, not the law, was preeminent (Donner: 1986). The local community absorbed and used Islam on its own terms rather than being transformed by it, with stress on the ruler's spiritual qualities consistent with the expression of sovereignty in the prior Srivijaya realm (see chapter 4) (Milner: 1982, 1983). Merah Silu, the first Pasai sultan, was proclaimed "God's Shadow on Earth" (*zill Allah fi'l-'alam*) by his subjects, which would be the title taken by subsequent Malay monarchs (Hill: 1960, 57–58). The sultan ruled on earth as God's agent, the "shadow of God," and by God's favor (*anugerah*) created a state of spiritual welfare, peace, and prosperity as his gift to humanity.

The monarch was also presented as a saintlike figure, as was appropriate to the Sufi tradition. This legitimation was made through mention of the regalia and its association with the Prophet, though the saintlike persona was also patterned on the earlier ideal of the Buddhist bodhisattva (Koentjaraningrat: 1992; Trimingham: 1971, 26; Reid: 1994, 166; Johns: 1957, 1961a, 1961b). In the Sufi model, the sultan realized his essential oneness with the Divine Being by means of his mystical powers and thus could guide his disciples along the path he had already walked. The *Hikayat* portrays several visitors and neighboring polities who recognized these qualities in the Pasai ruler. We already noted the episode of the Indic yogi, skilled in the magical arts, who unsuccessfully competed against the sultan in the performance of miracles. In his defeat he implicitly recognized the sultan's sanctity, or *keramat* (Arabic *karama*), the "magical gift of 'saints,'" and subsequently embraced the faith of Islam. According to the chronicle of the neighboring fifteenth-century polity of Melaka, the ruler of that polity later acknowledged this same "saintly" prowess by sending an Islamic manuscript to Pasai for the sultan's explanation; in the subsequent *Hikayat Patani*, the local ruler converted to Islam after he was cured of a skin disease by the healing powers of the ruler of Pasai (Roolvink: 1965; Teeuw and Wyatt: 1970, 71–75).

In addition to promoting the new ruler's personal prowess, the *Hikayat* associates spiritual empowerment with the place of rule. It develops an elaborate rationale for the selection of the court site, stressing magical properties which, when properly drawn upon by the ruler, tapping into the local spiritual powers, could enhance the collective well-being. Prosperity was therefore the result of the conjunction of person (the ruler) and place (the court). Of the two, the person was the more important, for a court center lost its potency during the ruler's absence, because the political center traveled with the ruler. Herein the traditional straits conceptualization of the potency of place and person dating from the Srivijaya era (see chapter 4) coincided with that of the early Middle Eastern Islamic tradition, as there was the potency of the caliph as the direct heir to Muhammad, but also the potency of the place, as in the importance of Mecca, Medina, Jerusalem, and Damascus as the spiritually endowed sacred places and governmental centers where the sacred and the secular coincided. In the later Baghdad-based Abbasid caliphate, Baghdad itself became the critical center relative to local expressions of authority, where local allegiance to the person of the caliph was questionable at best (Donner: 1986). In the *Hikayat,* not only could a court's location enhance a ruler's power, it could also be a hindrance, having harmful spiritual properties that negated his potency. Spirits could roam about the place, or could even make an individual their intermediary. In such situations, it could be prudent for a ruler to move his court to a more auspicious site. An example of these considerations appears in the *Hikayat Raja-Raja Pasai*'s account of the origin of the polity. Two young brothers, Merah Silu and Merah Hasum, emigrated from the nearby Semerlanga polity, where they were members of the royal family, reasoning that the place had become spiritually polluted by prolonged civil war: "If we remain in this place we too will share the fate [of Semerlanga] for no good at all can come to us from living here. Let us leave the city and search elsewhere for a good place which we can make our home."

Merah Silu, who would become king of the new polity of Pasai (r. 1275–1297), came to a river where, as already noted, "by the grace of God, he [was] able to turn worms into gold." Later, on a hunting expedition, his dog submitted to a magical mousedeer on high ground. Thus he reasoned that "this is the right place for me to build a city where my son . . . shall become ruler" (Hill: 1960, 113–25).

This passage encapsulates several of the points we have been discussing. Merah Silu's ability to turn worms into gold symbolizes his ability to create magically not only his own wealth but also that of his subjects, and it suggests he did not make undue economic/revenue demands on his subjects. Furthermore, the text stresses that Merah Silu was of the royal lineage of Semerlanga and therefore rightfully a raja. In addition, his personal wealth ensured his central role in the ceremonial exchanges that play such an important role in the *Hikayat* text.

On a more mundane level, Merah Silu developed his polity by first building a hinterland confederacy, then leading it to victory over surrounding groups, and finally establishing control over the coast. He then achieved new levels of prosperity for his society through trade with the international commercial community. The Pasai monarchs generally left marketplace administration to the "men of the marketplace" rather than a royal official, being more concerned with cultivating their connections with upstream societies and with neighboring coastal port-polities (Hill: 1960, 146). Nevertheless, the sultan's political and commercial successes brought new wealth to all. The new polity had rich resources for trade. The chronicle's list of the presents sent to the caliph of Mecca in return for the royal regalia suggests that at this time Pasai was a source of ambergris, camphor, eaglewood, benzoin, cloves, and nutmeg (Hill: 1960, 120). We also know from the chronicle and external sources that it was an important source of pepper. In addition, Anthony Reid suggests that the "worms into gold" episode is a reference to the early development of silk production at Pasai, which is documented in sixteenth-century Portuguese sources (Reid: 1988, 92–93). In return, Pasai received an array of goods from abroad, including the all-important textiles, which were used to mark status and convey a sense of hierarchy (Hill: 1960, 115ff).

The rulers of Samudra-Pasai were not democratic leaders, but neither were they oppressive dictators. In the archipelago world reflected in the Pasai chronicle, when an individual was bestowed with sovereignty (*daulat*) he became the common representative of his community. Both in theory and in practice, the ruler was dependent on ministers, chiefs, lesser royalty, and even commoner subjects. In the *Hikayat Raja-Raja Pasai* the importance of the community's access to royalty was especially symbolized at the times of succession. In this *Hikayat* episode as in other regional chronicles that would follow, especially in the early years there was open competition for the vacant throne, and a royal audience hall was normally the first building constructed in a contender's new court, a move the chronicles portray as a sign of openness and a key to competitive success. In the *Hikayat Raja-Raja Pasai*, it was the successful candidates' deep sense of community that led them to build these halls onto their palaces. By contrast, unsuccessful candidates' personal vanity led them to build only a palace, providing no communal space (Hill: 1960, 110, 116). Yet despite the provision of the audience hall, it is not clear how open the royal audiences actually were. Most of the participants were dignitaries and local chiefs, and acknowledgments of hierarchy loom large in chronicle records of such audiences. Furthermore, although advice taking was highly valued by monarchs and subjects alike, these audiences served more to keep the elite in line than as general forums of open discussion. It was the security of society that mattered, not the opinions of individuals.

This concern for social welfare is seen in other ways as well. The chronicle enumerates a corps of officers, subject to the chief minister, who patrolled night and day to check on thieves, people fighting, people committing adultery, people taking liberties with other men's wives or daughters, and people displaying symbols of status without permission. In effect, this corps was enforcing customary law and preserving social order, while protecting people and society from visual deceptions (Hill: 1960, 124, 136, 139ff). The officers were concerned not just with protecting innocent victims, but also with guarding against threats to the spiritual, social, and economic order. The chroniclers assumed that human society tends toward conflict if unchecked. To avoid this tendency for strife, there was a required ritual renunciation of individualism and a proclamation to channel personal power into the common well-being of the society centered in the ruler.

Even the ruler needed to develop restraint. In one deathbed scene in the *Hikayat Raja-Raja Pasai* the dying monarch warned his son against the problems that result when a ruler acts too impulsively and when he ignores the canons of Muslim morality.

> Do not transgress the commandments of God, the Exalted, or the sayings of the Prophet Muhammad, the Apostle of God. My child, you must not fail to heed well the counsel I am giving you. When there is anything you wish to do you must consult the eldest among your ministers. Do not hastily embark on any course of action. . . . So conduct yourself that you are always on your guard against the things which are not in accordance with Holy Law. Do not oppress or despoil the servants of God the Exalted by unjust treatment. Do not be backward in enjoining good and eschewing evil . . . for this mortal world will pass away and only the world to come will last for ever. (Hill: 1960, 133–34)

As for the polity's material welfare, Pasai's success resulted from its being a prominent port-polity in the straits and its role as a source of pepper. Both the importance of pepper and the need for unselfish behavior on the part of the ruler are seen in the following episode of the *Hikayat Raja-Raja Pasai*. As noted earlier, in the mid-fourteenth century Sultan Ahmad's own impulsive actions aborted an important diplomatic initiative with Majapahit. His son was engaged to a princess of Majapahit, but out of jealousy the sultan had him murdered. The distraught princess subsequently committed suicide (in response to her appeal for Divine intervention, her ship sank in a storm and she drowned—see below). Facing certain Majapahit reprisal, relates the chronicle, Sultan Ahmad broke all the bones in his hand as an act of contrition to God (also as a public statement to his followers) and admits that it was his own vanity that caused him to initiate the murder of both this and another son. He asks in despair: "You, my chiefs, why did you not stop me from murdering my sons?" One chief replies with this critical refrain:

> Whose pepper is it in the shed?
> Since from the stems the corns were parted.
> Whose place is it to mourn the dead?
> You are to blame that they've departed. (Hill: 1960, 156)

With the "corn from the stems" reference the speaker accuses the monarch not only of murder but of removing the community's material resources— pepper as well as his sons—for his own personal gain rather than the collective good. That is, he has betrayed the community and his leadership obligations to it. In response to the sultan's attempt to include his followers in his guilt, the speaker informs him that since he acted against the community's interests, he should now stand alone in facing the consequences (later he is said to have taken a core of followers with him anyway). Nevertheless, Majapahit eventually extracted vengeance upon the entire community, and the *Hikayat* makes the sultan's individual failure responsible for the collective harm.

THE ROLE OF CLOTH IN
FIFTEENTH-CENTURY SAMUDRA-PASAI

The *Hikayat* focuses not on divine intervention but on the local initiatives of a mediating monarch, whose personal efforts brought access to prosperity in this world and the next for those who chose to join his community. One of the demonstrations of this principle was the use of cloth in the ritual festivals celebrating the monarch's leadership. This cloth symbolized the realm's material prosperity while also marking social rank. The *Hikayat Raja-Raja Pasai* highlights the legitimating function of cloth in ceremonies and displays (Hill: 1960, 121ff). As was consistent with their contemporaries in the wider Eurasian world, they considered cloth magical, bestowing vitality, well-being, and fertility and connecting the living to spiritual or ancestral forces (Gordon: 2001). Cloth also enhanced the moral and legal obligations that bound partners to transactions. The chronicle frequently used references to textiles to set the stage for important actions and to demonstrate contemporary value judgments.

According to the chronicle, cloth exchanges were important from the very earliest days of Samudra-Pasai. Despite the early reference to Merah Silu turning worms into gold, cloth became valued above gold or silver, for those of lesser stature received gold and silver, while only those of highest status had their dignity proclaimed by presentations of cloth. For example, in a royal wedding celebration the "raja gave fine clothing to his chiefs, to the needy he presented gold and silver . . . to the state minister were given robes of finest material, and all the [other] people who came with him were rewarded with gold and silver" (Hill: 1960, 123).

Cloth is the focal point in descriptions of ceremonial events, which include elaborate references to the clothing and dress of participants. Royal audiences receive special attention in the chronicle, which describes at length the displays of clothing and dress by those in attendance. For contemporary audiences, these markers provided easy clues to the importance of those present. For example, on one occasion,

> The king ordered the palace to be decorated and the two young princesses to wear dresses of cloth-of-gold embroidered with precious stones . . . and to one daughter (of lesser status) he gave a skirt of silk bandanna cloth, a jacket red in color like the jambu flower, rings studded with gems and ear-pendants . . . [the place made for the most important sister to sit showed] that her status [was] much above that of her [other] sisters. (Hill: 1960, 121–22)

Another example of cloth as a symbol of rank appears in the initial investiture episode, when Merah Silu received the symbols of royal office that had been sent by the caliph of Mecca. The Islamic fakir who presented the regalia was said to have "donned the clothing appropriate to his position." On this same occasion the sultan "wore his robes of state," while the assembly of his chiefs sat in long rows arranged according to their rank in the state hierarchy (Hill: 1960, 117–19). As described in another part of the *Hikayat*, the sultan's "robes of state" included

> a cloth of fine yellow silk, with the back in iridescent colors, the border neatly worked in gold thread with a trellis pattern of . . . gold, the fringe decorated with tinkling bells; a coat shimmering like the rays of the sun . . . ; buttons encased in gold and bespangled with myriads of scarlet gems; a headcloth . . . [and] jewel-encrusted armlets; bracelets in the form of dragons, [their bodies] in seven coils; a kris inlaid with precious stones mounted in a scabbard of gold; a sash held the sword which could flash like lightning. He wore a jeweled guard and had a golden bow slung from his left shoulder . . . his coat flashed in the colors of the rainbow. (Hill: 1960, 140)

In the *Hikayat*'s account of diplomatic missions the exchange of ceremonial cloth was both the dramatic introduction and the climax. For example, in a game of one-upsmanship, the Pasai monarch sent the king and queen of Perlak and their two daughters "presents of fine robes" after the receipt of their gift of "fine clothing." This was a follow-up to an initial gift of gold and silver vessels to the Perlak ministers of state "each in turn according to his rank"—note that the cloth was gifted to the most distinguished, the royal family, while the lesser nobility received gold and silver gifts (Hill: 1960, 121–23). Once again, Majapahit is shown as having set the standard, in this case a coincidence of the diplomatic and ritualized exchange and ceremonial display of cloth, when the ruler of Majapahit sent the diplomatic mission to Pasai to secure a prince to wed his daughter:

> the fleet was decorated with the finest materials presented by the Emperor to the princess [to be given to the Pasai monarch, as a diplomatic or marital reciprocity for the Pasai ruler's agreement to allow his son to marry the Majapahit princess]; pieces from the king's regalia, cloths of the finest materials, ornaments of gold, silver, and gems, and costumes of various kinds. (Hill: 1960, 154)

Cloth also served as a way to define people, based on the traditions of material display rather than distinctions made on the basis of biological or linguistic difference. The foremost example of this is the story involving the son of Sultan Ahmad, Tun Abdul Jalil, who was so handsome that the daughter of the king of Majapahit fell in love with his portrait. She selected him out of ninety-three portraits of princes she had commissioned:

> if he dressed in Javanese costume he looked like a man of Java. If he dressed in [Thai] costume he looked like a man of the [Thai] state. If he wore the costume of India he looked like a man of India. If he wore the costume of Arabia, like an Arab. His renown spread to Java and became known to Princess Gemerenchang [also known as Raden Galuh/Galoh in Malay], daughter of the King of Majapahit. (Hill: 1960, 135)

These references to Tun Abdul Jalil—whose versatility in clothing enhanced his already notable bearing—acknowledged the differences in the cloth traditions among the societies that were active in the Straits. This understanding of clothing distinctions and its association as a focal asset of the young prince was so important to the chronicle authors that they repeated it a second time, when the prince was entrusted with the realm while his father made a trip to receive tribute from his outlying territories (Hill: 1960, 144).

The passage just mentioned and its cloth references also introduce the tale of Pasai's fall to Majapahit's forces, an event that happens near the close of the *Hikayat*'s tale. Sultan Ahmad, jealous of his son, has him murdered. The Princess Gemerenchang was coming to Pasai on a diplomatic mission to meet the handsome prince, and when informed of the prince's death she was shattered. She prayed to "God, the Exalted": "I want to be united with Tun Abdul

Jalil." In response, "God, the Exalted," sunk her ship and she drowned—it is intriguing that she is presented praying to the Muslim God in a Muslim fashion as "the Exalted," consistent with Pasai Islamic cultural standards, rather than to a Hindu-Buddhist Indic Divine, as would have been appropriate to the Majapahit court's religious patronage of that era, as discussed in chapter 8. Fearing Majapahit's certain reprisal, Sultan Ahmad broke every bone in his fingers as a sign of repentance. He subsequently fled his palace compound accompanied by a core of followers and the royal regalia, which would together ensure Pasai's future.

Insulted by these developments, the king of Majapahit sent four hundred ships against Pasai. His forces included troops supplied by all his allied and subordinate polities. Owing to their overwhelming numbers, Majapahit's troops temporarily occupied Pasai and carried away significant quantities of booty and prisoners, returning by way of Jambi and Palembang, which they also conquered and pillaged. The latter two port-polities then became direct vassals of Majapahit. However, after a period of Majapahit occupation followed by Pasai's vassalage to Majapahit, Pasai eventually regained its autonomy. The Pasai chronicle ends with the symbolically significant victory of Sumatra's allied forces over those of Majapahit, due to Pasai's noted trickery, which results in the losers "dressing down to the ankles in women's clothing." This final reference to clothing is a highly appropriate setting in an age in which cloth defined status. Improper dress—"dressing like women"—was the extreme indignity for a man and a powerful statement about the loss of personal worth (Hill: 1960, 163–64).

THE ROLE OF ISLAM AT SAMUDRA-PASAI

The realm's conversion to Islam receives special attention in the *Hikayat* as the capstone to a founding myth whose prior movements are firmly grounded in local tradition. The chronicle's account of this story begins with a falling-out among the elite at the port-polity of Semerlanga in northern Sumatra, as a result of which Merah Silu and his brother Merah Hasun leave the polity, wandering until they settle at the mouth of the Pasangan River. A quarrel breaks out between the brothers, and Merah Silu leaves. Upon the invitation of Megat Iskandar, a local Muslim chief, he travels upstream to the headwaters of the Pasangan River. There he becomes very wealthy, collecting worms that miraculously turn into gold when he boils them (standard practice in silk production, which was worthy of gold exchanges in contemporary marketplaces) in a highly symbolic portrayal of the region's entry into the international trade and the gold wealth derived in exchange for local productivity at the initiative of the first monarch. His magical powers, wealth, and organizational abilities make him very popular with the locals. After consultation with his subordinate chiefs, Megat Iskandar decides that Merah Silu would make a worthy head chief, or raja. This development allows the locals to break their relationship with a downriver raja (perhaps from the Perlak port), Sultan Maliku'l-Nasar, Merah Silu's competitor for the vacant Samudra-Pasai throne, who promptly but unsuccessfully attacks Merah Silu's upstream confederation. Merah Silu follows this victory with others and becomes raja over the entirety of the local riverine system territories.

One of the most significant aspects of this story is the dichotomy between upstream and downstream polities and the priority initially accorded to the upstream. The establishment of Samudra-Pasai begins when Merah Silu goes upstream from the coast and receives sovereignty by the recognition and consensus of the existing political authorities of the hinterland. Once acknowledged as their legitimate ruler, he leads the upstream forces to victory over the downstream, which is claimed by a coastal sultan, and thus assumes sovereignty over the entire riverine system. This pattern fits an enduring Sumatran tradition of basing ultimate sovereignty in the upstream hinterland, with legitimacy bestowed by group acclamation. Studies of the Minangkabau populations who migrated from their original Sumatra homeland to settle in the Negri Sembilan region on the western Malay Peninsula coast, and who are of similar heritage, indicate that the leader of the jungle peoples of the upstream was regarded as the original source of political legitimacy and held rights over all the land. After their arrival, there was a division of the community. Groups who wanted to leave the jungle to settle coastal areas came to the "head chief" (*batin*) to ask his consent. As holder of hereditary titles, the batin would assign the title *penghulu* (territorial chief) to one of the group and give him the duty of protecting these people who chose to live "outside" the jungle. Well into the twentieth century the Negri Sembilan batin was still performing rituals of sacred installation, burning incense and ritually bathing penghulu, and he was still regarded among the coastal chiefs as the mythical source of their title (Lewis: 1960; B. Andaya: 1993a; Masashi: 1994; Kathirithamby-Wells, 1993a; L. Andaya: 2008, 146–72).

Working from this indigenous perspective, it is appropriate, then, that Pasai's initial ruler received legitimate installation in this manner. Only then does he conquer the coast and receive additional sources of legitimacy in the form of the royal regalia and the people's conversion to Islam. According to the chronicle, Merah Silu's conversion happened when he had his dream of the Prophet Muhammad spitting into his mouth and thus converting him to Islam. Merah Silu awoke miraculously circumcised and with the ability to recite the *Quran* (i.e., in Arabic). Thus the Pasai monarch was converted by direct intervention of the Prophet, just as the Prophet himself received the message of God from the archangel Gabriel. In theory, then, the Pasai sultan was subordinate to God alone, and not to any mortal, except perhaps the Prophet.

Shortly after the sultan's conversion, a Muslim scholar delegated by the caliph arrived by boat to bestow the royal regalia. But as this scholar provided instruction in the faith it became clear that Merah Silu already understood the message of Islam, and thus the two entered into a prolonged dialogue as equals. The caliph's envoy then led the entire populace to convert, having called a great assembly of the people.

> [The envoy of the Caliph] ordered an assembly of chiefs and the people great and small, old and young, male and female. When they were all gathered together . . . the whole population willingly recited the words of the profession of faith, in all sincerity and with true belief in their hearts. . . . Among the people all strife and conflict ceased, and they did not weary of their zeal in spreading the faith of Islam. (Hill: 1960, 119)

Interestingly, the *Hikayat Raja-Raja Pasai* informs us that some members of Merah Silu's confederacy were unwilling to convert to Islam and moved instead to the upstream jungle: "There were in the city members [of the community who] would not embrace the religion of Islam. So they fled to the upper reaches of the river Pasangan. It is for that reason that the inhabitants of the [region] call themselves Gayau, and have so called themselves up to the present time" (Hill: 1960, 120; Bowen: 1993).

The aforementioned studies of the Negri Sembilan Minangkabau in western Malaya indicate similarly that the coming of Islam to the Malay Peninsula caused a permanent split of the inhabitants of the region after their original migration from Sumatra; those who became Muslims lived in clearings near the banks of rivers, while others retained their traditional jungle lifestyle in the upstream (Lewis: 1960; B. Andaya: 1993b; Kathirithamby-Wells: 1993a; Hefner: 1985, 3–43).

The *Hikayat Raja-Raja Pasai* notes that even after its conquest of the coast Pasai had steady contact with the upstream jungle groups. The Pasai ruler looked to this hinterland as both the origin of his legitimacy and the source of trade commodities; flow of production to the Pasai port was likely organized as an institutionalized reciprocity (subordinate chiefs required to supply the port with marketable commodities) or as an indigenous trade cycle in which the hinterland exchanged forest products for imported commodities, as described in chapter 1 (Dunn: 1975). Pasai's ruler undertook regular upstream holidays that allowed him to inspect villages and hamlets while enjoying himself hunting. On these trips he ritually feasted and participated in "merrymaking" with his upstream allies. In reality these were ceremonial renewals of the alliance between the downstream court and the upstream members of the riverine system community (Hill: 1960, 129). These upstream populations could be valuable allies, as was demonstrated when Thai forces attacked around 1290 (see chapter 7). Defeated in the initial battle, Thai warriors fled upstream, where they were slaughtered by Samudra-Pasai's upstream allies (Hill: 1960, 129).

There are several reasons why Merah Silu was able to make the local reciprocity networks work for him: (1) he was recognized as a raja via the proper channels and then proved to be more than a normal chief by his personal accomplishments; (2) he took the community to new levels of prosperity, achieved through international trade; and (3) at least in retrospect, his legitimacy was enhanced by his conversion, by divine intervention, to Islam.

Although international political, economic, and cultural considerations undoubtedly prompted his conversion, Merah Silu's turn to Islam may have been equally motivated by indigenous considerations. Islam was a new source of prestige for Samudra-Pasai's ruler. Interestingly, the individual previously claiming sovereignty, Sultan Maliku'l-Nasar, seems also to have converted, but (due to his lack of initiative) his power was confined to the coast, and he never received the upstream region's acknowledgment. Merah Silu overcame this by basing his initial legitimacy on his upstream connections and only then converting to Islam. Nevertheless, his conversion represented a significant break with the past, as Pasai's tradition makes no reference to the heritage of Srivijaya as its legacy, in contrast to the importance of a Srivijaya connection in the assertion of Melaka's heritage in the *Sejarah Melayu* (Wolters: 1970, 102, 244n70; Teeuw: 1964; Sweeney: 1967).

There was good reason for the break. By the thirteenth century the old networks were somewhat tarnished, due to the demise of the Srivijaya realm that had most recently been based at Jambi, thus allowing an alien Javanese presence along the east coast Sumatra passageway following the victories of the Singhasari monarch Kertanagara and his father in the 1280s. These Java-based military initiatives seem to have eliminated the last vestiges of the old Srivijaya coastal network, as well as challenging the Hindu-Buddhist traditions that had been such a significant part of earlier straits regional proclamations of sovereignty. To separate themselves from Hindu-Buddhist Majapahit, Pasai's rulers seemingly saw Islam to be a powerful alternative new source of ritual prestige and an especially powerful means of releasing supernatural energy in Sufi-inspired ceremonies (Reid: 1994, 138). The introduction of the mystical, less legally oriented Sufi tradition of Islam along the trade channels during the late thirteenth century thus was likely to have encouraged Samudra-Pasai's conversion (Gibb: 1929, 273–76; Reid: 1994, 169–73; Johns:

1961a, 1961b). Ibn Battuta's 1345–1346 account of Pasai reports that at that time the ruler of Pasai took a lively personal interest in the religious discussion of Sufi theologians resident at his court. The Sufi emphasis on magical and mystical possession was consistent with the Hindu-Buddhist past and therefore critical to this synthesis of the old with the new in Islam's emphasis on theocracy. Despite being a Muslim, Pasai's ruler could be a traditional chief and still participate in the broader Muslim and Indian Ocean worlds.

Thus we have seen that in Samudra-Pasai, as in many other places in island Southeast Asia, the upstream populations were not incorporated by force, but joined for their own reasons. The question of why hinterland-based polities would have integrated with the coast is a complex one. Historian Barbara Andaya notes that in the past historians have assumed too easily that it was coastal elites who became preeminent over their upriver neighbors (B. Andaya: 1997). Focusing on upstream populations' motives, she points out that the upstream people desired commodities that the coast could supply, and in particular she documents the demand for imported textiles (B. Andaya: 1989, 1997). The present chapter suggests that cultural dialogue was another part of the upstream-downstream glue. It appears that the coastal elite actively drew upon previous cultural patterns to formulate a common concept of community that included upriver and downriver populations. The *Hikayat Raja-Raja Pasai* documents that in the fourteenth and fifteenth centuries the elite also promoted the Islamic ideal that the sultan was the leader of an Islamic spiritual community/society. This in turn reinforced previous notions of magic- and possession-based sovereignty.

Yet conversion to Islam brought a new social order. As it had in Islam's earliest days in Arabia, commitment to the *Quran*'s authority entailed a commitment to the Islamic community, superseding earlier tribalism as well as the potential for self-indulgence. Those who made this commitment therefore accepted common laws of societal conduct. The recompense to those who committed to this new order was the promise of prosperity in this world and also, consistent with the focal message of the *Quran*, the implicit promise of a world to come, with a sense of a "day of judgment" in which the material wealth and human vanity of this world mattered little (Donner: 1998).

Pasai's rulers were empowered by their assertions of local Islamic authority. They claimed to have been conferred both legitimacy and religion by the Prophet himself, and they implicitly claimed (at least in the pages of the chronicle) to be able to hold their own as intellectual and spiritual equals of even the most prestigious and learned of foreign visitors. Together these increased the likelihood of the downriver court's acceptance among the upstream populations, who had had no need for regular interaction before. The rulers' ability to present themselves as empowered by these external connections also increased the likelihood of the downstream elite's acknowledgment of the importance of the upstream region. Previously the coastal population's only concerns had been that the upstream swidden groups should not raid their settlements and that they provide periodic supplies of upstream jungle products for export. But the economic ties would become increasingly important. By the end of the fifteenth century, Sumatra's downstream port-polities would find themselves wanting to regularize upstream cooperation so they could extend commercial pepper cultivation to fertile lands upriver. Either they needed to colonize the hinterland with downstream populations or they needed to encourage the upstream dwellers to expand their cultivation of the desired cash crops (Wicks: 1992, 228–38; Kathirithamby-Wells: 1986, 265–67; 1993; Hudson: 1967; Hall: 1995).

At the same time, the growing influence of the marketplace offered upstream populations the opportunity to secure cloth and other culturally valuable commodities in exchange for their pepper and produce. It was as the polity was seeking new ways to express authority in this evolving relationship that imported textiles assumed significance as marks of social distinction. Thus it was through a combination of religious, political, economic, social, and cultural factors that local society moved from a collection of relatively isolated population clusters to a more integrated public order participating collectively in broader networks (L. Andaya: 1993a, 1993b; B. Andaya: 1993b).

Islam linked this increasingly integrated area with the regions to its north and west, just as it would soon do in other parts of Southeast Asia (Andaya and Ishii: 1992). The common cultural variable was the Islamic faith among the trading populations who traveled to and sometimes settled in Southeast Asia's ports of trade.

However, though Southeast Asia's external economic and ideational interchanges certainly contributed to these developments, increased internal networking within the local societies comprising the Southeast Asian maritime region also contributed, even providing some of the opportunity for religious conversion (Manguin: 1979; Andaya and Ishii: 1992, 514–15). The conversion of Samudra-Pasai on the Sumatra coast was merely one of the first of a stream of such conversions, and by the fifteenth century the exchange of Islamic symbols, along with the material goods and services of commercial trade, would be reinforcing the linkages among the people who shared the Straits of Melaka and the Java, South China, and Sulu seas, not as one united "island world," but as a series of linked subregional networks (Miksic: 1990; Hall: 2008).

In 1512–1515, Portuguese traveler Tomé Pires would report that foreign merchants in archipelago port towns were accompanied by "chiefly Arab *mullas*"—who could have been Islamic scholars, Sufi mystics, or preachers—who collectively undermined the established authorities (Johns: 1981). Building on the fragmentary writings left by the earliest Sufis and court-based scholars and chroniclers, one can partially reconstruct the intellectual and spiritual environment of these port-polities. One can also explore the nature of their contacts, both with their archipelago hinterlands and with scholars in India or Arabia. By the painstaking study of who, where, when, and under whose (if anyone's) patronage these scholars operated, the hope is that we may one day be able to make more meaningful statements about the process of Islamization (Braginsky: 1998, 2004).

As we have been showing, conversion to Islam coincided with a tendency for Straits port-polities to interact more directly with their interiors. In Java, as discussed in chapter 8, new Islamic north coast ports—notably Demak—would successfully confront the Hindu-Buddhist hinterland society of the Majapahit polity (Robson: 1981). Another important development was the rise of Melaka in the early fifteenth century, which we will examine next. We will then look at Banda in the eastern archipelago and Cebu in the Philippines to gain comparative perspective on the developments of this period.

FIFTEENTH-CENTURY MELAKA

The Straits of Melaka port-based Malay state of Melaka (Malacca) was founded by a Malay prince, the Srivijaya heir, who shifted his court there from what is now Singapore (previously known to the Chinese as Tamusik) around 1390 (Wolters: 1970). Within fifty years Melaka would become the wealthiest commercial port in Asia, as the connecting hub in the India-to-China trade, and the most important international source of Indonesian archipelago spices. Melaka's initial commercial success was due to its special diplomatic relationship with China's Ming court. Merchants wishing to trade in China's ports were given special treatment if they first made stopovers in Melaka. In return, Melaka was obligated to keep the Straits of Melaka free of piracy and thereby ensure the regular flow of Western luxuries into China's marketplace, for the consumption of China's elite as well as for taxation by China's government.

Zheng He, the Ming maritime admiral, visited Melaka several times between 1409 and the early 1430s with his fleet of ships, in part to reinforce Melaka's position as China's favored Southeast Asian port of trade. When the Ming voyages ended in the 1430s, Melaka's ruler converted to Islam to encourage Muslim traders, then dominant among that era's commercial sojourners, to use his port. His patronage of Islam was also a means to legitimize and extend his control over other Straits region ports.

In his early fifteenth-century account of one of Zheng He's voyages, the Chinese scribe Ma Huan described Melaka as a busy trading center with a transient population and makeshift residences (Mills: 1970, 109–14). By contrast, in the early sixteenth-century accounts of the first Portuguese visitors, Melaka was a major urban center with settled residential communities of foreigners among whom the Gujarati and Tamil (Keling) from India, the Javanese from the archipelago, and the Chinese were the most prominent. By this time, every foreign community was assigned its own "suburban" residential neighborhood. Each of the major foreign communities also had its own "chief of port" (*shahbandar/syahbandar*) who received merchants on their arrival; presented them to the civilian head of state (*bendahara*); found them lodging, storage, and shops for their goods; and, up to the late fifteenth century, acted as their trade broker in return for 1 percent of the value of their sales. The shahbandar also provided visiting merchants with small boats and elephants for local transport, and in time of war he might gather, arm, and command his community, along with its slaves and other dependents, to fight on Melaka's behalf, as Melaka did not have a large standing army of its own (Cortesao: 1944, 286–87; Heng: 1990).

Many of the "Gujarati" merchants were not actually from Gujarat; rather, the term referred to any who had come from Sri Lanka or India's west coast and beyond (Pearson: 1976). These merchants normally had trade links to Middle East ports such as those on the Saudi Arabian Peninsula and in the Red Sea region (Aden and Hormuz), with access to Mamluk Egypt, and an assortment of Persian Gulf ports, which were linked to post-Mongol polities that would become the Ottoman Turk and Iranian realms. All the Gujarati merchants were Muslims, and the elite among them were termed *adhiraja*, a Malay title of nobility, seemingly as an acknowledgement that there was a local mix of the resident Gujarati merchant elite and the Malay political aristocracy. Similarly, contemporary elite Muslim merchants resident in Java's ports were also distinguished by reference to the adhiraja title. The most notable among the Gujarati merchants lived in the "rich merchant" (orang kaya) quarter of Upeh (see map 9.1). Gujarati merchants in Melaka sought to acquire China's products and the drugs, spices, and woods that arrived from the eastern Indonesian archipelago. In exchange they supplied Gujarati cotton and products from the Middle East.

"Kelings" from south India's Tamil region, as well as Indians from Kelinga, associated with present-day Orissa, were from India's southeast coast. These people were mostly Hindu (though some were converting to Islam) (Ricci: 2010), and their leaders were distinguished by their *naina* title. The

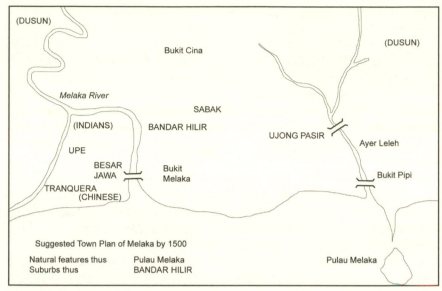

Map 9.1.   Melaka City, ca. 1500

term comes from the Sanskrit *Nayana*, meaning leader or guide. The Keling shahbandar had authority over all traders from the Bay of Bengal region, including Bengalis and Burmese, who brought cotton textiles to Melaka and, in the case of the Burmese, rice, which they exchanged for Southeast Asia's spices. From the 1450s, the Kelings were in favor locally, since the Sultan Muzaffar Shah (1446–1459) was the son of a Tamil princess. Consequently, they held five of the positions on the Committee of Ten, the members of which established the value of ship cargoes in the presence of the *Tumenggung* (chief of police) immediately prior to the latter's collection of taxes. Like the Gujarati elite, major Keling merchants resided in the Upeh rich merchant zone, except that the Keling resided near the seafront, while the Gujaratis lived on the inland side. At the end of the century, Naina Suryadeva, a powerful Keling merchant, shared with a Muslim merchant of Chinese heritage, based in the port of Gresik on Java's north coast, the local monopoly on the nutmeg and clove shipments from Banda and the Malukus. Naina Suryadeva was also separately sending his own junks to Siam, Bengal, Palembang, Pegu (Myanmar), and China (Wade: 1997; Thomaz: 2000).

The "Javanese" merchants at Melaka were Muslims connected to Java's prosperous north coast *pasasir* ports and were represented by their own shahbandar. They included Java-based merchants of Chinese heritage and some ethnic Malay merchant nomads. "Javanese" ships sailed not only to Java but also to Sumatra, Borneo, the Malukus, Banda, and Luzon in the Philippines. Most of the "Java" merchants lived on the edge of the Bandar Hilir district with their chief Tuan "Colascar," who came from Gresik. Another group, hailing from Tuban, Japara, Sunda, and Lampung, lived in the Upeh quarter with their chief Utimuti Raja, though apart from the Keling, Chinese, and Gujarati residential enclaves. This second group appears to have been more prosperous than the first, or at least held in higher regard by Melaka's rulers. "Javanese" merchants specialized in the import of foodstuffs, such as rice, to feed the Melaka residents and to provision their Melaka-based ships, as well as other visiting vessels, since Melaka did not have adequate adjacent land to supply local dietary needs. The Javanese also supplied Melaka with Indonesia's spices. Finally, some of the small-scale Javanese merchant nomads, ethnically inclusive of Malays, lived on their small boats along the Melaka shoreline and sold their produce in the "Javanese market."

The "Chinese," who were the most numerous of the foreigner groups, occupied the Kampong Cina residential district and also areas close to the city's commercial center. Their shahbandar represented not only merchants from China, but also the interests of Champa-based merchants, those from the Vietnam (Kauchi) coastal ports, Japan (more specifically the Ryukyus), and China's ports. References to the local Chinese community in the local *Sejarah Melayu* chronicle distinguished between Chincheu (Quanzhou, or Hokkiens, who were frequently Muslim converts) and Chinas (Cantonese, who were not). In both cases, the Melaka communities included both permanent and sojourning residents, who maintained houses, centers of worship, and warehouses. The most elite of the merchants, who owned or fitted out their own ships or were financiers, also had rural estates on the edges of the city (*dusun*), which doubled as valued recreational space.

These four communities did not cover the full range of commercial activity. Various ethnically diverse populations also filled positions as salesmen, craftsmen, sailors, fishermen, and artillerymen. Those who were technologically skilled resided in Melaka's core business district (Ujong Pasir) and in Melaka's suburbs. Bengalis were especially prominent as tailors, fishermen, and laborers; Peguans from lower Burma were sailors and pilots; "Armenians" were also present. This last term referred inclusively to all Middle Eastern Jews and Christians, the latter primarily being Nestorian Christians and others from Mesopotamia. The Jews were further distinguished as "white" (Middle Eastern) or "black" (deriving from the Malabar coast in India's southwest). There were also small communities of Yemeni and Persians, also involved in trade with the major Southeast Asian ports of trade (Lambourn: 2003; Ho: 2006; Subrahmanyam: 1999). Originating from the opposite direction was a small community of Luzon-connected Muslim merchants, of mixed Filipino-Chinese ethnicity, who resided in Minjan, a small port northwest of Melaka where they ran several tin mines and also periodically dispatched ships to China, Japan, and the Philippines (Thomaz: 1993).

Melaka was in theory an open marketplace free of royal monopolies, yet it imposed certain royal regulations and taxes. Resident merchants and Melaka-based sojourners who had resident families paid a 3 percent tax on imports, while other non-Melaka-based sojourners were subject to other regimes. Those sojourners who came from countries to the east (*negeri di-bawah angin*), including island Southeast Asia, were exempt from direct customs duties but required to participate in the local "reciprocal buying" (*beli-belian*) system. Specifically, they were required to sell 25 percent of their goods directly to the sultan's trade representatives (*hamba raja*, the "king's servitors" who managed the sultan's business) at 20 percent less than the current market price and to buy commodities from the sultan's shops at 20 percent higher than the market price (B. Andaya: 1978). In contrast, ships arriving from countries to the west (*negeri di-atas angina*), including India, the Bay of Bengal, and the Middle East, were charged a flat 6 percent fee on their imports, probably because they brought the most desired products: India's cotton textiles. There is no evidence that Melaka's taxation system discriminated between Muslims and non-Muslims, as was common in India's ports during this era. Rather, the goal was to manage the foreign trade communities and promote trade. It was only in the next century, after the arrival of Europeans, that it became common in Straits of Melaka ports (as a response to the Portuguese seizure of Melaka and their uniform taxation of all Asian traders) to base taxes on Islamic law (*fiqh*), which enjoined the rightful additional taxation of non-Muslims. In the fifteenth century, Melaka law (*Undang-undang Melaka*) was still based on local custom, though the "Law of Allah" (known in Arabic as *Sharia* and in Malay as *Itulah adatnya negeri, tetapi pada hikum Allah*) might be applied in extreme cases when harsher punishment seemed appropriate (Wake: 1983; Winstedt and Jong: 1956; Kheng: 1998).

Despite the diverse array of ethnic groups we have discussed, merchants were loyal to their families or to personal contracts rather than to any sense of a shared corporate commercial community. Rich merchants maintained residences in Melaka, where they transacted their business, and they sent trade representatives with their ships. Not all the wealthy merchants owned ships, as most overseas trade was conducted as silent partnerships in which a shipowner contracted with other merchant-financiers to share a voyage's expenses at a rate dependent on the destination, with all investors sharing in the profits on the ship's return.

In other cases, small-scale merchant/sojourners could lease a "compartment" (*petak*) in a ship, which might go for a freight charge equivalent to 20 percent of the merchandise value. If ships were lost, all investors lost, but if ships were successful there were normally profits of 35–50 percent on voyages to Southeast Asia, 80–90 percent on India missions, and up to 200 percent on China ventures (Thomaz: 2000, 33). Trade profits were reinvested in merchandise, or in the purchase of slaves (*belati*) who worked in the shipyards, served on ship crews, transported merchandise, hauled ships onto the beach, and performed various other labor. Funds could also be spent on "slaves of debt" (*ulur*, *orang berhutang*), who were "household" or personal slaves. Common to the Malay tradition, and in competition with local Malay elite, those of the greatest social and political status in Melaka regardless of their ethnicity had the largest number of dependents of this type. There was also a substantial amount of conspicuous consumption. Tomé Pires comments: "And true it is that this part of the world is richer and more prized than the world of the Indies, because the smallest merchandise here is gold, which is least prized, and in Melaka they consider it merchandise . . . in Melaka they prize garlic and onions more than musk, benzoin, and other precious things" (Cortesao: 1944, 286–87).

Though Melaka would fall to the Portuguese in 1511, the period of its hegemony saw the development of important social patterns that would have later consequences. For example, during the fifteenth century the Melaka-resident Chinese communities retained their distinctness as Chinese rather than acculturate, as was happening at that time among numbers of Chinese communities resident in other Straits of Melaka ports (Chang: 1991). Perhaps the difference was that Melaka's Chinese community had continuing opportunities for direct interaction with the Chinese marketplace, because Melaka was more important as an international entrepôt, and as a destination rather than an intermediary in the regional market system. In the Sumatra and north Java coast ports, Chinese were more likely to depend on trade relationships with their hinterlands. Samudra-Pasai and other north Sumatra port-polities were the source of pepper, which came from their upstream hinterlands. In Java, port-polities needed access to Java's rice, which they could exchange in the Melaka marketplace or among the port-polities of the eastern Indonesian archipelago. On the north coast of Java and elsewhere there was a layering of maritime diasporas that distinguished between the newly arrived and the longstanding resident, and also among the nonassimilated, the assimilating, and the assimilated communities (Hall: 2008). These issues of community distinction were also prominent in the eastern Indonesian archipelago, where the value of local spice exports attracted a variety of sojourners, some based in Melaka and north Java and others in the Philippines and Borneo. In the eastern Indonesian Spice Islands, locally based sojourning communities and merchant elite emerged in the fifteenth century and competed as transporters and traders of the internationally valued spices against the seasonally resident sojourning diasporas who arrived from ports in the west and north, with significant consequences to the future of the region (Kathiriathamby-Wells and Villiers: 1990; L. Andaya: 1993a, 1993b; Ellen: 2003).

BANDA AND THE EMERGING EASTERN INDONESIAN COMMUNITIES OF EXCHANGE

Unlike Melaka, fourteenth-century Banda was not the heir to a previous dominating entrepôt as Melaka was to Srivijaya. Nor could it, like Melaka, claim to hold special privileges relative to accessing the Chinese marketplace, with Ming China as its patron. While Banda's spices were in high demand among international traders, it was on the geographic periphery of the international trade mainstream, dependent on the seasonal visits of outsiders and the initiatives of its own sojourning community to market its spices in the international marketplace. But like Melaka and Samudra-Pasai, Banda would become a commercial intermediary, as the source of exotic products of islands even less accessible to international traders.

Banda was the central island among several Banda Islands in the eastern Indonesian archipelago that were the source of nutmeg and mace. In notable contrast to Melaka, there was no significant year-round foreign residency in Banda until late in the sixteenth century. There was a small community of shahbandars, using the same title that in Melaka designated that port-polity's chiefs of trade. But in Banda the shahbandar title applied collectively to the residential community of Muslim merchants of Javanese origin, but in most cases of Chinese heritage, who had settled locally during the fourteenth and early fifteenth centuries (Villiers: 1981, 729; Cortesao: 1944, 206). These shahbandars initially supplied Banda's spices to the small number of sojourning merchants who made the long voyage to Banda and back on the seasonal monsoon winds.

Up to the late fourteenth-century Ming era, Chinese merchant-seafarers had also traveled there by way of the Sulu Sea. However, from the late fourteenth century onward Chinese traders seemed disinterested in direct trade, being content to secure Banda's spices from intermediary ports (Ptak: 1992, 1993, 1998a). The majority of the traders traveling to Banda in the fifteenth century were Javanese Muslims, of mixed Chinese, Javanese, and Malay heritage, based in north coast Java ports such as Tuban, Demak, Gresik, and Surabaya. After arriving in Banda, bringing rice from Java and Indian cloth, along

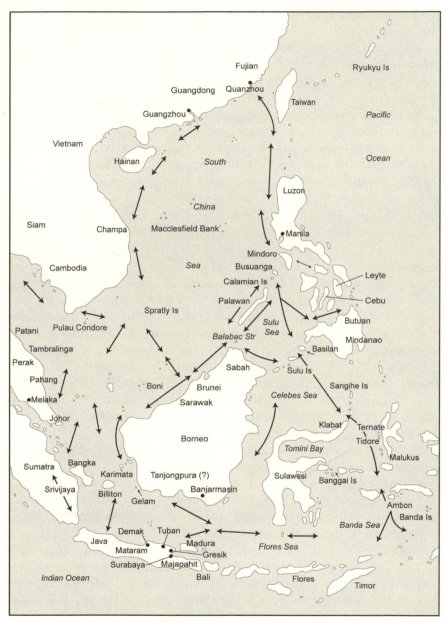

Map 9.2. Maritime Trade Networking in Eastern Southeast Asia, ca. 1200–1500

with luxury items from China and the West, these sojourners would lay over for several months waiting for favorable return winds. Some of these Java-based merchants eventually took local wives and settled on the Banda coast, where they collectively took the shahbandar title and networked with hinterland chiefs to ensure their control over local nutmeg and mace in the mountainous interior, and thus monopolized the Banda marketplace.

By the late fifteenth century these shahbandars kept other foreign traders from establishing permanent residential compounds similar to those found in fifteenth-century Melaka and commonly in other important regional ports of trade, including those in the neighboring Malukus (L. Andaya: 1991, 1993a, 1993b). Banda's residential coastal trade elite, partnering with hinterland chiefs, had direct control over the production and exchange of nutmeg and mace, products unique at that time to the Banda Islands. The shahbandar community also controlled local access to the imported commodities received at Banda's coastal ports (Cortesao: 1944, 207). This monopoly was possible because Banda society was traditionally communal and had no monarch. Even community chiefs were the most among equals, whose major delegated authority was negotiating with outsiders in the community's interests.

In the fifteenth century, due to the increased volume of the international trade, in their desire to avoid direct contact with outsiders and the potentially disruptive consequences to local society, the local communities allied with the shahbandar, who were empowered to act as the communities' delegated agents in the negotiation of trade with the increasing numbers of visiting foreign merchants. The shahbandar thus became a coastal ruling oligarchy of elders, while the hinterland society retained its communalism. These shahbandar would also become known to visiting merchants as orang kaya (rich men), a term commonly applied in that era to merchant elite in other archipelago ports of trade (Kathirathamby-Wells: 1986, 1993b).

Normally in other Southeast Asian marketplaces, such as Melaka, residential orang kaya merchant elite faced opposition from traditional noncommercial aristocracies and visiting traders. In both Samudra-Pasai and Melaka, as described above, residential merchants based in the downstream port had to network with upstream chiefs or other traditional political elite to allow them some degree of control over the flow of local production from the port's hinterland into the port of trade's international marketplace. In Banda the orang kaya had no such local competitors; they were the only functional aristocracy. From their base on the coast they exclusively negotiated the terms of trade with visiting merchants who were unwilling and unable to challenge the orang kaya monopoly over access to local production (Villiers: 1981, 729; Cortesao: 1944, 206). The Banda shahbandar/orang kaya's power rested on their capacity to represent the interests of the hinterland's collective village societies, which they acquired by popular consent rather than by force. The port-resident commercial specialists redistributed shares of the trade-derived wealth to the villagers in return for deliveries of locally grown spices.

In early archipelago places other than Banda, powerful sojourning merchants might have been able to buy off a local ruler, ally with one local faction against another, or impose their will by force, but in Banda the local merchant elite and the local producing communities were in unison, to their joint advantage. Visiting foreign merchants never challenged the local orang kaya trade monopoly, because of the efficiency by which they received the valued local spices and their own incapacity or lack of interest in mounting a military attack against such a diffuse situation. At the beginning of the sixteenth century, a Keling merchant based in Melaka and a Javanese merchant of Chinese heritage from Gresik sent most of the sojourning ships to Banda annually—there were eight ships annually from Melaka and four ships from Gresik (Cortesao: 1944, 447).

Banda occupied a strategic position in the eastern archipelago trade routes. According to Tomé Pires, at the beginning of the fifteenth century Java- and Melaka-based traders would sail to the Banda Islands each year, taking with them cargoes of cotton and silk cloth from Gujarat, the Coromandel, and Bengal, as well as Chinese silk, Java rice, Chinese and Thai ceramics, ivory, and Javanese gongs. The best of the cloth from India remained in Java's north coast ports, where it was exchanged for Java's rice, other food supplies, and Java's own less expensive coarse cotton cloth (Wisseman Christie: 1993; Lombard: 1990). The food imports from Java were critical, because Banda's soil was of limited fertility and because its producers had by then specialized in the cultivation of mace and nutmeg, and depended on rice imports instead of sago to provide the staple of their daily diet.

Some of the Indian cottons and other exotic international products as well as also lesser-quality Javanese cloth were reexported under the direction of the Banda orang kaya to the nearby neighboring Maluku, using "Bandanese" crews, which in reality were an assortment of ethnicities who called the Banda coast their home. The Banda orang kaya trade elite's dominance of this particular leg of the trade was possible because of the monsoon wind currents. The Maluku were just a twelve- to fifteen-day voyage beyond Banda, yet the extra distance was crucial for traders making the six-month voyage from the western Java Sea to Banda and back. Spending extra days at sea would have made the trip twice as long for the larger junks of the Java Sea trade because they would have had to lay over until the next seasonal winds. Thus it was Banda's smaller ships that supplied the linkage between Banda and the Maluku. There, in addition to the cloth, they reexported ivory and other commodities that they exchanged for Maluku cloves, which they would then resell to the foreign merchants making their annual visits to Banda. Bandanese crews would sometimes sail to Java and Melaka themselves, but to do so was risky, since Banda ships were less seaworthy than those of the major Southeast Asian traders. Bandanese voyages to Melaka and back often took two or three years and their small junks were regularly lost (Villiers: 1981, 733–34).

By the end of the fifteenth century Southeast Asians from Sulawesi and its nearby islands west of Banda were also voyaging throughout the Indonesian archipelago. These included traditional Sulawesi-based sojourners, Buginese (Bugis) and Makasserese, both notorious slave traders, who now also became legitimate traders in spices, which they exchanged for Indian cloth and other foreign commodities (L. Andaya: 1993a, 1993b; B. Andaya: 1993b; Ellen: 2003; Cummings: 2007, 2011).

Banda, as well as the neighboring Maluku and Sulawesi islands, represents local response in the eastern Indonesian archipelago to the new fifteenth-century international trading opportunities. In contrast to Samudra-Pasai and Melaka, both of which were strategically adjacent to the international trade mainstream, Banda was on the trade route's periphery and consequently was in a much stronger position, at least at that time, to dictate the terms of trade locally. Because of the value of what Banda had to offer, paired with the difficulty in reaching Banda, the powerful Melaka- or Java-based shipowners who sent most of the visiting ships to Banda chose not to challenge the local preeminence of the Banda orang kaya merchant elite (Manguin: 1991). Banda's society reaped the benefits of the initial opportunities afforded by the new trading relationships without substantially altering the traditional communal social order.

Any new element of hierarchy was isolated on the periphery of traditional society. By minimizing its involvement with the external marketplace, except as this external marketplace improved the local standard of living, and by securing the agency of the initially alien orang kaya shahbandars to ensure their insularity, Banda's society did not require an elaborate overhaul of its existing social and political structure to accompany its new economic specialization. Nor did Banda's society have to convert to a new religion more conducive to new social, economic, and political realities, as was the case with Samudra-Pasai and Melaka becoming Islamic sultanates.

Shifting focus to the northwest, fifteenth-century Cebu in the Philippines provides an example of a Sulu Sea society trying to cope with the new age of trade. Here, in contrast to Banda, there was a strong existing tradition of upstream-downstream hierarchical chieftainship that is more similar to the origins of the Samudra-Pasai and Melaka polities.

MARITIME TRADE IN THE FIFTEENTH-CENTURY
SULU SEA REGION OF THE EASTERN
ARCHIPELAGO WORLD ca. 1500: THE CASE OF
CEBU IN THE PHILIPPINES

Archaeologists make the case that trade played a key role in stimulating major changes in Philippine society in the pre-European age. As has been noted in earlier chapters, archeologists assume that Chinese traders were establishing bases in the Philippines as early as the eleventh and twelfth centuries CE. Chinese traders had early settlements in Laguna and on Mindoro, and when the Spanish arrived in Manila in the early sixteenth century they found some twenty Chinese traders residing there with their wives (Hutterer: 1974). This was likely the norm in other early Philippines regional ports, and archeologists assume that an intensive and extensive network of native trade existed to distribute imports and to gather the forest products desired by Chinese traders. These trade activities necessitated formal regulation, and this encouraged the rise of local chiefs (datu) who controlled and protected networks of barangay (villages). In addition, recent archaeological excavations document urban settlements of over five hundred households in the Laguna (Manila) area, as well as in sites on the Mindoro, Mindanao, and Cebu coasts (Junker: 1999).

The Laguna, Mindoro, and Cebu sites especially demonstrate the rapid growth of trade centers—in response to the opportunities and demands afforded by foreign trade—as populations from the interior and other islands congregated around ports, whose locally made brass artillery protected against the piracy rampant in this region's sea channels (Hutterer: 1974). Each of these early urban sites is associated with significant deposits of Chinese porcelain dating to the late Song and early Ming eras (twelfth through sixteenth centuries) (Junker: 1999). Excavations in the Cebu City region, for example, revealed multiple levels of Chinese porcelains predating the Spanish incursions, including large quantities of early Ming blue-and-white ceramics dating at least one century prior to the arrival of the Spanish (Hutterer: 1973).

Magellan's world voyage anchored at Cebu in 1522 to take on provisions. Antonio Pigafetta, the chronicler of this voyage, provided the first extensive Western accounts of Philippine island trade (Nowell: 1962). The information from his account is worth exploring in some detail. Magellan's crew had asked the ruler of Limasawa, a small island off the southern tip of Leyte, to direct them to a port where they could obtain food, and the ruler named three ports, adding that Cebu was the largest and the one with the most trade (Nowell: 1962, 144). At Cebu the Spanish encountered a population of almost two thousand (Nowell: 1962, 160) and an extensive entrepôt trade based on the exchange of Chinese articles for Southeast Asian products. Humabon, the ruler of Cebu, initially informed the Spanish that it was the custom of all ships that entered the port to pay him tribute, and that it was also customary for the ruler of the port to exchange presents with the captains of all ships that came to trade—his demand was quickly dropped after a Muslim merchant based in the Thai Ayudhya realm, mistaking the Spanish for the Portuguese, informed Humabon that his visitors had recently conquered the great emporium of Melaka and part of India.

It may be noticed that this practice of ritualized exchange between ruler and commercial populations was common in Asian ports of the time. The gift giving created a symbolic bond of friendship, in an attempt to mitigate the potential for conflict during the subsequent commercial transactions (Foster: 1977; Junker: 1999). Not only had the Cebuanos adopted this practice, but they were also excellent hosts to the Spanish, being accustomed to the arrival of foreigners. Humabon and his nephew repeatedly provided Magellan and his men with food, invited them to meals, and entertained them with examples of local music and dance (Nowell: 1962, 153–55). The ruler's collection and redistribution of tribute, as well as his mediation and facilitation of trade exchanges, were key to his position, and he applied these roles to the Spanish. Humabon's brother, reportedly called a *bendara* (bendahara), facilitated their trade (Nowell: 1962, 162; Cortesao: 1944, 167, 193–94). In addition, Humabon took Spanish goods under his personal care along with the four Spaniards assigned to trade the goods (Nowell: 1962, 156). The Cebuanos traded rice, pigs, and other food provisions for small Spanish articles, but they especially desired to acquire Spanish iron (Wheatley: 1959b, 117; Bronson: 1992). In these exchanges the Cebuanos impressed the Spanish with their use of sophisticated measures; local merchants carried about small wooden balances marked off into units equivalent to roughly one-fourth pound, one-third pound, and one pound (Nowell: 1962, 156).

We have already noted evidence that Chinese porcelain was one of Cebu's principal import items. Pigafetta notes the frequent use of Chinese porcelains by prominent members of Cebu society, both in common household activities and as a means of displaying a person's wealth and social status. For example, Humabon ate turtle eggs from Chinese porcelain dishes and served the Spanish explorers meat on Chinese porcelain platters (Nowell: 1962, 149, 154). Porcelains were also used in local religious ceremony as storage containers for myrrh, storax, and benzoin, and these containers were prominently displayed in the funeral services of wealthy Cebuanos (Nowell: 1962, 168). Other imports that impressed the Spanish explorers included three Ming Buddha images made of grayish white jades; variously sized brass gongs said to have been manufactured in China (these were played by local musicians to entertain Magellan's crew and were also used in religious ceremonies); and cotton and silk clothing, imported from China, that was worn by Cebu elites. Pigafetta also records the arrival of the previously noted Muslim merchant from Thailand who landed with a cargo of gold and slaves for trade (Nowell: 1962, 148–49).

Cebu also had a regular trade connection to Ayutthya, as demonstrated by the presence of the Thai porcelain, which accounts for roughly one-third of the ceramics recovered at Cebu (Hutterer: 1973). This is consistent with the patterns of the ceramic trade in Southeast Asia from roughly 1430 to 1580, when the Ming restriction on the export of Chinese blue-and-white porcelains provided a market opportunity for Thai, Cham, and Vietnamese manufacturers (for more on this, see chapter 7). There are few corresponding examples of native pottery, and that which has been found is of poor quality compared to that of the earlier levels of habitation; it would seem, then, that Cebu's local pottery production largely ceased as imported ceramics became readily available (Hutterer: 1973, 42).

As for Cebu's exports, they included gold, slaves, and food supplies. It is likely that Cebu's gold came from other parts of the Sulu Sea region, or from farther abroad, since Cebu itself was not known to have produced gold; by this time, gold was a standard medium of international exchange (as well as also copper cash), which could account for its availability at Cebu. Pigs were raised locally, and Pigafetta's list of the indigenous products normally exchanged at Cebu's port also includes rice, millet, sugar cane, palm wine, and various fruits that grew in Cebu's hinterland (Nowell: 1962, 153, 175). Cinnamon, ginger, and silk articles, all reportedly from the Malukus, were also marketed at Cebu, although it is not clear whether they were brought by Cebuanos or others (Nowell: 1962, 175; L. Andaya: 1993a, 1993b; Junker: 1999).

Like in Pasai, personal adornments obtained through international trade could be used to mark status. For example, while Humabon's retainers were clothed only in a short piece of palm tree cloth, Humabon wore an embroidered scarf on his head, a necklace of great value, and two large gold earrings inlaid with precious gems (Nowell: 1962, 154–66). His wife dressed in a black and white cotton cloth, covered her shoulders with a large silk scarf crossed with gold stripes, and "wore a large hat of palm leaves in the manner of a parasol, with a crown about it of the same leaves, like the tiara of the Pope" (Nowell: 1962, 160–61). Humabon also promised Magellan two large gold earrings, two armlets, two anklets, and gems to wear in his ears, as appropriate to someone of Magellan's rank (Nowell: 1962, 162).

Cebu's foreign trade thus brought Humabon status and wealth. It seems from Pigafetta's commentary that Humabon was at the apex of a sequence of datu relationships, that is, personal alliances among chiefs who led barangay upstream-downstream networks and were therefore responsible for the flow of local agricultural goods to Humabon's port for the entrepôt trade. Pigafetta specifically mentions two barangay settlements along the Cebu coast, Mandaui and Lalutan (Liloan), that were subordinate to Humabon; archeological evidence suggests there were others (Nowell: 1962, 164; Hutterer: 1973). The impression of early Spanish visitors to the area was that such alliances were subject to flux, and that populations often moved from place to place according to the current hierarchy of a region (Fenner: 1976). For example, at the time of the initial Spanish visit in the early sixteenth century Humabon was competing with a rival chief, named Lapulapu, who ruled the Maton and Bulaia barangay on the neighboring island of Mactan and commanded a force of fifteen hundred fighting men (Nowell: 1962, 169). Whichever of these two chiefs controlled the strait separating the two islands would dominate regional commerce and the wealth associated with the international trade. It is for this reason that Humabon enlisted the support of Magellan's crew in hopes of establishing his supremacy over Lapulapu's alliance network, and the ensuing battle resulted in Magellan's death (Steinberg: 1971, xi; Fenner: 1976).

The Cebu alliance network ruled by Humabon is best thought of as a developing polity that, though participating in the external commercial networks, was incapable of linking the riverine systems of the Sulu Sea maritime realm into a continuous political entity focused on a single port or its elite (L. Andaya: 1993a, 1993b). Humabon's authority was confined to the developing population center of Cebu; beyond that center his commercial and political dominance depended on his ability to undertake direct military intervention to subjugate the chiefs (datu) of other developing and potentially rival centers on the Cebu coast and on neighboring islands. Even in his own realm Humabon's authority was based on fragile personal alliance networks with subordinate datu who ruled other coastal barangay and their upstream interiors. There was certainly a degree of integration between the coast and its hinterland, demonstrated by the broad upstream distribution of Chinese and Thai ceramics dating to this era. Pigafetta's account of the Magellan expedition's visit implies that loyalties to Humabon were based upon the chief's personal strength, itself a product of the wealth he had achieved in his role as the principal facilitator of trade.

Humabon made great displays of his trade-derived wealth in his use of Chinese ceramics, in his wearing of foreign clothing and jewelry, and in his association with visiting foreigners, including Chinese, Thai, and Europeans. The Spanish were amazed by the extent of Humabon's understanding of international trade as well as by his expectations of traders who participated in his marketplace. Yet such awareness is not surprising, since Humabon's personal administration of Cebu's entrepôt trade was the source of his political power. Humabon mediated and monopolized the outward flow of locally produced foods as well as those spices acquired in the Malukus that found their way into Cebu's marketplace. He also dominated the internal redistribution of foreign goods—for instance the Chinese and Thai ceramics, Indian cloth, and Chinese and European metals—from his port to those dwelling in his subordinate upstream, whose production of local foodstuffs made possible the flow of Maluku spices to his port. While Humabon's direct authority would appear to have been confined to the coast, he was able to exercise his hegemony over the Cebu upstream via the strategic position of his court center relative to the indigenous and external networks of exchange.

It is the movement beyond such a system based on personal alliance to a more structured and less personal state system involving a more direct integration of the upstream hinterlands and coastal populations, and especially a more formal subordination of the hinterland to the coastal populations, which is characteristic of the emerging states in maritime Southeast Asia at the end of the fifteenth century. This was also true of the Southeast Asian mainland societies of Burma, Thailand, and Vietnam as discussed in previous chapters.

10

Maritime Trade and State Development, ca. 1250–1500

Chapters 7 through 9 have focused on the regional consequences of the upsurge in East-West trade that took place from roughly 1250 when the establishment of the Mameluke dynasty in Egypt brought stability to the Red Sea passage from the Indian Ocean to the Mediterranean. Then, in 1368, the founders of the Ming dynasty overthrew the Mongol Yuan dynasty, bringing the collapse of the overland caravan route across the central Asian steppes that the Yuan had stabilized. The Ming established their initial capital at Nanjing, a city on the Yangtze River in China's commercial heartland, and in the early years of the dynasty the maritime route between East and West that passed through Southeast Asia boomed.

On the western end the Mameluke dynasty contracted with Venetian merchants to facilitate the flow of Asian goods into the growing European markets of the post-crusade era; on the eastern end the Ming began to solicit trade by sending maritime expeditions into Southeast Asia. Southeast Asians responded by expanding their marketing of pepper, tin, and spices, and new emporia emerged as well. In the fourteenth century, the Southeast Asia trade was no longer dominated by strategic ports on the southeastern Sumatra and Java coasts; though Java continued to play an important commercial role, the commodity source regions on the northern end of Sumatra; the Burma, Thai, and Vietnam regions of the mainland; and the Spice Islands of the eastern Indonesian archipelago became more direct participants in the international trade route (Schottenhammer: 2001). During the fourteenth century, Southeast Asian port-polities dependent on commercial revenues rose in the island realm at Samudra-Pasai in northern Sumatra, Melaka on the Malay Peninsula,

Brunei in northwestern Borneo, Cebu in the Philippines, and Makassar on Sulawesi. There were also significant mainland commercial ports, including the ones at Pegu and elsewhere in lower Burma and the ones associated (after 1351) with the Thai center at Ayudhya on the Chaophraya River. In that same era the Cham port of Thi Nai was the major stopover on the Vietnam coastline for international shipping going to and coming from China and intersecting there with ships based in Java Sea, Gulf of Thailand, and Straits of Melaka emporia to the south and ships sailing to Borneo, the Philippines, and the Sulu Sea region and beyond to the east.

These long-distance carriers serviced lesser secondary regional ports, which in several cases, as described in the above chapters, evolved as major emporia that displaced their former commercial nodes to stand alone as the primary ports among ever-changing linked secondary centers. Beginning in the early fifteenth century Angkor was also succeeded by a new Khmer center, at the intersection of the Bassac River and Tonle Sap near present-day Phnom Penh, which provided more direct access to the sea via the Mekong River—the Khmer realm had previously depended on overland transit to the South China Sea via the Cham and Dai Viet realms.

In addition to the proliferation of new regional ports, during the fourteenth to early sixteenth centuries Southeast Asia participated in a new pattern of world trade that linked the continents of Asia and Europe in an even more direct exchange of goods. The new pattern left no single part of the world as the dominant center of the trading network. Each zone, along with the interconnected sea route from China to western Europe, was important to the whole system. The long voyages that had once transported goods to faraway markets were now broken down into several consecutive smaller voyages undertaken by Chinese, Javanese, Indian, Burmese-Mon, Persian-Arab, Italian, and Jewish traders based variously in Europe, the Middle East, India, Southeast Asia, and China. There was extensive exchange within regions, and each region in turn overlapped one or more of the others. Each zone of trade was dominated by a few seafaring peoples who sought profit from the transport of goods in that zone. The dominant ports in the zone became the chief distributors of foreign goods in their region as well as the source of local products for traders from other zones. The people of the Southeast Asian hinterlands were brought into contact with the outside world via such dominant ports, and thus it was that they entered into the mainstream of the new regional history in this period.

There were at least six if not seven zones of trade through which goods from China had to pass before they reached northeastern Europe, via a route extending from China past India, through the Middle East, and around Italy and northwest Europe to the Baltic Sea, Poland, and Russia (Chaudhuri:

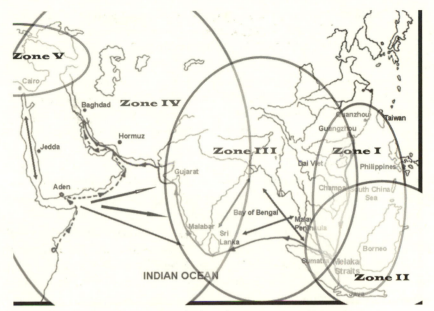

Map 10.1.   Indian Ocean Networked Trade Zones, ca. 1400–1500

1985; Meilink-Relofszk: 1962). Moving east to west, the first zone had its center in southern China, and included ports in the northern Philippines and along the Vietnam coast and the Gulf of Thailand down the east coast of the Malay Peninsula. In this zone, traders of a variety of ethnicities carried goods in junks from one port to another (Hall: 2006). To the south, this first zone made contact with a second zone centered in the ports of Tuban, Gresik, Japara, and Demak in Java. The second zone, which was controlled largely by multiethnic commercial groups based in Java's ports, extended eastward to the Spice Islands and the southwestern ports of Sulawesi, northward along the south and east coast of Borneo to the island of Mindanao and beyond, and westward to the ports of the east coast of Sumatra. There, at Melaka and the northeastern ports of Sumatra, it intersected with a third zone centered on India.

The third zone encompassed ports along the two coasts of India, especially in southern India and Sri Lanka, Gujarat, and Bengal. It connected with the western Indonesian archipelago in the east and the Red Sea in the west. The fourth zone focused upon Alexandria and included other ports of the eastern Mediterranean and the Middle Eastern realm. Italian merchants dominated the fifth zone, and via the Mediterranean they distributed Asian goods to the sixth zone, which was centered on the Iberian Peninsula at the western end

of the Mediterranean. From there, goods were redistributed to northwestern
Europe and onward to the Hanseatic traders of the northern seas. The Hanse
commercial network, which would be a seventh zone, carried goods farther
to the east and northeast.

An alternative way of viewing Southeast Asia's trade at the beginning of
the fourteenth century—and one more immediately relevant to this conclud-
ing chapter—is to perceive the region in terms of five commercial zones of
maritime trade as introduced in chapter 1. Each of the five was a prosperous
and independent regional picture of prosperity. Going from west to east, the
first zone comprised a Bay of Bengal regional trade network that began on
the Coromandel Coast of southern India and Sri Lanka and included Burma,
the west coast of the upper Malay Peninsula, and the northern and western
coasts of Sumatra. The second commercial zone began with the new Sultanate of Melaka, which included the Thai and Vietnam coastlines between Melaka and China to the east and overlapped the eastern Bay of Bengal network
to its west, and the western Java Sea and South China Sea networks to its
east. The third trade zone encompassed the Vietnam coastline, southern
Sumatra, and the regions bordering the Gulf of Thailand, including Thailand,
Cambodia, and the Malay Peninsula's eastern coast, linking with Melaka and
the Java and South China seas. The Java Sea network was the fourth Southeast Asian trade zone and included the Lesser Sunda Islands, the Maluku,
Banda, Timor, the western coast of Borneo, Java, the southern coast of Suma-
tra, and Melaka. The fifth zone, which was the back-door passageway to the
Spice Islands from the China and Vietnam coastlines, centered in the Sulu
Sea region and included the Philippines coasts of Luzon, Mindoro, Cebu, and
Mindanao; the Brunei region of Borneo's north coast; the eastern Indonesian
archipelago's Spice Islands; and south China's ports.

The first of the five zones, comprising the northern and western coasts of
Sumatra, became important in the post-1300 era due to increasing world
demand for pepper. In particular, the Samudra-Pasai entrepôt became the
principal supplier of pepper to Western and Eastern traders, supplementing
the pepper exports of India's southwestern Malabar Coast, because that
region's more limited productive capacity could not keep up with the rising
Western and Eastern demand and, based on common consumer belief that
Malabar pepper was superior to that of Sumatra, was more expensive. Meanwhile, the port of Pegu, located in the Irrawaddy River delta of lower Burma,
began to take part in the commerce involving northern Sumatra, the Straits
of Melaka, and the Bay of Bengal, especially as a supplier of rice meant to
provision the commercial populations from the East and the West who were
frequenting the Straits of Melaka's new pepper ports (Furnivall: 1939; Tun:
1959; Aung-Thwin, 2011).

The second commercial zone was the Straits of Melaka. In the fourteenth century this region was still in a state of transition and was a bone of contention between the Thais to the north and the Javanese to the east. However, by the fifteenth century, immediately prior to the European incursion, this region would become the most important of the commercial zones. Its transformation was due to the rise of Melaka at the turn of the fifteenth century. Founded by the prince who claimed to be a successor to the rulers of the Srivijayan maritime empire of earlier times, Melaka's rise was initially due to the initiatives by the Ming dynasty at the end of the fourteenth century to fill what they perceived to be a political void in the area and to contain piracy, which was jeopardizing the steady flow of commerce into south China's ports (Wolters: 1970). In so doing, they hoped to revitalize the Tang-era China-centered tributary trade system (Levathes: 1994, 22–26; Chang: 1991, 22–26; Wade: 2005). By the 1430s, however, Melaka's prosperity would depend less on Chinese support and more on interaction with Javanese and other Southeast Asia–based merchants and their networks. Java-based sojourners continually dominated the flow of spices from the eastern Indonesian archipelago to Melaka, which was used as a trade intermediary through which to market Javanese rice and Java Sea spices as well.

Thus, in the fifteenth century Melaka provided another singular entrepôt at the intersection of the Bay of Bengal, South China Sea, and Java Sea regional networks. Yet it was also somewhat independent of China. The Ming effort to recreate the tributary system ultimately failed, not only because of debate within China itself (Yoshinobu: 1983; Schottenhammer: 1999), but also because the old tributary system was no longer valid. Instead, Melaka's rise to prominence by the fifteenth century depended equally, and perhaps more, on the complexity of the multicentered trade in the Indian Ocean and the practicality at that time of establishing a single Southeast Asian entrepôt as the clearinghouse for this Indian Ocean trade. It was appropriate that this central entrepôt should be in Southeast Asia, because Southeast Asia was then the source of the most demanded commodities, the most important consumer marketplace for imported textiles and ceramics, and the exchange point for a variety of commodities derived from China, the Middle East, and various secondary sources of supply.

The available records tell us little about the men who traded from Melaka, but we know a good deal about Melaka's leaders. They took great care to make their new port attractive to international traders. As with its predecessors, Melaka's residency patterns ebbed and flowed with the monsoons. Traders and other groups maintained permanent warehouse and residency compounds, the forerunners to the European "factories" that were later established there. However, except for a few year-round representatives of the major trading establishments, the population in these compounds was at best seasonal. Meanwhile, a special governing body and judicial system gave visiting merchants and their goods protection while in the port. The main court officials, including the *bendahara* (prime minister), *laksamana* (admiral of the monarch's fleet), *syahbandar* (harbor master), and *temenggung* (minister of justice, defense, and palace affairs) all facilitated trade in various ways. Melaka's port regulations aided the local exchange of goods so merchants would not find themselves overly burdened and so they would not need to prolong their stays so long as to risk losing the appropriate monsoon wind for their return voyage.

At the same time, there were regular customs duties, fixed weights and measures, and fixed units of coinage, all of which helped provide local stability (Thomaz: 1993, 2000). Malay nobles did not take part in the affairs of the marketplace, leaving this to the merchants themselves, but they did command the fleet of ships that policed the Straits to keep them free from piracy. In addition, vessels powered by oar rather than sail patrolled the Straits, so that they could tow becalmed ships into port. Furthermore, in the tradition of Srivijaya, Melaka's success also persuaded local chiefs to enter the traditional Straits alliance between ruler and ruled. Under this arrangement, potential rivals and pirates were kept in line by means of periodic redistributions of wealth to those who remained subordinate to the port-polity instead of conducting acts of piracy or disloyalty (Milner: 1982).

Melaka almost immediately achieved international economic prominence. Heavy naval traffic came from western Asia. India-based ships arrived regularly from the Gujarat, Malabar, and Coromandel coasts, as well as from Bengal and Myanmar. Goods included luxury items from the Middle East such as rosewater, incense, opium, and carpets, as well as seeds and grains, and Malabar merchants from India's southwest coast brought pepper and Middle Eastern goods. But the bulk of the fifteenth-century cargoes coming from west of Sri Lanka were made up of cotton cloth from the Gujarat and Coromandel coasts (Barnes: 2002). In addition, vessels from Bengal brought quantities of foodstuffs, rice, cane sugar, dried and salted meat and fish, preserved vegetables, and candied fruits, as well as the local white cloth fabrics. The Pegu-based polity in lower Burma also supplied foodstuffs, rice and sugar, and ships. In return, spices, gold, camphor, tin, sandalwood, alum, and pearls were sent northwest from Melaka. Malabar and Sumatran pepper were also carried back to Bengal, along with some opium from Middle Eastern countries (Meilink-Roelofsz: 1962, 61ff; Wake: 1967).

While China may have discouraged official tributary trade with the south after the 1430s, there was still an ample, unofficial, and privately financed trade conducted by junks, and reexports westward from China via Melaka included porcelain, musk, quicksilver, copper, vermillion, and large quantities of raw and woven silks, damask, satin, and brocade (Ptak: 1998; Vogel: 1993; Heng: 2001, 2009). Privately financed trade from China also included pottery, camphor, and pearls, as well as the less valuable alum, saltpeter, sulfur, iron, and copper and iron utensils. Regular shipping also came from Thailand, Vietnam, Japan, and the Philippines, which contributed foodstuffs, jungle goods, and a variety of other trade items (Wade: 2004; Wang: 1970; Chan: 1968).

In addition, Melaka drew on trade within the archipelago (the fifth zone, which will be described further below). This trade had become highly profitable, and the spices of the Maluku—nutmeg, mace, and cloves—had assumed global importance. Intra-archipelago trade was at that time dominated by merchant-seafarers based in the Muslim-ruled ports of Java's north coast, but eastern archipelago sojourners known collectively as the Bugis were becoming a factor. From the Straits polities themselves—notably from Kedah on the west coast of the Malay Peninsula and Samudra-Pasai on the northwest coast of Sumatra—came tin, gold, jungle products, and pepper, in return for cloth, opium, and foodstuffs. By the end of the fifteenth century, when the first Portuguese missions reached Asia, Melaka was the commercial hub of Asian trade. Early arriving Portuguese, whose home ports in the Atlantic must have seemed poor and provincial by Melaka's cosmopolitan standards, were awed by what they saw. They left with impressive accounts of the bustling Melaka urban center.

In the words of the early fifteenth-century Portuguese scribe Tomé Pires, Southeast Asia was "at the end of the monsoon, where you find what you want, and sometimes more than you are looking for" (Cortesao: 1944, 2:228). When Europeans came to Southeast Asia in the early sixteenth century, they saw Melaka as more than a marketplace. It was a symbol of the wealth and luxury of Asia. They were eager to circumvent the monopoly of Venice on the priceless spice trade, and the great wealth and luxury available in this trading had enticed them halfway around the world in their tiny, uncomfortable ships on an extraordinarily hazardous journey. When the Portuguese entered the Indian Ocean in the early 1500s, therefore, their objective was to seize Melaka, which they rightfully considered to be the dominant center of contemporary Asian trade (McRoberts: 1991).

The third trade zone was centered around Thailand and the lower coast of Vietnam, what Leonard Andaya has recently detailed as the Sea of Melayu (L. Andaya: 2008), including the upper Malay Peninsula's eastern coast and the mainland regions bordering the Gulf of Thailand, and the east coast of Sumatra. The Thai state of Ayudhya developed in the first half of the fourteenth century in the lower Chaophraya valley and thrived as a result of new foreign contacts. Though it was initially hostile to the rise of Melaka in the south, which it viewed as an intruder into the Thai political and economic sphere, Ayudhya began to export rice to Melaka in the fifteenth century while also being a commercial center for trade with the Philippines and China (Kasetsiri: 1976; Vickery: 2004). Thai participation in Southeast Asian trade is well documented by deposits of their porcelains at the sites of numerous Southeast Asian ports active during the post thirteenth-century era (Roxanna Brown: 2008b; Miksic: 2010a). Meanwhile, following the demise of Angkor in the thirteenth and fourteenth centuries, the remnants of the Khmer civilization of Cambodia established a new base at the edge of the Mekong Delta, which provided them with a commercial link to the Malay populations on the north fringe of the South China Sea (Wolters: 1966b).

The Sulu Sea region comprised the fourth commercial zone. In this region the western coasts of Luzon, Mindoro, Cebu, and Mindanao, along with the Brunei region of Borneo's north coast, all served to varying degrees as facilitators of trade between China and the Spice Islands to the south and east (Ptak: 1992). These Spice Islands were the source of nutmeg, mace, cloves, sandalwood, and other more exotic commodities, such as parrots and birds of paradise, all of which flowed through the Sulu Sea to China and Thailand in the north, as well as to the central Vietnam coastline, Java, and Melaka in the west.

The Chinese presence was not new—Chinese traders had established these bases in the Philippines during the eleventh and twelfth centuries (Hutterer: 1974). The first mission to the Chinese court from the Philippines arrived in 1003. In 1007, envoys were again sent by the ruler of Butuan in northwest Mindanao, requesting that the Song court bestow upon them the same class of flags that Cham envoys had received in 1004. The request was rejected because Butuan, the Chinese reasoned, was beneath Champa in commercial importance (Wolters: 1983, 58).

By the fourteenth century an intensive and extensive network of native trade had evolved to distribute imports and gather the forest products desired by Chinese traders. This trade in both its internal and external dimensions stimulated major changes in Philippine society. It called for formal regulation of commercial contact between indigenous populations and the foreign traders and encouraged the formation of village clusters (*barangay*) that were controlled and protected by local chiefs (datu) (Hutterer: 1974, 297). Archeological research has revealed population clusters of over five hundred households in the Manila area dating to the pre-Spanish period, as well as other clustered residential sites on the Mindoro, Mindanao, and Cebu coasts. Each of these communities' trade links with China are demonstrated by the communities' association with significant deposits of Song and Ming porcelain dating to the thirteenth and fourteenth centuries. The archeological remains of early Laguna, Mindoro, and Cebu societies especially document the rapid growth of trade centers as people from the interior and other islands congregated around ports fortified with brass artillery—to protect against the piracy rampant in this region's sea channels—in response to the opportunities and demands afforded by foreign trade (Hutterer: 1974, 296; 1973). The Brunei coast of Borneo was important to the Chinese in its own right, for it was Borneo's jungles that provided bird's nests, camphor, and other gums and resins used in China for pharmacological purposes (Nichol: 1983).

The Java Sea network was the fifth Southeast Asian trade zone and included the Lesser Sunda Islands, the Malukus, Banda, Timor, the western and southern coasts of Borneo, Java, and the southern coast of Sumatra. Eastern Java had emerged as the strongest among the archipelago's political systems by the thirteenth century and came to facilitate the Java Sea spice trade (Wisseman Christie: 1998b; Robson: 1995; Wicks: 1992). The new east Java–based state of Majapahit that came into existence at the end of the thirteenth century established a loose hegemony over the eastern and western archipelagos. Because Java had limited control over the straits maritime realm, there was a rise in piracy in the Straits of Melaka and along the southern Borneo coast in the fourteenth century. It was due either to this piracy or to the weakness of Java that Malay populations with Chinese support established Melaka at the end of the fourteenth century. Owing to the rise of Melaka, Chinese traders could now avoid the Borneo coast route to Java and acquire the spices from the Java-based merchants at Melaka or, alternatively, from Sulu Sea entrepôts via the Philippines.

By the fifteenth century, these new patterns of trade had brought about a different type of state in Southeast Asia. The increasing importance of local products, spices, pepper, and various forest products in the international trade, and the intensity of Javanese, Chinese, and India-based shipping in the area that resulted in more competition among Southeast Asia's ports, encouraged a policy of territorial expansion that was actively pursued by important states in the Straits of Melaka and South China Sea regions. The extension of control over territory that produced marketable products was essential to these polities in order to prevent the flow of products to rival ports. This is clearly demonstrated in the Dai Viet conquest of its Cham rival Vijaya in 1471 as detailed in chapter 7, and the subsequent physical relocation of Cham ceramics artisans to Dai Viet ceramics production centers near its Van Don port of trade. This was notable because it effectively ended the fluid exchange network that had prevailed in the centuries-old Jiaozhi Ocean system networking south China with the Vietnam coastline and beyond. As in this case, the loose federations of port-polities that had characterized earlier times disappeared in other sectors of the trade network too, as only one port, often also the seat of government in the island realm, came to dominate in each of the new states (Li: 2006). Functional power was extended from this port center over nearby ports as well as their upstream hinterlands. Samudra-Pasai, Melaka, and Pedir, the dominant ports of the Straits of Melaka region during the late fifteenth century, had varying control over their interiors and competed for commercial and political dominance over other port-polities on the two coasts of the straits (Cortesao: 1944, 139).

The extension of power by these port-polities was different in nature from that of the earlier Srivijaya age, for now a state's authority over other river systems penetrated deeper into their upstream hinterlands (Kathirithamby-Wells and Villiers: 1990). This contrasts with the case of Funan, which we saw in chapter 2. Funan's rulers were most interested in providing entrepôt facilities for foreign traders, utilizing alliances with Funan's supporters to ensure the security of and continuous provisioning of its ports. On the other hand, Funan's rulers were less interested in mobilizing the flow of substantial quantities of local products from their upstream hinterlands to their downstream coastal ports, being content to provide a neutral commercial facility for the exchange of Western, Chinese, and Southeast Asian products. Port fees and foreign products acquired by the Funan ruler in his ports had been redistributed to the ruler's two groups of supporters, the leaders of the Malay seamen who facilitated the flow of trade goods from the Isthmus of Kra in the west and to China's ports in the north, and the chiefs of the hinterland populations, who provisioned the port with foodstuffs that sustained the international sojourners during their seasonal stopovers.

These upstream and hinterland redistributions had reinforced the magical relationship between the ports' ruler and his upstream allies. Funan was not engaged in administratively annexing the lands and people of its hinterland and was concerned only with recognition of its authority by its potential rivals. For these reasons, the Funan ruler shared his spiritual prowess with his loyal followers. As discussed in chapter 2, the Funan ruler's legitimacy was rooted in that region's traditional understanding of chieftainship (pon), in which a network of client populations and chiefs owed their loyalty to that one among them who had demonstrated spiritual superiority. Similarly, as O. W. Wolters described the early Srivijaya polity, "the [Srivijaya] ruler was much more than a hoarder of material wealth . . . his influence promoted sensations of psychological well-being among his followers, for his person was the effective ceremonial centre" (Wolters: 1979a, 24).

By the fifteenth century, in contrast, there was new interest in more directly controlling the hinterland peoples, their production, and their access to foreign trade. This interest in establishing direct control changed the political structure of early Southeast Asian riverine system states. From their earlier grounding in localized Indic religiomystical systems that structured the relationship of the subordinate regions to the center, Southeast Asia's major polities had transformed themselves into states that were characterized by the downstream center's military administrative control over smaller upstream communities in its hinterland (Reid: 1988, 1994; Lieberman: 2003).

In the new era, access to Chinese and Western markets by a series of potentially competitive regional ports could no longer be dominated by a single regional entrepôt that successfully achieved Chinese dynastic designation as its "most favored" port-polity. New marketing options were serviced by the even more diverse multiethnic communities of Southeast Asia–based traders (Hall: 2008). Furthermore, the trading had become more intensive (in volume) and extensive (in the variety of items offered). Southeast Asia's trade was by the fifteenth century more than a peddling trade in luxury items. The new commercial port-polities of the Straits of Melaka region, for example, depended upon rice and other food imports to feed their cosmopolitan populations. A bulk trade in rice, salt, dried fish, pepper, and spices provisioned these developing commercial centers (Reid: 1988, 1995). In addition, as the volume of trade grew, revenue from it became an increasingly vital source of state income, even in land-based rice states such as Ayudhya, Dai Viet, and Java (Lieberman: 2003; Moertono: 1968; Baker: 2003). The increased demand for Southeast Asian products called for new delivery mechanisms, while the state's increased dependence on trade income called for new methods of control. The old mechanisms, so often dependent upon personal alliances and oaths of allegiance between courts and their hinterland chiefs, or perhaps even relying totally on the natural flow of products from the interior to the coast, were insufficient to meet the demand for Southeast Asian products in the new commercial age. To increase the flow of hinterland products to the coast, a greater degree of coast-hinterland economic and political unity was necessary, and this depended on more formalized commercial and cultural networking among and with hinterland populations.

MARITIME TRADE AND STATE DEVELOPMENT IN SOUTHEAST ASIA AT THE DAWN OF THE SIXTEENTH CENTURY

At the dawn of the European incursions, Southeast Asia's populations faced a dichotomy. The networks of international maritime exchange provided potential for a high degree of commercial and political integration, yet there was still a low level of state development among most of these populations.

Manpower, not land, was the state's principal asset. State elites were at the apex of alliance networks, acting as patrons of their populations, yet they were not the leaders of centralized polities. In other words, their states did not have administrative centers that dominated and effectively integrated subordinate population centers under elaborate systems of administration, justice, and protection.

In the Southeast Asian island world of the early sixteenth-century European sources, the initial efforts of local chiefs such as Humabon or Lapulapu to subordinate other chiefs (datu) involved the redistribution of a chief's own treasury for the purpose of drawing others under his authority. In the Straits of Melaka region the trend toward more integrated states realized itself in the political systems of Samudra-Pasai in the fourteenth century, and even more in the case of fifteenth-century Melaka, as described in chapter 9. Movement toward this level of integration had also been achieved a century earlier by Majapahit. Compared to earlier polities, the successful new maritime realm societies featured greater internal order, including greater societal integration and cultural consensus focused in a preeminent court as well as alliances between commercial sectors and rulers. The resulting political and economic strength allowed rulers to monopolize the production and redistribution of major commodities. Banda provides an interesting parallel to the Straits of Melaka realm in that there it was the commercial elite (the orang kaya) rather than the traditional political elite who assumed the leading role in mobilizing and monopolizing the production and distribution of fifteenth-century Banda's nutmeg and mace.

Before the entry of Europeans into Asia in the early sixteenth century, the increasing importance of internal trade in local products, spices, pepper, and various forest products, together with the intensity of competition among Southeast Asia's ports, had encouraged the important states in the island world and mainland to pursue a policy of territorial expansion to prevent the flow of these products to rival ports. The federations of port towns characteristic of earlier times disappeared, as the new states typically tolerated only one dominant port. Power extended from this port center over nearby ports and their interiors. The states also developed new product delivery mechanisms as well as greater agricultural productivity to sustain the expenses of the new centralizing states and their administrative hierarchies.

For this, a greater degree of upstream-downstream unity was necessary to increase the flow of hinterland products to the coast. Earlier entrepôts had been concerned only with extending their control over other ports and had not been interested in or able to effectively annex the lands and people of the rival ports' upstreams. By contrast, the emerging fifteenth-century polities' authority penetrated more deeply into the hinterlands even of the rival river systems. There was a parallel change in governance structure. Previously, statecraft had been based on the religiomystical loyalty of the subordinate regions to the center, but now states also sought to establish military-administrative control over the small communities in the upstream hinterland. Thus, by the beginning of the sixteenth century there had emerged a substantial group of Southeast Asians who had been freed from subsistence agriculture and traditional social structures, were preoccupied with trade and commerce, and were part of a new, cosmopolitan, urban, commercial society.

The emergence of this group, whose activities have been richly evident in the closing chapters of this book, as in other recent studies by regional specialists, belies the assumption of many late nineteenth- and early twentieth-century historians that at the beginning of the sixteenth century there were no elements of Western capitalism in Southeast Asia and particularly that there was "no native middle group carrying out trade on its own account" (Meilink-Roelofsz: 1962, 8–9). Sixteenth- and seventeenth-century European explorers had actually been surprisingly perceptive about Southeast Asian society and its cultural milieu. But historians of the nineteenth and twentieth century molded Southeast Asia's history to fit the preconceived assumption that Southeast Asians had accomplished nothing except when foreigners such as the Chinese, the Indians, and later the Europeans had imposed themselves and provided direction to the otherwise helpless native populations. In this view, Indians and Chinese had helped Southeast Asians to become civilized in earlier times, and from the sixteenth century onward it was the Europeans' turn to lift Southeast Asian civilization to new heights, especially introducing Southeast Asia to the capitalist economic and social order (Abu-Lughod: 1989; Frank: 1998; Modelski and Thompson: 1996; Bentley: 1993).

This book challenges such views throughout. In the early chapters we saw the importance of local dynamics in the rise of states like Funan, Srivijaya, and the kingdoms of central and eastern Java. We saw that even the earliest of these states were often built on the products of trade networks. But trade could be a double-edged sword. One major consequence of the growing foreign demand for Southeast Asian products from the thirteenth century onward, an era previous to any significant European presence, was the emergence in maritime Southeast Asia of indigenous commercial groups (orang kaya) who began to challenge the rule of previous elites, though in some places they assumed prominence as the supporters of these elites. Banda, a kingless state, was administered by the coastal merchant (orang kaya) oligarchy that was delegated as commercial agents of the traditional communal communities of the upstream.

The emergence of assorted trade-related diasporas added complexity to the political picture. In Melaka, for example, a social contract prevailed between the ruler and subject populations. The court's chronicle saw this relationship as the source of a stable political and economic environment based in the court's leadership over the networked residential districts of the port. But the early Portuguese account by Tomé Pires cites the networked rather than unitary government of Melaka as significantly contributing to Melaka's fall to the Portuguese. Some of the unassimilated merchant diasporas did not remain loyal to the Melaka monarch when it became clear that the Portuguese forces were militarily superior. Reasoning that a relationship with the Portuguese would be critical to the continuance of their leading commercial role in Melaka's lucrative trade, they quickly transferred their loyalty to the Portuguese, thus replacing one political alliance with another (Thomaz: 2000; L. Andaya: 2008, 77–81). Nevertheless, while this development aided the Europeans, it also fit an ongoing pattern of shifting alliances, favoring the political authority holding the most power, which was consistent with the traditionally fragile Malay political systems outlined above.

Overall, it could be said that trade was the engine that drove political development in the fifteenth-century coastal world of Southeast Asia. Local land-based rulers initially patronized trade and traders, utilizing trade-derived revenues to build a more centralized and continuous state order. When their commercial elites began to challenge the rulers' authority, the indigenous land-based rulers were forced to assume an even more direct relationship with trade, in some instances establishing royal monopolies over the flow of trade within their domains (Birch: 1875–1884, 87–88). Above all, Southeast Asian rulers needed trade-derived revenues to finance their lavish monarchies and imported luxuries to sustain their politically critical ritualized redistributions to their loyal following. Increased trade volumes also led to the rise of Chinese and other foreign middlemen.

It was once thought that the rise of these middlemen was a consequence of the Europeans' initiation of the capitalist economic order, which encouraged Chinese and others to facilitate the flow of goods from the interior to the European coastal enclaves. However, it now appears that it was the rulers themselves who initially encouraged Chinese and other foreign traders to move into their states as allies in their struggle for political dominance against traditional landed and religious elite. Java's rulers used foreign merchants as delegated revenue collectors in their hinterlands, and there as in other cases they were an alternative to the native commercial classes linked to the ruler's regional opponents who might challenge the authority of the traditional political oligarchy. Thus it was that Humabon solicited Magellan's crew's support against Lapulapu in the attempt to consolidate his political and economic hold over the Cebu and Mactan coasts, noted in chapter 9. In doing so, he was consistent with the earlier monarchs of Srivijaya, who had previously recruited Straits of Melaka maritime diasporas as their periodic supporters.

All this revolved around a shifting array of networked political centers that provided economic and political leadership and also served as the source of a common cultural identity among their subordinate populations. Early Southeast Asian centers were the primary node among a chain of patron-client relationships, with the state-level center attempting to maintain itself economically, politically, and culturally against the centrifugal forces of secondary regional alliance networks. The local level, reinforced by kinship and economic ties, had permanence, but the primary center was vulnerable. At the secondary level, the immediate clients of local patrons or "big men"—for example, landed elites or tribal chiefs—would remain loyal to their leaders until the local civilization was destroyed. However, when the state center demonstrated the least sign of weakness, its clients rapidly began to express their independence.

Yet though the networked state center was vulnerable, its loss was crucial to the local society, for the center provided unity among the various competing local units, if not on a political and economic level then at least in a cultural sense. In the early Southeast Asian world, with the loss of central authority regional, units competed with each other to become the new center, building new networks of economic and political alliance and underscoring these economic and political relationships by establishing new sources of cultural legitimacy. They did this, for example, by converting from syncretic Hindu and Buddhist religious systems to the Islamic and Theravada Buddhist religious traditions (or, in the case of Dai Viet, to the local synthesis of the Vietnamese and sinic Neoconfucian traditions). Legitimacy might also be substantiated by fabricating links with eras of past glory, as in the case of Melaka looking backward to the Srivijayan age. Centers that failed to initiate such new networked linkages languished as their populations lapsed into more isolated and internalized secondary economic, political, and social realms.

Even the agrarian populations subordinate to these state centers were far from static. In the thirteenth through fifteenth centuries, a return to an older order of existence might have been desired but was impossible to achieve because the structure of societies, their economic and social organizations, and their perceptions of the world had been affected by the penetration of new commercial and cultural concerns from the outside. There were new expectations among the local societies that had to be fulfilled. For instance, during the glory years of indigenous participation in the supralocal patterns of trade, the local peasantry had achieved a new standard of living. Consequently, they expected the continued redistribution of wealth from the state centers and the provision of or access to certain trade goods like ceramics, spices, and cloth that had become necessities of life.

Within the new fourteenth- and fifteenth-century Southeast Asian centers, the traditional societies and foreign cultures continually intersected on mainland Southeast Asia and in the island realm (as depicted in figure 10.1). Though these interactions sometimes precipitated open conflict, it was also within such networked centers that the synthesis of traditional and modern took place, if indeed the process of change can be reduced to this opposition. Among some secondary segments of the indigenous population, foreign cultures were fully accepted and traditional ways of doing things were rejected as being backward and the cause of economic and political instabilities. This was the case in the new Islamic ports of trade on Java's north coast, which during the fifteenth century separated from the Majapahit state and its rich Javanese traditions. Others chose the opposite course, totally rejecting new opportunities or cultures while reaffirming their old cultural norms, in which state elite explained difficulties that arose as being due to corruptions to the traditional system and stressed the need to return to the "pure" cultural forms of a past golden age (Vickery: 1977; Whitmore: 2006; Aung Thwin: 2005). A third group attempted a middle way between the other two, selecting the best of its own society while accommodating those foreign ways considered necessary to survival in the ever more complex world order. In such polities indigenous political and economic leaders came to terms with their past and present to articulate a future for their world.

This tendency toward multiculturalism was especially pronounced by 1500 in coastal centers such as Melaka, which had emerged to be what Anthony Reid has called a "cosmopolis" (Reid: 1999a, 2004). In Reid's view, by the early 1500s Southeast Asian centers of international exchange were characterized by their heterarchy rather than hierarchy. That is, the major port communities were composed of residents who had clear understandings of their differing ethnicities, lived in separate ethnic compounds, were productive as ethnic communities, and negotiated trade as understood ethnic communities. They were more or less equals in the price-making marketplace, which had continuing elements of the traditional reciprocity and redistribution networks that were still foundational to the hinterland monarchies.

Victor Lieberman asserts a similar characteristic of the transition from what he calls Southeast Asia's "charter states" to a new post-1500 age (Lieberman: 2003). Lieberman notes that the hinterland courts of the Southeast Asian mainland had by that time similarly developed their own distinctive cultural forms, which were conveyed in written texts and political and religious institutions that reinforced the local sense of membership in a shared culture that was, however, different than that of their neighbors. Thus Bur-

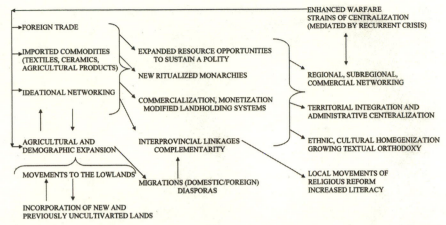

Figure 10.1. Southeast Asian Development and Interactions, ca. 1400–1500 (adapted from Lieberman: 2003, 65)

mese and Thai lived side by side, but no longer engaged in the peaceful cultural exchanges that had been common in the earlier age, and engaged in periodic warfare that had material consequences rather than the lofty symbolic or plunder ambitions of the past. They were segregated polities that had goals of territorial annexation to acquire control over ongoing productive human and economic resources. In this new order there was less concern that the monarch was magically empowered or that war was not about territorial annexations, but driven by local networked reciprocity and redistribution expectations. There was now a more secular monarchy in Dai Viet, but even there spirituality remained important, and it was now articulated in different ways in new Southeast Asian Islamic and Buddhist monarchies, which were foundational to what Reid has called "the new age of commerce" (Reid: 1988, 1994).

Abbreviations Used in References and in Citations

ARE	*Annual Reports on Epigraphy* (Archaeological Survey of India, various)
BEFEO	*Bulletin de l'Ecole Francaise d'Extreme-Orient* (Hanoi, Saigon, Paris)
BKI	*Bijdragen tot de Taal-, Land-, en Vokenkunde (van Nederlandsch-Indie), uitgegeven door het Koninklikj Instituut voor Taal-, Land-, en Volkenkunde (van Nederlandsch-indie)* (s'Gravenhage, Leiden)
BSOAS	*Bulletin of the School of Oriental and African Studies* (London)
EI	*Epigraphica Indica* (Archaeological Survey of India, various)
EZ	*Epigraphia Zeylanica* (Columbo)
IC	*Inscriptions du Cambodge*, Coedes: 1937–1966
JAS	*Journal of Asian Studies* (Ann Arbor)
JESHO	*Journal of the Economic and Social History of the Orient* (Leiden)
JMBRAS	*Journal of the Malay/Malaysian Branch of the Royal Asiatic Society* (Singapore, Kuala Lumpur)
JRAS	*Journal of the Royal Asiatic Society* (London)
JSEAH	*Journal of Southeast Asian History* (Singapore)
JSEAS	*Journal of Southeast Asian Studies* (Singapore)
RIMA	*Review of Indonesian and Malaysian Affairs* (various)
SII	*South Indian Inscriptions* (Archaeological Survey of India, various)
TBG	*Tijdschrift voor Indische Taal-, Land- en Volkenkunde*

uitgegeven door het Koninklijk Bataviaasch Genotschap (Batavia, s'Gravenhage)

TT   *Dai Viet Su Ky Toan Thu* [Complete Book of the Chronicle of Dai Viet] (Hanoi: NXB Khao Hoc Xa Hoi, 1998).

References

Abraham, Meera. 1988. *Two Medieval Merchant Guilds of South India*. New Delhi: Manohar.

Abu-Lughod, Janet. 1989. *Before European Hegemony: The World System AD 1250–1350*. New York: Oxford University Press.

Aelast, Arjan Van. 1995. "Majapahit Picis, The Currency of a 'Moneyless' Society 1300–1700." *BKI* 151 (3): 357–93.

Aeusrivongse, Nidhi. 1976. "*Devaraja* Cult and Khmer Kingship at Angkor." In *Explorations in Early Southeast Asian History*, ed. Hall and Whitmore, 107–49. Ann Arbor, MI: Center for South and Southeast Asian Studies.

Andaya, Barbara Watson. 1978. "The Indian Saudagar Raja (the King's Merchant) in Traditional Malay Courts." *JMBRAS* 51 (1): 13–36.

———. 1989. "Cloth Trade in Jambi and Palembang during the Seventeenth and Eighteenth Centuries." *Indonesia* 48:26–46.

———. 1993a. *To Live as Brothers, Southeast Sumatra in the Seventeenth and Eighteenth Centuries*. Honolulu: University of Hawaii Press.

———. 1993b. "Cash Cropping and Upstream-Downstream Tensions: The Case of Jambi in the Seventeenth and Eighteenth Centuries." In *Southeast Asia in the Early Modern Era*, ed. Reid, 91–122. Ithaca, NY: Cornell University Press.

———. 1997. "Raiding Cultures and Interior-Coastal Migration in Early Modern Island Southeast Asia." In *Empires, Imperialism, and Southeast Asia: Essays in Honour of Nicholas Tarling*, ed. Brook Barrington. Monash, Australia: Center for Southeast Asian Studies, 1–16.

———. 2003. "Aspects of Warfare in Premodern Southeast Asia." *JESHO* 46 (2): 139–42.

Andaya, Barbara Watson, and Yoneo Ishii. 1992. "Religious Developments in Southeast Asia, c. 1500–1800." In *Cambridge History of Southeast Asia*, ed. Tarling, vol. 1, 508–71. Cambridge: Cambridge University Press.

Andaya, Barbara Watson, and Hiroshue Masashi. 1994. "Port Polities and Hinterlands in North Sumatra." Unpublished paper presented at the Thirteenth International Conference of the Association of Historians of Asia, Tokyo.

Andaya, Leonard Y. 1991. "Local Trade Networks in Maluku in the Sixteenth, Seventeenth, and Eighteenth Centuries." *Cakalele: Maluku Research Journal* 2 (2): 71–96.

———. 1993a. "Cultural State Formation in Eastern Indonesia." In *Southeast Asia in the Early Modern Era*, ed. Reid, 23–41. Ithaca, NY: Cornell University Press.

————. 1993b. *The World of Maluku: Eastern Indonesia in the Early Modern Period*. Honolulu: University of Hawaii Press.

————. 2008. *Leaves of the Same Tree: Trade and Ethnicity in the Straits of Melaka*. Honolulu: University of Hawaii Press.

Aoyagi, Yogi, and Gakuji Hasebe, eds. 2002. *Champa Ceramics Production and Trade—Excavation Report of the Go Sanh Kiln Sites in Central Vietnam*. Tokyo: Study Group of Go Sanh Kiln Sites in Central Vietnam, Tokyo University Foreign Studies.

Appadurai, Arjun, and Carol Appadurai Breckenridge. 1976. "The South Indian Temple: Authority, Honour, and Redistribution." *Contributions to Indian Sociology* (New Series) 10 (2): 187–211.

Auboyer, J. 1977. "Aspects de l'art bouddhique au pays khmer aux temps de Jayavarman VII." In *Mahayana Art after AD 900*, ed. William Watson, 66–74. London: Percival David Foundation of Chinese Art.

Aung Thwin, Michael. 1976a. "The Problem of Ceylonese-Burmese Relations in the Twelfth Century and the Question of an Interregnum in Pagan: 1165–1174 AD." *JSS* 64 (1): 53–74.

————. 1976b. "Kingship, the *Sangha*, and Society in Pagan." In *Explorations in Early Southeast Asian History*, ed. Hall and Whitmore, 205–56. Ann Arbor, MI: Center for South and Southeast Asian Studies.

————. 1979. "The Role of Sasana Reform in Burmese History: Economic Dimensions of a Religious Purification." *JAS* 38 (4): 671–92.

————. 1983. "Divinity, Spirit, and Human: Conceptions of Classical Burmese Kingship." In *Centers, Symbols, and Hierarchies: Essays on the Classical State of Southeast Asia*, ed. Lorraine Gesick, 45–86. New Haven, CT: Yale University Southeast Asia Program.

————. 1985. *Pagan: The Origins of Modern Burma*. Honolulu: University of Hawaii Press.

————. 1987. "Heaven, Earth and the Supernatural World: Dimensions of the Exemplary Centre in Burmese History." In *The City as a Sacred Center: Essays on Six Asian Contexts*, ed. Bardwell Smith and Holly Baker Reynolds, 88–102. Oxford: Oxford University Press.

————. 1990. *Irrigation in the Heartland of Burma: Foundations of the Precolonial Burmese State*. Oxford, OH: Ohio University Press.

————. 1991. "Spirals in Early Southeast Asian and Burmese History." *Journal of Interdisciplinary Studies* 21 (4): 575–602.

————. 1998. *Myth and History in the Historiography of Early Burma*. Athens, OH: Institute of Southeast Asian Studies.

————. 2002. "Lower Burma and Bago in the History of Burma." In *The Maritime Frontier of Burma*, ed. Gommans and Leider, 25–58. Leiden, Netherlands: KITLV.

————. 2005. *The Mists of Ramanna: The Legend that Was Lower Burma*. Honolulu: University of Hawaii Press.

————. 2011. "A New/Old Look at 'Classical' and 'Post-Classical' Southeast Asia/Burma." In *New Perspectives in the History and Historiography of Southeast Asia, Continuing Explorations*, ed. Aung-Thwin and Hall. London: Routledge.

————. Forthcoming. *Ava and Pegu: A Tale of Two Kingdoms—Burma in the Fifteenth Century*.

Aung-Thwin, Michael, and Kenneth R. Hall, eds. 2011. *New Perspectives in the History and Historiography of Southeast Asia, Continuing Explorations*. London: Routledge.

Aymonier, Etienne. 1891a. *Les Tchames et leur religions*. Paris: Ernest Leroux.

————. 1891b. "Premiere etude sur les inscriptions Tchames." *JA* 17 (1): 5–187.

————. 1900–1904. *Le Cambodge*. Paris: Ernest Leroux.

Baker, Chris. 2003. "Ayutthaya's Rise: From Land or Sea?" *JSEAS* 34 (1): 41–62.

Bandaranayake Senake et al., eds. 1990. *Sri Lanka and the Silk Road of the Sea*. Columbo: National Commission for UNESCO.

Barnes, Ruth. 2002. "Indian Trade Textiles: Sources and Transmission of Design." Unpublished paper presented at the University of Michigan–Ann Arbor.

Barrett Jones, Antoinette M. 1968. "Two Old Javanese Copper-plate Inscriptions of Balitung." Unpublished MA thesis, University of Sydney.

———. 1984. *Early Tenth Century Java from the Inscriptions, A Study of Economic, Social and Administrative Conditions in the First Quarter of the Century*. Dordrecht, Netherlands: Foris Publications.

Barth, A., and A. Bergaigne. 1885–1893. *Inscriptions sanscrites de Campa et du Cambodge*. Paris: Imprimerie Nationale.

Basham, A. L. 1954. *The Wonder that Was India*. London: Sidgwick and Jackson.

Bautier, R. H. 1971. *The Economic Development of Medieval Europe*. New York: HBJ.

Begley, Vimala, et al. 1996–2004. *The Ancient Port of Arikamedu, New Excavation and Researches*. 2 vols. Paris, Pondichery: L'Ecole Francaise d'Extreme-Orient.

Bellwood, Peter. 1997. *Pre-History of the Indo-Malaysian Archipelago*. Honolulu: University of Hawaii Press.

Bellwood, Peter, and Ian Glover, eds. 2004. *Southeast Asia From Pre-History to History*. London: RoutledgeCurzon.

Bentley, Jerry H. 1993. *Old World Encounters: Cross-Cultural Contacts and Exchanges in Pre-Modern Times*. New York: Oxford University Press.

Bernet-Kempers, A. J. 1959. *Ancient Indonesian Art*. Cambridge, MA: Harvard University Press.

Birch, Walter de Gray, ed. and trans. 1875–1884. *The Commentaries of the Great Alfonso D'Albuquerque, Second Viceroy of India*. London: Hakluyt Society.

Bishop, Paul, David Sanderson, et al. 2004. "OSL and Radiocarbon Dating of a pre-Angkorian Canal in the Mekong Delta, Southern Cambodia." *Journal of Archaeological Science* 31:319–36.

Blair, Emma Helen, and James Alexander Robertson, eds. 1903–1909. *The Philippine Islands, 1493–1898*. Cleveland, OH: A.H. Clark.

Boechari. n.d. *Prasasti Kalirungan*. Unpublished manuscript, Jakarta National Museum.

———. 1965. "Epigraphy and Indonesian Historiography." In *An Introduction to Indonesian Historiography*, ed. Soedjatmoko et al., 50–60. Ithaca, NY: Cornell University Press.

———. 1966. "Preliminary Report on the Discovery of an Old Malay Inscription at Sodjomerta." *Madjalah Ilmu-Ilmu Sastra Indonesia* 2–3:241–51.

———. 1967–1968. "Rakryan Mahamantri I Hino: A Study of the Highest Court Dignitary of Ancient Java up to the Thirteenth Century AD." *Journal of the Historical Society, University of Singapore*, 7–20.

———. 1968. "Sri Maharaja Mapanji Garasakan; a New Evidence on the Problem of Arlanga's Partition of His Kingdom." *Majalah Ilmu-ilmu Sastra* 4:1–26.

———. 1979. "Some Considerations on the Problem of the Shift of Mataram's Centre of Government from Central to East Java in the Tenth Century." In *Early South East Asia: Essays in Archaeology, History and Historical Geography*, ed. R. B. Smith and W. Watson, 473–91. Oxford: Oxford University Press.

Boisselier, Jean. 1952. "Reflexions sur l'art du Jayavarman VII." *BSEI* 27 (3): 261–73.

———. 1966. *Le Cambodge, Asie du Sud-Est*. Vol. 1. Paris: A. & J. Picard & Cie.

———. 1970. "Pouvoir royal et symbolisme de architectural: Nak Pean et son importance pour la royaute Angkorienne." *Arts Asiatiques* 21:92–109.

Bonatz, Dominik. 2006. "Kerinci-Archaeological Research in the Highlands of Jambi on Sumatra." In *Uncovering Southeast Asia's Past*, ed. Elisabeth A. Bacus, Ian C. Glover, and Vincent C. Pigott, 310–24. Singapore: University of Singapore Press.

Boomgaard, Peter. 2007. *Southeast Asia, An Environmental History*. Oxford: ABC-CLIO.

Boon Kheng, Cheah. 1998. "The Rise and Fall of the Great Melakan Empire: Moral Judgement in Tun Bambang's *Sejarah Melayu*." *JMBRAS* 71:104–21.

Bourdieu, Pierre. 1977. *Outline of a Theory of Practice*. Cambridge: Cambridge University Press.

Bourdonneau, Eric. 2003. "Culturalisme et historiographie du Cambodge ancien: a propos de la hierarchisation des sourced de l'histoire khmere." *Moussons* 7:39–70.

———. 2004. "The Ancient Canal System of the Mekong Delta: A Preliminary Report." In *Fishbones and Glittering Emblems: Southeast Asian Archaeology 2002*, ed. A. Kiristrom and A. Kallen, 257–70. Stockholm: Museum of Far Eastern Antiquities.

Bourge, H. de Mestier du. 1970. "La premiere moitie du XIe siecle au Cambodge: Suryavarman Ier sa vie et quelques aspects des institutions son epoque." *JA* 258 (3–4): 281–314.

Bowen, John R. 1993. *Muslims through Discourse: Religion and Ritual in Gayo Society*. Princeton, NJ: Princeton University Press.

Braginsky, Vladirmir. 1998. "Sufi Boat Symbolism: Problems of Origin and Evolution." *Indonesia and the Malay World* 26:50–64.

———. 2004. *The Heritage of Traditional Malay Literature*. Leiden, Netherlands: KITLV.

Brandes, J. L. A. (ed. N. J. Krom). 1913. *Oud-Javaansche Oorkonden*. The Hague: *Verhandelinen van het Bataviaasch Genootschap van Kunsten en Wetenschappen* 60.

Briggs, Lawrence Palmer. 1951. "The Ancient Khmer Empire." *Transactions of the American Philosophical Society*, New Series, 41, 1, 1–295.

Brocheux, Pierre. 1995. *The Mekong Delta*, Madison, WI: Center for Southeast Asian Studies.

Bronson, Bennet. 1977. "Exchange at the Upstream and Downstream Ends: Notes towards a Functional Model of the Coastal State in Southeast Asia." In *Economic Exchange and Social Interaction*, ed. Hutterer, 39–52. [Place? Publisher?]

———. 1992. "Patterns of the Early Southeast Asian Metals Trade." In *Early Metallurgy, Trade and Urban Centres*, ed. Glover et al., 63–114. Bangkok: White Lotus.

———. 1996. "Chinese and Middle Eastern trade in southern Thailand during the 9th century A.D." In *Ancient Trades and Cultural Contacts in Southeast Asia*, ed. A. Srisuchat, 181–200. Bangkok: Office of the National Culture Commission.

Bronson, Bennet, and Jan Wisseman. 1976. "Palembang as Srivijaya: The Lateness of Early Cities in Southern Southeast Asia." *Asian Perspectives* 19 (2): 220–39.

Brown, Robert L. 1996. *The Dvaravati Wheels of the Law and the Indianization of South East Asia*. Leiden, Netherlands: E. J. Brill.

Brown, Roxanna. 1988. *The Ceramics of South-East Asia*. Singapore: Oxford University Press.

———. 2008a. "Champa Prisoners as Chu-Dau Potters?" Paper abstract, Third International Conference of Vietnamese Studies, Hanoi.

———. 2008b. *The Ming Gap and Shipwreck Ceramics in Southeast Asia: Towards a Chronology of Thai Trade Ware*. Bangkok: River Books.

———. 2010. "Gap? Data from Shipwreck Cargoes." In *Southeast Asia in the Fifteenth Century: The China Factor*, ed. G. Wade and Sun Laichen. Singapore: National University of Singapore Press.

Brown, Roxanna, and Sten Sjostrand. 2000. *Turiang: A Fourteenth Century Wreck in Southeast Asian Waters*. Pasadena, CA: Pacific Asia Museum.

Buchari. 1963. "A Preliminary Note on the Study of the Old-Javanese Civil Administration." *Madjalah Ilmu-Ilmu Sastra Indonesia* 1:122–33.

Burger, D. H. 1956. *Structural Changes in Javanese Society: The Supra-Village Sphere*. Trans. L. Palmier. Ithaca, NY: Cornell Modern Indonesia Project.

Burma Archaeological Department. 1972. *She Haung Myanma Kyauksa Mya* [Ancient Burmese Inscriptions]. Rangoon, Burma: Burma Archaeological Department.

Cadiere, Leopold, 1989. *Religious Beliefs and Practices of the Vietnamese*. Trans. Ian W. Mabbett. Victoria: Centre of South East Asian Studies.

Caldwell, Ian, and Ann Appleby Hazlewood. 1994. "The Holy Footprint of the Venerable Gautama; A New Translation of the Pasir Panjang Inscription." *BKI* 150 (3): 457–79.

Callenfels, P. V. Stein. 1924. "Stukken Betrekking Hebbend op Oud Javaansche Opschriften in de Bibliotheque Nationale to Paris." *Oudheidkundig Verslag*, 23–27.

Casparis, J. G. de. 1941. "Nogmaals de Sanskrit-inscriptie op den steen van Dinojo." *TBG* 81:499–514.

————. 1950. *Inscripties uit de Cailendra-Tijd. Prasasti Indonesia I*. Bandung, Indonesia: A. C. Nix.

————. 1956. *Prasasti Indonesia II: Selected Inscriptions from the Seventh to the Ninth Century AD*. Bandung, Indonesia: A. C. Nix.

————. 1961. "New Evidence on Cultural Relations between Java and Ceylon in Ancient Times." *Artibus Asiae* 24:241–48.

————. 1967. "The Date of the Grahi Buddha." *JSS* 55 (1): 31–40.

————. 1975. *Indonesian Palaeography; A History of Writing in Indonesia from the Beginnings to c. AD 1500*. Leiden, Netherlands: E. J. Brill.

————. 1981. "Pour une histoire social de l'ancienne Java, principalement au Xième S." *Archipel* 21:125–54.

————. 1986. "The Evolution of the Socio-economic status of the East Javanese Village and Its Inhabitants." In *Papers of the Fourth Indonesian-Dutch History Conference*, ed. Sartono Kartodirdjo, 3–24. Yogakarta, Indonesia: Gadja Mada University Press.

Cayron, Jun G. 2006. *Stringing the Past: An Archaeological Understanding of Early Southeast Asia Glass Bead Trade*. Quezon City: University of the Philippines Press.

Chaffee, John. 2008. "At the Intersection of Empire and World Trade: The Chinese Port City of Quanzhou (Zaitun), Eleventh to Fifteenth Centuries." In *Secondary Cities*, ed. Hall, 99–122. Lanham, MD: Lexington.

Chakravarti, Ranabir. 1989. "Overseas Trade in Horses in Early Medieval India: Shipping and Piracy." In *Prachi Prabha, Perspectives in Indology: Essays in Honour of Professor B. N. Mukherjee*, ed. D. G. Battacharya and Devendra Handa, 343–60. New Delhi, Sundeep Prakashan.

————. 1999. "Early Medieval Bengal and the Trade in Horses: A Note." *JESHO* 42 (2): 194–211.

Chamberlain, James R., ed. 1991. *The Ram Kamheng Controversy: Collected Papers*. Bangkok: Siam Society.

Chan, Hok-lam. 1968. "The 'Chinese Barbarian Officials' in the Foreign Tribute Missions to China During the Ming Dynasty." *Journal of the American Oriental Society* 88:411–18.

Chandler, David P. 1983. "Going Through the Motions: Ritual Aspects of the Reign of King Duang of Cambodia (1848–1860)." In *Centers, Symbols, and Hierarchies: Essays on the Classical States of Southeast Asia*, ed. Lorraine Gesick, 106–24. New Haven, CT: Yale University Southeast Asia Program.

————. 1992. *A History of Cambodia*. Boulder, CO: Westview.

Chandler, David P., and I. W. Mabbett. 1995. *The Khmers*. Oxford: Blackwell.

Chang, Pin-tsun. 1991. "The First Chinese Diaspora in Southeast Asia in the Fifteenth Century." In *Emporia, Commodities and Entrepreneurs in Asian Maritime Trade, c. 1400–1750*, ed. Roderich Pak and Dietmar Rothermund, 13–28. Stuttgart: Steiner Verlag.

Changli, Zhu. 1993. "The Southern Overland Silk Route Eco-Cultural Exchanges between China, India, and Burma." *Indica* 30 (1–2): 23–45.

Charney, Michael. 1997. "Shallow-draft Boats, Guns, and the Aye-ra-wa-ti, Continuity and Change in Ship Structure and River Warfare in Precolonial Myanmar." *Oriens Extremus* 40 (1): 16–49.

Chatterjee, B. R. 1933. *India and Java*. Calcutta: Greater India Society.

Chaudhuri, K. N. 1985. *Trade and Civilisation in the Indian Ocean: An Economic History from the Rise of Islam to 1750*. Cambridge: Cambridge University Press.

Christie, A. H. 1979. "Lin-i, Fu-nan, Java." In *Early South East Asia*, ed. Smith and Watson, 281–87. London: Oxford University Press.

Chulalongkorn University, eds. 1984. *The Inscription of King Ramkhamhaeng the Great*. Bangkok: Chulalongkorn University.

Chutintaranond, Sunait, ed. 2002. *Recalling Local Pasts: Autonomous Histories in Southeast Asia*, Chiang Mai, Thailand: Silkworm.

Clark, Hugh. 1995. "Muslims and Hindus in the Culture and Morphology of Quanzhou from the Tenth to the Thirteenth Century." *Journal of World History* 6 (1): 54–63.

Clark, Joyce, ed. 2007. *Bayon, New Perspectives*. Bangkok: River Books.

Coedes, George. 1906. "La Stele de Ta-Prohm." *BEFEO* 6:44–81.

———. 1911. "Les deux inscriptions de Vat Thipdei." *Melanges d'Indianisme, offert par ses eleves a M. Sylvain Levi*. Paris: Leroux, 213–29

———. 1931. "Deux inscriptions Sanskrites du Fou-nan." *BEFEO* 31:1–12.

———. 1937–1966. *Inscriptions du Cambodge*. Hanoi, Paris: Ecole Francaise d'Extreme Orient.

———. 1940a. "Les hopitaux de Jayavarman VII." *BEFEO* 40:344–47.

———. 1940b. "Les sites d'etape a la fin du XIIe siecle." *BEFEO* 40:347–49.

———. 1941. "La Stele du Prah Khan d'Angkor." *BEFEO* 41:256–301.

———. 1943. "L'Inscription de Sdok Kak Thom." *BEFEO* 43:57–134.

———. 1960. "Le portrait dans l'art khmer." *Artibus Asia* 7 (3): 179–88.

———. 1961. *Recueil des inscriptions du Siam. Deuxieme partie. Inscriptions de Dvaravati, Crivijaya et de Lavo*. Bangkok: Vijiranana Library.

———. 1962. *Recueil des Inscriptions du Siam, Deuxieme Partie: Inscriptions de Dvaravati, de Crivijaya et de Lavo*. Bangkok: Siam Society.

———. 1966a. "Les Mons de Dvaravati." In *Essays Offered to G. H. Luce by his Friends in Honour of his Seventy-fifth Birthday*, ed. Shin, Ba, Jean Boisselier, and A. B. Griswold, 122–16. Ascona, Switzerland: Artibus Asiae.

———. 1966b. *The Making of Southeast Asia*. Berkeley: University of California Press.

———. 1968. *The Indianized States of Southeast Asia*. Ed. Walter F. Vella. Honolulu: University of Hawaii Press.

Coedes, G., and L. C. Damais. 1992. *Sriwijaya: History, Religion, and Language of an Early Malay Polity*. Ed. P. Y. Manguin. Kuala Lumpur: Malaysian Branch of the Royal Asiatic Society.

Coedes, George, and P. Dupont. 1943–1946. "Les steles de Sdok Kak Thom, Phnom Sandak et Prah Vihar." *BEFEO* 43:56–154.

Colless, Brian E. 1975a. "Majapahit Revisited: External Evidence on the Geography and Ethnology of East Java in the Majapahit Period." *JMBRAS* 48(2): 124–61.

———. 1975b. "A Note on the Names of the Kings of Java in the Ming History." *BKI* 131 (4): 487–89.

Cooler, Richard M. 2010. "The Pre-Pagan Period: The Urban Age of the Mon and the Pyu." Chapter 2 in *The Art and Culture of Burma* (online publication). www.seasite.niu.edu/burmese/Cooler/BurmaArt_TOC.htm (accessed July 12, 2010).

Cortesao, A. 1944. *A Translation of the Suma Oriental of Tome Pires, an Account of the East, from the Red Sea to Japan, Written in Malacca and India in 1512–1515*. London: Hakluyt Society.

Creel, H. G. 1965. "The Role of the Horse in Chinese History." *American Historical Review* 70 (3): 647–72.

Creese, Helen. 1997. *In Search of Majapahit: The Transformation of Balinese Identities*. Monash: Centre for South and Southeast Asian Studies.

Cummings, William P. 2007. *A Chain of Kings: The Makassarese Chronicles of Gowa and Talloq*. Leiden: KITLV Press.

———. 2011. *The Makassar Annals*. Leiden: KITLV Press.

Cuong Tu, Nguyen. 1998. *Zen in Medieval Vietnam: A Study and Translation of the Thien Uyen Tap Anh*. Honolulu: University of Hawaii Press.

Dai Viet Su Toan Thu (TT), Complete Book of the Chronicle of Dai Viet. 1998. 4 vols. Hanoi: NXB Khoa Hoc Xa Hoi.

Dalsheimer, N. and P. Y. Manguin. 1998. "Visnu mirres et rereseaux marchands en Asie du Sud Est: nouvelle donnees archeologiques sur le Iermillenaire apr. JC." *BEFEO* 85:87–123.

Damais, L. C. 1952– 1954. "Etudes d'epigraphie Indonesienne, III. Liste des principales inscriptions datees de l'Indonesie." *BEFEO* 46:1–105.

———. 1955. "Etudes d'epigraphie Indonesienne, IV. Discussion de Ia date des inscriptions." *BEFEO* 47:7–290.

———. 1968. "L'epigraphie Musulmane dans le SudEst Asiatique." *BEFEO* 54 (2): 353–415.

———. 1970. *Répertoire onomastique de l'épigraphie javanaise jusqu'à Pu Sindok sri Isanawik-rama dharmmotungadewa: Étude d'épigraphie indonésienne.* Paris: École Française d'Extrême-Orient, 378–86.

Davidson, Jeremy N. C. S. 1975. "Recent Archaeological Activity in Viet-Nam." *Journal of the Hong Kong Archaeological Society* 6:80–99.

Day, Tony. 2002. *Fluid Iron, State Formation in Southeast Asia,* Honolulu: University of Hawaii Press.

Dhida, S. 1999. *Dvaravati. The Initial Phase of Siam's History.* Bangkok: Muang Boran Publishing.

Diem, Allison I. 1998–2001. "The Significance of Pandanan Shipwreck Ceramics on Evidence of Fifteenth Century Trading Relations within Southeast Asia." *Bulletin of the Oriental Ceramics Society of Hong Kong* 12:28–36.

———. 1999. "Ceramics from Vijaya, Central Vietnam: Internal Motivations and External Influences (Fourteenth–Late Fifteenth Centuries)." *Oriental Art* 45 (3): 55–64.

———. 2001. "Vietnamese Ceramics from the Pandanan Shipwreck Excavation in the Philippines." *Taoci, Revue Annuelle de la Societe Francaise d'Etude de la Ceramique Orientale* 2:87–93.

———. 2010. "The Significance of Cham Ceramic Evidence for Assessing Contacts Between Vijaya and Other Southeast Asian Polities During the Fourteenth and Fifteenth Centuries CE." In *The Cham of Vietnam: History, Society, and Art,* ed. Bruce Lockhart and Tran Ky Phuong. Singapore: National University of Singapore Press.

Dijk, L. C. van. 1983. "Dutch Relations with Borneo in the Seventeenth Century." *BMJ* 5 (3).

Doanh, Ngo Van. 2002. *Champa Ancient Towers: Reality and Legend.* Hanoi: The Gioi.

Donner, Fred M. 1986. "The Formation of the Islamic State." *Journal of the American Oriental Society* 106:283–96.

———. 1998. *Narratives of Islamic Origins: The Beginnings of Islamic Historical Writing.* Princeton, NJ: Darwin Press.

———. 1999. "Muhammad and the Caliphate, Political History of the Islamic Empire up to the Mongol Conquest." In *The Oxford History of Islam,* ed. John L. Esposito, 1–61. Oxford: Oxford University Press.

Dove, Michael. 1985. "The Agroecological Mythology of the Javanese and the Political Economy of Indonesia." *Indonesia* 39:1–36.

Drakard, Jane. 1982. "Upland-Downland Relationships in Barus: A Northwest Sumatran Case Study." In *The Malay-Islamic World of Sumatra,* ed. J. Maxwell, 74–95. Clayton, Australia: Monash Centre for Southeast Asian Studies.

———. 1989. "An Indian Port: Sources for the Earlier History of Barus." *Archipel* 37:53–83.

———. 1990. *A Malay Frontier: Unity and Duality in a Sumatran Kingdom.* Ithaca, NY: Cornell University Southeast Asia Program.

———. 1999. *A Kingdom of Words: Language and Power in Sumatra.* New York: Oxford University Press.

Dunn, F. L. 1975. *Rain Forest Collectors and Traders, A Study of Resource Utilization in Modern and Ancient Malaya.* Malaysian Branch of the Royal Asiatic Society (MBRAS), monograph 5. Kuala Lumpur: MBRAS.

Dupont, Pierre. 1942. "Le Buddha de Grahi et l'ecole de C'aiya." *BEFEO* 42:105–13.

Duroiselle, C. 1960. *Epigraphia Birmanica,* 1:II. Rangoon: Superintendent, Government Printing.

Dvaravati, S. Dhida. 1999. *The Initial Phase of Siam's History.* Bangkok: Muang Boran Publishing.

Ellen, Roy. 2003. On the Edge of the Banda Zone: Past and Present in the Social Organization of a Moluccan Trading Network. Honolulu: University of Hawaii Press.

Fenner, Bruce L. 1976. *Colonial Cebu: An Economic-Social History, 1521–1896.* Unpublished PhD dissertation, Cornell University.

Ferrand, Gabriel. 1913. *Relatons de voyages et texts geogaphiques arabes, persans et turks relatifs a l'Extreme-Orien du VIIIe siecles, traduits, revus et annotes.* Paris: Ernest Leroux.

———. 1922. *L'empire sumatranais de Crivijaya.* Paris: Paul Geuthner.

Filliozat, Jean. 1967–1968. "Agastya et la propagation du Brahmanisme." *Adyar Library Bulletin* 31–32:442–49.

Finot, Louis. 1903a. "L'inscription sancrite de Say-fong." *BEFEO* 3:18–33.

———. 1903b. "Panduranga." *BEFEO* 3:630–54.

———. 1904a. "Inscriptions du Quang Nam." *BEFEO*, 4:83–115.

———. 1904b. "L'Inscription de Preah Khan." *BEFEO* 4:672–75.

———. 1909. "Nouvelles inscriptions de Po Klaun Garai." *BEFEO* 9:205–9.

———. 1912. "L'inscription de Ban That." *BEFEO* 12:1–28.

———. 1915. "L'inscription de Sdok Kak Thom." *BEFEO* 15 (2): 53–106.

Finot L., and V. Goloubew. 1923. "Le symbolisme de Nak Pean." *BEFEO* 23:401–5.

Flecker, Michael. 2001. "A Ninth-Century AD Arab or Indian Shipwreck in Indonesia: First Evidence for Direct Trade with China." *World Archaeology* 32 (3): 335–54.

———. 2002. "The Archaeological Excavation of the Tenth-Century Intan Shipwreck." British Archaeological Reports International Series 1047. Oxford: Archaoepress.

———. 2009. "Maritime Archaeology in Southeast Asia." In *Southeast Asian Ceramics: New Light on Old Pottery*, ed. John Miksic, 35–47. Singapore: Southeast Asian Ceramics Society.

Fletcher, Roland, Mike Barbetti, Pottier Christophe, Damian Evans, Matti Kummu, Terry Lustic, and Dan Penny. 2008. "The Water Management Network of Angkor, Cambodia." *Antiquity* 82:658–70.

Foster, Brian. 1977. "Trade, Social Conflict, and Societal Integration: Rethinking Some Old Ideas on Exchange." In *Economic Exchange and Social Interaction*, ed. Hutterer, 3–22. Ann Arbor, MI: Center for South and Southeast Asian Studies.

Francis, Peter, Jr. 2002. *Asia's Maritime Bead Trade from ca. 300 BC to the Present*. Honolulu: University of Hawaii Press.

Frank, Andre Gunder. 1998. *ReORIENT: Global Economy in the Asian Age*. Berkeley: University of California Press.

Frasch, Tilman. 1998. "The Buddhist Network in the Bay of Bengal: Relations between Bodhgaya, Burma, and Sri Lanka, c. 300–1300." In *From the Mediterranean to the China Sea*, ed. Claude Guillot, Denys Lombard, and Roderich Ptak, 69–92. Wiesbaden, Germany: Harrassowitz.

Furnivall, J. S. 1939. "Europeans in Burma in the Fifteenth Century." *JBRS* 29(3): 236–49.

Gaspardone, E. 1965. "L'inscripition de Vo-canh et les debuts du Sanskrit en Indonchine." *Sinologica* 8 (3): 129–36.

Gay, Bernard, 1988. "Vue Nouvelle Sur la Composition Ethnique du Campa." In *Actes du Seminaire Sur le Campa Organise a l'Universite de Copenhague le 23 Mai 1987*. Paris: Centre d'Histoire et Civilisation de la Peninsule Indochinoise, 49–58.

Geertz, Clifford. 1963. *Agricultural Involution*. Berkeley: University of California Press.

———. 1968. *Islam Observed*. Chicago: University of Chicago Press.

———. 1978. "The Bazaar Economy. Information and Search in Peasant Markets." *American Economic Review* 68:28–32.

———. 1980. *Negara: The Theatre State in Nineteenth Century Bali*. Princeton, NJ: Princeton University Press.

Geiger, Wilhelm, trans. 1930. *The Culavamsa: Being the More Recent Part of the Mahavamsa*. English trans. C. M. Rickmers. London: Oxford University Press.

Giap, Tran Van. 1932. "Le Bouddhisme en Annam." *BEFEO* 32:206–56.

Gibb, H. A. R. 1929/1957. *The Travels of Ibn Battuta*. New York: Robert M. McBride and Company.

Giles, H. A., trans. 1923/1959. *The Travels of Fa-hsien, 399–414, or Record of the Buddhist Kingdoms*. Cambridge: Cambridge University Press.

Gill, Moshe. 2003. "The Jewish Merchant in the Light of the Eleventh-Century Geniza Documents." *JESHO* 42 (3): 249–72.

Glover, Ian, Pornchai Suchitta, and John Villiers, eds. 1992. *Early Metallurgy, Trade and Urban Centres in Thailand and Southeast Asia*. Bangkok: White Lotus.

Goitein, S. D. 1974. *Letters of Medieval Jewish Trader*. Princeton, NJ: Princeton University Press.

Goloubew, V. 1927. "Le cheval Balaha." *BEFEO* 27:223–238.

Gommans, Joseph J., and Jacques Leider, eds. 2002. *Maritime Frontier of Burma: Exploring Political, Cultural, and Commercial Interaction in the Indian Ocean World 1200–1800*. Leiden, Netherlands: KITLV.

Gonarz, Domik. 2006. "Kerinci Archaeological Research in the Highlands of Jambi on Sumatra." In *Uncovering Southeast Asia's Past*, ed. Elisabeth A. Bacus, Ian C. Glover, and Vincent C Pigott, 310–24. Singapore: National University of Singapore Press.

Gordon, Stuart, ed. 2001. *Robes of Honor: The Medieval World of Investiture*. New York: Palgrave.

———. 2008. *When Asia Was the World*. Philadelphia: DaCapo Books.

Griswold, A. B., and Prasert na Nagara. 1971. "The Inscription of King Rama Gamhen of Sukhodaya (1292 AD): Epigraphic and Historical Studies, no. 9." *Journal of the Siam Society* 59 (2): 179–228.

Groeneveldt, W. P. 1887. "Notes on the Malay Archipelago and Malacca." In *Miscellaneous Papers Relating to Indochina and the Indian Archipelago*, ed. R. Rost, vol. 1, 126–262. London: Trubner.

Groslier, Bernard-Philippe. 1962. *The Art of Indochina*. New York: Crown.

———. 1973. *Inscriptions du Bayon*. Mémoires Archéologiques, III-2. Paris: EFEO.

———. 1979a. *Angkor et l e Cambodge au XVIe siecle d'apres les sources Portugaises et Espagnoles*. Annales du Musee Guiment 63. Paris:.Musee Guiment.

———. 1979b. "La Cite Hydraulique Angkorienne: exploration ou suresploitation du sol?" *BEFEO* 56:161–202.

Guillon, Emmanuel, ed. 2001. *Cham Art, Treasures of the Da Nang Museum, Vietnam*. Bangkok: River Books.

Guillot, Claude. 1998–2003. *Histoire de Barus, Sumatra: le site de Lobu Tua/sous la direction de Claude Guillot*. Paris: Association Archipel.

Guillot, C., Lukman Nurhakim, and Sonny Wibisono. 1994. *Banten avec l'Islam: Etudes archaeologique de Banten Girang (Java-Indonesie) 932?–1526*. Paris: l'Ecole Francaise d'Extreme Orient.

Gunawardana, R. A. L. H. 2001. "Cosmopolitan Buddhism on the Move: South India and Sri Lanka in the Early Expansion of Theravada in Southeast Asia." In *Fruits of Inspiration, Studies in Honour of Prof. J. G. de Casparis*, ed. Marijke J. Klokke and Karel R. van Kooij, 135–55. Gonda Indoogicla Studies XI. Groningen, Netherlands: Egbert Forsten.

Gutman, P. 1978. "The Ancient Coinage of Southeast Asia." *Journal of the Siam Society* 66 (1): 9–20.

Guy, John S. 1986. *Oriental Ceramics in South-East Asia, Ninth to Sixteenth Centuries*. Singapore: Oxford University Press.

———. 1993–1994. "The Lost Temples of Nagapattinam and Quanzhou: A Study in Sino-Indian Relations." *Silk Road Art and Archaeology* 3:291–310.

———. 2000. "Vietnamese Ceramics from the Hoi An Excavation: The Cu Lao Cham [Fifteenth-Century] Ship Cargo." *Orientations* (September): 125–28.

———. 2001. "Tamil Merchant Guilds and the Quanzhou Trade." In *Emporium of the World*, ed. Schottenhammer, 283–308. Leiden, Netherlands: Brill.

———. 2009. "Artistic Exchange, Regional Dialogue and the Cham Territories." In *Champa and the Archaeology of My-Son*, ed. Hardy et al., 127–54. Singapore: NUS Press.

Hall, D. G. E. ed. 1961. *Historians of South East Asia*. London: Oxford.

Hall, Kenneth R. 1975. "Khmer Commercial Development and Foreign Contacts under Suryavarman." *JESHO* 18:318–336.

———. 1976. "State and Statecraft in Early Srivijaya." In *The Origins of Southeast Asian Statecraft*, ed. Hall and Whitmore, 61–105. Ann Arbor, MI: Center for South and Southeast Asian Studies.

———. 1978. "International Trade and Foreign Diplomacy in Early Medieval South India." *JESHO* 21 (1): 75–98.

———. 1980. *Trade and Statecraft in the Age of the Colas*. Delhi: Abhinav.

———. 1981. "Trade and Statecraft in the Western Archipelago at the Dawn of the European Age." *JMBRAS* 54(1): 21–47.

———. 1985. *Maritime Trade and State Development in Early Southeast Asia.* Honolulu: University of Hawaii Press.

———. 1992. "An Economic History of Early Southeast Asia." In *Cambridge History of Southeast Asia,* ed. Tarling, vol. 1, 183–275. Cambridge: Cambridge University Press.

———. 1995. "Upstream and Downstream Networking in Seventeenth Century Banjarmasin." In *From Buckfast to Borneo, Studies in Honour of Robert Nichol,* ed. A. V. M. Horton and V. T. King, special issue. *Indonesia Circle,* 489–504.

———. 1996a. "The Southeast Asian Textile Trade, 1400–1800." *JESHO* 39 (2): 87–135.

———. 1996b. "Ritual Networks and Royal Power in Majapahit Java." *Archipel* 52:95–118

———. 1999. "Coinage, Trade, and Economy in South India and Its Bay of Bengal Neighbors." *Indian Economic and Social History Review* 36(4): 431–59.

———. 2000. "Personal Status and Ritualized Exchange in Majapahit Java." *Archipel* 59:51–96.

———. 2001a. "Unification of the Upstream and Downstream in Southeast Asia's First Islamic Polity: The Changing Sense of Community in the Fifteenth-Century *Hikayat Raja-Raja Pasai* Court Chronicle." *JESHO* 42 (2): 198–229.

———. 2001b. "Ritual Transitions and Kingship in Fifteenth-Century Java: A View from the Candi Panataran Complex." In *Structural Change in Early South India,* ed. Hall, 276–312. New Delhi: Oxford University Press.

———. 2003. "The Early Historical Texts, Breaking into Them and Breaking out of Them: A Case Study of the Old Javanese Pararaton." Texts and Contexts in Southeast Asia, part 2, 1–18. Yangon, Myanmar: Universities Historical Research Centre.

———. 2004a. "Temple Networks and Royal Power in Southeast Asia." In *The World in 1000,* ed. James Heitzmann and Wolfgang Schenkluhn, 183–213. Lanham, MD: University Press of America.

———. 2004b. "Local and International Trade and Traders in the Straits of Melaka Region: 600–1500." *JESHO* 47 (2): 213–60.

———. 2005. "Traditions of Knowledge in Old Javanese Literature, 1000–1500." *JSEAS* 36 (1): 1–27.

———. 2006. "Multi-Dimensional Networking: Fifteenth-Century Indian Ocean Maritime Diaspora in Southeast Asian Perspective." *JESHO* 49 (4): 454–81.

———. 2008. "Coastal Cities in an Age of Transition: Upstream-Downstream Networking and Societal Development in Fifteenth- and Sixteenth-Century Maritime Southeast Asia." In *Secondary Cities and Urban Networking,* ed. Hall, 176–204. Lanham, MD: Lexington Press.

———. 2010a. "Ports-of-Trade, Maritime Diasporas, and Networks of Trade and Cultural Integration in the Bay of Bengal Region of the Indian Ocean: c. 1000–1500." In *Empires and Emporia, The Orient in World-Historical Space and Time,* ed. Jos Gommans, 109–45. Leiden, Netherlands: E. J. Brill.

———. 2010b. "Indonesia's Evolving International Relationships in the Ninth to Early Eleventh Centuries: Evidence from Contemporary Shipwrecks and Epigraphy." *Indonesia,* Fall 2010.

———. 2010c. "Buddhist Conversions and the Creation of Urban Hierarchies in Cambodia and Vietnam, c. 1000–1200." In *The Growth of Non-Western Cities,* ed. Hall. Lanham, MD: Lexington.

———. 2011. "Sojourning Communities, Ports-of-Trade, and Commercial Networking in Southeast Asia's Eastern Regions, 1000–1400." In *New Perspectives on the History and Historiography of Southeast Asia,* ed. Aung-Thwin and Hall. London: Routledge, 2011.

Hall, Kenneth R., ed. 2008. *Secondary Cities and Urban Networking in the Indian Ocean Realm, c. 1400–1800.* Lanham, MD: Lexington Press.

———. 2010. *The Growth of Non-Western Cities: Primary and Secondary Urban Networking, c. 900–1900.* Lanham, MD: Lexington Press.

Hall, Kenneth R., and John K. Whitmore, eds. 1976. *Explorations in Early Southeast Asian History, The Origins of Southeast Asian Statecraft.* Ann Arbor, MI: Center for South and Southeast Asian Studies.

Hardjowardojo, P. Pitono, trans. (into Indonesian). 1965. *Pararaton*. Jakarta: Bhratara.

Hardy, Andrew. 2009. "Eaglewood and the Economic History of Champa and Central Vietnam." In *Champa*, ed. Hardy et al., 107–26. Singapore: NUP.

Hardy, Andrew, Mauro Cucarzi, and Patrizia Zolese, eds. 2009. *Champa and the Archaeology of My Son (Vietnam)*. Singapore: National University of Singapore Press.

Hartwell, Robert. 1967. "The Evolution of the Early Sung Monetary System, AD 960–1025." *Journal of the American Oriental Society* 87 (3): 280–89.

Harvey G. E. 1925. *History of Burma from the Earliest Times to the Beginning of the English Conquest*. London: Longman Green.

Hefner, Robert W. 1985. *Hindu-Javanese, Tengger Tradition and Islam*. Princeton, NJ: Princeton University Press.

———. 1990. *The Political Economy of Mountain Java*. Berkeley: University of California Press.

Heine-Geldern, Robert. 1942. "Conceptions of State and Kingship in Southeast Asia." *Far Eastern Quarterly* 2:15–30.

Heng, Derek Thiam Soon. 2001. "The Trade in Lakawood Products between South China and the Malay World from the Twelfth to Fifteenth C. AD." *JSEAS* 32 (2): 133–49.

———. 2008. "Structures, Networks, and Commercial Practices of Private Chinese Maritime Traders in Island Southeast Asia in the Early Second Millennium AD." *International Journal of Maritime History* 20 (2): 27–54.

———. 2009. *Sino-Malay Trade and Diplomacy from the Tenth through Fourteenth Century*. Athens, OH: Ohio University Press.

Heng, Leong Sua. 1990. "Collecting Centres, Feeder Points and Entrepôts in the Malay Peninsula, c. 1000 BC–AD 1400." In *Southeast Asian Port and Polity*, ed. Kathirithamby-Wells and Villiers, 17–39. Singapore: Singapore University Press.

Hickey, Gerald C. 1982. *Sons of the Mountains: Ethnohistory of the Vietnamese Central Highlands to 1954*. New Haven, CT: Yale University Press.

Higham, Charles, 2001. *The Civilization of Angkor*. Berkeley: University of California Press.

Hill, A. H. 1960. "Hikayat Raja-Raja Pasai." *JMBRAS* 33 (2): 1–215.

Himanshu Prabha Ray, 1994. *The Winds of Change: Buddhism and the Maritime Links of Early South Asia*. Delhi: Oxford University Press.

———. 2003. The Archaeology of Seafaring in Ancient South Asia. Cambridge World Archaeology. Cambridge: Cambridge University Press.

Himanshu Prabha Ray and Jean-Francois Salles, eds. 1996. *Tradition and Archeology: Early Maritime Contacts in the Indian Ocean*. Delhi: Monohar.

———. 1999. *Archaeology of Seafaring, The Indian Ocean in the Ancient Period*. Delhi: Pragati Publications.

Hirth, E., and W. W. Rockhill. 1911. *Chau Ju-kua: His Work on the Chinese and Arab Trade in the Twelfth and Thirteenth Centuries, Entitled Chu-fan-chi*. St. Petersburg: Imperial Academy of Sciences.

Hirth, F. 1885. *China and the Roman Orient*. Shanghai: Kelly and Walsh.

Ho, Enseng. 2002. "Weaving Community, Writing Transregional Consciousness." Unpublished paper presented at the University of Michigan, Ann Arbor, November.

———. 2006. *Graves of Tarim: Genealogy and Mobility across the Indian Ocean*. Berkeley: University of California Press.

Hoadley, Mason C. 1971. "Continuity and Change in Javanese Legal Traditions: The Evidence of the Jayapattra." *Indonesia* 11 (April): 95–109.

Holt, Claire. 1967. *Art in Indonesia: Continuity and Change*. Ithaca, NY: Cornell University Press.

Howard, Angela F. 1989. "Buddhist Sculpture of Pujiang, Sichuan: A Mirror of the Direct Link between Southwest China and India in the High Tang." *Asian Art* 42:49–61.

Huber, Edouard. 1911. "L'epigraphie de la dynastie de Dong-du'o'ng." *BEFEO* 11:268–311.

Hucker, Charles O. 1975. *China's Imperial Past*. Palo Alto, CA: Stanford University Press.

Hudson, A. B. 1967. *Padju Epat: The Ethnography and Social Structure of a Maanyan Dyak Group in Southeastern Borneo*. Unpublished PhD dissertation, Cornell University.

Hudson, Robert, Nyein Lwin, and Win Maung. 2001. "The Origins of Bagan." *Asian Perspectives* 40:48–78.

Hultzsch, E. 1902–1903. "A Vaishnava Inscription at Pagan." *Epigraphica Indica* 7:197–98.

Hunter, Thomas M., Jr. 1996. "Ancient Beginnings: The Spread of the Indic Scripts." In *Illuminations: The Writing Traditions of Indonesia*, ed. Ann Kumar and John H. McGlynn. Jakarta: Lontar.

Hutterer, Karl L. 1973. *An Archaeological Picture of a Pre-Spanish Cebuano Community*. Cebu City: University of San Carlos.

———. 1974. "The Evolution of Philippine Lowland Societies." *Mankind* 9:287–99.

———. 1977. "Prehistoric Trade and the Evolution of Philippine Society: A Reconsideration." In *Economic Exchange and Social Interactions in Southeast Asia*, ed. Hutterer. Ann Arbor, MI: Center for South and Southeast Asian Studies.

Hutterer, Karl L., ed. 1977. *Economic Exchange and Social Interaction in Southeast Asia: Perspectives from Prehistory, History and Ethnography*. Ann Arbor, MI: Center for South and Southeast Asian Studies.

Ishii, Yoneo, 1986. *Sangha, State and Society: Thai Buddhism in History*. Honolulu: The University of Hawaii Press.

———, ed. 1978. *Thailand, A Rice Growing Society*. Honolulu: University of Hawaii Press.

Jacq-Hergoualc'h, Michel. 2002. "The Mergui-Tenasserim Region in the Context of the Maritime Silk Road." In *Maritime Frontier of Burma*, ed. Gommans and Leider, 79–92. Leiden, Netherlands: KITLV.

Jacques, C. 1976. "A propos de l'esclavage dans l'ancien Cambodge." In *Actes du 29e Congrès international des Orientalistes*, ed. B. P. Lafont, 1:71–76. Asie du Sud-Est continentale 1, Paris.

———. 1978. "Auteur de quelques toponymes de l'inscription du Prasat Tapan Run K. 598: la capitale Angkorienne, de Yasovarman Ier a Suryavarnan Ier." *BEFEO* 65:281–321.

———. 1990. *Angkor*. Paris: Borbas.

———. 1997. *Angkor, Cities and Temples*. Bangkok: River Books.

———. 2006. *Ancient Angkor*. Bangkok: River Books.

———. 2007. "The Historical Development of Khmer Culture from the Death of Suryavarman II to the Sixteenth Century." In *Bayon, New Perspectives*, ed. Joyce Clark, 28–49. Bangkok: River Books.

Jacques, C., and Philippe Lafond. 2007. *The Khmer Empire: Cities and Sanctuaries from the Fifth to the Thirteenth Centuries*. Bangkok: River Books.

Johns, Anthony. 1957. "Malay Sufism." *JMBRAS* 30 (2): 8–160.

———. 1961a. "Sufism in Indonesia." *Journal of Southeast Asian History* 2 (2): 10–23.

———. 1961b. "The Role of Sufism in the Spread of Islam to Malaya and Indonesia." *Journal of the Pakistan Historical Society* 9:143–60.

———. 1964. "The Role of Structural Organization and Myth in Javanese Historiography." *JAS* 24 (1): 91–99.

———. 1967. "From Buddhism to Islam." *Comparative Studies in Society and History* 11:40–50.

———. 1981. "From Coastal Settlement to Islamic School and City: Islamization in Sumatra, the Malay Peninsula, and Java." *Hamdard Islamicus, Quarterly Journal of Studies and Research in Islam* 4:3–28.

Junker, Laura Lee. 1999. *Raiding, Trading, and Feasting: The Political Economy of Philippine Chiefdoms*. Honolulu: University of Hawaii Press.

Kaplan, D. 1963. "Men, Monuments, and Political Systems." *Southwestern Journal of Anthropology* 19 (4): 397–410.

Kasetsiri, Charnvit. 1976. *The Rise of Ayudhya: A History of Siam in the Fourteenth and Fifteenth Centuries*. Kuala Lumpur: Oxford University Press.

———. 1992. "Ayudhya: Capital-Port of Siam and Its Chinese Connection in the Fourteenth and Fifteenth Centuries." *Journal of the Siam Society* 80 (1): 75–80.

Kathirithamby-Wells, J. 1986. "Royal Power and the 'Orang Kaya' in the Western Archipelago." *Journal of Southeast Asian Studies* 27 (2): 256–67.

———. 1993a. "*Hulu-hilir* Unity and Conflict: Malay Statecraft in East Sumatra before the Mid-Nineteenth Century." *Archipel* 45:77–96.

———. 1993b. "Restraints on the Development of Merchant Capitalism in Southeast Asia before c. 1800." In *Southeast Asia in the Early Modern Era*, edited by Reid. Ithaca, NY: Cornell University Press, 123–48.

Kathirithamby-Wells, J., and John Villiers, eds. 1990. *The Southeast Asian Port and Polity*. Singapore: Singapore University Press.

Kee-long, So. 1998. "Dissolving Hegemony or Changing Trade Pattern? Images of Srivijaya in the Chinese Sources of the Twelfth and Thirteenth Centuries." *JSEAS* 29 (2): 295–308.

Kennedy, Victor. 1970. "An Indigenous Early Nineteenth Century Map of Central and Northeast Thailand." In *In Memorian Phya Anuman Rajadhon*, ed. Tej Bunag and M. Smithis. Bangkok: Siam Society, 315–48.

Kheng, Cheah Boon. 1998. "The Rise and Fall of the Great Melakan Empire: Moral Judgment in Tun Bambang's *Sejarah Melayu*." *JMBRAS* 71:104–21.

Khôi, Lê Thành. 1955. *Le Viet Nam*. Paris: E'ditions de Minuit.

———. 1981. *Histoire du Vietnam des origines à 1858*. Paris: Sudestasie.

Kinney, Ann R. 2003. *Worshipping Siva and Buddha: The Temple Art of East Java*. Honolulu: University of Hawaii Press.

Kirsch, A. Thomas. 1976. "Kinship, Genealogical Claims, and Societal Integration in Ancient Khmer Society: An Interpretation." In *Southeast Asian History and Historiography*, ed. C. D. Cowan and O. W. Wolters, 190–202. Ithaca, NY: Cornell University Press.

Klokke, M. J., and K. R. Kooij, eds. 2001. *The Fruits of Inspiration: Studies in Honour of Prof. Dr J. G. de Casparis, Retired Professor of the Early History and Archeology of South and Southeast Asia at the University of Leiden, the Netherlands, on the occasion of his Eighty-Fifth birthday*. Groningen, Netherlands: Egbert Forsten.

Ko, Taw Sein. 1892. *The Kalyani Inscriptions*. Rangoon: Government Printing Office.

Koentjaraningrat. 1992. "The Hindu-Buddhist and Islamic Civilizations of Indonesia." In *Disciplines croisees hommage a Bernard Philippe Groslier*, ed. Georges Condominas, 149–61. Paris: Ecole des Hautes Etudes en Sciences Sociales.

Koestoro, Lucas P., Pierre-Yves Manguin, and Soeroso. 1994. "Kota Kapur (Bangka Indonesia): A Pre-Sriwijayan Site Re-ascertained." In *Southeast Asian Archaeology 1994*, ed. Pierre-Yves Manguin, 61–81. Hull, UK: Centre of Southeast Asian Studies.

Krom, N. J. 1931. *Hindoe-Javaansche Geschiendenis*. The Hague: M. Nijhoff.

Kulke, Hermann. 1978. *The Devaraja Cult*. Ithaca, NY: Cornell University Southeast Asia Program.

———. 1980. "Early State Formation and Ritual Policy in Eastern Java." In proceedings, Eighth International Association of Historians of Asia Conference, Kuala Lumpur.

———. 1986. "The Early and the Imperial Kingdom in Southeast Asian History." In *Southeast Asia in the Ninth to Fourteenth Centuries*, ed. Marr and Milner, 1–22. Singapore: Institute for South East Asian Studies..

———. 1991. "Epigraphical References to the 'City' and the 'State' in Early Indonesia." *Indonesia* 52:3–22.

———. 1993. "Kadatuan Srivijaya—Empire or Kraton of Srivijaya? A Reassessment of the Epigraphical Evidence." *BEFEO* 81(1): 159–80.

———. 1999. "Rivalry and Competition in the Bay of Bengal in the Eleventh Century and Its Bearing on Indian Ocean Studies." In *Commerce and Culture in the Bay of Bengal*, ed. Om Prakash and Denys Lombard, 17–35. New Delhi: Manohar.

Kummu, Matti. 2009. "Water Management in Angkor: Human Impacts on Hydrology and Sediment Transportation." *Journal of Environmental Management* 90, 3:1413–21.

Laichen, Sun. 2003. "Military Technology Transfers from Ming China and the Emergence of Northern Mainland Southeast Asia (c. 1390–1527)." *JSEAS* 34 (3): 495–517.

Lajonquiere, E. Lunet de. 1911. "Carte archeologique de l'ancien Cambodge." *Publications de l'Ecole Francaise d'Extreme Orient* 9. Insert.

Lamb, Alastair. 1961. "Kedah and Takuapa: Some Tentative Historical Conclusions." *Federated Museums Journal* 6:69–81.

———. 1964. "Takuapa: The Probable Site of a Pre-Malaccan Entrepôt in the Malay Peninsula." In *Malayan and Indonesian Studies*, ed. John Bastin and R. Roolvink, 76–86. Oxford: Clarendon Press.

Lambourn, Elizabeth. 2003. "From Cambay to Samudera-Pasai and Gresik—The Export of Gujarat Grave Memorials to Sumatra and Java in the Fifteenth Century." *Indonesia and the Malay World* 31 (July), 221–89.

———. 2008a. "Tombstones, Texts and Typologies—Seeing Sources for the Early History of Islam in Southeast Asia." *JESHO* 51 (2): 252–86.

———. 2008b. "India from Aden: *Khutba* and Muslim Urban Networks in Late Thirteenth-Century India." In *Secondary Cities and Urban Networking*, ed. Hall, 55–97. Lanham, MD: Lexington.

Lansing, John Stephen. 1991. *Priests and Programmers: Technologies of Power in the Engineered Landscape of Bali*. Princeton, NJ: Princeton University Press.

Le Tac. 1961. *Annam Chi Luo'c*. Hue: University of Hue.

Leger, Daniel. 1998. "L'esclavage en pays bahnar-lao (Centre Vietnam)." In *Formes exteres de dependence*, ed. Georges Condominas, 101–63. Paris: Ecole Pratiques des Haute Etudes en Sciences Sociales.

Leong Sua Heng. 1990. "Collecting Centres, Feeder Points and Entrepôts in the Malay Peninsula, c. 1000 BC–AD 1400." In *The Southeast Asian Port and Polity*, ed. Kathirithamby-Wells and Villiers, 17–39. Singapore: Singapore University Press.

Levathes, Louise E. 1994. *When China Ruled the Seas: The Treasure Fleet of the Dragon Throne 1405–1437*. New York: Oxford University Press.

Lewis, Diane. 1960. "Inas, A Study of Local History." *JMBRAS* 33:65–94.

Li Hui-lin. 1979. *Nan-fang ts'ao-mu chuang, A Fourth Century Flora of Southeast Asia*. Hong Kong: Chinese University Press.

Li Tana. 2006. "A View from the Sea: Perspectives on the Northern and Central Vietnamese Coast." *Journal of Southeast Asian Studies* 37 (1): 83–102.

———. 2010. "The Ming Factor and the Emergence of the Viet in the Fifteenth Century." In *Southeast Asia in the Fifteenth Century, the Ming Factor*, ed. Geoff Wade and Laichen Sun. Singapore: National University of Singapore Press.

Lieberman, Victor. 1980. "The Political Significance of Religious Wealth in Burmese History." *JAS* 39:753–69.

———. 2003. *Strange Parallels: Southeast Asia in a Global Context, 800–1830*. Cambridge: Cambridge University Press.

Liere, W. I. van. 1980. "Traditional Water Management in the Lower Mekong Basin." *World Archaeology* 11 (3): 265–80.

Liu, Xinru. 1988. *Ancient India and Ancient China: Trade and Religious Exchanges AD 1–600*. Delhi: Oxford University Press.

———. 1995. "Silks and Religions in Eurasia, c. AD 600–1200." *Journal of World History* 6 (1): 25–48.

———. 1996. *Silk and Religion: An Exploration of Material Life and the Thought of People*. Delhi: Oxford University Press.

Lo, Jung-pang. 1955. "The Emergence of China as a Sea Power during the Late Sung and Early Yuan Periods." *Far Eastern Quarterly* 14 (4): 489–503.

Lockhart, Bruce, and Tran Ky Phuong, eds. 2010. *New Scholarship on Champa*. Singapore: NUP.

Lombard, Denys. 1990. *Le Carrefour javanais: essai d'histoire global*. 3 vols. Paris: Editions de l'Ecole des hautes etudes en sciences socials.

Lombard, Denys, and Jean Aubin, eds. 1988/2000. *Marchands et homes d'affaires asiatiques dans l'Ocean Indien et la Mer de Chine 13e–20e siecles*. Paris: Editions de l'Ecole des hautes etudes en sciences socials. Translated and republished as *Asia Merchants and Businessmen in the Indian Ocean and the China Sea*, New Delhi: Oxford University Press.

Luce, G. H., trans. 1920. "The Shwegugyi Pogoda Inscription." *Journal of the Burma Research Society* 10:72–74.

———. 1922. "A Cambodian (?) Invasion of Lower Burma—A Comparison of Burmese and Talaing Chronicles." *Journal of the Burma Research Society* 12 (1): 39–45.

———. 1937. "The Ancient Pyu." *Journal of the Burma Research Society* 27 (3): 239–53.

———. 1959. "The Early *Syam* in Burma's History: A Supplement." *Journal of the Siam Society* 47 (1): 59–101.

———. 1965. "Some Old References to the South of Burma and Ceylon." In *Felicitation Volumes of Southeast-Asian Studies Presented to His Highness Prince Dhaninivat*, 2:269–82. Bangkok: Siam Society.

———. 1966. "The Career of Htilaing Mm (Kyanzittha), the Unifier of Burma AD 1084–1113." *Journal of the Royal Asiatic Society*, new series 1–2:53–68.

———. 1969–1970. *Old Burma, Early Pagan*. Locust Valley, NY: J. J. Augustin.

Mabbett, I. W. 1977a. "The 'Indianization' of Southeast Asia: Reflections on the Prehistoric Sources." *JSEAS* 8 (1): 1–14; 8 (2): 143–61.

———. 1977b. "Varnas in Angkor and the Indian Caste System." *JAS* 36 (3): 429–42.

———. 1978. "Kingship in Angkor." *Journal of the Siam Society* 66 (2): 1–58.

———. 1983. "Some Remarks on the Present State of Knowledge about Slavery at Angkor." In *Slavery and Bondage*, ed. Reid, 289–314. London: University of Queensland Press.

Mabbett, Ian W., and David P. Chandler. 1995. *The Khmers*. Oxford and Cambridge, MA: Blackwell.

Majumdar, R. C. 1927. *Champa*. Vol. 1 of *Ancient Indian Colonies in the Far East*. Lahore, Pakistan: Punjab Sanskrit Book Depot.

———. 1927/1985. *Champa: History and Culture of an Indian Colonial Kingdom in the Far East*. Delhi: Gian Publishing House.

———. 1937. *Suvarnadvipa. Ancient Indian Colonies in the Far East*. Calcutta: Modern Publishing Syndicate.

Malleret, Louis. 1956–1963. *L'archeologie du delta du Mekong*. Paris: L'Ecole francaise d'Extreme Orient.

Manguin, Pierre-Yves. 1976. "La traversee de la mer de Chine meridienale, des detroits Canton, jus-qu'au 17e siecle (La question des iles Paracels)." *Actes du XXIXe Congres international des Orientalistes* 2, 110–15.

———. 1979. "Etudes Cain II. L'introduction de l'Islam au Campa." *BEFEO* 66:255–87.

———. 1980. "The Southeast Asian Ship: An Historical Approach." *JSEAS* 11 (2): 266–76.

———. 1982. "The Sumatran Coastline in the Straits of Bangka: New Evidence." *SPAFA Digest* 3 (2): 24–29.

———. 1991. "Merchant and the King: Political Myths of Southeast Asian Coastal Politics." *Indonesia* 52:41–54.

———. 1993a. "Palembang and Sriwijaya: An Early Malay Harbour-City Rediscovered." *JMBRAS* 66:23–46.

———. 1993b. "The Vanishing *Jong*: Insular Southeast Asian Fleets in Trade and War (Fifteenth to Seventeenth Centuries)." In *Southeast Asia in the Early Modern Era*, ed. Reid, 197–213. Ithaca, NY: Cornell University Press.

———. 1994. "Trading Ships of the South China Sea: Shipping Techniques and Their Role in the History of the Development of Asian Trade Networks." *JESHO* 36:253–80.

————. 2004. "The Archaeology of the Early Maritime Polities of Southeast Asia." In *Southeast Asia from Prehistory to History*, ed. I. C. Glover and Peter Bellwood, 282–313. London: RoutledgeCurzon.

————. 2009. "The Archaeology of Fu Nan in the Mekong River Delta: The Oc Eo Culture of Vietnam." In *Arts of Ancient Viet Nam, From River Plain to Open Sea*, ed. Nancy Tingley, 103–18. New Haven, CT: Yale University Press for the Asia Society.

Manguin, Pierre-Yves, and Agustijanto Indrajaya. 2006. "The Archaeology of Batujaya (West Java, Indonesia): An Interim Report." In *Uncovering Southeast Asia's Past*, ed. Elisabeth A. Bacus, Ian C. Glover, and Vincent C Pigott, 245–57. Singapore: National University of Singapore Press.

Manguin, Pierre-Yves, and Vo Si Khai. 2000. "Excavatons at the BaThe/Oc Eo complex (Viet Nam), A Preliminary Report on the 1998 Campaign." In *Southeast Asian Archeeology 1998: Proceedings of the Seventh International Conference of the European Association of Southeast Asian Archaeologists*, ed. W. Lobo, 107–22. Hull, UK: Center for Southeast Asian Studies.

Mannikka, Eleanor. 2000. *Angkor Wat: Time, Space, and Kingship*. Honolulu: University of Hawaii Press.

Marr, David G., and A. C. Milner, eds. 1986. *Southeast Asia in the Ninth to Fourteenth Centuries*. Singapore: Institute for South East Asian Studies.

Masashi, Hiroshue. 1994. "Port Polities and Hinterlands in North Sumatra." Unpublished paper presented to the Thirteenth International Conference of the Association of Historians of Asia, Tokyo, September.

Maspero, Georges, 1910. "Le protectorat general d'Annam sous les T'ang." *BEFEO* 10:539–682.

————. 1918. "La frontiere de l'Annam et du Cambodge." *BEFEO* 18 (3): 29–36.

————. 1928. *Le Royaume de Champa*. Paris: Van Ouest. English trans. Walter E. J. Tips. *The Champa Kingdom: The History of an Extinct Vietnamese Culture*. Bangkok: White Lotus Press.

Maxwell, T. S. 2007. "Religion at the Time of Jayavarman VII." In *Bayon*, ed. Clark, 72–121. Bangkok: River Books.

McKinnon, E. Edwards. 1979. "A Note on the Discovery of Spur-Marked Yueh Type Sherds at Bukit Seguntang Palembang." *JMBRAS* 52 (2): 50–58.

————. 1984. "Kota Cina: Its Context and Meaning in the Trade of Southeast Asia in the Twelfth to Fourteenth Centuries." Unpublished PhD dissertation, Cornell University.

————. 1985. "West Java's Increasing Involvement in Overseas Trade in the Thirteenth–Fourteenth centuries." *SPAFA Digest* 6 (1): 28–33.

————. 2006. "Mediaeval Landfall Sites in Acheh, North Sumatra." In *Uncovering Southeast Asia's Pasts*, ed. Elisabeth A. Bacus, Ian C. Glover, and Vincent C. Pigott, 325–34. Singapore: National University of Singapore Press.

McRoberts, Robert W. 1991. "A Study in Growth: An Economic History of Melaka 1400–1510." *JMBRAS* 64:47–77.

Meilink-Roelofsz, M. A. P. 1962. *Asian Trade and European Influence in the Indonesian Archipelago between 1500 and about 1630*. The Hague: Martinus Nijhoff.

Meulen, J. Van der, S. J. 1975. "Ptolemy's Geography of Mainland Southeast Asia and Borneo." *Indonesia* 19 (April): 16–22.

————. 1977. "In Search of Ho-ling." *Indonesia* 23 (April): 87–111.

Miksic, John N. 1990. "Settlement Patterns and Sub-Regions in Southeast Asian History." *Review of Indonesian and Malaysian Affairs* 24:86–129.

————. 1992. "Survei permukaan situs Trowulan 1991 dan perkotaan di Indoneisa pada zaman kelasik." Paper presented at Pertemuan Ilmiah Arkeologi ke-VI. Published 1994. "Recent Research at Trowulan: Implications for Early Urbanization in Indonesia." In *Pertemuan Ilmiah Arkeologi VI*, 357–66. Jakarta: Pusat Penelitian Arkeologi Nasional.

————. 1993–1994. "Double Meditation Platforms at Auradhapura and the Pendopo of Ratu Boko." *Saraswati Esai-Esai Arkeologi Kalpataru Majalah Arkeologi* 10:23–31.

————. 1994. "Recently Discovered Chinese Green Glazed Wares of the Thirteenth and Fourteenth

Centuries in Singapore and Riau Islands." In *New Light on Chinese Yue and Longquan Wares: Archaeological Ceramics Found in Eastern and Southern Asia, AD 800–1400*, ed. Ho Chui Mei, 229–50. Hong Kong: The University of Hong Kong.

———. 2000. "Heterogenetic Cities in Premodern Southeast Asia." *World Archaeology* 32 (1): 106–20.

———. 2003a. "Introduction: The Beginning of Trade in Ancient Southeast Asia: The Role of Oc-Eo and the Lower Mekong Delta." In *Art and Archaeology of Funan: Pre-Khmer Kingdom of he Lower Mekong Valley*, 1–33. Bangkok: Orchid Press.

———. 2003b. "The Manjusrigraha Inscription of Candi Sewu, Saka 714/AD 792." In *Text and Contexts in Southeast Asia*, part 2, 19–42. Yangon: Universities Historical Research Centre.

Miksic, John, ed. 2010a. *Southeast Asian Ceramics, New Light on Old Pottery*. Singapore: Southeast Asian Ceramics Society.

———. 2010b. "Kilns of Southeast Asia." In *Southeast Asian Ceramics*, 48–69.

———. 2010c. "Research on Ceramic Trade, within Southeast Asia and between Southeast Asia and China." In *Southeast Asian Cereamics*, 71–99.

Miksic, John N., and C. T. Yap. 1992. "Compositional Analysis of Pottery from Kota Cina, North Sumatra: Implications for Regional Trade during the Twelfth to Fourteenth Centuries." *Asian Perspectives* 31 (1): 57–76.

Miksic, John N., and Endang Sri Hardiati Soekatno, eds. 1995. *The Legacy of Majapahit*. Singapore: National Heritage Board.

Mills, J. V. G, trans. 1970. *Ying- yai Sheng-lan of Ma Huan* (1433). Cambridge: Hakluyt Society.

Milner, A. C. 1982. *Kerajaan: Malay Political Culture on the Eve of Colonial Rule*. Tucson, AZ: Association for Asian Studies.

———. 1983. "Islam and the Muslim State." In *Islam in South-East Asia*, ed. M. B. Hooker, 23–49. Leiden, Netherlands: E. J. Brill.

Modelski, George, and William R. Thompson. 1996. *Leading Sectors and World Powers: The Chronicular* Tijdstrom B.V.

Moron, Eleanor, 1977. "Configurations of Time and Space at Angkor Wat." *Studies in Indo-Asian Art and Culture* 5:217–67.

Morrison, Kathleen D., and Laura L. Junker, eds.. 2002. *Forager-Traders in South and Southeast Asia*. Cambridge: Cambridge University Press.

Mus, Paul. 1937. "Angkor at the Time of Jayavarman VII." *Indian Arts and Letters* 2:65–75.

———. 1975. *India Seen from the East: Indian and Indigenous Cults in Champa*. Trans. I. W. Mabbett and D. Chandler. Clayton, Victoria: Monash University.

Naerssen, F. H. van. 1937. "Inscripties van het Rijksmuseum voor Volkenkunde te Leiden." *BKI* 97:507–8.

———. 1938. "De Brantas en haar waterwerken in den Hindu-Javaanschen tijd." *De Ingenieur* 53:A65–A66.

Naerssen, F. H. van, and R. C. de Iongh. 1977. *The Economic and Administrative History of Early Indonesia*. Leiden, Netherlands: E. J. Brill.

Naerssen, F. H. van, Th. G. Th. Pigeaud, and P. Voorhoeve. 1977. *Catalogue of Indonesian Manuscripts*, part 2. Copenhagen: Royal Library.

Nakamura, Rie, 2009. "*Awar-Ahier*: Two Keys to Understanding the Cosmology and Ethnicity of the Cham People (Ninh Thuan Province, Vietnam)." In *Champa*, ed. Hardy et al., 78–106. Singapore: NUS Press.

Nguyen, Cuong Tu. 1997. *Zen in Medieval Vietnam, A Study and Translation of the Thien Uyen Tap Anh*. Honolulu: University of Hawaii Press.

Nicholl, Robert. 1983. "Brunei Rediscovered, A Survey of Early Times." *JSEAS* 14 (1): 32–45.

Nilakanta Sastri, K. A. 1932. "A Tamil Merchant Guild in Sumatra." *TBG* 72:314–27.

———. 1949. *History of Srivijaya*. Madras: Madras University Press.

Noorduyn, J. 1975. "The Eastern Kings in Majapahit." *BKI* 131 (4): 479–87.

————. 1978. "Majapahit in the Fifteenth Century." *BKI* 134 (2–3): 207–74.

Noorduyn, J., and H. Th. Verstappen. 1972. "Purnavarman's River Works Near Tugu." *BKI* 128:298–307.

Nowell, Charles E., ed. 1962. *Magellan's Voyage around the World: Three Contemporary Accounts.* Evanston, IL: Northwestern University Press.

O'Brien, K. P. 1988. "Candi Jago as a Mandala; Symbolism of its Narratives (Part I)." *Review of Indonesian and Malayan Affairs* 22 (2): 1–61.

————. 1990. "Candi Jago: a Javanese Interpretation of the Wheel of Existence?" *Review of Indonesian and Malaysian Affairs* 24 (Winter): 23–85.

O'Conner, Richard A. 1995. "Agricultural Change and Ethnic Succession in Southeast Asian States: A Case of Regional Anthropology." *Journal of Asian Studies* 54 (4): 968–96.

O'Connor, Stanley J. 1968. "Si Chon: An Early Settlement in Peninsular Thailand." *JSS* 56 (1): 1–18.

————. 1972. *Hindu Gods of Peninsular Siam. Artibus Asiae* Supplementum XXVIII. Ascona, Switzerland: Artibus Asiae Publishers.

————. 1985. "Metallurgy and Immortality at Candi Sukuh." *Indonesia* 39:53–70.

O'Reilly, Dougald J. W. 2007. *Early Civilizations of Southeast Asia.* Lanham, MD: Altamira Press.

Osborne, Milton. 1966. "Notes on Early Cambodian Provincial History: Isanapura and Sambhupura." *France-Asie/Asia* 20 (4): 433–49.

Paranavitana, S. 1944. "Negapatam and Theravada Buddhism in South India." *Journal of the Greater India Society* 11 (1): 17–25.

————. 1966. *Ceylon and Malaysia.* Colombo: Lake House Publishers.

Paris, Pierre, 1931. "Anciens canaux reconnus sur photograhies aeriennes dans les provinces de Ta Kev et de Chau-Duc." *BEFEO* 31: 221–23.

————. 1941. "Ancienc canaux reconnus sur photographies aeriennes dans les provinces de Takeo, Chau-Duc, Long-Xuyen et Rach-Gia." *BEFEO* 41: 365–70.

Park, Hyunhee. 2010. "Port-City Networking in the Indian Ocean Commercial System Represented in Geographic and Cartographic Works in China and the Islamic West from 750 to 1500." In *The Growth of Non-Western Cities*, ed. Hall. Lanham, MD: Lexington.

Parker, Geoffrey. 1988. *The Military Revolution.* Cambridge: Cambridge University Press.

Paul, J. Gilman d'Arcy. 1967/1992. *Notes on the Customs of Cambodia by Chou Ta-kuan.* Bangkok: Social Science Association Press. Translation of Paul Pelliot, 1951, *Memoires sur les coutumes.*

Peacock, B. A. V. 1974. "Pillar Base Architecture in Ancient Kedah." *JMBRAS* 47 (1): 66–86.

Pearson, M. N. 1976. *Merchants and Rulers in Gujarat: the Response to the Portuguese n the Sixteenth Century.* Berkeley: University of California Press.

Pelliot, Paul. 1903. "Le Fou-Nan." *BEFEO* 3:248–303.

————. 1904. "Deux itineraries de Chine en Inde a la fin du VIIIe siecle." *BEFEO* 4:271–88.

————. 1925. "Quelques textes chinois concernant l'Indochine hindouisee." *Etudes Asiatiques* 2:243–63.

————. 1951. *Memoires sur les coutumes du Cambodge de Tcheou Ta-Kouan.* Paris: Adrien-Maisonneuve./English Translation, 2007. Daguan Zhou. *Notes on the Customs of Cambodia: A Record of Cambodia.* Trans. Peter Harris and David Chandler. Chiangmai: Silkworm Books.

Phalgunadi, I Gust Putu. 1996. *Pararaton: A Study of the South-East Asia Chronicle.* New Delhi: Sandeep Prakashan.

Phuong, Tran Ky. 2009. "The Architecture of the Temple-Towers of Ancient Champa (Central Vietnam)." In *Champa and the Archaeology of My Son*, ed. Hardy et al.

Pigafetta, Antonio. 1962. "First Voyage around the World." In *Magellan's Voyage around the World: Three Contemporary Accounts*, ed. Charles E. Nowell. Evanston, IL: Northwestern University Press.

Pigeaud, Th. G. Th. 1924. De Tantu Panggĕlaran, Oud-Javaansch proza-geschrift, uitgegeven, vertaald en Toegelicht. The Hague: Boek- en Steendrukkerij.

————. 1960–1963. *Java in the Fourteenth Century: A Study in Cultural History*. 5 vols. The Hague: Martinus Nijhoff.

Poerbatjarak R. Ng. Dr. 1936. "Vieroordonden in koper." *TBG* 76:373–90.

————. 1940. "Oorkonde van Krtarajasa uit 1296 AD (Penanggoengan)." *Inscripties van Neder-landsch-Indie* 33–49.

Polanyi, Karl. 1957. "The Economy as Instituted Process." In *Trade and Market in the Early Empires*, ed. K. Polanyi, C. Arensberg, and H. W. Pearson, 243–70. New York: Free Press.

Polo, Marco. 1958. *The Travels of Marco Polo*, ed. and trans. Ronald E. Latham. Middlesex: Penguin.

Przluski, Jean. 1925. "La princesse a l'odeur de poisson et la nagi dans les tradition de l'Asie Orien-tale." *Etudes Asiatiques* 2:265–84.

Ptak, Roderick. 1992. "The Northern Trade Route to the Spice Islands: South China Sea–Sulu Zone–North Moluccas (Fourteenth to Early Sixteenth Century)." *Archipel* 43:27–56.

————. 1993. "China and the Trade in Cloves, circa 960–1435." *Journal of the American Oriental Society* 113:1–13.

————. 1998a. "From Quanzhou to the Sulu Zone and Beyond: Questions Related to the Early Four-teenth Century." *JSEAS* 29:269–94.

————. 1998b. "Possible Chinese Reference to the Barus Area (Tang to Ming)." In *Histoire de Barus. Le Site de Lobu Tua*, ed. Claude Guillot, 119–47. Paris: Association Archipel.

————. 1999. "Wang Dayuan on Kerala." In *Explorations in the History of South Asia: Essays in Honour of Dietmar Rothermund*, ed. Georg Berkemer, Tilman Frasch, Hermann Kulke, and Jurgen Lutt, 39–52. New Delhi: Manohar.

Quach-Langlet, Tam. 1988. "Le Cadre Geographique de l'Ancien Campa." In Actes du Seminaire Sur le Campa Organise a l'Universite de Copenhague le 23 Mai 1987. Paris: Centre d'Histoire et Civilisation de la Peninsule Indochinoise, 28–48.

Ras, J. J. 2001. "Sacral Kingship in Java." In *Fruits of Inspiration*, ed. Klokke et al., 373–88. Groningen, Netherlands: Egbert Forsten.

Ravaisse, Paul. 1922. "Deux inscriptions coufiques du Campa." *JA* 20 (2): 247–89.

Ray, Himanshu P. 1994. *Winds of Change: Buddhism and the Maritime Links of Early South Asia*. Delhi: Oxford University Press, 1994.

————. 2003. *The Archaeology of Seafaring in Ancient South Asia*. Cambridge University Press.

Redfern, William A., III. 2002. "Hoi An in the Seventeenth and Eighteenth Centuries: An International Entrepôt." Unpublished masters thesis, University of Michigan–Ann Arbor.

Reid, Anthony. 1988, 1994. *Southeast Asia in the Age of Commerce, 1450–1680*; I, *The Lands Below the Winds*; II, *Expansion and Crisis*. New Haven, CT: Yale University Press.

————. 1999a. "A Saucer Model of Southeast Asian Identity." *Southeast Asian Journal of Social Science* 27 (1): 7–23.

————. 1999b. *Charting the Course of Early Modern Southeast Asia*. Chiangmai: Silkworm Books.

————. 2004. "Cosmopolis and Nation in Central Southeast Asia." ARI Working Paper 22, National University of Singapore Asian Research Institute.

Reid, Anthony, ed. 1983. *Slavery, Bondage and Dependency in South-East Asia*. London: University of Queensland Press.

————. 1993. *Southeast Asia in the Early Modern Era, Trade, Power, and Belief*. Ithaca, NY: Cornell University Press.

Reynolds, Frank E. 1978. "The Holy Emerald Jewel: Some Aspects of Buddhist Symbolism and Political Legitimation in Thailand and Laos." In *Religion and Legitimation of Power in Thailand, Laos, and Burma*, ed. Smith, Bardwell, 175–93. Chambersburg, PA: Anima Books.

Ricci, Ronit. 2010. "Islamic Literary Networks in South and Southeast Asia." *Journal of Islamic Studies* 21 (1): 1–28.

Ricklefs, M. C. 1967. "Land and the Law in the Epigraphy of Tenth-Century Cambodia." *JAS* 26 (3): 411–420.

————. 1976. "Javanese Sources in the Writing of Modern Javanese History." In *Southeast Asian*

History and Historiography: Essays Presented to D. G. E. Hall, ed. C. D. Cowan and O. W. Wolters, 332–44. Ithaca, NY: Cornell University Press.

———. 1981. *A History of Modern Indonesia*. Bloomington: Indiana University Press.

———. 1998. *The Seen and Unseen Worlds in Java, 1726–1749: History, Literature, and Islam in the Court of Pakubuwana II*. Honolulu: University of Hawaii Press; Sydney: Allen and Unwin.

———. 2006. *Mystic Synthesis in Java: A History of Islamization from the Fourteenth to the Early Nineteenth Centuries*. Norwalk, CT: Eastbridge.

Robson, Stuart O. 1978. "Notes on the Early Kidung Literature." *BKI* 135 (2–3): 300–322.

———. 1979. "Notes on the Early Kidung Literature." *BKI* 135:300–22.

———. 1981. "Java at the Crossroads, Aspects of Javanese Cultural History in the Fourteenth and Fifteenth Centuries." *BKI* 137:259–92.

———. 1995. *Desawarnana: (Nagarakrtagama) by Mpu Prapanca*. Leiden, Netherlands: KITLV.

———. 1997. "Thailand in Old Javanese Sources." *BKI* 153 (3): 431–35.

Rockhill, W. W. 1913–1917. "Notes on the Relations and Trade of China with the Eastern Archipelago and the Coasts of the Indian Ocean during the Fourteenth Century." *Toung Pao* 14 (4): 473–76; 16:61–150.

Roolvink, R. 1965. "The Answer of Pasai." *JMBRAS* 38:124–39.

Roomy, Dawn F. 2003. "Kendi in Cultural Context." *SPAFA Journal* 13 (2): 5–16.

Sahai, Sachchidanand. 1970. *Les institutions politiques et l'organisation administrative du Cambodge Ancien (VIe–XIIIe Siecles)*. Paris: EFEO.

———. 1977. "Fiscal Administration in Ancient Cambodia." *South East Asian Review* 1–2: 123–38.

Sahlins, Marshall. 1972. *Stone Age Economics*. Chicago: Aldine.

Said, Edward. 1979. *Orientalism*. New York: Vintage.

Salmon, Claudine. 2002. "Srivijaya la Chine et les marchands chinois (Xe–XIIe s.) Quelques reflexions sur la societe de l'empire sumatranais." *Archipel* 63:57–78.

Sanderson, David, Paul Bishop, et al. 2003. "Luminescence Dating of Anthropologically Reset Canal Sediments from Angkor Borei, Mekong Delta, Cambodia." *Quaternary Science Review* 22:111–21.

Sapardi Djoko Damono, et al., trans. 2004. *Babad Tanah Jawi*. Jakarta: Lontar Foundation.

Sarkar, H. B. 1971–1972. *Corpus of the Inscriptions of Java (up to 928 AD)*. Calculta: Firma K. L. Mukhopadhyay.

Sarkar, K. Kumar. 1956. "The Earliest Inscription of Indochina." *Sino-Indian Studies* 5 (2): 77–87.

Schafer, Edward H. 1954. *The Empire of Min*. Rutland, VT: Charles E. Tuttle.

———. 1967. *The Vermilion Bird: Tang Images of the South*. Berkeley: University of California Press.

Schnitger F. M. 1937. *The Archaeology of Hindoo Sumatra*. Leiden, Netherlands: Brill.

———. 1939. *Forgotten Kingdoms in Sumatra*. Leiden, Netherlands: Brill.

Schottenhammer, Angela. 1999. "The Maritime Trade of Quanzhou (Zaitun) from the Ninth through the Thirteenth Century." In *Archaeology of Seafaring*, ed. Ray and Salles, 271–90. Delhi: Pragati Publications.

Schottenhammer, Angela, ed. 2001. *The Emporium of the World: Maritime Quanzhou, 1000–1400*. Leiden, Netherlands: Brill.

Schrieke, B. J. O. 1955–1957. *Indonesian Sociological Studies, I: Selected Writings; II: Ruler and Realm in Early Java*. The Hague: W. van Hoeve.

Schweyer, Anne-Valérie. 1998. "Le dynastie d'Indrapura (Qu?ng Nam, Viet Nam)." In *Southeast Asian Archaeology 1998*, ed. Wibke Lobo, Wibke and Stefanie Reimann, 205–17. Proceedings of the Seventh International Conference of the European Association of Southeast Asian Archaeologists, Berlin, Centre for South to East Asian Studies, University of Hull, Special Issue of Ethnologisches Museum, Staatliche Museen zu Berlin, Stiftung Preussischer Kulturbesitz.

———. 1999a. "Chronologie des inscriptions publiées de Campa, Études d'épigraphie cam I." *BEFEO* 86:321–44.

————. 1999b. "La vaisselle en argent de la dynastie d'Indrapura (Qu?ng Nam, Vi?t Nam, Études d'épigraphie cam—II." *BEFEO* 86:345–55.

————. 2005. "Po Nagar de Nha Trang." *Aséanie* 14:109–40; 15:87–119.

————. 2007. "The Confrontations of the Khmers and Chams in the Bayon Period." In *Bayon*, ed. Clark, 50–71. Bangkok: River Books.

Sedov, L. A. 1963. "On the Problem of the Economic System in Angkor Cambodia in the IX–XII Centuries." Trans. Antonia Glasse. *Narody Asii i Afriki, Istoria, Ekonomika, Kul'tura* 6 (Akademija Nauk SSR): 73–81.

Sedyawati, Edi. 1994. *Ganesa Statuary of the Kadiri and Sinhasari Periods: A Study of Art History.* Leiden, Netherlands: KITLV.

Sen, Tansen. 2003. *Buddhism, Diplomacy and Trade: The Realignment of Sino-Indian Relations, 600–1400.* Honolulu: University of Hawaii Press.

Seong, Tan Yeok. 1964. "The Sri Vijayan Inscription of Canton (AD 1079)." *Journal of Southeast Asian History* 5 (2): 17–24.

Setten van der Meer, N. C. van. 1979. *Sawah Cultivation in Ancient Java: Aspects of Development during the Indo-Javanese Period, Fifth to Fifteenth Century.* Canberra: Australian National University Press.

Sharrock, Peter. 2007. "The Mystery of the Face Towers." In *Bayon*, ed. Joyce Clark, 230–81. Bangkok: River Books.

Shin, Leo K. 2007. "Ming China and Its Border with Annam." In *The Chinese State at the Border*, ed. D. Lary, 91–104. Vancouver: University of British Columbia Press.

Shiro, Momoki. 1998a. "Dai Viet and the South China Sea Trade from the Tenth to the Fifteenth Century." *Crossroads* 12 (1): 1–34.

————. 1998b. "Was Champa a Pure Maritime Polity? Agriculture and Industry Recorded in Chinese Documents." "Eco-History and Rise/Demise of the Dry Areas in Southeast Asia," 1998 Core University Seminar, Kyoto University and Thammasat University.

————. 1999. "A Short Introduction to Champa Studies." In *The Dry Areas in Southeast Asia*, Fukui Hayao, 65–74. Kyoto: Center for Southeast Asian Studies, Kyoto University.

————. 2008. "Was Dai Viet a Rival of Ryukyu." In *China and Southeast Asia*, ed. Geoff Wade, 59–70. Singapore/London: Routledge.

Shorto H. L. 1961. "A Mon Genealogy of Kings: Observations on the *Nadana Aramabhakantha*." In *Historians of South-East Asia*, ed. D. G. E. Hall, 163–72. Ithaca, NY: Cornell University Press.

————.1963. "The 32 *Myos* in the Medieval Mon Kingdom." *Bulletin of the School of Oriental and African Studies* 26 (3): 127–41.

————. 1967. "The Dwatau Sotapan, a Mon Prototype of the 37 Nats." *BSOAS* (30): 127–41.

Sims-Williams, Nicholas. 1994. "The Sogdian Merchants in China and India." In *Cina e Iran: Da Alessandro Magno alla Dinastia Tang*, ed. Alfredo Cadonna and Lionello Lanciotti, 45–67. Firenze: Leo S. Olschiki Editore.

Slametmuljana. 1976. *A Story of Majapahit.* Singapore: Singapore University Press.

Smith, R. B. and W. Watson, eds. 1979. *Early South East Asia: Essays in Archaeology, History and Historical Geography.* London: Oxford University Press.

So, Billy Kee-long. 1998. "Dissolving Hegemony or Changing Trade Pattern: Srivijayan Images in the Chinese Sources of the Twelfth and Thirteenth Centuries." *JSEAS* 29 (2): 295–308.

Sox, David Griffith. 1972. *Resource-Use Systems of Ancient Champa.* Unpublished masters thesis, University of Hawaii–Manoa.

Spencer, George W. 1983. *The Politics of Expansion: The Chola Conquest of Sri Lanka and Sri Vijaya.* Madras, India: New Era.

Spinks, B. N. 1956. "Siam and the Pottery Trade of Asia." *Journal of the Siam Society* 44 (2): 61–111.

Spiro, Milford E. 1967. *Burmese Supernaturalism.* Philadelphia: Institute for the Study of Human Issues.

Stadtner, Donald. 2003. "The Fallacy of Pyu Art." Unpublished paper presented at the Traditions of Knowledge in Southeast Asia conference hosted by the Universities Historical Research Centre in Yangon, Burma, 17–19 December.

Stargardt, Janice. 1971. "Burma's Economy and Diplomatic Relations with India and China from Early Medieval Sources." *JESHO* 14 (1): 28–62.

Stark, Miriam T. 1998. "The Transition to History in the Mekong Delta: A View from Cambodia." *International Journal of Historical Archaeology* 2–3:175–203.

———. 2003. "Angkor Borei and the Archaeology of Cambodia's Mekong Delta." In *Art and Archaeology of Funan: Pre-Khmer Kingdom of the Lower Mekong Valley*, ed. James CM Khoo, 87–105. Bangkok: Orchid Press.

———. 2004. "Pre-Angkorian and Angkorian Cambodia." In *Southeast Asia From Pre-History to History*, ed. Peter Bellwood and Ian Glover, 89–119. London: Routledge.

———. 2006a. "Funan to Angkor. Collapse and Regeneration in Ancient Cambodia." In *After the Collapse*, ed. G. M. Schwartz and J. J. Nichols, 144–67. Tucson: University of Arizona Press.

———. 2006b. "Textualized Places: Pre-Angkorean Khmer and Historicized Archeology." In *Excavating the Relation between History and Archeology in the Study of PreModern Asia*, ed. N. Yoffe and B. Crowell, 307–26. Tucson: University of Arizona Press.

Stark, Miriam, and Bong Sovath. 2001. "Recent Research on Emerging Complexity in Cambodia's Mekong." *Indo-Pacific Prehistory Association Bulletin* 21:85–98.

Stein, R. 1947. "La Lin-yi." *Han-Hiue (Bulletin du centre d'etudes sinologques de Pekin)* 2:1–54.

Steinberg, David Joel, et al. 1971. *In Search of Southeast Asia*. New York: Praeger.

Stern, Philippe. 1942. *L'art du Champa (ancien Annam) et son evolution*. Paris: Adrien-Maison-neuve.

———. 1965. *Les monuments khmers du style de Bayon et Jayavarman VII*. Paris: Presses Universitaires de France.

Stevenson, John, and John Guy. 1997. *Vietnamese Ceramics: A Separate Tradition*. Chicago: Art Media Resources.

Strachan, Paul. 1989. *Imperial Pagan*. Honolulu: University of Hawaii Press.

Stutterheim, W. F. 1913. "Transcriptie van een defecte ooorkonde op bronzen platen uit het Malang-sche." *Oudheidkundig Verslag* 67:172–215.

———. 1929. *A Javanese Period in Sumatra History*. Surakarta, Indonesia: de Bliksem.

Stutterheim, W. F. ed. 1940. *Oudheidkundige Dienst in Nederlansch-Indie. Inscripties van Nederlandsch-Indie*. Batavia: Koninglijk Bataviaasch Genootschap van Kunsten en Wetenschappen.

Subbarayalu, Y. 1998–2003. "The Tamil Merchant-Guild Inscription at Barus: A Rediscovery." In *Histoire de Barus*, ed. Guillot, 25–33. Paris: Association Archipel.

Subrahmanyam, Sanjay. 1999. "Persianization and Mercantilism: Two Themes in Bay of Bengal History." In *Commerce and Culture in the Bay of Bengal, 1500–1800*, ed. Om Prakash and Denys Lombard, 47–85. New Delhi: Monohar.

Sumio, Fukami. 2004. "The Long Thirteenth Century of Tambralinga, from Javaka to Siam." *Memoirs of the Toyo Bunko* 62:45–79.

Sundberg, Jeffrey Roger. 2004. "The Wilderness Monks of Abyayagirivihara and the Origins of Sino-Javanese Exoteric Buddhism." *BEFEO* 160(1): 95–123.

Supomo, S. 1976. "The Image of Majapahit in Later Javanese and Indonesian Writing." In *Perceptions of the Past in Southeast Asia*, ed. Anthony Reid and David Marr, 171–85. Singapore: Heinemann Educational Books.

———. 1997. "From Sakti to Shahada. The Quest for New Meanings in a Changing World Order." In *Essays on Scripture, Thought, and Society: A Frestschrift in Honour of Anthony H. Johns*, ed. Peter Riddell and A. Street, 218–36. Leiden, Netherlands: Brill.

Sweeney, P. L. 1967. "The Connection between the Hikayat Raja-Raja Pasai and the Sejarah Melayu." *JMBRAS* 40 (2): 94–105.

Takakusu, J. 1896. *A Record of the Buddhist Religion as Practiced in India and the Malay Archipelago (671–695 AD) by I-Tsing*. Oxford: Oxford University Press.

Tambiah, Stanley J. 1976. *World Conqueror and World Renouncer: A Study of Buddhism and Polity in Thailand against a Historical Background*. Cambridge: Cambridge University Press.

Tan, Yvonne. 2006. "Cirebon Wreck." *Southeast Asia Ceramics Museum Newsletter* 3(7): 1.

———. 2007. "Cirebon Cargo of Yue Ceramic Vessels." *Asian Art Magazine*, May 2007, as posted on www.seaceramics.org.sg/articles_cargo.html (accessed March 25, 2010).

Tarling, Nicholas, ed. 1992. *The Cambridge History of Southeast Asia*. Cambridge: Cambridge University Press,

Tasaka, Kodo. 1952. "Islam in Champa." In Japanese. *Tohogaku* 4:52–60.

Taylor, Keith W. 1976. "Madagascar in the Ancient Malayo-Polynesian Myths." In *Explorations in Early Southeast Asian History*, ed. Hall and Whitmore, 149–92. Ann Arbor, MI: Center for South and Southeast Asian Studies.

———. 1983. *The Birth of Vietnam*. Berkeley: University of California Press.

———. 1986. "Authority and Legitimacy in Eleventh Century Vietnam." In *Southeast Asia in the Ninth to Fourteenth Centuries*, ed. Marr and Milner, 139–76, Singapore: Institute of Southeast Asian Studies.

———. 1992. "The Early Kingdoms." In *Cambridge History of Southeast Asia*, ed. Nicholas Tarling, 1:137–182. Cambridge: Cambridge University Press.

Teeuw, A. 1964. "Hikayat Raja-Raja Pasai and Sejarah Melayu." In *Malayan and Indonesian Studies: Essays Presented to Sir Richard Winstedt on his Eighty-fifth Birthday*, ed. John Bastin and R. Roolvink, 222–34. London: Clarendon Press.

———. 2001. "Kahulunan and Sri Kahulunan." In *Fruits of Inspiration*, ed. Klokke and van Kooij, 525–38. Groningen: Egbert Forsten.

Teeuw, A. and D. K. Wyatt, eds. 1970. *Hikayat Patani: The Story of Patani*. The Hague: KITLV.

Thomaz, Luis Filipe Reis. 1979. *A Study of the Arab Texts Containing Material on South-East Asia*. Leiden, Netherlands: Brill.

———. 1993. "The Malay Sultanate of Melaka." In *Southeast Asia in the Early Modern Era*, ed. Reid, 69–90. Ithaca, NY: Cornell University Press.

———. 2000. "Malaka et ses communautes marchandes au tournant du 16e siecle." In *Marchands et homes d'affaires asiatiques dans l'Ocean Indien et la Mer de Chine 13e–20e siecles*, ed. Denys Lombard and Jean Aubin, 31–48. Paris: Editions de l'Ecole des Hautes Etudes en Sciences Socials. Translation, "Melaka and Its Merchant Communities at the Turn of the Sixteenth Century." In Lombard and Aubin, 2000, 25–48.

Tibbets, G. R. 1979. *A Study of the Arab Texts Concerning Material on Southeast Asia*. Leiden: Brill.

Tingley, Nancy, ed. 2009. *Arts of Ancient Viet Nam, from River Plain to Open Sea*. New Haven, CT: Yale University Press for the Asia Society.

———. 2009. "The Archaeology of Fu Nan in the Mekong River Delta: The Ec Eo Culture of Vietnam." In *Arts of Ancient Viet Nam*, 19–175.

Trautmann, Thomas R. 1973. "Consanguineous Marriage in Pali Literature." *Journal of the American Oriental Society* 93 (2): 158–80.

Trimingham, J. S. 1971. *The Sufi Orders in Islam*. Oxford: Clarendon Press.

Tun, Than. 1959. "History of Burma, 1300–1400." *Journal of the Burma Research Society* 42 (2): 119–35.

Veerdonk, Jan van den. 2001. "Curses in Javanese Royal Inscriptions from the Singhasari-Majapahit Period, AD 1222–1486." *BKI* 157 (1): 97–111.

Vickery, Michael. 1977. *Cambodia after Angkor, the Chronicular Evidence from the Fourteenth to Sixteenth Centuries*. Unpublished PhD dissertation, Yale University.

———. 1985. "The Reign of Suryavarman I and Royal Factionalism at Angkor." *JSEAS* 16 (2): 226–44.

―――. 1986. "Some Remarks on Early State Formation in Cambodia." In Marr and Milner, eds., 95–115. Singapore: Institute for Southeast Asian Studies.

―――. 1998. *Society, Economics, and Politics in Pre-Angkor Cambodia, The Seventh–Eighth Centuries*. Tokyo: The Centre for East Asian Cultural Studies for UNESCO.

―――. 2003–2004. "Funan Reviewed: Deconstructing the Ancients." *BEFEO* 90–91:101–43.

―――. 2004. "Cambodia and Its Neighbors in the Fifteenth Century." Asia Research Institute Working Paper Series 27. Singapore: Asia Research Centre.

―――. 2009. "A Short History of Champa." In *Champa and the Archaeology of My Son (Vietnam)*, ed. Hardy, et al., 45–60. Singapore: National University of Singapore Press.

Villiers, John. 1981. "Trade and Society in the Banda Islands in the Sixteenth Century." *Modern Asian Studies* 15 (4): 723–50.

Vo Si Khai. 2003. "The Kingdom of Funan and the Culture of Oc-Eo." In *Art and Archaeology of Funan: Pre-Khmer Kingdom of the Lower Mekong Valley*, ed. James C. M. Khoo, 35–86. Bangkok: Orchid Press.

Vogel, Hans Ulrich. 1993. "Cowry Trade and Its Role in the Economy of Yunnan: From the Ninth to the Mid-Seventeenth Century." *JESHO* 36 (3): 211–52; 36 (4): 309–53.

Vogel, J. Ph. 1925. "The Earliest Sanskrit Inscriptions of Java." *Publicaties van de Oudheidkundige Dienst in Nederlandsch-Indie* 1:15–35.

Wachtel, L. Michael, 1998. *Defining Champa: The Other Classical State of Southeast Asia*. Unpublished masters thesis, University of Michigan–Ann Arbor.

Wade, Geoff. 1994. "The *Ming Shi-Lu* (Variable Records of the Ming Dynasty) as a Source for Southeast Asian History—Fourteenth to Seventeenth Centuries." Unpublished PhD dissertation, University of Hong Kong.

―――. 1997. "Melaka in Ming Dynasty Texts." *JMBRAS* 70 (1): 31–69.

―――. 2000. "The *Ming Shi-lu* as a Source for Thai History Fourteenth to Seventeenth Century." *JSEAS* 31 (2): 249–94.

―――. 2003. "The *Ming shi* Account of Champa." Asia Research Institute Working Paper Series 3. Singapore: Asia Research Institute.

―――. 2004. "Ming China and Southeast Asia in the 15th Century: A Reappraisal." Asia Research Institute Working Paper Series 28. Singapore: Asia Research Institute.

―――. 2005. "The Zheng He Voyages: A Reassessment." *JMBRAS* 78 (1): 37–58.

―――. Southeast Asia in the Ming Shi-lu. Online Internet research site. www.epress.nus.edu.sg/ms/ (accessed August 8, 2010).

Wade, Geoff and Laichen Sun, eds. 2010. *Southeast Asia in the Fifteenth Century, the Ming Factor*. Singapore: National University of Singapore Press, in press.

Wake, Christopher. 1967. "Malacca's Early Kings and the Reception of Islam." *JSEAS* 5 (2): 104–28.

―――. 1983. "Melaka in the Fifteenth Century: Malay Historical Traditions and the Politics of Islamization." In *Melaka: The Transformation of a Malay Capital c. 1400–1980*, ed. Kernial Singh Sandhu and Paul Wheatley, vol. 1, 128–61. Kuala Lumpur: Oxford University Press, Kuala Lumpur.

Wales, H. G. Quaritch. 1969. *Dvaravati*. London: Bernard Quaritch.

Wang, Gungwu, 1958. "The Nanhai Trade: A Study of the Early History of Chinese Trade in the South China Sea." *JMBRAS* 31, 2.

―――. 1968a. "Early Ming Relations with Southeast Asia: A Background Essay." In *The Chinese World Order: Traditional China's Foreign Relations*, ed. John K. Fairbank, 34–62. New Haven, CT: Harvard.

―――. 1968b. "The First Three Rulers of Malacca." *JMBRAS* 41:11–22.

―――. 1970. "China and Southeast Asia 1402–1424." In *Studies in the Social History of China and Southeast Asia*, ed. J. Chen and N. Tarling, 375–402. Cambridge: Cambridge University Press.

————. 1998. *The Nanhai Trade: The Early History of Chinese Trade in the South China Sea*. Singapore: Times Academic Press (reprint and update of the 1958 original).

Wee, Vivienne. 1988. "Material Dependence and Symbolic Independence: Constructions of Melayu Ethnicity in Island Riau, Indonesia." In *Ethnic Diversity and the Control of Natural Resources in Southeast Asia*, ed. A. T. Rambo, K. Gillogly, and K. L. Hutterer, 197–226. Ann Arbor, MI: Center for South and Southeast Asian Studies.

Wheatley, Paul. 1959. "Geographical Notes on Some Commodities Involved in Sung Maritime Trade." *JMBRAS* 32 (2): 5–140.

————. 1961. *The Golden Khersonese, Studies in the Historical Geography of the Malay Peninsula before AD 1500*. Kuala Lumpur: Malaysian Branch of the Royal Asiatic Society.

————. 1965. "Agricultural Terracing." *Pacific Viewpoint* 6 (2): 123–44.

————. 1975. "Satyanrta in Suvarnadvipa: From Reciprocity to Redistribution in Ancient Southeast Asia." In *Ancient Civilizations and Trade*, ed. Jeremy Sabloff and G. C. Lamberg-Karlovsky, 227–83. Albuquerque: University of New Mexico Press.

————. 1979. "Urban Genesis in Mainland South-East Asia." In *Early South East Asia*, ed. Smith and Watson, 288–303. London: Oxford University Press.

————. 1983. *Nagara and Commandery: Origins of the Southeast Asian Urban Traditions*. Chicago: University of Chicago Department of Geography.

Wheeler, Charles. 2001. "Cross-Cultural Trade and Trans-Regional Networks in the Port of Hoi An: Maritime Vietnam in the Early Modern Era." Unpublished PhD dissertation, Yale University.

————. 2006. "One History, Two Regions: Cham Precedents in the History of the H?i An Region." In *Vi?t Nam: Borderless Histories*, ed. N. Tran and Anthony Reid, 163–93. Madison: University of Wisconsin Press.

————. 2008. "Missionary Buddhism in a Post-Ancient World: Monks, Merchants, and Colonial Expansion in Seventeenth-Century Cochinchina (Vietnam)." In *Secondary Cities and Urban Networking*, ed. K. Hall, 205–31. Lanham, MD: Lexington Press.

Whitmore, John K. 1983. "Vietnam and the Monetary Flow of Eastern Asia, Thirteenth to Eighteenth Centuries." In *Precious Metal Flows in the Later Medieval and Early Modern Worlds*, ed. John F. Richards, 363–93. Durham, NC: Carolina Academic Press.

————. 1985. *Ho Quy Ly, and the Ming (1371–1421)*. New Haven, CT: Yale Center for International and Area Studies, Council on Southeast Asian Studies.

————. 1986. "Elephants Can Actually Swim: Contemporary Chinese Views of Late Ly Dai Viet." In *Southeast Asia in the Ninth to Fourteenth Centuries*, ed. Marr and Milner, 97–113. Singapore: ISEAS.

————. 1997/1999. "Literati Culture and Integration in Dai Viet, c. 1430–c. 1840." *Modern Asian Studies* 31 (3): 665–87. Reprinted in *Beyond Binary Histories*, ed. Victor Lieberman. Ann Arbor: University of Michigan Press.

————. 2004. "The Two Great Campaigns of the Hong-Duc Era (1470–1497) in Dai Viet." *South East Asian Research* 12 (1): 127–30.

————. 2005. "China Policy in the New Age: Le Thanh-tong and Northern Relations." Unpublished paper presented at the Association for Asian Studies Annual Meeting, Chicago.

————. 2006. "The Rise of the Coasts: Trade, State, and Culture in Early Dai Viet." *JSEAS* 37:103–22.

————. 2008. "Secondary Capitals of Dai Viet: Shifting Elite Power Bases." In *Secondary Cities and Urban Networking*, ed. K. Hall, 155–75. Lanham, MD: Lexington Press.

————. 2010a. "Paperwork: The Rise of the New Literati and Ministerial Power and the Effort Toward Legibility in Dai Viet." In *Southeast Asia in the 15th Century, the Ming Factor*, ed. Geoff Wade and Laichen Sun, 104–25. Singapore: NUP.

————. 2010b. "The Last Great King of Classical Southeast Asia: 'Che Bong Nga' and Fourteenth Century Champa." In *The Cham of Vietnam: History, Society and Art*, ed. Bruce Lockhart and Tran Ky Phuong. Singapore: National University of Singapore Press, 168–203.

————. 2011a. "Van Don, the 'Mac Gap' and the End of the Jiaozhi Ocean System: Trade and State in Dai Viet, c. 1450–1550." In *The Gulf of Tongking in History: Soundings in Time and Space*. Philadelphia: University of Pennsylvania Press.

————. 2011b. "The Thirteenth Province: Internal Administration and External Expansion in Fifteenth Century Vietnam." In *Asian Expansions*, ed. Geoff Wade.

Wicks, Robert S. 1985. "Ancient Coinage of Mainland Southeast Asia." *JSEAS* 16 (2): 196–99.

————. 1986. "Monetary Developments in Java Between the Ninth and Sixteenth Centuries: A Numismatic Perspective." *Indonesia* 42:42–77.

————. 1992. *Money, Markets, and Trade in Early Southeast Asia: The Development of Indigenous Monetary Systems to AD 1400*. Ithaca, NY: Cornell University Southeast Asia Program.

Winichakul, Thongchai. 1994. *Siam Mapped: A History of the Geo-Body of a Nation*. Honolulu: University of Hawaii Press.

Winstedt, R. O., and de Josselin de Jong. 1956. "The Maritime Laws of Malacca." *JMBRAS* 29 (3): 22–59.

Wisseman, Jan. 1977. "Markets and Trade in Pre-Majapahit Java." In Hutterer, ed., 197–212. Ann Arbor, MD: Center for South and Southeast Asian Studies.

Wisseman Christie, Jan. 1982. *Patterns of Trade in Western Indonesia: Ninth through Thirteenth Centuries AD*. Unpublished PhD thesis, University of London.

————. 1986. "Negara, Mandala, and Despotic State: Images of Early Java." In *Southeast Asia in the Ninth to Fourteenth Centuries*, ed. Marr and Milner, 65–93. Singapore: ISEAS.

————. 1991. "States without Cities: Demographic Trends in Early Java." *Indonesia* 52:23–40.

————. 1992. "Trade and Settlement in Early Java: Integrating the Epigraphic and Archaeological Data." In *Early Metallurgy, Trade, and Urban Centres*, ed. Glover et al., 181–95. Bangkok: White Lotus.

————. 1992–1993. "Trade and Value in Pre-Majapahit Java." *Indonesia Circle* 59–60:3–17.

————. 1993. "Texts and Textiles in Medieval Java." *BEFEO* 80, 1:181–211.

————. 1994. "*Wanua, thani, paraduwan:* The 'Disintegrating' Village in Early Java?" In *Texts from the Islands: Oral and Written Traditions of Indonesia and the Malay World*, ed. Wolfgang Marschall, vol. 4, 27–42. Berne, Switzerland: University of Berne.

————. 1995. "State Formation in Early Maritime Southeast Asia: A Consideration of the Theories and the Data." *BKI* 151 (2): 25–88.

————. 1996. "Money and Its Uses in the Javanese States of the Ninth to Fifteenth Centuries AD." *JESHO* 39 (3): 243–86.

————. 1998a. "The Medieval Tamil-Language Inscriptions in Southeast Asia and China." *JSEAS* 29 (2): 239–68.

————. 1998b. "Javanese Markets and the Asian Sea Trade Boom of the Tenth to Thirteenth Centuries AD." *JESHO* 41 (3): 344–81.

————. 1999. "Asian Sea Trade between the Tenth and the Thirteenth Centuries and Its Impact on the States of Java and Bali." In *Archaeology of Seafaring, The Indian Ocean in the Ancient Period*, ed. Himanshu Ray, 221–70. Delhi: Pragati Publications.

————. 2001. "Revisting Mataram." In *Fruits of Inspiration*, ed. Klokke and van Kooij, 24–54. Groningen, Netherlands: Egbert Forsten.

Wittfogel, Karl. 1957. *Oriental Despotism, A Comparative Study of Total Power*. New Haven: Yale University Press.

Wolters, O. W. 1958. "Tambralinga." *Bulletin of the School of the Asian and African Studies* 21:587–607.

————. 1966a. "A Note on the Capital of Srivijaya during the Eleventh Century." In *Essays Offered to G. H. Luce by his Friends in Honour of his Seventy-fifth Birthday*, ed. Ba Shin, Jean Boisselier, and A. B. Griswold, 225–39. Ascona, Switzerland: Artibus Asiae.

————. 1966b. "The Khmer King at Basan (1371–1373) and the Restoration of the Cambodian Chronology during the Fourteenth and Fifteenth Centuries." *Asia Major* 12 (1): 44–64.

———. 1967. *Early Indonesian Commerce: A Study of the Origins of Sri Vijaya*. Ithaca, NY: Cornell University Press.

———. 1970. *The Fall of Srivijaya in Malay History*. Ithaca, NY: Cornell University Press.

———. 1973. "Jayavarman II's Military Power: The Territorial Foundations of the Angkor Empire." *Journal of the Royal Asiatic Society* 21–30.

———. 1979a. "Studying Srivijaya." *JMBRAS* 52 (2): 1–52.

———. 1979b. "Khmer 'Hinduism' in the Seventh Century." In *Early South East Asia*, ed. Smith and Watson, 427–41. New York: Oxford University Press.

———. 1982. *History, Culture, and Region in Southeast Asian Perspectives*. Singapore: Institute of South East Asian Studies.

———. 1983. "A Few Miscellaneous Pi-chi Jottings on Early Indonesia." *Indonesia* 36 (October): 46–62.

———. 1986. "Restudying Some Chinese Writings on Sriwijaya." *Indonesia* 42:1–42.

———. 1999. *History, Culture, and Region in Southeast Asian Perspectives*. Rev. ed. Ithaca, NY: Cornell University Southeast Asia Program.

Woodward, Hiram W., Jr. 1975. *Studies in the Art of Central Siam, 950–1350 AD*. Unpublished PhD dissertation, Yale University.

———. 1981. "Tantric Buddhism at Angkor Thom." *Ars Orientalis* 12:57–68.

Wyatt, David K. 1975. *The Crystal Sands: the Chronicles of Nagara Śrī Dharrmarāja*. Data Paper 98. Ithaca, NY: Southeast Asia Program.

———. 1984. *Thailand, A Short History*. New Haven, CT: Yale University Press.

———. 1994. "Mainland Powers on the Malay Peninsula." In *Studies in Thai History*. Chiang Mai: Silkworm, 22–48.

———. 2001. "Relics, Oaths, and Politics in Thirteenth-Century Siam." *JSEAS* 32 (1): 3–66.

———. 2003. *A Short History of Thailand*. 2nd ed. New Haven, CT: Yale University Press.

Xinru Liu. 1988. *Ancient India and Ancient China: Trade and Religious Exchange, AD 1–600*. Delhi: Oxford University Press.

Yang, Bin, 2003. "The Southwest Silk Road: Overland Trade via Burma." Unpublished paper presented at the Association for Asian Studies Annual Meeting, New York, March.

———. 2004. "Horses, Silver, and Cowries: Yunan in Global Perspective." *Journal of World History* 15 (3): 281–322.

Yoshinobu, Shiba. 1983. "Sung Foreign Trade: Its Scope and Organization." In *China Among Equals: The Middle Kingdom and Its Neighbors*, ed. Morris Rossabi, 89–115. Berkeley: University of California Press.

Yule, Henry, ed. and trans. 1903. *The Book of Ser Marco Polo the Venetian Concerning the Kingdoms and Marvels of the East*. 3rd ed. New York: Scribner's.

———. 1913–1916. *Cathay and the Way Thither*. London: Hakluyt Society.

Zhao, Gang, 2008. "Restructuring the Authority of the Ancestor: Zhu Yuanzhang's role in the Evolution of Ming Maritime Policy, 1400–1600." In *Long Live the Emperor!: Uses of the Ming Founder across Six Centuries of East Asian History*, ed. S. Schneewind. Minneapolis, MN: Society for Ming Studies.

Zoetmulder, P. J. 1974. *Kalangwan. A Survey of Old Javanese Literature*. The Hague: Martinus Nijhoff.

———. 1982. *Old Javanese-English Dictionary*. The Hague: Martinus Nijhoff.

Index

About the Author

Kenneth R. Hall, PhD Michigan, is professor of history at Ball State University (Muncie, Indiana), teaching courses in comparative world civilizations. He previously taught at Elmira College, (SUNY) Binghamton University, Tufts University, Massachusetts College of the Liberal Arts/Williams College, and the University of Chicago, with postdoctoral appointments at the University of Michigan, New York University, the University of Hawai'i, the University of Chicago, and Gadjah Madah University. He has published numbers of articles in professional journals and collected volumes, as well as *Maritime Trade and State Development in Early Southeast Asia* (1985), *Trade and Statecraft in the Age of the Colas* (1980/1997), and an extended chapter on "The Economic History of Early Southeast Asia" in *The Cambridge History of Southeast Asia* (1992/2001). He edited *The Growth of Non-Western Cities: Primary and Secondary Urban Networking, c. 900–1900* (2010), *Secondary Cities and Urban Networking in the Indian Ocean Realm, c. 1400–1800* (2008), *Maritime Diasporas in the Indian Ocean and East and Southeast Asia, 960–1775* (2006), and *Structural Change and Societal Integration in Early South India* (1991/1995) and coedited *New Perspectives in the History and Historiography of Southeast Asia, Continuing Explorations* (with Michael Aung-Thwin, 2011) and *Explorations in Early Southeast Asian History: The Origins of Southeast Asian Statecraft* (with John K. Whitmore, 1976). He serves on the advisory board of the *Journal of the Economic and Social History of the Orient* and is editor of the Lexington Press/Rowman & Littlefield Comparative Urban Studies series.